For Reference

Not to be taken from this room

		DATE	

The History of
Rock
and
Roll

A Selective Discography

The History of
Rock
and
Roll

A Selective Discography

MIREK KOCANDRLE

G.K. HALL & CO.
BOSTON

Library of Congress Cataloging-in-Publication Data

Kocandrle, Mirek.
　　The history of rock and roll.

　　Includes index.
　　1. Rock music--Discography.　I. Title.
ML156.4.R6K64 1988　　　789.9'12454　　　88-21200
ISBN 0-8161-8956-0

This publication is printed on permanent/durable acid-free paper
MANUFACTURED IN THE UNITED STATES OF AMERICA

Contents

Contents

Contents

Preface

The main aim of this work is to present a historical and chronological overview of all important rock'n'roll styles in one source, something that the various surveys, playlists, and other forms of rock literature, however useful, have never done. *The History of Rock and Roll* is meant to provide the fan, collector, disc jockey, music educator, or historian abundant information and delight.

No limits were set on this project except one--that it contain the artistically and commercially most notable works in rock music. Jazz and classical music were the only styles consciously omitted because they are huge topics on their own and beyond the scope of this book. The fifty-five categories and numerous subsections included represent the established styles recognized in the music industry today, although a few are my own creation.

Most available resources on rock'n'roll are organized alphabetically, an arrangement that is useful for identification of artists and their work, but that does not allow the researcher to chart the evolution of different styles of music. As the accompanying figure illustrates, no style is independent of those that came before it; artists borrow elements from existing styles and incorporate them into new ones, creating forms of music rich with the history of earlier styles. Because an appreciation of the evolution of rock is crucial to the understanding of the music, the main headings and subcategories in this work, as well as the entries for each musician or group within them, are listed chronologically. Under each musician or group, records are listed by release date; singles appear first, followed by albums. Where the dates of early releases were not available, titles are grouped alphabetically at the beginning of each list.

Defining the style of a particular musician or group is a most difficult task, for artists and bands can change style from record to record. Artists and groups known for playing in different styles, therefore, are classified by the style to which they made the greatest contribution. In most cases this means they are listed under the style in which they first began playing, as this is usually where they made their major contribution. Sometimes, however, a group or performer later adopts a style for which it becomes better known. Fleetwood Mac illustrates this point; it started out playing blues but later switched to a pop sound, and is now linked with this later style. In such cases, I have classified the performer or band under its prevailing, recognized style.

Artists who have left a group to perform on their own, or continue to play with the group while pursuing independent careers, are listed under the name of the group as solo performers. Phil Collins, for example, who has had a brilliant solo career, is to be found under Genesis, with whom he still sometimes performs.

The selection of recordings is based on a grading system ranging from A to F. I have tried to include all records worthy of grades of B and better, based on artistic contribution to a particular style. In addition, I have placed asterisks before some names and titles to denote exceptional artistic quality, an innovative contribution to an idiom or style, and/or recordings essential to a comprehensive collection. Records rated lower than B are included if they were extremely popular even though they could not be considered artistically superior, or if they are the only record in print to represent an artist or style. The listings are current through 1987.

Imported and out-of-print works are also included, both "for the record" and for those fans who will make the extra effort to search for these gems way back in grandma's attic, in the dusty bins of a store, or at flea markets. I have made no special attempt to distinguish these titles, nor to note those that have been reissued; any reputable record store can obtain imports and check to find out if a record is still in print or has been reissued.

Deciding what artists and bands to include was not easy, and I had to choose those I felt made the greatest contribution to rock'n'roll. I wanted to list many of the recordings that are just now being released, as well as many other up-and-coming performers. This book is only the beginning of the charting of the path of rock'n'roll, a task that will need continous updating and further research as time goes on.

Bibliography

Hibbard, Don J., and Kaleialoha, Carol. *The Role of Rock.* Englewood Cliffs, N.J.: Prentice-Hall, 1983.
The discography in the back of this book was probably the major inspiration and model for my work. It defines styles in chronological order, lists LPs, but gives no dates. On average, it lists two to three albums per artist or group; some styles, artists, and groups are omitted.

Pareles, John, and Romanowski, Patricia. *Encyclopedia of Rock'n'Roll.* Rolling Stone Press, 1983.

Fairly comprehensive, contains lots of trivia but no obvious definition of styles. The format is alphabetical, so the evolution of the music cannot be traced. The singles listings are partial, neither singles nor LPs are rated, and some artists and groups are not included.

Marsh, Dave, and Swenson, John. *Rolling Stone Record Guide.* Rolling Stone Press, 1983.

Rates records (LPs only) according to their artistic merit, which makes it an invaluable book. Alphabetical format, with no clear definitions of style. Mentions many minor artists. Lists only records in print, mentions and describes some singles. Some artists are omitted.

Gillet, Charlie. *The Sound of the City.* New York: Random House, 1984.

Excellent book covering the early years and foundations of Rock'n'Roll. Defines early styles only and ends with 1971. Lists no albums.

Nite, Norm L. *Rock On.* 3 vols. New York: Harper and Row, 1985.

Alphabetical format listing singles only. No definition of styles.

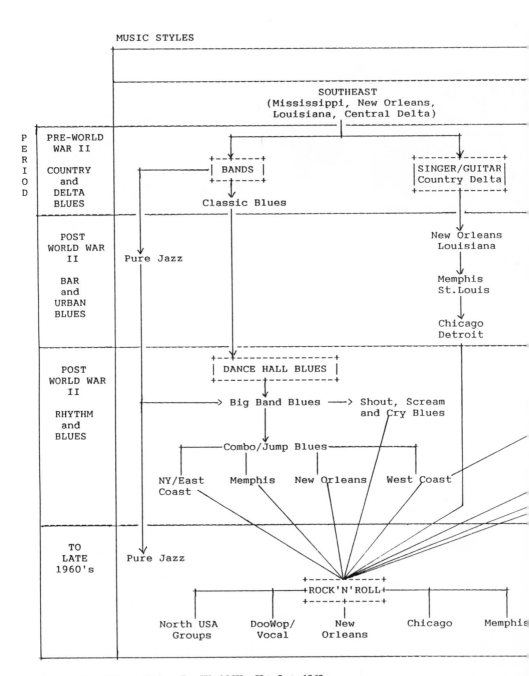

MUSIC STYLES

Progression of Music Styles: Pre-World War II to Late 1960s

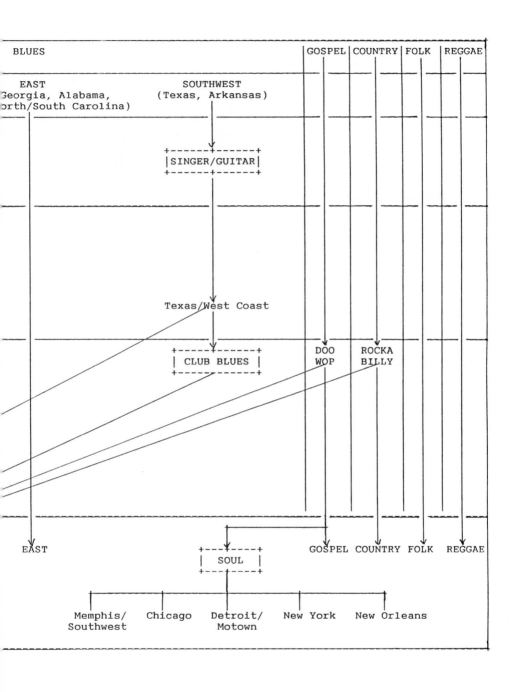

Ragtime

*Scott Joplin (1868-1917)

Maple Leaf Rag (1899)
The Entertainer (1902)

*Keith Nichols Plays Scott Joplin &
   Classic Rag Masters* (One Up)
Ragtime Piano Roll Classics (BYG)
The Scott Joplin Golden Gift Box
   (Nonesuch)
Scott Joplin Rags (Sonet)

*Jelly Roll Morton (1885-1941)

Perfect Rag
King Porter Stomp (1924)

Jelly Roll Morton (DJM)
Jelly Roll Morton (Milestone)
Jelly Roll Morton, 1923-24 (Classic
   Jazz)
King of New Orleans Jazz (RCA
   Victor)
The Library of Congress Recordings,
   Vols. 1-12 (Classic Jazz Masters)
Louis Armstrong & King Oliver
   (Milestone)
New Orleans Memories
   (Commodore-Fontana)
New Orleans Rhythm Kings
   (Milestone)
Stomps & Joy (RCA Victor)

Al Jolson (1886-1950)

Ragging the Baby to Sleep (1912,
   Victor)

Henry Thomas (1874-1949?)

Ragtime Texas (1974, Heroin)

Boogie-Woogie

*Meade Lux Lewis (1904-64)

Honky Tonk Train Blues (1927,
   Paramount)

Barrelhouse Piano (Storyville)
Blues Piano--Chicago Plus
   (Columbia)
Cat House Piano (Verve)
*Lewis, Ammons, Johnson-Boogie-
   Woogie Trio* (Storyville)
Meade Lux Lewis (Archives of Folk
   and Jazz)
Meade Lux Lewis (Atlantic)
Meade Lux Lewis (Decca)
Meade Lux Lewis (Stinson)
Meade Lux Lewis (Tops)
*Meade Lux Lewis, Boogie at the
   Philharmonic* (Clef)
*Meade Lux Lewis, Piano Jazz-
   Boogie-Woogie Style* (Swaggie)
*Meade Lux Lewis, Yancey's Last
   Ride* (Verve)
*Original Boogie-Woogie Piano
   Giants* (Columbia)
Ridin' in Rhythm (World Records)
Tell Your Story (Oldie Blues)

*Jimmy Yancey (1894-1951)

Chicago Solos (Joker)
The Immortal Jimmy Yancey (Oldie
   Blues)
Jimmy and Mama Yancey (Atlantic)
Jimmy Yancey (Oldie Blues)
Lost Recordings Date (Riverside)
Lowdown Dirty Blues (Atlantic)
Chicago Piano 1972 (Atlantic)

Cow Cow Davenport (1894-1955)

Cow Cow Davenport 1976 (Magpie)
Cow Cow Blues 1977 (Oldie Blues)

Albert Ammons (1907-49)

Boogie-Woogie Stomp (Swaggie)

The Complete Library of Congress
  Boogie-Woogie Recordings (Jazz.
  P)
Jug Session (Emarcy)
*King of Blues and Boogie-Woogie
  (Oldie Blues)
*Spirituals to Swing (1938,
  Vanguard)
Cafe Society Swing & Boogie Woogie
  (1939, Swingfan)
Boogie-Woogie Piano Stylings (1946,
  Mercury)

Clarence "Pine Top" Smith (1907-29)

Boogie-Woogie (1928, Vocalion)

Pine Top Smith (Vocalion)
Pine Top Smith (Brunswick)

Piano Red

(Willie Perryman, 1911-)

Boogie Honky-Tonk (Oldie Blues)
Dr. Feelgood Alone (Arhoolie)
Percussive Piano (Euphonic)
Rockin' with Red/Red's Boogie
  (RCA Victor)

Pete Johnson (1904-67)

Joe Turner & Pete Johnson
  (EmArcy)
Jumpin' with Pete Johnson
  (Riverside)
Master of Blues & Boogie-Woogie
  (Oldie Blues)
Pete Johnson (Blue Note)
Spirituals to Swing--1967 (1967,
  Columbia)

Classic Blues

Mamie Smith (188?-1946)

Crazy Blues (1920, Okeh)

Stars of the Apollo Theatre
  (Columbia)
Women of the Blues (RCA)

Clara Smith (1894-1935)

Nobody Knows the Way I Feel This
  Morning (1920, Columbia)
Freight Train Blues (1924,
  Paramount)

*Ma (Gertrude) Rainey (1886-1939)

Deep Moaning Blues (1920s,
  Paramount)
See See Rider (1920s, Paramount)
Those Dogs of Mine (1920s,
  Paramount)
Traveling Blues (1920s, Paramount)

*Immortal (Milestone)
*Ma Rainey (Biograph)
*Ma Rainey (Milestone)
*Ma Rainey, Vols. 1-8 (Rarities)
*Oh My Babe Blues (Biograph)
*Queen of the Blues (Biograph)

*Alberta Hunter (1887-)

Down-Hearted Blues (1920s,
  Paramount)
Songs We Taught Your Mother
  (1961, Bluesville)
Remember My Name (1978,
  Bluesville)
Amtrak Blues (1980, Columbia)

Bertha "Chippie" Hill (1905-50)

Trouble in Mind (1920s,
  Paramount)
Panama Limited Blues (1925,
  Rosetta)

Victoria Spivey (1906-76)

Black Snake Blues (1920s, Okeh)

Recorded Legacy of the Blues
  (Spivey)

Sara Martin (1884-1955)

Jug Band Blues (1922, Okeh)

*Bessie Smith (1894-1937)

Downhearted Blues (1923,
  Columbia)
Yellow Dog (1923, Columbia)
Nobody Knows You When You Are
  Down and Out (1929,
  Columbia)

Bessie Smith Story (Columbia)
*Any Woman's Blues (1970,
  Columbia)
*The Empress (1971, Columbia)
*Empty Bed Blues (1971, Columbia)
*The World's Greatest Blues Singer
  (1971, Columbia)
*Nobody's Blues But Mine (1972,
  Columbia)

Trixie Smith (1885-1943)

Freight Train Blues (1924,
  Paramount)
Railroad Blues (1925, Paramount)

Ida Cox (1889-)

Chicago Bound Blues (1923,
  Paramount)

Blues Ain't Nothin' Else But
  (Miletone)
Blues for Rampart Street (Riverside)
Hard Times Blues (Fontana)
Ida Cox, Vols. 1-2 (Fountain)

Anthologies

The Great Blues Singers (Riverside)
*Mean Mothers-Independent Women's
  Blues*, Vol. 1 (Rosetta)

Women of the Blues (RCA Victor)
*Women's Railroad Blues-Sorry But I
  Can't Take You* (Rosetta)

Pre-World War II Country and Delta Blues

MISSISSIPPI AND CENTRAL STATES

*Charlie Patton (1887-1934)

Frankie and Albert (ca. 1929-34, Yazoo)
Mississippi Boll Weevil Blues (ca. 1929-34, Yazoo)
*Pony Blues (ca. 1929-34, Yazoo)
A Spoonful Blues (ca. 1929-34, Yazoo)
Stone Pony Blues (ca. 1929-34, Yazoo)
34 Blues (ca. 1929-34, Yazoo)

Charlie Patton & Country Blues (Original Jazz Library)
**The Founder of the Delta Blues* (Yazoo)

*Lonnie Johnson (1889-1970)

*He's a Jelly Roll Baker (1942, Bluebird)

The Blues of . . . (Swaggie)
**Eddie Lang and Lonnie Johnson,* Vols. 1-2 (Swaggie)
Lonnie Johnson (RCA)
**Mr. Johnson's Blues* (Swaggie)
**Tomorrow Night* (King)
**The Originator of Modern Guitar Blues* (1980, Blues Boy)

*Big Bill Broonzy (1893-1958)

*Banker's Blues (1930, ARC)
Take Your Hands Off Her (1949, Mercury)

Big Bill Broonzy (Queen)
Big Bill Broonzy (RCA)

Big Bill's Blues (CBS)
**Young* (1968, Yazoo)
**Do That Guitar Rag* (1972, Yazoo)
1932-42 (1973, Biograph)

*Mississippi John Hurt (1893-1966)

*Stack-O-Lee (1928, Okeh)
*Candy Man Blues (1930, Okeh)
*C:C. Rider (1930, Okeh)

Folk Songs and Blues (Piedmont)
Mississippi John Hurt (Piedmont)
**Best of . . .* (1965, Vanguard)
Mississippi John Hurt--Today (1966, Vanguard)
The Immortal Mississippi John Hurt (1968, Vanguard)
His First Recordings (1972, Biograph)
**1928 Sessions* (1975, Yazoo)
**Monday Morning Blues* (1981, Flyright)

Fury Lewis (1893-1981)

Billy Lions and Stack O'Lee (1928, Vocalion)
*Good Looking Girl Blues (1928, Vocalion)
*John Henry (1928, Vocalion)

**In His Prime Time-1920s* (1975, Yazoo)

Tampa Red

(Hudson Whittaker, 1900-)

*Its Tight Like That (1929, Vocalion)

Bluebird No. 11 (Bluebird)
**The Guitar Wizard, 1935-53* (Blues Classics)
You Can't Get That Stuff No More (Oldie Blues)
**The Guitar Wizard* (1975, RCA)

Bo Carter (1893-1964)

*Banana in Your Fruit Basket
(Yazoo)
*Greatest Hits, 1930-40 (1968, Yazoo)
*Twist It Babe (1972, Yazoo)

Son House

(Eddie House, 1902-)

*The Legendary 1941-42 Recordings
(Folklyric)
*Son House and Blind Lemon
Jefferson (Biograph)
Son House and Robert Pete Williams
(Roots)
The Vocal Intensity (Roots)
*Son House (1973, Arhoolie)

Mississippi Fred McDowell (1904-72)

*You've Got to Move (1930,
Arhoolie)

Leevee Camp Blues (O.J.L.)
*Mississippi Delta Blues (1964,
Arhoolie)
*Mississippi Fred McDowell (1967,
Arhoolie)
I Do Not Play No Rock and Roll
(1969, Capitol)
Keep Your Lamp Trimmed and
Burning (1973, Arhoolie)

*Robert Johnson (1912-38)

*Dust My Broom 1936 (Columbia)

*King of the Delta Blues Singers, Vol.
1: 1935 (1961, Columbia)
*King of the Delta Blues Singers, Vol.
2: 1936 (1970, Columbia)

Sonny Boy Williamson

(John Lee Williamson, 1914-48)

*Good Morning, Little Schoolgirl
(1937, Blues Classic)

*Sugar Mama (1937, Blues Classic)

*Sonny Boy Williamson, Vols. 1-3
(Blues Classic)
Sonny Boy Williamson, Vols. 1-2
(RCA)

Bukka White (1906-77)

*Fixin' to Die (1940, Columbia)
Jitterbug Swing (1940, Columbia)

Parchman Farm (1940, Columbia)
Mississippi Blues (1960, Takoma)
*Sky Songs, Vols. 1-2 (1965,
Arhoolie)
Big Daddy (1974, Biograph)

Sleepy John Estes (1903-77)

Drop Down Mama (1941,
Bluebird)
*Someday Baby (1941, Bluebird)

The Blues of . . ., Vols. 1-2
(Swaggie)
1935-37 (Collector's Classics)
*1929-40 (1961, Folkways)

Jesse Fuller (1896-1976)

*San Francisco Bay Blues (1954,
Prestige)

The Lone Cat (1961, GTJ)
San Francisco Bay Blues (1963,
Prestige)
Brother Lowdow (1972, Fantasy)

*Big Boy Arthur Crudup (1904-74)

*That's All Right (1946, Bluebird)

Look on Yonder's Wall (1968,
Delmark)
Crudup's Mood (1970, Delmark)
*The Father of Rock'n'Roll (1971,
RCA)

Leroy Carr (1905-35)

*How Long, How Long Blues (1928, Vocalion)

1934 (1973, Biograph)

Robert Pete Williams (1914-)

Free Again (Prestige)
Rural Blues (Fantasy)
When I Lay My Burden Down (Sonet)
Angola Prisoner's Blues (1960, Arhoolie)
Those Prison Blues (1960, Arhoolie)
Louisiana Blues (1980, Takoma)

Anthologies

From Spirituals to Swing, Carnegie Hall 1936 (Vanguard)
Mississippi Blues (Yazoo)
The Mississippi Blues, Vols. 1-3 (O.J.L.)

EAST AND SOUTHEAST

*Elizabeth Cotten (1893-)

*Freight Train (1930, Folkways)
*Shake Sugaree (1967, Folkways)

Folksongs and Instrumentals with Guitar (1958, Folkways)
Elizabeth Cotten, Vol. 2: *Shake Sugaree* (1967, Folkways)

*Reverend Gary Davis (1896-1972)

American Street Songs (Riverside)
Pure Religion and Bad Company (1960) (77)
The Singing Reverend (1963, Stinson)
The Guitar and Banjo of . . . (1964, Prestige)
1935-49 (1970, Yazoo)
When I Die I'll Live Again (1972, Fantasy)

A Little More Faith (1973, Prestige)
O'Glory (1973, Adelphi)

Blind Blake

(Arthur Blake, 1895-1940)

*Bootleg Rum Dum Blues (1926, Biograph)

Bootleg Rum Dum Blues (1926 Biograph)
No Dough Blues' (1926, Biograph)
Rope Stretchin' (1926, Biograph)
Search Warrant Blues (1926, Biograph)

Blind Boy Fuller

(Allen Fulton Fuller, 1909-41)

1935-40 (1966, Blues Classics)

Sonny Terry (1911-86)

Blues Is My Companion (Verve)
Harmonica and Vocal Solos (1952, Folkways)

Brownie McGhee (1915-)

Traditional Blues, Vols. 1-2 (Folkways)

Sonny Terry and Brownie McGhee

Hootin' and Hollerin' (Olympic)
Sing (1958, Folkways)
Best of . . . (1960, Prestige)
Live at the Second Fret (1962, Prestige)
Back to New Orleans (1977, Fantasy)
Midnight Special (1977, Fantasy)

Stick McGhee (1917-61)

*Drinkin' Wine Spo-Dee-O-Dee (1947, Harlem)
*Tennessee Waltz Blues (1951, Atlantic)

Highway of Blues (1958, Audio-
Lab)

Pink Anderson (1900-74)

Pink Anderson, Vols. 1-3
(Bluesville)

Josh White (1915-69)

Josh White, Vols. 1-2 (Stinson)

LOUISIANA,
SOUTHWEST, AND WEST

*Leadbelly

(Huddie Ledbetter, 1889-1949)

Give Me Li'l Water Sylvie (1936,
Elektra)
*Goodnight Irene (1936, Elektra)
*Midnight Special (1936, Elektra)
*Rock Island Line (1936, Elektra)
Take This Hammer (1936, Elektra)

*Blues Songs by the Lonesome Blues
Singer* (Royale)
Good Morning Blues (Biograph)
His Guitar, His Voice, His Piano
(Capitol)
Keep Your Hands Off Her (Verve)
Leadbelly's Legacy (Folkways)
Rock Island Line (Folkways)
Take This Hammer (Verve)
*Leadbelly's Library of Congress
Recordings* (1950, Elektra)
Leadbelly's Last Sessions, Vols. 1-2
(1953, Folkways)
Leadbelly Sings Folk Songs (1968,
Folkways)
Leadbelly (1969, Capitol; 1973,
Fantasy)

*Blind Lemon Jefferson

(Lemon Jefferson, ca. 1897-1930)

*Black Snake Moan (1926,
Paramount)
*Booger Rooger Blues (1929,
Paramount)
*Long Lonesome Blues (1929,
Paramount)
*See That My Grave Is Kept Clean
(1929, Paramount)

Black Snake Moan (Milestone)
Blind Lemon Jefferson, Vols. 1-3
(Roots)
Blind Lemon Jefferson, Vol. 2
(Milestone)
Blind Lemon Jefferson, 1926-29
(Biograph)
Blind Lemon Jefferson (1975,
Milestone)

Mance Lipscomb (1895-1976)

Mance Lipscomb, Vols. 1-6
(Arhoolie)
Trouble in Mind (Reprise)
Texas Sharecropper and Songster
(1960, Arhoolie)
Texas Songster, Vols. 2-6 (1964-74,
Arhoolie)
*You'll Never Find Another Man Like
Mance* (1964, Arhoolie)
New Orleans Street Singer
(Folkways)
Possum Up a Simmon Tree (1971,
Arhoolie)

Snooks Eaglin (1936-)

John Henry
*Rock Me Mama
*That's All Right
*This Train

Juke Boy Bonner (1932-78)

Legacy of the Blues (Sonet)
The Struggle (Arhoolie)

I'm Going Back to the Country
(1968, Arhoolie)

ARKANSAS

*Roosevelt Sykes (1901-)

*Honeydripper (1936, Decca)
*44 Blues (1930, Victor)

Country Blues Piano Ace, 1929-32
(1971, Yazoo)

Post-World War II Bar and Urban Blues

General Anthologies

Barefoot Rock and You Got Me
(Duke)
*Fourteen Golden Recordings from
the Vault of Duke Records*, Vol. 1
(ABC)
*Fourteen Golden Recordings from
the Vaults of Vee Jay Records*
(ABC)
Golden Age of Rhythm and Blues
(Chess)
Great Bluesmen (Vanguard)
Great Bluesmen at Newport
(Vanguard)
Lake Michigan Blues, 1934-41
(Nighthawk)
Please Warm My Wiener (Yazoo)
Risky Business (King)
Story of the Blues (Columbia)
Super Super Blues Band (Checker)
Texas Guitar--From Dallas to L.A.
(Atlantic)
*Windy City Blues: The Transition
from 1935 to 1953* (Nighthawk)
Blues at Newport (1963, Vanguard)
Alladin Magic (1979, United
Artists)
Walking Blues (1979, Flyright)
*Rhythm and Rock: Best of Chess,
Checker, Cadet* (1981, Chess)
Shagger's Delight (1981, Ripete)
Bachelor Blues (1982, Neon)
Okeh Rhythm and Blues (1982,
Epic)
Wizards of the Southside (1982,
Chess)

NEW ORLEANS AND LOUISIANA

Champion Jack Dupree (1909-)

*Cabbage Greens (1940, Okeh)
*Rampart Street Special (1959, Atlantic)

Blues from the Gutter (Atlantic)
Cabbage Greens (Okeh)
Champion Jack Dupree (Everest)
Woman Blues of Champion Jack Dupree (1961, Folkways)
Blues at Montreux (1973, Atco)
Happy to Be Free (1973, Crescendo)
Tricks (1973, Crescendo)
Rub a Little Boogie, 1945-53 (1982, Krazy Kat)

*Slim Harpo

(James Moore, 1924-70)

*I'm a King Bee (1957, Excello)
*Blues Hang-Over (1960, Excello)
*Raining in My Heart (1961, Excello)
*Baby Scratch My Back (1966, Excello)
Tip Ou It (1967, Excello)
Te-Ni-Nee-Ni-Nu (1968, Excello)

Baby Scratch My Back (Excello)
Best of . . . (Excello)
**Slim Harpo Knew the Blues*, Vols. 1-2 (Excello)
Slim Harpo Sings Raining in My Heart (Excello)
**Blues Hangover* (1978, Flyright)
**Got Love If You Want It* (1978, Flyright)
**He Knew the Blues* (1978, Sonet)

*Lightnin' Slim

(Otis Hicks, 1913-74)

*Bad Luck (1954, Excello)

I Can't Live Happy (1954, Feature)
New Orleans Bound (1954, Feature)
*Rock Me Mama (1954, Excello)
*Lightnin' Blues (1955, Excello)
*Sugar Plum (1955, Excello)
Hoo Doo Blues (1958, Excello)
I'm a Rollin' Stone (1958, Excello)
I've Grown (1958, Excello)
*G.I. Slim (1959, Excello)
*Rooster Blues (1959, Excello)
Bed Bug Blues (1960, Excello)
*Cool Down Baby (1960, Excello)
*Nothin' But the Devil (1960, Excello)
Tom Cat Blues (1960, Excello)
Hello Mary Lee (1962, Excello)
I'm Tired Waitin' Baby (1962, Excello)
Mind Your Own Business (1962, Excello)
You're Old Enough to Understand (1962, Excello)
*Winter Time Blues (1963, Excello)

Mean Old Lonesome Train (Excello)
Rooster Blues (Excello)
The Feature Sides 1954 (Flyright)
High and Low (1970, Excello)
**The Early Years* (1977, Flyright)
**Trip to Chicago* (1978, Flyright)

Earl King

**Those Lonely Lonely Nights* (1979, Ace)
**Trick Bag* (1985, Score)

Lonesome Sundown

(Cornelius Green, 1928-)

*Lost without Love (1955, Excello)
*My Home Is a Prison (1955, Excello)
Don't Say a Word (1957, Excello)
Gonna Stick To You Baby (1957, Excello)
I'm a Mojo Man (1957, Excello)

*I Stood By (1957, Excello)
Lonesome Lonely Blues (1962, Excello)
Hoodoo Woman Blues (1964, Excello)
I Got a Broken Heart (1964, Excello)
Please Be on That "519" (1964, Excello)

Bought Me a Ticket (Flyright)
Lonesome Sundown (Excello)
Been Gone Too Long (1977, Joliet)

*Jimmy Reed (1925-76)

*Bright Lights, Big Lights (1955, Vee Jay)
You Don't Have to Go (1955, Vee Jay)
*Ain't That Lovin' You Baby (1956, Vee Jay)
*Big Boss Man (1957, Vee Jay)
Honest I Do (1957, Vee Jay)
*Baby What You Want Me to Do (1960, Vee Jay)

Best of . . . (Vee Jay)
Found Love (Vee Jay)
Greatest Hits, Vols. 1-2 (Kent)
History of . . ., Vols. 1-2 (Trip)
I'm Jimmy Reed (Vee Jay)
New Jimmy Reed Album (Bluesway)
Root of My Blues (Kent)
Jimmy Reed at Carnegie Hall (1962, Vee Jay)
High and Lonesome (1980, Charly)
Upside Your Head (1980, Charly)

Paul Gayten

Creole Gal, 1947-57 (Route 66)

*Lazy Lester

(Leslie Johnson, 1933-)

I Hear You Knocking (1957, Excello)

I'm a Lover, Not a Fighter (1957, Excello)
*Lester's Stomp (1957, Excello)
*Sugar Coated Love (1957, Excello)
*They Call Me Lazy (1957, Excello)
Through the Goodness of My Heart (1957, Excello)
*Patrol Blues (1961, Excello)
*Whoa Now (1961, Excello)
*You Got Me Where You Want Me (1961, Excello)
*Lonesome Highway Blues (1963, Excello)

They Call Me Lazy (1976, Flyright)
Poor Boy Blues (1978, Flyright)

Vince Monroe (1919-82)

Give It Up (or Tell Where It's At) (1956, Excello)
*Hello Friends, Hello Pal (1956, Excello)
*On the Sunny Side of Love (1956, Excello)
*Ain't Broke, Ain't Hungry (1963, Instant)

Boogie Jake

(Mathew Jacob, 1929-)

Early Morning Blues (1958, Excello)
I Don't Know Why (1958, Excello)
Bad Luck and Trouble (1959, Minit)
Chance for Your Love (1960, Minit)

Gonna Head for Home (1976, Flyright)

Silas Hogan (1911-)

Born in Texas (1960, Reynaud)
Let Me Be Your Hatchet (1960, Reynaud)
*Airport Blues (1962, Excello)

*Trouble at Home Blues (1962, Excello)

Blues Live in Baton Rouge (Excello)
Louisiana Blues (Arhoolie)
Swamp Blues (Excello)
Trouble (Excello)

Jimmy Anderson

*I Wanna Boogie (1961, Zynn)
*Naggin' (1961, Excello)
Goin' Crazy over T.V. (1964, Excello)

Moses "Whispering" Smith (1932-)

Cryin' Blues (1958, Excello)
Mean Woman Blues (1958, Excello)

Over Easy (Excello)

Tabby Thomas (1929-)

Church Members Ball (1953, Delta)
Thinking Blues (1953, Delta)
Tomorrow (1955, Feature)
*Hoodoo Party (1962, Excello)
*Popeye Train (1962, Excello)
Roll On Ole Mule (1962, Excello)
Keep on Trying (1966, Excello)
Play Girl (1966, Excello)

25 Years with the Blues (Blues Unlimited)

Charles Sheffield

*Kangaroo (1961, Excello)
*Rock'n'Roll Train (1961, Excello)
*It's Your Voodoo Working (1962, Excello)

Katie Webster (1939-)

*Baby, Baby (No Bread, No Meat) (1959, Excello)
I Need You Baby, I Need You (1959, Zynn)

On the Sunny Side of Love (1959, Rocko)
Sea of Love (1959, Decca)

Whooee Sweet Daddy (1977, Flyright)

Henry Gray (1925-)

I'm Lucky, Lucky Man (1970, Blues Unlimited)
You're My Midnight Dream (1970, Blues Unlimited)

They Call Me Little Henry (Bluebeat)

Anthologies

Delta Blues Heavy Hitters, 1927-1931 (Herwin)
New Orleans Jazz and Heritage Festival (Island)
Gonna Head for Home--Jay Miller Sessions (1976, Flyright)
Rooster Crowed for Day--Jay Miller Sessions (1976, Flyright)
Ace Story, Vols. 1-3 (1981, Ace)

TEXAS AND WEST COAST

*T-Bone Walker

(Aaron Thibeaux Walker, 1910-75)

*Call It Stormy Monday (1943, Black & White)
Hypin' Woman Blues (1947, Black & White)
I Want a Little Girl (1947, Black & White)
Lonesome Woman Blues (1947, Black & White)
T-Bone Shuffle (1947, Black & White)

His Original 1945-50 Performances (Black & White)
Singing the Blues (Imperial)
Sings the Blues (Imperial)

11

Stormy Monday Blues (1968, Stateside)
The Truth (1968, Brunswick)
Funky Town (1969, Statesidey)
Good Feelin' (1970, Polydor)
Dirty Mistreater (1973, Bluesway)
I Want a Little Girl (1973, Delmark)
Very Rare (1974, Warner Bros.)
T-Bone Blues (1975, Atlantic)
*T-Bone Walker (1975, Blue Note)
Classics of Modern Blues (1976, Blue Note)
T-Bone Jumps Again (1980, Charly)

*Lightnin' Hopkins

(Sam Hopkins, 1912-82)

*Big Mama Jump (1947, Alladin)
*Short Haired Woman (1947, Gold Star)
Baby Please Don't Go (1948, Gold Star)

And the Blues (Imperial)
Autobiography (Tradition)
Best (Tradition)
*Blues (Mainstream)
Down Home Blues (Souffle)
Fast Life Woman (Verve)
Lightnin' (Soul Parade)
Lightnin' Blues (Up Front)
Lightnin' Hopkins (Archives of Folk and Jazz)
Lightnin' Hopkins (Arhoolie)
Lightnin' Strikes (Tradition)
*Original Folk Blues (United Artists)
*Sings the Blues (Aladdin)
Soul Blues (Prestige)
*Strums the Blues (Aladdin/Score)
Gotta Move Your Baby (1960, Prestige)
Best of Texas Blues Band (1962, Prestige)
*Lightnin' Sam Hopkins (1962, Arhoolie)
Hootin' the Blues (1962, Prestige)
*Early Recordings (1963, Arhoolie)
Greatest Hits (1963, Prestige)

Texas Blues Man (1968, Arhoolie)
Talkin' Some Sense (1971, Jewel)
Double Blues (1972, Fantasy)
In Berkeley (1973, Arhoolie)
A Legend in His Own Time (1976, Blue Anthology)
Lightnin' (1977, Tomato)
*The Rooster Crowed in England (1977, LA)

*Clarence "Gatemouth" Brown (1924-)

*Didn't Reach My Goal (1949, Peacock)
*Mary Is Fine (1949, Peacock)
Okie Dokie Stomp (1949, Peacock)
Pale Dry Boogie (1949, Peacock)
You Got Money (1949, Peacock)

One More Mile (Demon)
Clarence "Gatemout" Brown Sings Louis Jordan (1974, Black and Blue)
Down South in Bayou Country (1975, Barclay)
Gate's on the Heat (1975, Blue Street)
Bogalusa Boogie Man (1976, Barclay)
*San Antonio Ballbuster (1979, Red Lightnin')
Alright Again (1982, Rounder)

*Willie Mae Thornton (1926-)

Ball and Chain (1953, Peacock)
*Hound Dog (1953, Peacock)
Little Red Rooster (1953, Peacock)

In Europe (1966, Arhoolie)
Big Mama Thornton (1967, Arhoolie)
Chicago Blues (1967, Arhoolie)
Ball and Chain (1968, Arhoolie)
Stronger than Dirt (1969, Mercury)
Jail (1975, Vanguard)
Mama's Pride (1978, Vanguard)

*Freddie King (1934-76)

*Have You Ever Loved a Woman
(1960, Federal)
*Hideway (1960, Federal)

Is a Blues Master (Cotillion)
17 Original Greatest Hits, 1934-76
(King)
Freddie King (1953, Parrot)
Freddie King (1954, Parrot)
Freddie King (1956, El-Bee)
My Feeling for the Blues (1970,
Cotillion)
Texas Cannonball (1972, A&M)
Woman Across the River (1973,
A&M)
Best of . . . (1975, MCA)
Larger Than Life (1975, RSO)
Hide Away (1976, Gusto)

*Johnny "Guitar" Watson (1935-)

*Gangster of Love (1962, Federal)
Ruben (1962, Federal)
Three Hours Past Midnight (1963,
King)
Space Guitar (1964, King)
Those Lonely, Lonely Nights (1964,
King)
A Real Mother for Ya (1976, DJM)
I Don't Wanna Be a Lone Ranger
(1976, DJM)

The Gangster Is Back (Red
Lightnin')
Very Best of . . . (MCA)
Bad (1966, Okeh)
Two for the Price of One (1967,
Okeh)
In the Fats Bag (1968, Okeh)
Gangster of Love (1973, Fantasy)
I Don't Want to Be a Lone Ranger
(1975, Fantasy)
Ain't That a Bitch (1976, DJM)
*Johnny "Guitar" Watson and the
Family Clone* (1981, DJM)
That's What Time It Is (1981,
Atlantic)

Jimmy McCracklin (1921-)

*The Walk (1958, Checker)

Let's Get Together (Imperial)
My Rockin' Soul (United Artists)
Rockin' Man, 1946-55 (Route 66)
High on Blues (1971, Stax)

Little Willie Littlefield (1931-)

It's Midnight (Route 66)
Little Willie Littlefield, Vols. 1-2
(1981, Chiswick)

Anthology

Texas Blues (Kent)

MEMPHIS AND ST. LOUIS

*B.B. King (1925-)

*Three O'Clock Blues (1951, RPM)
When My Heart Beats Like a
Hammer (1952, RPM)
Sweet Little Angel (1956, Kent)
*Please Accept My Love (1958,
Kent)
Sweet Sixteen (1960, Kent)
*Rock Me Baby (1964, Kent)
Don't Answer the Door (1966,
ABC)
Paying the Cost to Be the Boss
(1968, Blues Way)
*The Thrill Is Gone (1969, Blues
Way)
Why I Sing the Blues (1969, Blues
Way)
Ask Me No Questions (1971, ABC)
To Know You Is to Love You
(1973, ABC)
*I Like to Live the Love (1974,
ABC)

*Anthology of the Blues--B.B. King,
1949-50* (Kent)
B.B. King (Modern)
B.B. King Live (Kent)
Better Than Ever (Kent)

13

Blues in My Heart (Crown)
*From the Beginning (Kent)
Greatest Hits of . . . (Kent)
Incredible Soul of . . . (Kent)
*The Jungle (Kent)
Let Me Love You (Kent)
*Live, B.B. King on Stage (Kent)
Original "Sweet Sixteen" (Kent)
*Pure Soul (Kent)
Sings Spirituals (Crown)
*Underground Blues (Kent)
Mr. Blues (1963, ABC)
Confessin' the Blues (1965, ABC)
*Live at Regal (1965, ABC)
Blues Is King (1967, ABC)
B.B. King Story (1968, Blue
    Horizon)
Lucille (1968, ABC)
B.B. King Story, Vol. 2 (1969, ABC)
Boss of the Blues (1969, Kent)
Live and Well (1969, ABC)
Indianola Mississippi Seeds (1970,
    ABC)
*Live in Cook County Jail (1971,
    ABC)
Guess Who (1972, ABC)
L.A. Midnight (1972, ABC)
Best of . . . (1973, ABC)
To Know You Is to Love You (1973,
    ABC)
*Back in the Alley (1975, ABC)
Blues on Top of Blues (1975, ABC)
Completely Well (1975, ABC)
Lucille Talks Back (1975, ABC)
B.B. King Anthology (1976, ABC)
Kingsize (1977, ABC)
Midnight Believer (1978, ABC)
Take It Home (1979, ABC)
There Must Be a Better World
    Somewhere (1981, MCA)
Blues'n'Jazz (1983, MCA)

Albert King (1923-)

*Bad Luck Blues (1953, Parrot)
*Lonesome in My Bedroom (1953,
    Parrot)
Don't Throw Your Love on Me Too
    Strong (1961, King)

Laundromat Blues (1966, Stax)

Blues (Atlantic)
Years Gone By (Stax)
The Big Blues (1962, King)
Born under a Bad Sign (1967, Stax)
King of the Blues Guitar (1968,
    Atlantic)
I'll Play Blues for You (1972, Stax)
Truckload of Lovin' (1975, Utopia)
The Pinch (1977, Stax)
Chronical (1979, Stax)
New Orleans Heat (1979, Tomato)
Albert King Masterworks (1982,
    Atlantic)
Laundromat Blues (1985, Edsel)

*Junior Parker

(Herman Parker, 1927-71)

Feelin' Good (1953, Sun)
*Mystery Train (1953, Sun)
*Driving Wheel (1961, Duke)

*Driving (1960, Duke)
*Best of . . . (1962, Duke)
Junior Parker (1964, Bluesway)
Like It Is (1967, Mercury)
Outside Man (1970, Capitol)
Blue Shadows Falling (1972,
    Groove Merchant)
You Don't Have to Be Black (1973,
    People)
Love Ain't Nothing But Business
    (1974, People)
Junior Parker and Billy Love (1977,
    Charly)
Legendary Sun Performers (1978,
    Charly)
*I Wanna Ramble 1954-56 (1982,
    Duke-Ace)

Anthologies

Memphis Blues (Kent)
Lowdown Memphis Harmonica Jam,
    1950-55 (Nighthawk)

CHICAGO

*Muddy Waters (1915-83)

*Gypsy Woman (1949, Chess)
I Can't Be Satisfied (1949, Chess)
I Feel Like Going Home (1949, Chess)
Rollin' Stone (1950, Chess)
Honey Bee (1951, Chess)
She Moves Me (1952, Chess)
*Got My Mojo Working (1954, Chess)
*Hoochie Coochie Man (1954, Chess)
*I Just Wanna Make Love to You (1954, Chess)
I'm Ready (1954, Chess)
*Mannish Boy (1955, Chess)
Close to You (1958, Chess)

Afro-American Songs (Testament)
Best of . . . (Chess)
The Celebrated 1941-42 Library of Congress Recordings (Testament)
Down on Stovall's Plantation (Testament)
Electric Mud (Cadet)
More Real Folk Blues (Chess)
Muddy Waters at Newport (1960, Chess)
Fathers and Sons (1962, Chess)
Folk Singer (1964, Chess)
Real Folk Blues (1966, Chess)
Sail On (1968, Chess)
They Call Me Muddy Waters (1970, Chess)
Back in the Early Days (1971, Syndicate Chapter)
Good News (1971, Syndicate Chapter)
McKinley Morganfield and Muddy Waters Live (1971, Chess)
The London Muddy Waters Sessions (1972, Chess)
Can't Get No Grindin' (1973, Chess)
Hard Again (1977, Blue Sky)

Muddy Waters (1977, Chess)
Chicago Blues, 1946 (1981, Okeh)
Blues Roots, Vol. 2 (1982, Chess)
Chess Masters, Vols. 1-2 (1982, Chess)
Rolling Stone (1982, Chess)
Muddy Waters Sings Big Bill Broonzy (1986, MCA)

*Sonny Boy Williamson

(Rice Miller, 1899-1965)

Eyesight to the Blind (1951, Trumpet)
*One Way Out (1951, Chess)
*Bye Bye Bird (1953, Chess)
*Help Me (1953, Chess)
*Nights by Myself (1954, Trumpet)
*Don't Start Me Talking (1955, Chess)
*Fattening Frogs for Snakes (1957, Checker)

More Real Folk Blues (Chess)
The Real Folk Blues (Chess)
Bummer Road (1962, Chess)
This Is My Story (1965 Chess)
Sonny Boy Williamson (1966, Storyville)
The Original (1967, Blues Classics)
One Way Out (1974, Chess)
And the Animals (1975, Charly)
King Biscuit Time (1976, Arhoolie)
Sonny Boy Williamson (1977, Chess)

*Howlin' Wolf

(Chester Burnett, 1910-76)

*Back Door Man
*I Ain't Superstitious
*Killing Floor
*Little Red Rooster
*Spoonful
*How Many More Years (1951, Chess)
*Moanin' at Midnight (1952, Chess)

*Smokestack Lightnin' (1956, Chess)
*Sitting On Top of the World (1957, Chess)

Can't Put Me Out, Vol. 2 (Blues Ball)
Chester Burnett, aka Howlin' Wolf (Chess)
Chess Blues Masters (Chess)
From Early Till Late (Blue Night)
Going Back Home (Syndicate Chapter)
Heart Like Railroad Steel, Vol. 1 (Blues Ball)
The Legendary Sun Performers (Charly)
Howlin' Wolf (1964, Chess)
Moaning in the Moonlight (1964, Chess)
Poor Boy (1965, Chess)
Big City Blues (1966, United Artists)
Real Folk Blues (1966, Chess)
Evil (1967, Chess)
More Real Folk Blues (1967, Chess)
The London Sessions (1972, Chess)
The Back Door Wolf (1973, Chess)

*Elmore James (1918-63)

*It Hurts Me Too (1951, Chess)
*Dust My Blues (1955, Sue)
*I Believe I'll Dust My Broom (1959, Sue)
*The Sky Is Crying (1959, Fire)
*Shake Your Money Maker (1961, Charly)
*Standing at the Crossroads (1962, Sue)

Best of . . . (Chiswick)
Blues after Hours (Crown)
Got to Move (Charly)
History of . . ., Vols. 1-2 (Trip)
Original Folk Blues (United Artists)
Blues Masters (1966, Blue Horizon)
Tough (1970, Blue Horizon)
I Need You (1971, Sphere Sound)
The Legend (1971, Polydor)
Sky Is Crying (1971, Sphere Sound)
Street Talking (1973, Muse)

All Them Blues (1973, DJM)
Legend of . . . (1976, Kent)
Resurrection of . . . (1976, Kent)
One Way Out (1980, Charly)

*Little Walter Jacobs (1930-68)

*Juke (1952, Checker)
*My Babe (1955, Checker)

Best of . . . (Chess)
Blue Midnight (Roi du Blues)
Boss Blues Harmonica (Chess)
Hate to See You Go (Chess)
Little Walter (Chess)
Southern Feeling (Roi du Blues)
Super Blues (1967, Checker)
Confessin' the Blues (1976, Chess)

James Cotton (1935-)

Chicago Breakdown (TKM)
Cotton Crop Blues (1954, Verve)
James Cotton Blues Band (1967, Verve)
Cotton in Your Ears (1968, Verve)
Pure Cotton (1968, Verve)
100% Cotton (1974, Buddah)
Live and on the Move (1976, Buddah)

Otis Rush (1934-)

*I Can't Quit You Baby (1956, Cobra)
*So Many Roads, So Many Trains (1960, Chess)

Mourning in the Morning (Cotillion)
Right Place, Wrong Time (1976, Bullfrog)
Groaning the Blues (1980, Flyright)

Magic Sam

(Sam Maghett, 1937-69)

*I Just Want a Little Bit (1957, Delmark)

West Side Soul (1968, Delmark)

Black Magic (1969, Delmark)
Magic Rocker (1980, Flyright)

Buddy Guy (1936-)

*Knock on Wood (1960, Chess)
Buddy Guy (Chess)
In the Beginning (Red Lightnin')
Man and the Blues (1968,
Vanguard)
This Is . . . (1968, Vanguard)
I Was Walking through the Woods
(1977, Chess)

Koko Taylor (1935-)

*Wang Dang Doodle (1960, Chess)

I Got What It Takes (1975,
Alligator)
Southside Baby (1975, Black and
Blue)
The Earthshaker (1978, Alligator)
From the Heart of a Woman (1981,
Alligator)

Little Milton

(Milton Campbell, 1934-)

I'm a Lonely Man (1961, Chess)
So Mean to Me (1961, Checker)
*Grits Ain't Groceries (1965,
Checker)
*We're Gonna Make It (1965,
Checker)

Grits Ain't Groceries (Checker)
Little Milton (Chess)
If Walls Could Talk (1969, Chess)
Greatest Hits (1972, Chess)
Raise a Little Sand (1975, Red
Lightnin')
Blues Masters (1976, Chess)
Walking the Back Streets (1981,
Stax)
Age Ain't Nothing but a Number
(1983, MCA)

Otis Spann (1930-70)

Chicago Blues (Testament)
Blues Never Die (1964, Prestige)
Cryin' Time (1970, Vanguard)
*Otis Spann with Luther Johnson and
the Muddy Waters Band* (1973,
Muse)

Junior Wells

(Amos Blackmore, 1934-)

*Hoodoo Man (1965, Delmark)
Messin' with the Kid (1965,
Delmark)

Messing with the Blues (P-Vine)
Hoodoo Man Blues (1965,
Delmark)
It's My Life Baby (1966, Vanguard)
Blues Hit the Big Town (1967,
Delmark)
Sings at the Golden Bear (1968,
Blue Rock)
You're Tuff Enough (1968,
Mercury)
*Buddy Guy and Junior Wells Play the
Blues* (1972, Atlantic)
I Was Walking through the Woods
(1973, Chess)
Got to Use Your Head (1979, Blue
Ball)

*J.B. Lenoir (1929-67)

J.B. Lenoir (Chess)
Mojo Boogie (Flyright)
Chicago Golden Years (1969,
Chess)
Alabama Blues (1979, L&R)
Down in Mississippi (1979, L&R)

*Fenton Robinson (1935-)

Mellow Blues Genius (P-Vine)
Somebody Loan Me a Dime (1976,
Alligator)
I Hear Some Blues Downstairs
(1977, Alligator)

Hound Dog Taylor

(Theodore Roosevelt Taylor, 1915-75)

*Hound Dog Taylor and the
Houserockers* (1971, Alligator)
Natural Boogie (1974, Alligator)
Beware of the Dog (1976, Alligator)

Earl Hooker (1930-70)

Blues Guitar (P-Vine)
There's a Fungus among Us (1972,
Red Lightning')

*Paul Butterfield (1942-87)

*The Paul Butterfield Blues Band
(1965, Elektra)
*East-West (1966, Elektra)
*The Resurrection of Pigboy Crabshaw
(1968, Elektra)

Charlie Musselwhite (1944-)

*Stand Back (1967, Vanguard)
*Takin' My Time (1971, Arhoolie)
*Goin' Back Down South (1974,
Arhoolie)
*Stone Blues Down South (1974,
Vanguard)

Stefan Grossman (1945-)

Yazoo Basin Boogie (1975, Kicking
Mule)
Acoustic Music for Body and Soul
(1976, Kicking Mule)
*Stefan Grossman and John
Renbourn* (1978, Kicking Mule)

Anthologies

Best of the Chicago Blues
(Vanguard)
Blues Piano--Chicago Plus
(Atlantic)
Chicago Blues Anthology (Chess)

Chicago Slickers, 1948-1953
(Nighthawk)
Chicago, The Blues Today, Vols. 1-3
(Vanguard)
Living Chicago Blues, Vols. 1-6
(1978, Alligator)

DETROIT

*John Lee Hooker (1917-)

*Boogie Chillun (1948, Modern)
*Moaning Blues (1948, Modern)
*I'm in the Mood (1951, Modern)
*Boom Boom (1962, Vee Jay)

Detroit Special (Atlantic)
*Greatest Hits of . . . (United Artists)
House of the Blues (Chess)
How Long Blues (Riverside)
*I'm John Lee Hooker (Vee Jay)
I Want to Shout the Blues (Vee Jay)
John Lee Hooker (Archives Folk)
John Lee Hooker Alone (Specialty)
Slim's Stomp (Polydor)
Whiskey and Women (Trip)
Folklore of . . . (1962, Vee Jay)
It Serves You Right (1966, Impulse)
The Real Folk Blues (1968, Chess)
Urban Blues (1968, Setside)
Coast to Coast (1971, United
Artists)
Mad Man Blues (1971, Chess)
Boogie Chillun (1972, Fantasy)
Never Get Out of These Blues Alive
(1972, Fantasy)
Best of . . . (1974, Vee Jay)
Don't Turn Me from Your Door
(1974, Atco)
John Lee Hooker (1975, New
World)
The Cream (1978, Tomato)
Live (1978, Lynarz)
*This Is Hip (1980, Charly)
*Everybody's Rockin' (1981, Charly)
Hooker Alone, Vol. 1 (1981, Labor)
Hooker Alone, Vol. 2 (1982, Labor)
**John Lee Hooker Plays and Sings the
Blues* (1986, MCA)

Rhythm and Blues

Detroit Blues, 1948-1954
(Nighthawk)

General Anthologies

*Best of the Chicago Blues
(Vanguard)
*Chicago Blues Anthology (Chess)
*Great Bluesmen (Vanguard)
*The Mississippi Blues, Vols. 1-3
(O.J.L.)
*New Orleans Jazz & Heritage Festival
(Island)
*Please Warm My Weiner (Yazoo)
*Risky Blues (King)
*Story of the Blues (Columbia)
*From Spirituals to Swing (1936,
Vanguard)
*Tag Along--Jay Miller Sessions
(1976, Flyright)
*Living Chicago Blues, Vols. 1-3
(1978, Alligator)
*Shagger's Delight (1981, Ripete)
*Okeh Rhythm & Blues (1982, Epic)
*Atlantic R&B 1947-74, Vols. 1-7,
(1986, Atlantic)
*Atlantic Blues (1987, Atlantic)
*The Blues, Vol. 1: *Various Artists*
(1987, Chess)

DANCE-HALL BLUES

BIG BAND BLUES

World War II Jazz or Dance

Lionel Hampton (1913-)

*Flying Home (1943, Decca)

All American Award Concert
(Decca)
Golden Favorites (Decca)
Lionel Hampton's Best Records,
Vols. 1-6 (RCA)

Cootie Williams (1910-)

Sextet and Orchestra (1944, Phoenix)

Billy Eckstine (1914-)

*Mr. B and the Band (1976, Savoy)

Milton Larkin

Arnett Cobb and His Orchestra (Vogue)

End of World War II R&B Dance Bands

Johnny Otis (1921-84)

Barrel House Stomp (1949, Savoy)
*Double Crossing Blues (1950, Savoy)
*Mistrustin' Blues (1950, Savoy)
Rockin' Blues (1950, Savoy)
*Willie and the Hand Jive (1958, Capitol)

The Johnny Otis Show (Capitol)
The Original Johnny Otis Show (Savoy)
*Cold Shot (1969, Kent)
Live at Monterey (1971, Epic)
The New Johnny Otis Show (1981, Alligator)

Buddy Johnson (1912-)

*Did You See Jackie Robinson Hit the Ball? (1949, Decca)
I'm Just Your Fool (1954, Mercury)

Rock'n'Roll with Buddy Johnson (Mercury)
Walkin' (Mercury)

Tiny Bradshaw (1905-58)

Tiny Plays (King)
Tiny Bradshaw (1952, King)

Lucky Millinder (1900-)

Lucky Millinder (Tod)
Lucky Millinder and His Orchestra (Affinity)
Lucky Millinder Orchestra (1947, Decca)
Apollo Jump (1983, Carly)

Big Band Saxophonists

Paul Williams (1940-)

The Hucklebuck (1949, Savoy)

The Hucklebuck (Saxophonograph)

Willis Jackson

Gator Tail (1949, King)

Willis Jackson Quintet (Prestige)

Jimmy Forrest

Night Train (1952, United Artists)

Earl Bostic (1913-65)

Flamingo (1952, King)

Best of . . . (King)
Bostic Rocks (King)
Dance Time (King)
*Fourteen Original Greatest Hits (King)

Sam Butera

Easy Rocking (1952, Capitol)

The Big Horn (Capitol)

Red Prysock (1929-)

I Didn't Sleep a Wink Last Night (1952, Mercury)
Finger Tips (1955, Mercury)

Best of . . . (Verve)

Sil Austin (1929-)

Slow Walk (1956, Mercury)

Everything's Shaking (Mercury)
Slow Walk Rock (Mercury)

Maxwell Davis

Slow Walk (1956, Mercury)

Blue Tango (Score)
Maxwell Davis and His Tenor Sax (Aladdin)

Big Jay McNeely (1928-)

There Is Something on Your Mind (1959, Swinging)

Big Jay in 3-D (King)
Big Jay McNeely (Warner Bros.)
Big Jay McNeely Selection (Savory)
Deacon Rides Again (Imperial)

King Curtis

(Curtis Ousley, 1934-71)

*Soul Twist (1959, Enjoy)
Spanish Harlem (1963, Atco)
Something on Your Mind (1968, Atco)
Them Changes (1971, Atco)

One More Time (1961, Prestige)
The Best of . . . (1968, Atco)
Live at Fillmore West (1971, Atco)
Jazz Grove (1973, Prestige)
Atlantic Honkers (1986, Atlantic)

Sam "The Man" Taylor

Amos Milburn and His Orchestra (Alladin)
Cootie Williams and His Orchestra: Jazz Anthology (Bethlehem)
Louis Armstrong and His Orchestra (MCA)
Quincy Jones and His Orchestra (Fontana)

Ray Charles and His Orchestra (Fontana)
Woody Herman and the New Third Herd (Verve)

Electric Guitarists

*Eddie Durham (1906-)

*He Ain't Got Rhythm (1936, MCA)

Jimmie Lunceford: Jimmie's Legacy (MCA)

*Charlie Christian (1919-42)

Charlie Christian Live! (Jazz Archives)
Harlem Jazz Scene, 1941 (Esoteric)

*Les Paul (1915-)

Nola (1950, Capitol)
How High the Moon (1951, Capitol)
Mockin' Bird Hill (1951, Capitol)
Whispering (1951, Capitol)

New Sounds, Vol. 2 (1951, Capitol)
Les Paul Story, Vols. 1-2 (1974, Capitol)
The World Is Still Waiting for the Sunrise (1974, Capitol)
Chester and Lester (1977, RCA)
Guitar Monsters (1978, RCA)

SHOUT, SCREAM, AND CRY BLUES

*Joe Turner (1911-85)

Goin' Away Blues (1938, Vocalion)
Roll'em Pete (1938, Vocalion)
Cherry Red (1939, Vocalion)
Beale Street Blues (1940, Okeh)
How Long, How Long Blues (1940, Varsity)
*Joe Turner Blues (1940, Okeh)
Shake It and Break It (1940, Varsity)

Blues on Central Avenue (1941, Decca)
*Corrine, Corrina (1941, Decca)
*Lonesome Graveyard (1941, Decca)
*Lucille (1941, Decca)
*Piney Brown Blues (1941, Decca)
*Rock Me Mama (1941, Decca)
*Rocks in my Bed (1941, Decca)
  Wee Baby Blues (1941, Decca)
*I Got Love for Sale (1946, National)
*My Gal's a Jockey (1946, National)
*Rebecca (1946, Decca)
  Battle of the Blues (1947, National)
  Miss Brown Blues (1947, National)
  Old Piney Brown Is Gone (1948, Swing Time)
*Please Don't Talk Me to Death (1948, Modern)
  Win-o-Baby (1948, Swing Time)
*Still in the Dark (1950, Atlantic)
*Sweet Sixteen (1952, Atlantic)
*Honey Hush (1953, Atlantic)
*TV Mama (1953, Atlantic)
*Shake Rattle and Roll (1954, Atlantic)
*Flip Flop and Fly (1955, Atlantic)
*Hide and Seek (1955, Atlantic)
*Lipstick, Powder, and Paint (1956, Atlantic)
*Morning, Noon, and Night (1956, Atlantic)
*Rock a While (1956, Atlantic)

Big Joe Rides Again (Atlantic)
Early Big Joe, 1940-44 (MCA)
Have No Fear, Big Joe is Here (Savoy)
Joe Turner (Atlantic)
Jumpin' the Blues (Arhoolie)
Nobody In Mind (Pablo)
Kansas City Jazz (1941, Decca)
Kansas City Jazz (1956, Atlantic)
His Greatest Recordings (1971, Atlantic)
The Boss of the Blues (1981, Atlantic)
Rhythm & Blues Years (1986, Atlantic)

Wynonie Harris (1915-69)

Hurry, Hurry (1944, Decca)
Time to Change Your Town (1945, Apollo)
Who Threw the Whiskey in the Well (1945, Decca)
*Good Rockin' Tonight (1947, King)
*All She Wants to Do Is Rock (1949, King)
Drinkin' Wine, Spo-Dee-O-Dee (1949, King)
Bloodshot Eyes (1950, King)
Good Morning Judge (1950, King)
I Like My Baby's Pudding (1950, King)
Lovin' Machine (1951, King)

Good Rockin' Tonight (King)
Mr. Blues Is Coming to Town (Route 66)
Oh Babe (1982, Route 66)
Party after Hours (1956, Aladdin)
Battle of the Blues (1958, King)
Battle of the Blues, Vol. 2 (1958, King)
Good Rockin' Blues (1977, Gusto)

*Jimmy Rushing (1903-71)

Going to Chicago (Vanguard)
Listen to the Blues (Vanguard)
Every Day I Have the Blues (1973, Bluesway)
If This Ain't the Blues (1974, Vanguard)
The Essential Jimmy Rushing (1978, Vanguard)
Mister Five By Five (1980, Columbia)

*Roy Brown (1925-81)

*Good Rockin' Tonight (1947, De-Luxe)
*Boogie at Midnight (1949, De-Luxe)
  Rockin' at Midnight (1949, De-Luxe)
*Hard Luck Blues (1950, De-Luxe)

Love Don't Love Nobody (1950,
De-Luxe)
Big Town (1951, De-Luxe)
Good Rockin' Man (1951, De-
Luxe)
Everybody (1955, King)
Saturday Night (1955, Imperial)
I'm Sticking with You (1956,
Imperial)
Party Doll (1956, Imperial)

Blues Are All Brown (Bluesday)
Hard Luck Blues (King)
Roy Brown Sings 24 Hits (King)
Battle of the Blues, Vols. 1-2 (1958,
King)
Hard Times (1973, Bluesway)
Good Rockin' Tonight (1978, Route
66)
Laughing But Crying (1978, Route
66)

*Big Joe Williams (1903-)

Back to the Country (Testament)
Everyday I Have the Blues
(Roulette)
Tough Times (Arhoolie)
Thinking of What They Did To Me
(1969, Arhoolie)

Eddie "Cleanhead" Vinson (1917-)

*Kidney Stew Blues (1945, King)
I'm Weak, But I'm Willing (1949,
King)
Something Done Stole My Cherry
Red (1949, King)

Blues Rocks (Blues Time)
Cherry Red Blues (King)
Eddie "Cleanhead" Vinson
(Riverside)
The Original Cleanhead (Philips)
Wee Baby Blues (Black & Blue)
Jamming the Blues (1975, Black
Lion)

Jimmy Witherspoon (1923-)

*Ain't Nobody's Business (1947,
Swing Time)
*No Rollin' Blues (1949, King)

Ain't Nobody's Business (Black
Lion)
At the Renaissance (Vogue)
Singin' the Blues (World Pacific)
There's Good Rockin' Tonight
(Fontana)
A Spoonful of Blues (1957, RCA)
Best of . . . (1964, Prestige)

Bullmoose Jackson

(Benjamin Jackson, 1919-)

*I Want a Bow-Legged Woman
(1949, King)
Why Don't You Haul Off and Love
Me (1949, King)
I Love You, Yes I Do (1961, Seven
Arts)

Anthology of R&B, Vol. 1
(Columbia)
Bullmoose Jackson (King)
*Bullmoose Jackson and the Buffalo
Bearcats, 1947-52* (King)
18 King Size R&B Hits (Columbia)

Women of Shout, Scream, and Cry
Blues

*Ella Mae Morse (1924-)

*Cow-Cow Boogie (1942, Capitol)
*Mister Fire by Fire (1942, Capitol)
Invitation to the Blues (1944,
Capitol)
Patty-Cake Man (1944, Capitol)
Buzz Me (1945, Capitol)
*The House of Blue Lights (1946,
Capitol)
Pig Foot Pete (1947, Capitol)
Pine Top Schwartz (1947, Capitol)
Tennessee Saturday Night (1951,
Capitol)

A Sleepin' at the Foot of the Bed
(1952, Capitol)
Big Mamou (1953, Capitol)
Greyhound (1953, Capitol)
Smack Dab in the Middle (1955,
Capitol)
Rock'n'Roll Wedding (1956,
Capitol)

Barrelhouse, Boogie and the Blues
(1955, Capitol)
Morse Code (1957, Capitol)
Sensational (1985, Capitol)

*Ruth Brown (1928-)

*Teardrops from My Eyes (1950,
Atlantic)
*5-10-15 Hours (1952, Atlantic)
(Mama) He Treats Your Daughter
Mean (1953, Atlantic)
Mambo Baby (1954, Atlantic)
Oh What a Dream (1954, Atlantic)
*Lucky Lips (1956, Atlantic)
*This Little Girl's Gone Rockin'
(1958, Atlantic)

Along Comes Ruth (Philips)
Best of . . . (Atlantic)
Late Date with Ruth Brown
(Atlantic)
Ramblin' (RB)
Ruth Brown (Atlantic)
m*Teardrops from My Eyes*
(Atlantic)
Sugar Babe (1976, President)
Sweet Baby of Mine (1981, Route
66)
The Soul Survives (1982, Flair)

Faye Adams

Shake a Hand (1953, Herald)
Hurts Me to My Heart (1954,
Herald)

Original Golden Blues Greats, Vol. 5
(Liberty)
Shake a Hand (Warwick)
Softly He Speaks (Savoy)

Hurts Me to My Heart (1954,
Herald)
Faye Adams (1980, Savoy)

Big Maybelle

(Maybelle Smith, 1924-72)

Candy (1956, Savoy)

Big Maybelle Sings (Savoy)
The Last of . . . (Paramount)
The Gospel Soul of . . . (1968,
Brunswick)
The Great Soul Hits of . . . (1969,
Brunswick)

Varetta Dillard

Easy, Easy Baby (Savoy)
Mercy Mr. Percy (Savoy)

Little Esther Phillips (1935-)

Cupid's Boogie (1950, Savoy)
Ring-a-Ding-Doo (1952, Federal)
Release Me (1962, Lenox)
Set Me Free (1970, Atlantic)
What a Diff'rence a Day Makes
(1975, Kudu)

Esther Phillips (Atlantic)
Burnin' (1971, Atlantic)
From a Whisper to a Scream (1972,
Kudu)
Black-Eyed Blues (1973, Kudu)
Little Esther Phillips (1975, Power
Pak)
What a Difference a Day Makes
(1975, Kudu)
A Good Black Is Hard to Crack
(1981, Mercury)
Set Me Free (1986, Atlantic)

*La Vern Baker (1929-)

*Tweedle Dee (1954, Atlantic)
Bop-Ting-A-Ling/That's All I Need
(1955, Atlantic)
*I Can't Love You Enough (1956,
Atlantic)

*Jim Dandy (1956, Atlantic)
Tra-La-La (1956, Atlantic)
Voodoo Voodoo (1956, Atlantic)
*I Cried a Tear (1958, Atlantic)
*I Waited Too Long (1959, Atlantic)
Bumble Bee (1960, Atlantic)
*Saved (1961, Atlantic)
*See See Rider (1963, Atlantic)

Blues Ballads (Atlantic)
LaVern Baker (Atlantic)
LaVern Baker Sings Bessie Smith (Atlantic)
Let Me Belong to You (1970, Brunswick)
Her Greatest Recordings (1971, Atco)

COMBO AND JUMP BLUES

Roy Milton (1907-83)

Milton's Boogie (1945, Specialty)
*R.M. Blues (1945, Specialty)
I'm Grateful (1957, King)

Big Fat Mama (Jukebox Lil)
Grandfather of R&B (Jukebox Lil)
Roy Milton and His Solid Senders (Specialty)
Roy Milton Blues (Vivid)
Rhythm and Blues (Dooto)
Roots of Rock, Vol. 1 (Kent)

*Louis Jordan (1908-75)

Gee, But You're Swell (1937, Decca)
*Choo Choo Choo Boogie (1942, Decca)
I'm Gonna Move to the Outskirts of Town (1942, Decca)
G.I. Jive (1944, Decca)
Ain't Nobody Here but Us Chickens (1946, Decca)
Ain't That Just Like a Woman (1946, Decca)
*Let the Good Time Roll (1946, Decca)

Stone Cold Dead in the Market (1946, Decca)
That Chick's Too Young to Fry (1946, Decca)
*Saturday Night Fish Cry (1949, Decca)

Choo Choo Ch'Boogie (Philips International)
Let the Good Times Roll (Decca)
Louis Jordan (Blues Spectrum)
Louis Jordan (Decca)
Prime Cuts (Swing House)
Silver Star Series Presents Louis Jordan and His Orchestra (MCA)
Louis Jordan and His Tympany Five, Vol. 1 (1946, Decca)
Louis Jordan and His Tympany Five, Vol. 2 (1948, Decca)
Somebody Up There Digs Me (1957, Mercury)
Go Blow Your Horn (1958, Score)
Man, We're Wailing (1958, Mercury)
The Best of . . . (1975, MCA)

Amos Milburn (1927-80)

Down the Road a Piece (1946, Aladdin)
*Chicken Shack Boogie (1948, Aladdin)
*Bad, Bad Whiskey (1950, Aladdin)
Let's Rock a While (1951, Aladdin)
Rock, Rock, Rock (1952, Aladdin)
Let's Have a Party (1953, Aladdin)
Milk and Water (1954, Aladdin)
Juice, Juice (1956, Aladdin)

Amos Milburn (Blues Spectrum)
Amos Milburn and His Chicken Shackers (Route 66)
Return of the Blues Boss (Motown)
Party After Hours (1951, Aladdin)
Rockin' the Boogie (1951, Aladdin)
Let's Have a Party (1958, Score)

Jimmy Liggins

Cadillac Boogie (1947, Specialty)

I Can't Stop It (Route 66)

Joe Liggins (1916-)

Pink Champagne (1950, Specialty)

Joe and Jimmy Liggins: This Is How It All Began (Specialty)
Joe Liggins (Blues Spectrum)

*Professor Longhair

(Roy Byrd, 1918-80)

*Bye, Bye Baby (1949, Star Talent)
*Mardi Gras in New Orleans (1949, Star Talent)
*Professor Longhair's Boogie (1949, Star Talent)
*She Ain't Got No Hair (1949, Star Talent)
She Ain't Got No Hair [Baldhead] (1950, Mercury)
*Mardi Gras in New Orleans [Go to the Mardi Gras] (1959, Mercury)
Big Chief (1964, Mercury)

New Orleans Piano (1953, Atco)
Live on the Queen Mary (1975, Harvest)
Rock'n'Roll Gumbo (1975, Barclay)
Crawfish Fiesta (1980, Alligator)

*Fats Domino (1929-)

*Fat Man (1949, Imperial)
*Goin' Home (1952, Imperial)
Gong to the River (1953, Imperial)
*Ain't That a Shame (1955, Imperial)
*Blueberry Hill (1956, Imperial)
Blue Monday (1956, Imperial)
*I'm In Love Again (1956, Imperial)
*I'm Walking (1957, Imperial)
*Whole Lotta Loving (1958, Imperial)

Walkin' to New Orleans (1960, Imperial)

Cooking with Fats (Imperial)
Let's Dance with Domino (Imperial)
Rare Dominoes, Vols. 1-2 (Imperial)
Rock and Rollin' (Imperial)
Sings Million Record Hits (Imperial)
That Fabulous Mr. D. (Imperial)
Two Sensational Albums (Pickwick)
This Is Fats Domino (1956, Imperial)
Let's Play Fats Domino (1959, Imperial)
Cooking with Fats (1966, Liberty)
Legendary Masters Series (1972, United Artists)
Play It Again Fats (1973, United Artists)
Live at Montreux (1974, Atlantic)
Twenty Greatest Hits (1976, United Artists)
The Fats Domino Story, Vols. 1-6 (1977, United Artists)

Percy Mayfield (1938-)

*Please Send Me Someone to Love (1950, Specialty)

Best of . . . (Specialty)
Percy Mayfield (Tangerine S.)

*Jackie Brenston (1930-79)

Independent Woman (1951, Chess)
My Real Gone Rocket (1951, Chess)
*Rocket 88 (1951, Chess)
Hi Ho Baby (1952, Chess)
Starvation (1953, Chess)
Trouble up the Road (1960, Sue)
You Ain't the One (1960, Sue)
Down in My heart (1963, Mel-Lon)
Want You to Rock Me (1963, Mel-Lon)

Kings of Rhythm (1981, Flyright)

Wilbert Harrison (1929-)

This Woman of Mine (1952, Fury)
*Kansas City/K.C. Lovin' (1959, Fury)
*Let's Work Together (1969, Sue)

Soul Food Man (Chelsea)
Battle of the Giants (1962, Joy)
Kansas City (1962, Sphere)
Let's Work Together (1969, Sue)

*Lloyd Price (1934-)

*Lawdy Miss Clawdy (1952, Specialty)
Oooh-Oooh-Oooh (1953, Specialty)
Restless Heart (1953, Specialty)
Just Because (1957, ABC)
*Stagger Lee (1958, ABC)
I'm Gonna Get Married (1959, ABC)
*Personality (1959, ABC)
Lady Luck (1960, ABC)

The ABC Collection (ABC)
L. Price (Specialty)
Mr. Personality (ABC)
Original Hits (Sonet)
Sixteen Greatest Hits (1972, ABC)
Mr. Personality Revisited (1983, Charly)

Smiley Lewis

(Overton Amos Lemons, 1920-66)

*The Bells Are Ringing (1952, Imperial)
Shame, Shame, Shame (1952, Imperial)
*I Hear You Knockin' (1955, Imperial)
One Night (1957, Imperial)

Shame, Shame, Shame (1970, Liberty)
The Bells Are Ringing (1978, United Artists)
I Hear You Knockin' (1978, United Artists)

Down Yonder (1984, K.C.)

*Chuck Willis (1928-58)

I Feel So Bad (1952, Okeh)
My Story (1952, Okeh)
*C.C. Rider (1957, Atlantic)
*Betty and Dupree (1958, Atlantic)
*What Am I Living For [Hang Up My Rock and Roll Shoes] (1958, Atlantic)

His Greatest Recordings (Atco)
King of the Stroll (Atlantic)
Wails the Blues (Epic)
I Remember Chuck Willis (1963, Warner Bros.)
Chuck Willis--My Story (1980, Columbia)
Be Good or Be Gone (1985, Edsel)

Rosco Gordon

Booted (1953, Chess)
No More Doggin' (1953, RPM)
Just a Little Bit (1954, Vee Jay)

Best of . . . (Chiswick)
Keep On Doggin' (Mr. R&B)
Rosco Gordon (1971, Charly)

Guitar Slim

(Eddie Jones, 1926-59)

*The Things I Used to Do (1954, Specialty)

The Things I Used to Do (Specialty)

Little Willie John

(John Davenport, 1937-68)

All Around the World (1955, King)
Fever (1956, King)
Let Them Talk (1960, King)
Sleep (1960, King)

Fever (King)
Fifteen Original Hits (King)

Free at Last (King)
Talk to Me (King)
Little Willie John, 1953-62 (1977, King)

*Huey "Piano" Smith (1934-)

*Rockin' Pneumonia and the Boogie Woogie Flu (1957, Ace)
*Don't You Just Know It (1958, Ace)

For Dancing (Ace)
Havin a Good Time (Ace)
**Rockin' Pneumonia and the Boogie Woogie Flu* (Sue)
Rock'n'Roll Revival (Ace)
'T Was Night before Christmas (Ace)
**Huey Piano Smith and the Clowns* (1979, Vivid)

CLUB BLUES

*Nat King Cole (1919-65)

Sweet Lorraine (1940, Decca)
That Ain't Right (1941, Decca)
All For You (1943, Excelsior)
Got a Penny (1943, Premier)
Straighten Up and Fly Right (1944, Capitol)
I'm a Shy Guy (1945, Capitol)
(Get your Kicks on) Route 66 (1946, Capitol)
She's my Buddy's Chick (1946, Capitol)
(I Love You) For Sentimental Reasons (1947, Capitol)
The Geek (1948, Capitol)
Nature Boy (1948, Capitol)
Too Young (1951, Capitol)
Looking Back (1957, Capitol)
Send for Me (1957, Capitol)
Those Lazy-Hazy-Crazy Days of Summer (1963, Capitol)

Anatomy of a Jam Session (Black Lion)

From the Very Beginning (MCA)
King Cole Trio, Trio Days (Capitol)
Original Sounds (Up Front)
Nat King Cole Trio, Vols. 1-4, (1944-49, Capitol)
**Love Is the Thing* (1957, Capitol)
Wild Is Love (1960, Capitol)
Ramblin' Rose (1962, Capitol)
L-O-V-E (1965, Capitol)

*Cecil Gant (1913-51)

I Wonder (1944, Gilt-Edge)
Cecil's Boogie (1945, Gilt-Edge)
Nashville Jumps (1946, Bullet)
Ninth Street Jive (1946, Bullet)
Another Day, Another Dollar (1948, Bullet)
I'm a Good Man, But a Poor Man (1948, Bullet)
Shotgun Boogie (1950, Decca)
We're Gonna Rock (1950, Decca)
Owl Stew (1951, Decca)
Rock Little Baby (1951, Decca)
Rock the Boogie (1951, Four-Star)

Cecil Gant (Gilt-Edge)
The Incomparable Cecil Gant (Sound)
Killer Diller Boogie (Magpie)
Rock Little Baby (Flyright)
Rock the Boogie, 1944-47 (1983, Krazy Kat)

*Ivory Joe Hunter (1914-74)

Ain't That Loving You Baby
My Wish Come There
Blues at Sunrise (1941, Ivory)
Pretty Mama Blues (1942, Pacific)
Landlord Blues (1947, King)
Guess Who (1949, King)
I Almost Lost My Mind (1950, MGM)
I Need You So (1950, MGM)
I Quit My Pretty Mama (1950, King)
Empty Arms (1957, Atlantic)
Since I Met You Baby (1957, Atlantic)

Yes, I Want You (1958, Atlantic)
City Lights (1959, Atlantic)

I Got That Lonesome Feeling
(MGM)
Ivory Joe Hunter (Atlantic)
Ivory Joe Sings the Old & the New
(Atlantic)
16 of His Greatest Hits (King)
Return of . . . (1971, Epic)
*Seventh Street Boogie (1977, Route
66)
*Jumping at the Dew Drop (1980,
Route 66)

Johnny Moore's Three Blazers featuring Charles Brown

Drifting Blues (1945, Philo)
Rock with It (1950, Aladdin)

Drifting Blues (1983, Score)

Lowell Fulsom (1921-)

Come Back Baby (1949, Downbeat)
Three O'Clock Blues (1949,
Downbeat)
You Know That I Love You (1949,
Downbeat)
Blue Shadows (1950, Swingtime)
Every Day I Have the Blues (1950,
Swingtime)
Lonesome Christmas (1950,
Swingtime)
Black Nights (1965, Kent)
Make a Little Love (1967, Kent)
Tramp (1967, Kent)

In a Heavy Bag (Jewel)
I've Got the Blues (Jewel)
The O'l Blues Singer (Granite)
The Tramp (1967, Kent)
Lowell Fulsom (1975, Arhoolie)
*Lowell Fulsom (1977, Chess)

Johnny Ace (1929-54)

Cross My Heart (1952, Duke)
Follow the Rule (1952, Duke)

My Song (1952, Duke)
Aces Wild (1953, Duke)
The Clock (1953, Duke)
Saving My Love For You (1953,
Duke)
Never Let Me Go (1954, Duke)
Please Forgive Me (1954, Duke)
No Money (1955, Duke)
Pledging My Love (1955, Duke)
Anymore (1956, Duke)
Still Love You So (1956, Duke)

Johnny Ace Memorial Album (1956,
Duke)

Jesse Belvin (1933-60)

Dream Girl (1953, Specialty)
Earth Angel (1955, Specialty)
Girl of My Dreams (1955,
Specialty)
Goodnight My Love (1956,
Modern)
Funny (1959, RCA)
Guess Who (1959, RCA)

Golden Goodies, Vol. 8 (Roulette)

*Ray Charles

Confession Blues (1949, Everest)
Baby Let Me Hold Your Hand
(1951, Everest)
Roll with Me Baby (1952, Atlantic)
Hallelujah I Love Her So (1955,
Atlantic)
I've Got a Woman (1955, Atlantic)
What'd I Say (1959, Atlantic)
Come Rain or Come Shine (1960,
ABC)
Georgia on My Mind (1960, ABC)
Greenbacks (1960, ABC)
Sticks and Stones (1960, ABC)
Them That Got (1960, ABC)
Hit the Road Jack (1961, ABC)
I Can't Stop Loving You (1962,
ABC)
Bested (1963, ABC)
Crying Time (1966, ABC)
Let's Go Get Stoned (1966, ABC)

Here We Go Again (1967, ABC)
Eleanor Rigby (1968, ABC)
Don't Change On Me (1971, ABC)

Doing His Thing (Tangerine)
The Greatest Hits of . . . (Atlantic)
Hallelujah I Love Her So (Atlantic)
Ray Charles, Vols. 1-2 (Everest)
Ray Charles Story, Vols. 1-4
    (Atlantic)
The Great Ray Charles (1957,
    Atlantic)
What I'd Say (1959, Atlantic)
Genius of . . . (1960, Atlantic)
Genius Sings the Blues (1960,
    Atlantic)
The Greatest Ray Charles (1961,
    Atlantic)
*Modern Sounds in Country and
    Western Music*, Vols 1-2 (1962,
    ABC)
Ray Charles Live (1973, Atlantic)
*A Twenty-Fifth Anniversary in Show
    Business Salute to Ray Charles*
    (1973, Atlantic)
Renaissance (1975, Crossover)
True to Life (1977, Atlantic)
Brother Ray Is at It Again (1980,
    Atlantic)
The Right Time (1980, Atlantic)
A Life in Music (1982, Atlantic)
Wish You Were Here Tonight (1983,
    Columbia)

Ike and Tina Turner

(Ike Turner, 1931- ; Tina Turner,
1938-)

From the Beginning (Kent)
Please, Please, Please (Kent)
The World of Ike and Tina Turner
    (United Artists)

*Ike Turner solo

Ike Turner and His Kings of Rhythm
    (Ace)
Blues Roots (1972, United Artists)
I'm Tore Up (1978, Red Lightnin')

Kings of Rhythm (1981, Flyright)

Tina Turner solo. SEE UNDER
Early Rock and Soul Producers:
Phil Spector

SOUTH LOUISIANA R&B

*Guitar Gable and His Musical Kings

(Gabriel Perrodin, 1937-)

Irene (Excello)
Congo Mombo (1956, Excello)
Guitar Rhumbo (1956, Excello)
Life Problem (1956, Excello)
It's Hard But It's Fair (1957,
    Excello)
Walking in the Park (1957, Excello)
What's the Matter with My Baby
    (1957, Excello)
This Should Go On Forever (1958,
    Excello)

*Carol Fran

Emmitt Lee (1957, Excello)
I Quit My Knockin' (1957, Excello)
One Look at You Daddy (1957,
    Excello)

Classie Ballou

Hey! Pardner (1957, Excello)
Confusion (1957, Excello)
Crazy Mambo (1957, Excello)

Jay Nelson

A Fool That Was Blind (1958,
    Excello)
Rocka Me All Night Long (1958,
    Excello)

Leroy Washington (?-1966)

*Baby Please Come Home (1958,
    Excello)

Everyday (1958, Zynn)
Long Hair Knock Knees and Bow
Legs (1958, Excello)
*Wild Cherry (1958, Excello)

Leroy Washington (1981, Flyright)

James Freeman

You're Gonna Need Me (1957,
T.N.T.)

Hop Wilson (?-1975)

Broke and Hungry (1958, Excello)
Chicken Stuff (1958, Excello)

Hop Wilson Blues with Friends
(1981, Excello)

Juke Boy Bonner (1932-78)

Call Me Juke Boy (1960, Excello)
Can't Hardly Keep From Crying
(1960, Excello)

Tal Miller

Baby (1957, Hollywood)
Life's Journey (1957, Goldband)

*Guitar Jr.

(Lonnie Brooks, 1933-)

Family Rules (1957, Goldband)
*The Crowl (1958, Goldband)
I Got It Made (When I Marry
Shirley Mae) (1958, Goldband)
Roll Roll Roll (1958, Goldband)

*Jimmy Wilson (?-1965)

Please Accept My Love (1958,
Goldband)
Tin Pan Alley (1960, Big Town)

NEW ORLEANS R&B

*Jessie Hill (1932-)

Ooh Poo Pah Doo, Parts 1-2 (1960,
Minit)
Whip It on Me (1960, Minit)

Naturally (Blue Thumb)

*Showmen

Country Fool (1961, Minit)
It Will Stand (1961, Minit)

*Ernie K-Doe

(Ernest Kador, Jr., 1936-)

Do Baby Do (1956, Specialty)
Hello My Lover (1959, Minit)
*A Certain Girl (1961, Minit)
I Cried My Last Tear (1961, Minit)
*Mother-in-Law (1961, Minit)
Te-Ta-Te-Ta-Ta (1961, Minit)
Wanted $10,000 Reward (1961,
Minit)
Later for Tomorrow (1967, Duke)

Ernie K-Doe, Vol. 2 (Bandy)
Mother-in-Law (Bandy)

*Irma Thomas (1941-)

Ruler of My Heart (1962, Minit)
Time Is on My Side (1964,
Imperial)

Irma Thomas (Bandy)
Safe with Me (1979, RCS)
In between Tears (1980, Charly)

Neville Brothers

(*Aaron Neville, 1941- ; Art
Neville)

Hey Pocky Way (1966, Parlophone)
*Tell It Like It Is (1966, Parlophone)
Iko Iko (1980, A&M)
Mona Lisa (1980, A&M)

The Ten Commandments of Love
    (1980, A&M)

Wild Tchoupitoulas (1975, Island)
The Neville Bros. (1978, Capitol)
Fiyo on the Bayou (1981, A&M)
*Treacherous: A History of the Neville
    Bros., 1955-85* (1986, Rhino)
Uptown (1987, Rounder)

Hawketts with Art and Aaron Neville

Mardi Gras Mambo (1954)

Aaron Neville solo

Over You (1960, Minit)

*Lee Dorsey (1927-86)

Do Re Mi (1961, Fury)
*Ya Ya (1961, Fury)
*Ride Your Pony (1965, Minit)
*Get Out of My Life Woman (1966,
    Amy)
Holy Cow (1966, Amy)
*Working in the Coal Mine (1966,
    Amy)
Go Go Girl (1967, Amy)
My Old Car (1967, Amy)
Everything I Do Gonna Be Funky
    (1969, Amy)

New Lee Dorsey (Amy)
Ride Your Pony-Get Out of My Life
    (Fury)
Working in the Coal Mine (Fury)
Ya Ya (Fury)
Lee Dorsey (1966, Amy)
Yes We Can (1970, Polydor)
Night People (1978, ABC)

Carter Brothers

Booze in the Bottle (1965, Jewel)

Big Mac

Rough Dried Woman (1965, Jewel)

Meters

Cabbage Alley (1972, Reprise)
Rejuvenation (1974, Reprise)
Cissy Strut (1975, Island)
New Direction (1977, Warner Bros.)

Tommy Ridgely (1925-)

The New King of the Stroll (1976,
    Flyer)

Jean Knight

My Toot Toot (1985, Mirage)

*Dr. John

(Malcolm "Mac" Rebennack, 1941-)

*Storm Warning (1960, Rex
    Records)
*Gris Gris Gumbo Ya Ya (1968,
    Atco)
*I Walk on Gilded Splinters (1968,
    Atco)
*Right Place Wrong Time (1973,
    Atco)
*Such a Night (1973, Atco)

The Brightest Smile in Town
    (Demon)
Gris-Gris (1968, Atco)
Babylon (1969, Atco)
Remedies (1970, Atco)
The Sun, Moon, and Herbs (1971,
    Atco)
Gumbo (1972, Atco)
In the Right Place (1973, Atco)
Desitively Bonaroo (1974, Atco)
Hollywood Be Thy Name (1974,
    United Artists)
Cut Me While I'm Hot (1975, DJM)
City Lights (1979, Horizon)
Tango Place (1979, Horizon)
Dr. John Plays Mac Rebennack
    (1981, Clean Cuts)

Shirley and Lee

(Shirley Goodman, 1937- ; Lee Leonard, 1935-)

I'm Gone (1952, Aladdin)
Feel So Good (1956, Aladdin)
*Let the Good Times Roll (1956, Aladdin)
I've Never Been Loved Before (1960, Warwick)

Let the Good Times Roll (1960, Aladdin)
Best of . . . (1973, Ace)

Shirley Goodman solo

Shame, Shame, Shame (1975, Vibration)

Shame, Shame, Shame (1975, Vibration)

Gene and Eunice

(Gene Forest; Eunice Levy)

*Ko Ko Mo (1955, Aladdin)
Poco Loco (1959, Case)

Milburn, Hopkins, Gene & Eunice (Aladdin)
Clap Your Hands and Stomp Your Feet (1986, EMI)
It Will Stand (1986, EMI)
History of New Orleans R&B, Vols. 1-3 (1987, Rhino)
New Orleans Rarities (1987, Imperial)

*Chris Kenner (1929-)

*Sick and Tired (1957, Imperial)
Come Back and See (1961, Minit)
*I Like It Like That (1961, Minit)
Land of 1,000 Dances (1961, Minit)
Packing Up (1961, Minit)
*Something You Got (1964, Minit)

Land of Thousand Dances (1963, Atlantic)

*Bobby Marchan (1930-)

There Is Something on Your Mind (1960, Fury)

*Don Gardner with Dee Dee Ford

I Need Your Loving (1961, Fire)

Jesse Stone (1901-)

(Charles Calhoun, pseud.)

It Should Have Been Me
Idaho (1942, Columbia)
Hey Sister Lucy (1947, RCA-Victor)
Cole-Slaw (1949, RCA-Victor)
Money-Honey (1953)
Oh, That'll Be Joyful (1954, Atlantic)
Shake, Rattle, and Roll (1954)
Your Cash Ain't Nothin' but Trash (1954)
Night Life (1955, Atco)
Jamboree (1956, Groove)

Dance to Rock & Roll (1957, Atlantic)
Rock & Roll (1958, Atco)

*Hardrock Gunter

(Sidney Louie Gunter, 1918-)

*Birmingham Bounce (1949, Bama)
*Gonna Dance All Night (1950, Bama)
Lonesome Blues (1950, Bama)
My Bucket's Been Fixed (1950, Bullet)
Boogie Woogie on Saturday Night (1951, Decca)
I've Done Gone Hog Wild (1951, Decca)
Sixty Minute Man (1951, Decca)
I'll Give 'em Rhythm (1954, King)
I Put My Britches On Just Like Everybody Else (1955, King)

Jukebox, Help Me Find My Baby
(1956, Sun)
Whoo! I Mean Whee! (1957,
Emperor)
Let Me Be a Fool (1958, Cross
Country)
Is It Too Late (1959, Cullman)
Hillbilly Twist (1962, Starday)

Merrill Moore (1923-)

*Corrine, Corrina (1952, Capitol)
*House of Blue Lights (1953,
Capitol)
*Red Light (1953, Capitol)
*Fly Right Boogie (1954, Capitol)
*Down the Road a Piece (1955,
Capitol)
*Rock-Rockola (1955, Capitol)

Bellyful of Blue Thnunder (1967,
Ember)
Rough House 88 (1969, Ember)

Billy Vera and the Beaters (1944-)

Country Girl--City Man (1968,
Atlantic)
At This Moment (1981, Rhino)

By Request (1987, Rhino)

OTHER R&B

*Robert Cray

Who's Been Talking (1978, Tomato)
Bad Influence (1983, Hightone)
False Accusations (1985, Hightone)
August (1986, Hightone)
Strong Persuader (1986, Polygram)

T-Bone Burnett

(J. Henry Burnette, 1934-63)

Behind the Trap Door (Demon)
Trap Door (Demon)
Truth Decay (1980, Takoma)
Proof through the Night (1983, Dot)

Stevie Ray Vaughan and Double Trouble

Live Alive (1987, Epic)

James Carr

Dark End of the Street (Gold Wax)
Pouring Water on a Drowning Man
(Gold Wax)
James Carr (P-Vine)

At the Dark End of the Street (1987,
Blue Side Upside)

*Johnny Copeland

*Make My Home Where I Hang My
Hat* (Demon)
Texas Twister (Demon)
Copeland Special (1981, Rounder)

Cajun and Zydeco

General Anthologies

Louisiana Cajun Music, Vols. 1-5
*Zydeco Blues--Jay Miller Sessions
(1978, Flyright)

CAJUN

*Joseph Falcon (1900-65)

*Allons à Lafayette (1928,
  Columbia)
*Jole Blonde (1928, Columbia)
Mon Coeur T'Appelle (1928,
  Columbia)
Fe Fe Puchaux (1929, Columbia)
Ossun One-Step (Osson Two-Step)
  (1929, Columbia)

Leo Soileau (1904-80) and Mayuse Lafleur

Mama Where You At (Hey Mom)
  (1928, Victor)

Leo Soileau and Moise Roli

Easy Rider Blues (1929,
  Paramount)

Leo Soileau's Three Aces

Hackberry Hop (1935, Bluebird)
La Valse de Gueydan (1935,
  Bluebird)
Le Gran Mamou (1936, Bluebird)

Leo Soileau's Four Aces

La Blues de Port Arthur (1938,
  Decca)

Hackberry Ramblers [Riverside Ramblers]

Te Petite et Te Meon (1935,
  Bluebird)
*You've Got to Hi De Hi (1935,
  Bluebird)
*Wondering (1936, Bluebird)
Silver Star Stomp (1953, De Luxe)
Cajun Pogo (1963, Arhoolie)

*LeRoy "Happy Fats" LeBlanc and Rayne-Bo Ramblers

(LeRoy LeBlanc, 1915-)

Vain Toi Don à Ma Mort (1937,
  Bluebird)
Les Veuve à Kita la Coulee (1941,
  Bluebird)

*J.B. Fusilier

Ma Chere Basett (1936, Bluebird)

*Harry Choates (1922-51)

Going High (Draggin' the Bow)
*Allons à Lafayette (1946, Gold
  Star)
*Jole Blon (1946, Gold Star)
*Poor Hobo (1947, Gold Star)
*Bayou Pon Pon (1948, Gold Star;
  1950, Gold Star)
Devil on the Bayou (1948; 1950)

*The Fiddle King of Cajun Swing,
  1946-49* (1982, Arhoolie)

*Iry Le-June (1928-54)

*Evangeline Special (1948, Opera)
*Love Bridge Waltz (1948, Opera)
*Calcasieu Waltz (1949, Folk-Star)
*Teche Special (1950, Folk-Star)

The Legendary Iry Le June, Vols. 1-2
  (Goldband)

*Nathan Abshire (1913-)

Hey Mom (1961, Kajun)
Jolie Catin' (1961, Kajun)
*Mardi Gras Song (1961, Kajun)
Pine Grove Blues (1961, Kajun)
Pop Corn Blues (1961, Kajun)
La Banana au Nonc Adam (1962, Kajun)
*The La La Blues (1962, Kajun)
*Games People Play (1970, Swallow)

Nathan Abshire and the Pine Grove Boys

*Pine Grove Blues (1949, O.T.)
*Nathan Abshire and the Pine Grove Boys (1977, Flyright)

Nathan Abshire with Balfa Brothers

*Lemonade Song (1970, Swallow)
A Musician's Life (1970, Swallow)
Offshore Blues (1970, Swallow)
*Sur le Courtableau (1970, Swallow)
Tramp sur la Rue (1970, Swallow)
Valse de Bayou Teche (1970, Swallow)

The Good Times Are Killing Me (Swallow)
Pine Grove Blues (Swallow)
Balfa Brothers Play Traditional Cajun Music (1968, Swallow)
The Cajuns (1972, Sonet)

*Dewey Balfa

*Drumhard's Sorrow Waltz (1967, Swallow)
Lacassine Speical (1968, Swallow)
T'Ai Petite et T'Ai Meon (1968, Swallow)
La Valse de Bambocheurs (1968, Swallow)

Balfa Brothers Play Traditional Cajun Music (1968, Swallow)

*Chuck Guillory and His Rhythm Boys

*Tolan Waltz (1948, Colonial)
*Big Texas (1949, Modern)

*Lee Sonnier and His Acadian Stars

War Window Waltz (1948, Feature)

*Doc Guidry

(Oran Guidry, 1918-)

Chere Cherie (1953, Decca)
The Little Fat Man (1953, Decca)

Alex Brussard with Happy Fats

Le Sud de la Louisianne (1959)

Lawrence Walker (1908-68)

*Alberta (1936, Bluebird)
*What's the Matter Now (1936, Bluebird)
*Evangeline Waltz (1951, Lyric)
*Reno Waltz (1951, Lyric)

A Tribute to the Late Great Lawrence Walker (La Louisianne)
Jambalaya on the Bayou (1968, Flyright)

*Al Terry (190?-)

*I'll Be Glad When I'm Free (1946, Gold Star)
*God Was So Good (Cause He Let Me Keep You) (1951, Feature)
*Good Deal Lucille (1953, Hickory)
Watch Dog (1960, Hickory)

This Is Al Terry (Index)

*Jimmy Newman (1927-)

*I Made a Big Mistake (1951, Feature)
*Wondering (1951, Feature)

*Cry Cry Darling (1954, Dot)
Blue Darlin' (1955, Dot)
Daydreamin' (1955, Dot)
*A Fallen Star (1957, Dot)
You're Making a Fool Out of Me (1958, Dot)
Grin and Bear It (1959, Dot)
So Soon (1959, Dot)
*A Lovely Work of Art (1960, MGM)
Wanting You with Me Tonight (1960, MGM)
*Alligator Man (1961, Decca)
Everybody's Dyin' For Love (1961, MGM)
*Bayou Talk (1962, Decca)
*DJ for a Day (1963, Decca)
Artificial Rose (1965, Decca)
Back in Circulation (1965, Decca)
Back Pocket Money (1966, Decca)
Blue Lonely Winter (1967, Decca)
*Louisiana Saturday Night (1967, Decca)
Born to Love You (1968, Decca)
Boo Dan (1969, Decca)

Happy Cajun (Plantation)
Folk Songs of the Bayou Country (1963, Decca)
Jimmy C. Newman Sings Cajun (1974, La Louisianne)
Lacke Pas la Patate (1974, La Louisianne)
Jimmy Newman and Al Terry (1981, Flyright)

*Vin Bruce (1932-)

*Dans la Louisiane (1952, Columbia)
*Fille de la Ville (1952, Columbia)
*Le Delaysay (1961, Swallow)

Vin Bruce Sings Jole Blon & Cajun Classics (1961, Swallow)

Gene Rodrique

Dans le Coeur de la Ville (In the Heart of the Town) (1953, Folk-Star)
*Jolie Fille (1954, Meladee)
*Little Cajun Girl (1960)

LATER CAJUN

*Austin Pitre and the Evangeline Playboys

(Austin Pitre, 1918-81)

*Flumes Dans Faires (1959, Swallow)
Mamou Blues (1959, Swallow)
Opelousas Waltz (1959, Swallow)
Two Step de Bayou Teche (1959, Swallow)

Austin Pitre and the Evangeline Playboys (Swallow)
Back to the Bayou (1980, Sonet)

*Badeaux and the Louisiana Aces

*Valse de Joly Rogers (1961, Swallow)
*The Back Door (1962, Swallow)

D.L. Menard Sings the Back Door and His Other Cajun Hits (1980, Swallow)

*Richard Belton and the Musical Aces

*Just En Reve (1962)
*Un Autre Soir D'Ennui (Another Sleepless Night) (1967)
*The Cajun Streak (1974)

Modern Sounds in Cajun Music (Swallow)

Camay Doucet

*Hold My False Tooth (1976)

Mom I'm Still Your Little Boy
(1976)
Me and My Cousin (1977)

Cajun Goodies (Swallow)

PRE-ZYDECO

Amadie Ardoin (1900-38?)

*Berlin (Bluebird)
*Les Blues de la Prison (1930,
Decca)
*Les Blues de Voyages (1930,
Bluebird)
*La Valse de Gueydan (1930,
Brunswick)
*La Valse de Amities (1936,
Bluebird)

Amadie Ardoin (Old Timey)
Louisiana Cajun Music, Vol. 1: *First
Recordings--1920s* (Old Timey)

Dennis McGee (1893-)

*Mon Chere Bebe Creole (1928,
Columbia)
*Le Reel Cajun (1928, Columbia)

Early Recordings of. . . (Morning
Star)

ZYDECO

*Clarence Garlow (1911-)

*Bon Ton Roula (Let the Good
Times Roll) (1950, Macy)
*Crawfishin' (1953, Flair)
*Route 90 (1953, Flair)
*Foggy Blues (1976, Flyright)

*Boozoo Chavis

*Paper in My Shoe (1954, Folk-Star)
*Forty One Days (1955, Folk-Star)

*Clifton Chenier (1925-)

*Ay-Tete-Fee (Eh Tite Fille) (1955,
Specialty)
*Boppin' the Rock (1955)
*Bayou Drive (1957, Checker)
*The Big Wheel (1957, Argo)
*Rockin' Accordian (1958, Zynn)
*Louisiana Blues (1965, Arhoolie)
*Zydeco et Pas Sale (1965, Arhoolie)
*Oh' Lucille (1966, Arhoolie)

Bayou Blues (Specialty)
Louisisana Blues and Zydeco (1964,
Arhoolie)
Bon Ton Roulet (1966, Arhoolie)
King of the Bayous (1970, Arhoolie)
Bogalusa Boogie (1975, Arhoolie)
Boogie & Zydeco (1978, Maison de
Soul)

*Stanley "Buckwheat" Dural, Jr. (1947-)

Miss Hard to Get (1972)
I Bought a Raccoon (1979)

One for the Road (1979, Blues
Unlimited)

OTHER ZYDECO

Rockin' Dopsie and the Twisters

(Alton Rubin)

Rockin' Dopsie and Twisters (1977,
Rounder)

Fernest Arceneaux

Fernest and the Thunders (Blues
Unlimited)

Delton Broussard and the Lawtell
  Playboys

Wilfred Latour and His Travel
  Aces

Hiram "Lune" Sampy and the Bad
  Habits

Queen Ida Guillory and Her Bon
  Temps Band

Gospel

ROOTS OF GOSPEL AND GENERAL ANTHOLOGIES

Ain't That Good News (Specialty)
Gospel at Its Best (Peacock)
The Gospel Sound, Vols. 1-2
  (Columbia)
Great Golden Gospel Hits, Vols. 1-3
  (Savoy)
Great Gospel Gems, Vols. 1-2
  (Specialty)
In the Spirit, Vols. 1-2 (Original
  Jazz Library)
Negro Church Music (Atlantic)
Negro Religious Music, Vols. 1-2:
  Sanctified Singers (BC)
*The Old Time Song Service: Dr. C.J.
  Johnson* (Savoy)
Original Greatest Gospel Hits
  (Gusto)
*Precious Lord (The Greatest Gospel
  Songs of Thomas A. Dorsey)*
  (Columbia)
Tony Heilbut: The Gospel Sound,
  Vols. 1-2 (Columbia)
An Introduction to Gospel Song
  (1972, RBF)
The Music of Africa (1974, BBC-
  Horizon)
*White Spirituals from the Sacred
  Harp* (1977, New World)
All of My Appointed Time (1978,
  Stash)
Birmingham Qartet Anthology
  (1980, Clanka Lanka)
From Jubilee to Gospel (1980,
  JEMF)
*Bless My Bones: Memphis Gospel
  Radio, The Fifties* (1982, P-Vine)
Gospel Warriors (1987, Spirit Feel)

EARLY GOSPEL

*Blind Willie Johnson (1923-49)

Dark Was the Night and Cold the
  Ground
If I Had My Way
I Just Can't Keep from Crying
Keep your Lamp Trimmed and
  Burning
Let Your Light Shine on Me
Motherless Children
You're Gonna Need Somebody on
  Your Bond
Jesus Make Up My Dying Bed
  (1928, Columbia)

Blues (1957, Folkways)
1927-30 (1965, Folkways)
Praise God I'm Satisfied (1976,
  Yazoo)

*Rosetta Tharpe (1915-73)

Last Mile of the Way (Savoy)
99 1/2 Won't Do (Savoy)
Peace in the Valley (Savory)
Precious Lord (Savoy)
Precious Memories (Savoy)
Walking Up the King's Highway
  (Savoy)
Rock Me (1939, Savoy)
This Train (1939, Savoy)
Shout, Sister, Shout (1942, Savoy)

Precious Lord (Savoy)
Precious Memories (Savoy)
Singing in My Soul (Savoy)
What Are They Doin' in Heaven?
  (1961, ALA)
The Best of . . . (1979, Savoy)
Gospel Train (1980, MCA)

*Golden Gate Quartet (1930-50)

Precious Memories (Pathe
  Marconi)
St. Louis Blues (Pathe Marconi)

Negro Spirituals Anthology, Vol. 1
  (1962, Pathe Marconi)
Negro Spirituals Anthology, Vol. 4
  (1964, Pathe Marconi)
Thirty-Five Historic Recordings
  (1977, RCA)

Thomas A. Dorsey (1899-)

Georgia Tom & His Friends
  (Riverside)
Come On Mama (1974, Yazoo)

MODERN GOSPEL

General Anthologies

Ain't That Good News (Specialty)
Great Golden Gospel Hits, Vols. 1-3
  (Savoy)
Birmingham Quartet, 1923-53 (1980,
  Clanka Lanka)
*Bless My Bones: Memphis Gospel
  Radio, the Fifties* (1982, P-Vine)
*Powerhouse for God: Sacred Speech
  Chant and Song in an
  Appalachian Baptist Church*
  (1982, University of North
  Carolina Press)

FEMALE ARTISTS

*Mahalia Jackson (1911-72)

City Called Heaven
He Said He Would
He Was Alone
His Eye Is on the Sparrow
How Great Thou Art
*I'm on My Way to Cannan
*In the Upper Room
*Move On Up a Little Higher
The Old Rugged Cross
Onward Christian Soldiers
Precious Lord
Rock of Ages
Sometimes I Feel Like a Motherless
  Child

Standing Here Wondering Which
Way to Go
Summertime
Trouble with This World
Walking to Jerusalem

Best of . . . (Kenwood)
Christmas with . . . (Kenwood)
Every Time I Feel the Spirit
(Columbia)
How I Got Over (Columbia)
In the Upper Room (Kenwood)
Just As I Am (Kenwood)
Mahalia! (Kenwood)
World's Greatest Gospel Singer
(Kenwood)
Great Gettin' Up Morning (1959,
Columbia)
Bless This House (1963, Columbia)
In Concert (1967, Columbia)
Right Out of the Church (1969,
Columbia)
1911-1972 (1972, Kenwood)

Clara Ward (1924-73)

Gospel's Greatest Hits (Paramount)
Memorial Album (Savoy)
Redeemed (Duke)
That Old Landmark (Savoy)
Time Is Winding Up (Duke)
Lord Touch Me (Savoy)

Dorothy Love Coates (1930?-)

Ninety-Nine and a Half
You Better Run

*Best of Dorothy Love Coates and the
Original Gospel Harmonettes,*
Vols. 1-2 (Specialty)

Marie Knight

Songs of Gospel (Mercury)

Shirley Caesar (1939-)

Best of . . . with the Caravans
(Savoy)
I'll Go (Hob)

Shirley Caesar (Up Front)
Stranger on the Road (Hob)

Marion Williams (1927-)

The New Message (Atlantic)
Somebody Bigger Than You and I
(Gospel)
*Standing Here Wondering Which
Way to Go* (Atlantic)
*Lord, You've Been Mighty Good to
Me* (1982, John Hammond
Records)

Sallie Martin (1896-)

The Living Legend (Savoy)

Mavis Staples (1941-)

A Piece of the Action (1977,
Curtom)
Mavis Staples (1978, Stax)
Oh, What a Feeling (1979, Warner
Bros.)

Aretha Franklin (1942-)

The Gospel Sound of . . . (1964,
Checker)
Songs of Faith (1964, Checker)
Never Grow Old (1973, Checker)

MALE ARTISTS

*James Cleveland (1932-)

*Lord Remember Me
*The Love of God
*Peace Be Still

James Cleveland Sings Solos
(Savoy)
*James Cleveland with the Angelic
Choir,* Vol. 7 (Savoy)
*James Cleveland with the Cleveland
Singers: He Leadeth Me* (Savoy)
*James Cleveland with the Gospel All-
Stars: Out on the Hill* (1959,
Savoy)

*James Cleveland with the Angelic
    Choir*, Vol. 3: *Peace Be Still*
    (1963, Savoy)
Amazing Grace (1972, Atlantic)
It's a New Day (1982, Savoy)

Robert Anderson (1894-)

*If You Deny Yourself (Savoy)
*In Times Like These (Savoy)

Alex Bradford (1926-78)

*Best of . . . (Specialty)
The Gospel Beat Goes On
    (Nashboro)
He Lifted Me (Specialty)
Walking with the King (Gospel)

Reverend C.L. Franklin (?-1984)

I Love the Lord/I Heard the Voice
    (Chess)
*I Will Trust In the Lord/Your Mother
    Loves Her Children* (Checker)
Precious Lord, Parts 1-2 (Checker)

Brother Joe May (1910-67)

In Church (Nashboro)
Search Me Lord (Specialty)

Reverend Cleophus Robinson

The Best of . . . (Peacock)

GROUPS AND CHOIRS

*Ward Singers

Packing Up
Surely God Is Able

I Feel the Holy Spirit (Savoy)
*Lord, Touch Me (Savoy)
Meeting Tonight (Savoy)
Packin' Up (Savoy)
Surely God Is Able (Savoy)
*Best of . . . (1978, Savoy)

*Five Blind Boys of Mississippi

I'm a Soldier
Oh Why
Where There's a Will There's a Way

The Best of . . . (Peacock)
*The Original Five Blind Boys
    (Exodus)
*Precious Memories: A Tribute to
    Archie Brownlee* (Peacock)

Five Blind Boys of Alabama

Great Camp Meeting (Gospel)
Oh Lord Stand By Me (Specialty)

*Roberta Martin Singers (1907-69)

God Is Still on the Throne (Savoy)
Grace (Savoy)
He Has Done Great Things for Me
    (Savoy)
Here This Sunday (Kenwood)
Old Ship of Zion (Savoy)
Prayer Meeting (Kenwood)
R. Martin Singers (Savoy)
Twelve Inspirational Songs (Savoy)

*Dixie Hummingbirds

Bedside of a Neighbor
Let the Holy Ghost Fall on Me
My Prayer
This Evening
I Just Can't Help, It (1952,
    Peacock)
In the Morning (1952, Peacock)
Jesus Walked the Water (1952,
    Peacock)

*The Best of . . . (Peacock)
Every Day and Every Hour
    (Peacock)
*In the Morning (Peacock)
Move On Up a Little Higher (Hob-
    Gotham)
Prayer for Peace (Peacock)
We Love You Like a Rock (1979,
    MCA)

Pilgrims Travelers

How Jesus Died
Jesus Hits Like the Atom Bomb
Mother Bowed
Peace of Mind
Standing on the Highway

Best of . . ., Vols. 1-2 (Specialty)
Everytime I Feel the Spirit (Vee Jay)
Shake My Mother's Hand
(Specialty)

*Swan Silvertones

Glory to His Name (Specialty)
How I Got Over (Specialty)
I'm Rollin (Specialty)
Mary, Don't You Weep (Exodus)

Love Lifted Me (Specialty)
My Book (Specialty)
My Rock (Specialty)
The Swan Silverstones (Exodus)
The Swan Silvertones, Vols. 1-2
(Upfront)

*Soul Stirrers

By and By (Specialty)
Jesus Wash Away My Troubles
(Specialty)
The Love of God (Specialty)
Touch the Hem of His Garment
(Specialty)
Wonderful (Specialty)

Gospel Archives (Imperial)
Gospel Music, Vol. 1: *Soul Stirrers*
(Specialty)
*The Gospel Soul of Sam Cooke with
the Soul Stirrers*, Vols. 1-2
(Specialty)
The Original Soul Stirrers (Specialty)
*The Soul Stirrers Featuring Sam
Cooke* (Specialty)

Sensational Nightingales

Burying Ground (Peacock)
Prayed Too Late (Peacock)

Standing at the Judgement
(Peacock)

Best of . . . (Peacock)

Spirit of Memphis

If I Should Miss Heaven (Peacock)
The Spirit of Memphis Quartet
(1978, King)

Angelic Gospel Singers

The Angelic Gospel Singers
(Nashboro)

Caravans

The Caravans (Gospel)
He Won't Deny Me (Gospel)
I Won't Be Back (Gospel)
Jesus Will Fix It (Gospel)
Mary Don't You Weep (Gospel)
That Old Time Religion (Sharp)

Davis Sisters

The Famous Davis Sisters (Savoy)
Get Right with God (Hob-Gotham)
Jesus Gave Me Water (Savoy)
Plant My Feet On Higher Ground
(Savoy)
Shine on Me (Savoy)

Gospel Clefs

The Gospel Clefs (Savoy)

Bill Moss and the Celestials

I've Already Been to the Water
(Billesse)

Raymond Rasberry Singers

The Rasberry Singers (Savoy)

*Staple Singers

Best of . . . (Buddah)
Uncloudy Day (Vee Jay)

We'll Get Over (Stax)
Pray On (1967, Epic)

Dorothy Norwood

The Denied Mother (Savoy)

Harmonizing Four of Richmond, Virginia

The Harmonizing Four (Upfront)
Where He Leads Me (Hob-Gotham)

Highway QCs

*The Highway QCs, Vols. 1-2 (Upfront)

Swanee Quintet

*The Swanee Quintet (Nashboro)
*What about Me (Nashboro)

Violinaires

Please Answer this Prayer (Checker)

CONTEMPORARY GOSPEL

*Mighty Clouds of Joy

Burying Ground (Peacock)
I Came to Jesus (Peacock)
We Think God Don't Care (Peacock)

Changing Times
Family Circle (Peacock)
Live at the Music Hall (1962, Peacock)
Live! At the Apollo (1968, Peacock)
The Best of . . . (1970, Peacock)
Bright Side (1972, Peacock)
It's Time (1974, ABC)
Cloudburst (1980, Myrrh)

*Edwin Hawkins Singers

Oh Happy Day (1969, Buddah)

Best of . . . (Buddah)
Oh Happy Day (1970, Buddah)

*Rance Allen Group

Ain't No Need of Crying (Stax)
Truth Is Where It's At (Stax)
The Rance Allen Group (1971, Stax)
Brothers (1973, Stax)
Straight from the Heart (1978, Stax)
I Feel Like Going On (1979, Stax)
Smile (1979, Stax)
Our Best to You (1981, Stax)

*Supreme Angels

Lucky Old Sun (Nashboro)
Precious Lord (Nashboro)
You Can't Get to Heaven (by Living Like Hell) (Nashboro)

If I'm Too High (Nashboro)
People Get Ready (Nashboro)
*Supreme (1972, Nashboro)

Andrae Crouch (1942-)

Best of . . .
I'll Be Thinking of You (1987, Light)

Troy Ramey

Great Change

44

Doo-Wop

General Anthologies

Doo-Wop (Specialty)
Echoes of a Rock Era: The Groups,
  Vols. 1-2 (Rounder)
*Echoes of a Rock Era: The Middle
  Years* (Rounder)
*Echoes of a Rock Era: The Later
  Years* (Rounder)
*Allan Freed's Memory Lane (1962,
  Rounder)
Beach Beat Classics (1980, Ripete)
Beach Beat Classics, Vol. 2 (1980,
  Ripete)
The Beat of the Beach (1982, Arista)

WHITE HARMONY GROUPS

Ink Spots

If I Didn't Care (1939, Decca)
My Prayer (1940, Decca)
To Each His Own (1946, Decca)

Best of . . . (Decca)
The Ink Spot's Greatest Hits
  (Grand)

Mills Brothers

Paper Doll (1943, Decca)
You Always Hurt the One You
  Love (1944, Decca)
Daddy's Little Girl (1950, Decca)
Glow Worm (1952, Decca)
Queen of the Senior Prom (1957,
  Decca)
Cab Driver (1968, Dot)

Best of . . . (Decca)
Fortuosity (1968, Dot)

Four Freshmen

It's a Blue World (1952, Capitol)

Day By Day (1955, Capitol)
Graduation Day (1956, Capitol)

Freshmen Favorites (1956, Capitol)
In Person (1958, Capitol)
Voices In Love (1958, Capitol)

Four Lads

The Mocking Bird (1952, Okeh)
Istanbul (1953, Columbia)
Skokiaan (1954, Columbia)
Moments to Remember (1955,
  Columbia)
No, Not Much! (1956, Columbia)
Who Needs You (1957, Columbia)
There's Only One of You (1958,
  Columbia)

On the Sunny Side (1956,
  Columbia)

*Crew Cuts

Crazy 'bout You, Baby (1954,
  Mercury)
*Sh-Boom (1954, Mercury)
*Earth Angel (1955, Mercury)

Rock'n'Roll Bash
Crew Cuts on the Campus (1954,
  Mercury)

Diamonds

High Sign
Kathy-O
She Say (Oom Dooby Doom)
The Stroll
Walking Along
Why Do Fools Fall in Love (1956,
  Mercury)
Little Darlin' (1957, Mercury)

America's #1 Singing Stylists
  (Mercury)
Pop Hits (Wing)

Hi-Los

Now Hear This (1957, Columbia)

45

Suddenly It's Hi-Lo's (1957, Columbia)

McGuire Sisters

Goodnight, Sweetheart, Goodnight (1955, Coral)
Sincerely (1955, Coral)
Sugartime (1958, Coral)

By Request (1955, Coral)

Fontane Sisters

Hearts of Stone (1954, Dot)
Seventeen (1955, Dot)

Andrews Sisters

Best of . . . (1973, MCA)
Boogie Woogie Bugle Girls (1973, Paramount)
In the Mood (1974, Paramount)

EARLY DOO-WOP

*Ravens

Bye Bye Baby Blues (1946, King)
My Sugar Is So Refined (1946, King)
Old Man River (1946, National)
*Write Me a Letter (1948, National)
Count Every Star (1950, National)
I Don't Have to Ride No More (1950, National)
White Christmans (1950, National)
Rock Me All Night Long (1952, National)
Green Eyes (1954, National)

The Ravens (Harlem Hitparade)
Write Me a Letter (Regent)
The Greatest Group of All (1978, Savoy)

*Dominoes with Clyde McPhatter

(Clyde McPhatter, 1931-72)
SEE ALSO UNDER Early Rock and Soul Producers: Jerry Wexler

Do Something for Me (1951, Federal)
*Sixty Minute Man (1951, Federal)
The Bells (1952, Federal)
*Have Mercy Baby (1952, Federal)

Dominoes with Jackie Wilson

(Jackie Wilson, 1934-84)

*Can't Do Sixty No More (1954, Federal)
St. Therese of the Roses (1956, Federal)

Billy Ward and the Dominoes Sixteen Greatest Hits (King)
Billy Ward and the Dominoes (1956, Federal)
Billy Ward and the Dominoes (1957, Federal)
Sea of Glass (1957, Liberty)
Billy Ward and His Dominoes with Clyde McPhatter (1958, King)
Yours Forever (1958, Liberty)
The Dominoes--Featuring Jackie Wilson, Vols. 3-4 (1977, King)

Drifters with Clyde McPhatter

(Clyde McPhatter, 1931-72)
SEE ALSO UNDER Early Rock and Soul Producers: Jerry Wexler

*Money Honey (1953, Atlantic)
Honey Love (1954, Atlantic)
Such a Night (1954, Atlantic)
Adorable (1955, Atlantic)
*Ruby Baby (1955, Atlantic)
Whatcha Gonna Do (1955, Atlantic)
White Christmas (1955, Atlantic)

The Early Years (1971, Atco)
Bip Bam (1985, Edsel)

Hank Ballard and the Royals

Every Beat of My Heart (1952, Federal)
Get It (1953, Federal)

*Hank Ballard and the Midnighters

(Hank Ballard, 1936-)

Annie Had a Baby (1954, Federal)
Annie's Aunt Fanny (1954, Federal)
*Sexy Ways (1954, Federal)
*Work with Me Annie (1954, Federal)
It's Love Baby (1955, Federal)
*Roll with Me Henry (1955, Federal)
Teardrops on Your Letter (1959, King)
Twist (1959, King)
*Finger Poppin' Time (1960, King)
Let's Go, Let's Go, Let's Go (1960, King)
The Continental Walk (1961, King)
The Hoochi Coochi Coo (1961, King)
Nothin' But Good (1961, King)
Do You Know How to Twist (1962, King)

Finger Poppin' Time (King)
Greatest Jukebox Hits, Vols. 1-2 (King)
20 Original Greatest Hits (1955, King)
Their Greatest Hits, Vol. 1 (1957, Federal)
Their Greatest Hits, Vol. 2 (1958, Federal)

Hank Ballard solo

How You Gonna Get Respect (1968, King)
Let's Go Streaking (1974, King)

COOL OR NORTHERN STYLE

*Orioles

*It's Too Soon to Know (1948, National)
Tell Me So (1949, Jubilee)
*Crying in the Chapel (1953, Jubilee)

The History of R&B, Vol. 1 (Atco)
Sonny Til and the Orioles--Greatest Hits (Collectibles)

*Five Keys

*Glory of Love (1951, Aladdin)
*Ling Ting Tong (1952, Capitol)
Close Your Eyes (1955, Capitol)
I Wish I'd Never Learned to Read (1955, Capitol)
Out of Sight, Out of Mind (1956, Capitol)
Wisdom of a Fool (1956, Capitol)

Best of . . . (Aladdin)
Connoisseur Collection (Harlem Hitparade)
The Fantastic Five Keys (Capitol)
Fourteen Original Greatest Hits (King)
On Stage (Capitol)

Larks

*My Reverie (1951, Apollo)
It's Unbelievable (1961, Sheryl)
The Jerk (1964, Money)

Super Oldies (Capitol)

Spaniels

*Baby, It's You (1953, Chance)
*Goodnite Sweetheart, Goodnite (1954, Vee Jay)
Everyone's Laughing (1957, Vee Jay)
Fairy Tales (1970, Calla)
Great Googley Moo! (1981, Charly)

The Spaniels (Lost Nite)
Goodnight, It's Time to Go (1956,
    Vee Jay)
*Great Googley Moo! (1981, Charly)

Spiders

I Didn't Want to Do It (1954,
    Imperial)
Witchcraft (1955, Imperial)

Rhythm & Blues, End of an Era,
    Vol. 1 (Imperial)

DRAMATIC STYLE

*Clovers

Bald Headed Woman (1951,
    Atlantic)
*Don't You Know I Love You (1951,
    Atlantic)
Fool, Fool, Fool (1951, Atlantic)
One Mint Julep (1951, Atlantic)
Crawlin' (1952, Atlantic)
Hey Miss Fannie (1952, Atlantic)
I Played the Fool (1952, Atlantic)
*Ting-a-Ling (1952, Atlantic)
*Good Lovin' (1953, Atlantic)
I've Got My Eyes On You (1954,
    Atlantic)
Little Mama (1954, Atlantic)
*Lovey Dovey (1954, Atlantic)
Your Cash Ain't Nothing But Trash
    (1954, Atlantic)
Blue Velvet (1956, Atlantic)
*Devil or Angel (1956, Atlantic)
*From the Bottom of My Heart
    (1956, Atlantic)
*Love, Love, Love (1956, Atlantic)
Down the Alley (1957, Atlantic)
*Love Potion Number Nine (1959,
    United Artists)

Dance Party (Atlantic)
*The Original Love Potion Number
    Nine* (Gran Prix)
Their Greatest Recording (Atco)
*The Clovers (1956, Atlantic)

Love Potion Number Nine (1960,
    United Artists)
*Five Cool Cats (1984, Edsel)

*Harptones

*A Sunday Kind of Love (1953,
    Bruce)
Cry Like I Cried (1954, Paradise)
*Life Is But a Dream (1954,
    Paradise)
The Shrine of St. Cecilia (1954,
    Paradise)
The Masquerade Is Over (1955,
    Rama)
*My Memories of You (1959, Bruce)
*No Greater Miracle (1959,
    Warwick)
What Will I Tell My Heart (1961,
    Companion)
Love Needs a Heart (1982,
    Ambient)

*The Harptones (Emus)
The Harptones (Harlem Hitparade)
The Harptones, Vol. 2 (Relic)
Love Needs (1982, Epic)

*Five Royales

*Baby Don't Do It (1953, Apollo)
Help Me Somebody (1953, Apollo)
*Think (1953, Apollo)
Dedicated To the One I Love
    (1958, King)

All Time Hits (King)
*Dedicated To You (King)
*Seventeen Original Greatest Hits
    (King)

*Flamingos

*Golden Teardrops (1953, Chance)
I'll Be Home (1954, Checker)
I Only Have Eyes for You (1959,
    End)
Lovers Never Say Goodbye (1959,
    End)
Love Walked In (1959, End)

I Was Such a Fool (1960, End)
Nobody Loves Me Like You (1960, End)
Time Was (1961, End)
Boogaloo Party (1966, Philips)
Dealin' (1969, Polydor)
Buffalo Soldier (1970, Polydor)

Color Them Beautiful (Ronze)
The Flamingos (Checker)
Flamingo Favorites (End)
The Flamingos' Greatest Hits (Meka)
*Golden Goodies, Vols. 2-3, 6, 19 (Roulette)

Chords

*Sh'Boom (1954, Cat)

History of Rhythm & Blues, Vol. 2 (Atlantic)

El Dorados

My Lovin' Baby (1954, Vee Jay)
*At My Front Door (1955, Vee Jay)
Bim Bam Boom (1956, Vee Jay)
I'll Be Forever Loving You (1956, Vee Jay)

Crazy Little Mama (Vee Jay)

Moonglows

Baby Please (1953, Chance)
Ooh Rocking Daddy (1954, Chance)
*Sincerely (1955, Chess)
See Saw (1956, Chess)
*Ten Commandments of Love (1959, Chess)

Look It's Moonglows (Chess)
Rock, Rock, Rock (Chess)
The Return of Moonglows (1972, RCA)
*Moonglows (1977, Chess)

Crows

*Gee (1954, Rama)

I Love You So (1954, Rama)
Baby Doll (1955, Rama)

Oldies, But Goodies, Vol. 2 (Original Sound)

Penguins

*Earth Angel (1954, Dootone)
Be Mine or Be a Fool (1955, Mercury)

Decades of Golden Groups (Mercury)
*Cool Cool Penguins (1955, Dootone)

Platters

*Only You (1953, Mercury)
*The Great Pretender (1955, Mercury)
It Isn't Right (1956, Mercury)
*The Magic Touch (1956, Mercury)
*My Prayer (1956, Mercury)
You'll Never, Never Know (1956, Mercury)
He's Mine (1957, Mercury)
I'm Sorry (1957, Mercury)
*Smoke Gets in Your Eyes (1958, Mercury)
*Twilight Time (1958, Mercury)
Enchanted (1959, Mercury)
*Harbor Lights (1960, Mercury)
If I Didn't Care (1960, Mercury)
I'll Never Smile Again (1960, Mercury)
I Love You 1000 Times (1960, Musicor)
To Each His Own (1960, Mercury)
With This Ring (1967, Musicor)

More Encore of Golden Hits (Mercury)
Nineteen Hits (King)
Sixteen Greatest Hits (Trip)
The Platters, Vols. 1-2 (1956, Specialty)
Remember When? (1959, Mercury)
*Encore of Golden Hits (1960, Mercury)

Otis Williams and the Charms

(Otis Williams, 1936-)

*Hearts of Stone (1954, DeLuxe)
*Ling Ting Tong (1955, King)
Two Hearts (1955, DeLuxe)
Ivory Tower (1956, King)
*Ko Ko Mo (I Love You So) (1956, King)
United (1957, King)

Otis Williams and His Charms Sing Their All-Time Hits (King)
Sixteen Hits (1978, King)

*Cadillacs

*Gloria (1955, Josie)
*Speedo (1955, Josie)
Rudolph the Red-Nosed Reindeer (1956, Josie)
Woe Is Me (1956, Josie)
Zoom (1956, Josie)
My Girlfriend (1957, Josie)
Jay Walker (1959, Josie)
Peek-a-Boo (1959, Josie)
Please Mr. Johnson (1959, Josei)
What You Bet (1961, Josie)

The Crazy Cadillacs (Jubilee)
Cruisin' with the Cadillacs (Harlem Hitparade)
The Fabulous Cadillacs (Jubilee)
Twisting with the Cadillacs (Jubilee)

Nutmegs

Ship of Love (1955, Herald)
*Story Untold (1955, Herald)

Golden Goodies, Vol. 6 (Roulette)

*Five Satins

*In the Still of the Night (1956, Ember)
Oh Happy Day (1956, Ember)
To the Aisle (1957, Ember)
I'll Be Seeing You (1960, Ember)
Shadows (1960, Ember)

Two Different Worlds (1974, Kirshner)
Everybody Stand Up and Clap Your Hands (1976, Kirshner)
Memories of Days Gone By (1982, Elektra)

Best of . . . (Celebrity Showcase)
Five Satins' Greatest Hits, Vols. 1-3 (Relic)
Five Satins Sing (Ember)

Frankie Lymon and the Teenagers

The ABC's of Love (1956, Gee)
I'm Not a Juvenile Delinquent (1956, Gee)
I Promise to Remember (1956, Gee)
I Want You to Be My Girl (1956, Gee)
*Why Do Fools Fall in Love (1956, Gee)

Frankie Lymon (1942-68) solo

Goody Goody (1957, Gee)
Little Bitty Pretty One (1960, Roulette)

Frankie Lymon and the Teenagers (Gee)
Rock'n'Roll (Roulette)
Why Do Fools Fall in Love (1956, Gee)

Jacks [Cadets]

Why Don't You Write to Me (1955, RPM)
*Stranded in the Jungle (1956, Modern)

Rock'n'Roll Hits of the Fifties (United Artists)

Schoolboys

Please Say You Want Me (1956, Okeh)
*Shirley (1957, Okeh)

Heartbeats

*A Thousand Miles Away (1956, Hull-Rama)

Golden Goodies, Vols. 1-2, 5 (Roulette)

Charts

*Deserie (1957, Everlast)

Oldies, But Goodies, Vol. 2 (Original Sound)

Lee Andrews and the Hearts

Long Lonely Nights (1957, Chess)
*Teardrops (1957, Chess)
Try the Impossible (1958, United Artists)

NEO DOO-WOP

*Dells

Darling Dear, I Know-Christine (1953, Chess)
*Oh What a Night (1955, Vee Jay)
Always Together (1968, Vee Jay)
Stay in My Corner (1968, Vee Jay)
*There Is (1968, Vee Jay-Chess)
I Can Sing a Rainbow-Love Is Blue (1969, Vee Jay)
Give Your Baby a Standing Ovation (1972, Vee Jay)
The Love We Had (Stays on My Mind) (1972, Vee Jay)

The Dells' Greatest Hits (Trip)
Oh, What a Night (Vee Jay)
There Is (Cadet)
The Mighty, Mighty Dells (1974, Cadet)

*Del-Vikings

*Come Go with Me (1957, Dot)
Whispering Bells (1957, Dot)
Cool Shake (1958, Dot)

Come Go with Del-Vikings (Universe)
*Come Go with Me (Dot)
The Del-Vikings and the Sonnets (Crown)
Newies and Oldies (Fee Bee)
Swinging, Singing Del-Vikings Record Session (Mercury)
*They Sing, They Swing (Mercury Universe)

Crests

Sweetest One (1957, Coed)
*Sixteen Candles (1958, Coed)
Isn't It Amazing (1960, Coed)
Step by Step (1960, Coed)

Sheppards

*Island of Love (1959, Solid Smoke)
Tragic (1960, Solid Smoke)

The Sheppards (1980, Solid Smoke)

Diamonds

*The Stroll (1957, Mercury)

The History of R&B, Vol. 1 (Atlantic)

Little Anthony and the Imperials

(Anthony Gourdine, 1941-)

Take Me Back (1956, DCP)
*Tears on My Pillow (1958, End)
*Shimmy, Shimmy Ko-Ko Bop (1960, End)
Goin' Out of My Head (1964, DCP)
Hurt So Bad (1965, DCP)
I'm on the Outside (Looking In) (1965, DCP)
I'm Falling in Love with You (1974, Avco)

Forever Yours (Roulette)
The Very Best of . . . (United Artists)

We Are the Imperials (End)
Out of Sight, Out of Mind (1969,
  United Artists)

*Dion and the Belmonts

(Dion DiMucci, 1939-)

The Chosen Few (1958, Laurie)
Don't Pity Me (1958, Laurie)
I Wonder Why (1958, Laurie)
No One Knows (1958, Laurie)
*A Teenager in Love 1959, (Laurie)
That's My Desire (1960, Laurie)
*Where or When (1960, Laurie)
Beribau (1967, Columbia)
Mr. Movin' Man (1967, Columbia)

Belmonts

*Tell Me Why (1961, Sabina)
Come On Little Angel (1962,
  Sabina)

Dion solo

Little Diane (1962, Laurie)
Lovers Who Wander (1962, Laurie)
Ruby Baby (1963, Laurie)
*Runaround Sue (1962, Laurie)
Sandy (1962, Laurie)
The Wanderer (1962, Laurie)
Donna the Prima Donna (1963,
  Laurie)
Drip Drop (1963, Laurie)
Abraham, Martin and John (1968,
  Columbia)
Clean Up Your Own Backyard
  (1969, Warner Bros.)
Born to Be with You (1975,
  Columbia)

Dion Sings the 15 Million Seller
  (1966, Laurie)
*Sixty Greatest of Dion and the
  Belmonts* (1971, Laurie)
Dion's Greatest Hits (1973,
  Columbia)
*Everything You Always Wanted to
  Hear by Dion and the Belmonts*
  (1973, Laurie)

Danny and the Juniors

(Danny Rapp, 1941-83)

*At the Hop (1957, Singular)
*Rock and Roll Is Here to Stay
  (1958, ABC)

Rock and Roll Is Here to Stay (1958,
  Singular)
Twistin' All Night Long (1958,
  Swan)

Rays

*Silhouettes (1957, Cameo)
Magic Moon (1961, XYZ)

Golden Goodies, Vol. 16 (Roulette)

Silhouettes

*Get a Job (1958, Ember)

Golden Goodies, Vol. 7 (Roulette)

Impalas

*Sorry (I Ran All the Way Home)
  (1959, Cub)

Elegants

*Little Star (1958, Apt)

Oldies But Goodies, Vol. 5
  (Roulette)

Chantels

*Maybe (1958, End)
*Look In My Eyes (1961, Carlton)
Golden Goodies, Vols. 2, 3, 6, 10, 11
  (Roulette)

LATE DOO-WOP

*Jive Five

*My True Story (1961, Ambient)

These Golden Rings (1962, Ambient)
I'm a Happy Man (1965, Ambient)
Bench in the Park (1966, Ambient)
Sugar (1968, Ambient)
I Want You to Be My Baby (1970, Ambient)
*Here We Are! (1982, Ambient)

Shep and the Heartbeats [Shep and the Limelites]

Crazy for You (1956, Hull)
*A Thousand Miles Away (1956, Hull)
*Daddy's Home (1961, Hull)

Capris

*There's a Moon Out Again (1958, Ambient)

*There's a Moon Out Again (1981, Epic)

Marcels

*Blue Moon (1961, Epic)

*Blue Moon (Epic)

Volumes

*I Love You (1962, Chex)

Earls

*Life Is But a Dream (1961, Rome)
*Remember Then (1963, Old Town)

Persuasions

A Cappella (1968, Straight)
*We Came to Play (1971, Capitol)
*Street Corner Symphony (1972, Capitol)
We Still Ain't Got No Band (1973, MCA)
More Than Before (1974, A&M)
*Chirpin' (1977, Elecktra)
Comin' at Ya (1979, Flying Fish)

*Force M.D.'s

*Chillin' (1986, Tommy Boy)

LATER R&B GROUPS

*Friends of Distinction

*Going in Circles (1969, RCA)
*Grazin' in the Grass (1969, RCA)
*Let Yourself Go (1969, RCA)

*Grazin' (1969, RCA)
*Love or Let Me Be Lonely (1970, RCA)

*Fifth Dimension

I'll Be Loving You Forever (1965, Soul City)
Go Where You Wanna Go (1967, Soul City)
*Up, Up and Away (1967, Soul City)
*Stoned Soul Picnic (1968, Soul City)
*Aquarius [Let the Sunshine In] (1969, Soul City)
*Sweet Blindness (1969, Soul City)
*Wedding Bell Blues (1970, Soul City)
(Last Night) I Didn't Get to Sleep at All (1972, Soul City)

*Up, Up and Away (1967, Soul City)
*The Magic Garden (1968, Soul City)
*Stoned Soul Picnic (1968, Soul City)
*The Age of Aquarius (1969, Soul City)
Greatest Hits on Earth (1972, Arista)

*Artistics

*I'm Gonna Miss You (1966, Brunswick)
*Girl I Need You (1967, Brunswick)

*I'm Gonna Miss You (1967, Brunswick)

Manhattans

*I Wanna Be (Your Everything)
   (1964, Carnival)
*Searchin' for My Baby (1965,
   Carnival)
*Baby I Need You (1966, Carnival)
*Follow Your Heart (1966, Carnival)
*Can I (1967, Carnival)
  From Atlanta to Goodbye (1968,
   Deluxe)
  If My Heart Could Speak (1968,
   Deluxe)
  Don't Take Your Love from Me
   (1974, Columbia)
  Hurt (1975, Columbia)
  I Kinda Miss You (1976, Columbia)
*Kiss and Say Goodbye (1976,
   Columbia)
  It Feels So Good (to Be Loved So
   Bad) (1977, Columbia)
  Am I Losing You (1978, Columbia)
*Shining Star (1980, Columbia)

Dedicated (1966, Carnival)
For You and Yours (1967, Carnival)
With These Hands (1968, King)
Million To One (1969, King)
There's No Me without You (1973,
   Columbia)
It Feels So Good (1977, Columbia)
Follow Your Heart (1981, Solid
   Smoke)

Country Music

GENERAL ANTHOLOGIES

All about Trains (RCA)
Anthology of the Banjo (Tradition)
Country & Western Classics: Duets
   (Time-Life)
*Country & Western Classics: The
   Women* (Time-Life)
Eighteen King Size Country Hits
   (Columbia)
Folk Music in America, Vols. 1-15
   (Library of Congress)
60 Years of Country Music (RCA)
*The Smithsonian Collection of
   Classic Country Music, 1922-76,*
   Vols. 1-8 (Smithsonian
   Institution)
Texas Country (United Artists)
Country Gospel Song (1971, RBF)
*Going Down the Valley: Vocal and
   Instrumental Style in Folk Music
   from the South* (1977, New
   World)
Super Country Hits of the 1940s
   (1978, Gusto)

EARLY STRING BANDS AND BALLADEERS

A.C. "Eck" Robertson

Arkansas Traveller (1922, Okeh)
*Sallie Gooden (1922, Okeh)

Henry Whitter with George Banman Grayson

*The Wreck of the Southern Old 97
   (1923, Okeh)

John Carson (?-1935)

*The Little Old Log Cabin in the
   Lane (1923, Okeh)

Carl T. Sprague

*When the Work's All Done This
Fall (1925)
The Boston Burglar (1926)
The Two Soldiers (1926)

Original Recordings, 1925-29 (FV)

Ernest V. Stoneman and the Blue Ridge Corn Shuckers

(Ernest V. Stoneman, 1893-)

The Sinking of the Titanic (1925,
Okeh)

*Ernest V. Stoneman and the Blue
Ridge Corn Shuckers* (Rounder)

Gid Tanner and His Skillet Lickers

*Bully of the Town (1927, Columbia)
*A Corn Licker Still in Georgia
(1927, Columbia)
*Pass Around the Bottle and We'll
Take a Drink (1927, Columbia)

The Kickapoo Medicine Show
(Rounder)
The Skillet Lickers, Vol. 2 (County)

*Uncle Dave Macon (1870-1952)

Chewing Gum (1924, Columbia)
Hill Billie Blues (1924, Columbia)
Keep My Skillet Good and Greasy
(1924, Columbia)
Bully of the Town (1926, Columbia)
Mountain Dew (1926, Columbia)

*Uncle Dave Macon, 1926-39--Wait
Till the Clouds Roll By*
(Historical)

*Vernon Dalhart (1883-1948)

The Prisoner's Song (1924, Victor)
The Wreck of the Old 97 (1917,
Edison)
The Death of Floyd Collins (1926,
Victor)

Ballads and Railroad Songs (Old
Homestead)
The First Singing Cowboy on Record
(Mark 56)

Bradley Kincaid (1894-)

The Blue Tail Fly (1928)
The First Whippoorwill Song
(1928)
Legend of the Robin Red Breast
(1928)
Letter Edged in Black (1928)
Sweet Betsy from Pike (1928)

*Mountain Ballads and Old-Time
Songs* (Old Homestead)

*Charlie Poole and the North Carolina Ramblers

(Charlie Poole, 1892-1931)

*Don't Let You Deal Go Down
(1925, Columbia)

*Charlie Poole and the North
Carolina Ramblers* (County)
Legend of Charlie Poole
Old time Songs, Vols. 1-2

*Gus Cannon (1883-1979)

*Poor Boy, Long Ways from Home
(1927, Herwin)
*Big Railroad Blues (1928, Herwin)
*Viola Lee Blues (1928, Herwin)
*Walk Right In (1929, Herwin)

*Cannon's Jug Stomper/Gus Cannon
as Banjo Joe, 1927-30* (Herwin)

Crook Brothers String Band

Going Across the Sea (1928,
Victor)
Jobbin' Gettin' There (1928,
Victor)

Uncle Jimmy Thompson

Billy Wilson (1926, Victor)
Karo (1926, Victor)

Sam and Kirk McGhee

Old Masters Runaway (1927, Victor)
Brown's Ferry Blues (1934, Victor)

Sam and Kirk McGee from Sunny Tennessee (Bear Family)

DeFord Bailey (?-1982)

Muscle Shoal Blues (1927, Victor)
Pan American Blues (1927, Victor)

Carson Robinson

Just a Melody (Old Homestead)

Dock Boggs

Dock Boggs: His Twelve Original Recordings (Folkways)

Grayson and Whitter

The Recordings of . . . (County)

Riley Puckett

Waitin' for the Evening Mail (County)

Jean Ritchie

Precious Memories (Folkways)

Carolina Tar Heels

Can't You Remember? (Bear Family)

Anthologies

Anthology of American Music, Vol. 2: *Social Music* (Folkways)
Anthology of American Folk Music, Vol. 1: *Ballads* (Folkways)
Anthology of American Folk Music, Vol. 3: *Songs* (Folkways)
Echoes of the Ozarks, Vols. 1-3 (County)
Folk Music of the United States: Anglo-American Songs and Ballads (Library of Congress)
Folk Music of the United States: Child Ballads Traditional, Vols. 1-2 (Library of Congress)
Mountain Blues (County)
Nashville--The Early String Bands, Vol. 2 (County)
Round the Heart of Old Galax, Vols 1-3 (County)
String Bands, Vols. 1-2 (Old Timey)

SEE ALSO Folk Music

THE DEPRESSION YEARS

Jimmie Rodgers (1897-1933)

*Mississippi Moon (1927, RCA)
Sleep Baby Sleep (1927, RCA)
The Soldier's Sweetheart (1927, RCA)
*Blue Yodel #9 (1928, RCA)
The One Rose (1928, RCA)
*Waiting for a Train (1928, RCA)
Fifteen Years Ago Today (1933, RCA)
*Southern Cannonball (1933, RCA)

This Is Jimmie Rodgers (RCA)
Country Music Hall of Fame: Jimmie Rodgers (1962, RCA)
Short but Brilliant Life of Jimmie Rodgers (1963, RCA)
My Time Ain't Long (1964, RCA)
Best of the Legendary Jimmie Rodgers (1965, RCA)
Never No Mo' Blues (1969, RCA)
Train Whistle Blues (1969, RCA)
My Rough and Rowdy Ways (1975, RCA)
A Legendary Performer (1978, RCA)

*Carter Family

I'm Thinking Tonight of My Blue
 Eyes
Wabash Cannonball
Will the Circle Be Unbroken
Bury Me under the Weeping Willow
 (1927, RCA)
Keep on the Sunny Side (1928,
 Camden)
Wildwood Flower (1928, Camden)
Will You Miss Me When I'm Gone
 (1928, Camden)

Country & Western Classics (Time-
 Life)
On Border Radio (JEMF)
Happiest Days of All (1975,
 Camden)
Lonesome Pine Special (1975,
 Camden)
'Mid the Green Fields of Virginia
 (1975, RCA)
*More Golden Gems from the Original
 Carter Family* (1975, Camden)
*The Original and Great Carter
 Family* (1975, Camden)
Smoky Mountain Ballads (1976,
 Camden)
Legendary Performers (1979, RCA)

Darby and Tarlton

*Birmingham Jail (1927, RCA)
*Columbus Stockade Blues (1927,
 RCA)

Darby and Tarlton (Old Timey)

*Delmore Brothers

*Brown's Ferry Blues (1930, RCA
 Bluebird)
*Gonna Lay down My Old Guitar
 (1932, RCA Bluebird)
*Nashville Blues (1936, RCA
 Bluebird)
*Blues Stay Away From Me (1949,
 RCA Bluebird)

Best of . . . (Starday)

Delmore Brothers (Decca-Old Time
 Classics)
Delmore Brothers, 1933-41 (RCA
 Bluebird-Country)

Arthur Smith (1898-)

*Blackberry Blossom (1935, RCA
 Bluebird)
*Chitlin Cookin' Time in Cheatham
 County (1935, RCA Bluebird)
*Fiddler's Dream (1935, RCA
 Bluebird)
*Indian Creek (1935, RCA Bluebird)
*Smith's Rag (1940, RCA Bluebird])

*Fiddlin' Arhtur Smith and His
 Dixieliners*, Vols. 1-2 (County)

*Roy Acuff (1903-)

*Great Speckled Bird (1936,
 Columbia)
*Fire Ball Mail (1938, Columbia)
*Mule Skinner Blues (1938,
 Columbia)
*Night Train to Memphis (1938,
 Columbia)
*Wabash Cannonball (1938,
 Columbia)
*Wreck on the Highway (1938,
 Columbia)

Greatest Hits (1970, Columbia)

Louvin Brothers

In the Pines (1955, Capitol)
*Let Her Go, God Bless Her (1955,
 Capitol)
A Tiny Broken Heart (1955,
 Capitol)
*When I Stop Dreaming (1955,
 Capitol)

The Family Who Prays (Capitol)
Tragic Songs of Life (Rounder)

Blue Sky Boys

Bluegrass Mountain Music, 1930s and 40s (RCA Camdaen)

Roy Hall and His Blue Ridge Entertainers

Roy Hall and His Blue Ridge Entertainers, 1939-41 (County)

Grandpa Jones (1913-)

16 Greatest Hits (King)

J.E. Mainer (1898-)

J.E. Mainer's Mountaineers, Vols. 1-2 (Old Timey)
A Variety Album (King)

Wade Mainer

Wade Mainer and the Sons of the Mountaineers (County)

Monroe Brothers

Feast Here Tonight (RCA Bluebird)
Bill and Charlie Monroe (1969, MCA)

Anthology

Steel Guitar Classics (Old Timey)

MODERN VARIATIONS ON "OLD TIME COUNTRY"

*New Lost City Ramblers

New Lost City Ramblers, Vols. 1-5 (1958-63, Folkways)
Songs from the Depression (1959, Folkways)
American Moonshine and Prohibition (1962, Folkways)

Mike Seeger (1933-)

American Folk Song (1957, Folkways)
Old Time Country Music (1962, Folkways)
Tipple, Loom and Rail (1966, Folkways)

Gail Davies

The Game (1979, Warner Bros.)
I'll Be There (1980, Warner Bros.)

SINGING COWBOYS

*Gene Autry (1907-)

Rudolph the Red Nosed Reindeer
Someday You'll Want Me To
South of the Border
Do It Right Daddy Blues (1931, Columbia)
That Silver-Haired Daddy of Mine (1931, Columbia)
Back to Old Smoky Mountain (1932, Columbia)
Mississippi Valley Blues (1932, Columbia)
Moonlight and Skies (1932, Columbia)
Why Don't You Come Back to Me (1932, Columbia)

Back in the Saddle Again (CBS Encore)
Columbia Historic Edition (Columbia)
Gene Autry's Country Music Hall of Fame Album (Columbia)

*Tex Ritter (1907-74)

Goodbye Old Paint (Capitol)
Rye Whiskey, Rye Whiskey (1933, ARC)
Everyday in the Saddle (1942, Capitol)
High Noon (1953, Capitol)

Hillbilly Heaven (1961, Capitol)

An American Legend (Capitol)
Best of . . . (Capitol)
Blood on the Saddle (1960, Capitol)
Hillbilly Heaven (1961, Capitol)

*Sons of the Pioneers

Cool Water (1937, RCA)
Tumbling Tumbleweeds (1937, RCA)
Room Full of Roses (1937, RCA)

Best of . . . (RCA)
Columbia Historic Edition (Columbia)
Songs of the Hills and Plains (JEMF-AFM)
Lucky U Ranch Radio Broadcast (1951, JEMF-AFM)

*Patsy Montana (1914-)

*I Want to Be a Cowboy's Sweetheart (1935, Columbia)

The Cowboys' Sweetheart (German Cattle)
The Very Early Patsy Montana and the Prairie Ramblers (German Cattle)

Marty Robbins (1925-)

*That's All Right (1954, Columbia)
*White Sport Coat (1957, Columbia)
*El Paso (1959, Columbia)

Gunfighter Ballads and Trail Songs (1959, Columbia)
All-Time Greatest Hits (1972, Columbia)

Anthologies

Cowboy Songs, Ballads, and Cattle Calls from Texas, 1941-48 (Library of Congress)
Legendary Songs of the Old West (Columbia)

WESTERN SWING

*Bob Wills and His Texas Cowboys

(Bob Wills, 1906-)

Maidens Prayer (1935, Columbia)
Osage Stomp (1935, Columbia)
*Big Beaver (1940)
*San Antonio Rose (1940, Columbia)
Blue Yodel #1 (1941, Columbia)
*Twin Guitar Special (1941, Columbia)

Country and Western Classics (Time-Life)
The Tiffany Transcriptions, Vol. 1 (Kaleidoscope)
24 Great Hits (Polydor)
Bob Wills and His Texas Playboys (1958, MCA)
Bob Wills Sings and Plays (1963, Liberty)
King of the Western Swing (1968, MCA)
Best of . . . (1969, MCA)
Living Legend (1969, MCA)
Plays the Greatest String Band Hits (1969, MCA)
In Person (1971, MCA)
Anthology (1973, Columbia)
For the Last Time (1974, United Artists)
Father and Sons (1975, Epic)
Remembering . . . (1976, Columbia)

Milton Brown and His Musical Brownies

(Milton Brown, 1903-36)

Chinatown, My Chinatown (1935, Decca)
El Rancho Grande (1935, Decca)
Taking Off (1935, Decca)

Pioneer Western Swing Band, 1903-36 (MCA)

Taking Off (British String)

Asleep at the Wheel

Miles and Miles of Texas (1973, Liberty)

Let Me Go Home Whiskey (1975, Capitol)

My Baby Thinks She's a Train (1975, Capitol)

Hank Thompson: Best of . . . (Capitol)

Hot As I Am (Rambler)

Okeh Western Swing (Epic)

Pasture Prime (Demon)

Texas Gold (1975, Capitol)

Wheelin' and Dealin' (1976, Capitol)

The Wheel (1977, Capitol)

Anthologies

Roy Newman and His Boys, 1934-38, Vol. 1 (Original Jazz Library)

Western Swing, Vol. 2 (Old Timey)

Western Swing, Vol. 4: *The 1930s* (Old Timey)

Western Swing, Blues, Boogie and Honky Tonk, Vol. 8: *The 1940s and 1950s* (Old Timey)

Comin' Right at Ya (1973, Liberty)

Okeh Western Swing (1982, Epic)

BLUEGRASS

*Bill Monroe with Lester Flatt and Earl Scruggs

(Bill Monroe, 1911-)

The Original Bluegrass Band (Rounder)

*Bill Monroe and His Blue Grass Boys

*Kentucky Waltz (1934, Decca)

*Blue Moon of Kentucky (1940, Decca)

*Little Cabin Home on the Hill (1940, Victor)

*Mule Skinner Blues (1940, Victor)

*Blue Grass Breakdown (1942, Victor)

*Molly and Tenbrooks (1942, Victor)

*Summertime Is Past and Gone (1942, Victor)

*Sweetheart You Done Me Wrong (1942, Victor)

*Blue Grass Ramble (1945, Columbia)

*Cheyenne (1945, Columbia)

*Get Up John (1945, Columbia)

*Gotta Travel On (1945, Columbia)

*Memories of You (1945, Columbia)

*Uncle Pen (1945, Columbia)

Mr. Bluegrass (MCA)

The Classic Bluegrass Recordings, Vol. 1 (1945, County)

The Classic Bluegrass Recordings, Vol. 2 (1949, County)

Bluegrass Special (1963, MCA)

I'll Meet You in Church Sunday Morning (1964, MCA)

The High, Lonesome Sound of Bill Monroe (1966, MCA)

Bill Monroe's Greatest Hits (1968, MCA)

Uncle Pen (1972, MCA)

Bean Blossom (1973, MCA)

Lester Flatt and Earl Scruggs

(Lester Flatt, 1914- ; Earl Scruggs, 1924-)

Foggy Mountain Breakdown (1948, Mercury)

Roll in My Sweet Baby's Arms (1948, Mercury)

Salty Dog Blues (1948, Mercury)

Flint Hill Special (1951, Mercury)

Country & Western Classics (Time-Life)

The World of . . . (1972, Columbia)

Don't Get Above Your Raisin' (1978, Rounder)
Golden Era (1978, Rounder)

Earl Scruggs solo

Banjoman (1977, Sire)

*Stanley Brothers

*Molly and Tenbrooks (1948, Rick-R-Tone)
*Mountain Dew (1950, Starday)
*Clinch Mountain Backstep (1958, King)
*Gathering Flowers for the Master's Bouquet (1958, King)
*Have You Someone (in Heaven Awaitin')? (1958, King)
*How Mountain Girls Can Love (1958, King)
*I'm a Man of Constant Sorrow (1958, King)
*It's Raining Here This Morning (1958, King)
*Keep a Memory (1958, King)
*Little Birdie (1958, King)
*Little Maggie (1958, King)
*The Memory of Your Smile (1958, King)
*Midnight Ramble (1958, King)
*Rank Stranger (1958, King)
*The White Dove (1958, King)
*Wildwood Flowere (1958, King)

Their Original Recordings (Melodeon)
The Best of . . . (1975, King)
For the Good People (1975, King)
The Stanley Bros. and the Clinch Mountain Boys Sing the Songs They Like Best (1975, King)
Good Old Camp Meeting Songs (1976, King)
Sixteen Greatest Hits (1977, Starday)
The Stanley Bros. and the Clinch Mountain Boys (1977, King)
Sixteen Greatest Gospel Hits (1978, Gusto)

Twenty Bluegrass Originals (1978, Gusto Deluxe)
The Columbia Sessions, 1949-50 (1980, Rounder)
I Saw the Light (1980, Gusto)
Old Country Church (1981, Gusto)

NEW GRASS

*Country Gentlemen

*The Fields Have Turned Brown (1967, Rebel)
*Get in Line Brother (1967, Rebel)
*The Long Black Veil (1967, Rebel)

The Gospel Album (Rebel)
Yesterday and Today, Vols. 1-3 (Rebel)
The Country Gentlemen, Vols. 1-4 (1960-73, Folkways)

*Osborne Brothers

The Best of . . . (MCA)
The Osborne Brothers (Rounder)
The Osborne Brothers and Red Allen (Rounder)

Larry Sparks

The Best of Larry Sparks and the Lonesome Ramblers (Rebel)
Bluegrass Old and New (Old Homestead)

J.D. Crowe and the New South

J.D. Crowe & New South (1975, Rounder)

Dillards

Back Porch Bluegrass (1963, Electra)

Bluegrass and New Grass Anthologies

Bluegrass for Collectors (RCA)

The Rich-R-Tone Story, Vol. 5: *The*
    Early Days of Bluegrass
    (Rounder)
Country Music and Bluegrass at
    Newport (1963, Vanguard)
Friends of Old-Time Music (1964,
    Folkways)
Country Cooking: Fourteen
    Bluegrass Instrumentals (1971,
    Rounder)
Sixteen Greatest Original Bluegrass
    Hits (1977, Starday)
Thirty Years of Bluegrass (1977,
    Gusto)
Twenty Bluegrass Originals:
    "Hymns" (1978, Gusto)

HONKY-TONK AND HILLBILLY BOOGIE

Al Dexter (1902-)

*Pistol Packin' Mama (1943, Okeh)

Ted Daffan and His Texans

(Ted Daffan, 1912-)

Born to Lose (1943, Okeh)
*No Letter Today (1943, Okeh)

*Floyd Tillman (1914-)

*They Took the Stars out of Heaven
    (1942, Columbia)
*Each Night at Nine (1943,
    Columbia)
*I Gotta Have My Baby Back (1949,
    Columbia)
I'll Keep On Loving You (1949,
    Columbia)
I Love So Much It Hurts (1949,
    Columbia)
*Slippin' Around (1949, Columbia)

*The Best of ... (Columbia)

*Ernest Tubb (1914-)

Slippin' Around (1941, Decca)
*Walking the Floor Over You (1941,
    Decca)
Have You Ever Been Lonely (1943,
    Decca)
I'll Get Along Somehow (1943,
    Decca)
My Tennessee Baby (1943, Decca)
Our Baby's Book (1943, Decca)
Take Me Back and Try Me One
    More Time (1943, Decca)
You Nearly Lose Your Mind (1943,
    Decca)
Driftwood on the River (1946,
    Decca)
Rainbow at Midnight (1946, Decca)
Tomorrow Never Comes (1946,
    Decca)
Half a Mind (1958, MCA)
Mr. Juke Box (1958, MCA)
Thanks a Lot (1963, MCA)
Waltz Across Texas (1965, MCA)
Another Story (1966, MCA)

Greatest Hits (1958, MCA)
The Ernest Tubb Story (1959, MCA)
Ernest Tubb and His Texas
    Troubadours (1975, Vocalion)

Delmore Brothers

(Alton Delmore, 1908-64; Rabon
Delmore, 1916-52)

*Freight Train Boogie (1945, King)
*Hillbilly Boogie (1945, King)
*Barnyard Boogie (1947, King)
Blues Stay Away from Me (1949,
    King)

The Best of ... (Starday-Gusto)

*Merle Travis (1917-)

*Divorce Me C.O.D. (1946, Capitol)
*Nine Pounds Hammer (1946,
    Capitol)
*Sixteen Tons (1946, Capitol)

Dark as a Dungeon (1947, Capitol)
*Fat Gal (1947, Capitol)
I'm a Natural Born Gamblin' Man
(1947, Capitol)
*So Round, So Firm, So Fully Packed
(1947, Capitol)
*Steel Guitar Rag (1947, Capitol)
Sweet Temptation (1947, Capitol)
Three Times Seven (1947, Capitol)

*Merle Travis' Guitar (1956, Capitol)
*The Best of . . . (1967, Capitol)

Moon Mullican (1909-67)

*Jole Blon (1947, King)
*Cherokee Boogie (1950, King)
*Grandpa Stole My Baby (1950,
King)
I'm Mad at You (1950, King)
Well Oh Well (1950, King)
*I'll Sail My Ship Alone (1951, King)
*Mona Lisa (1951, King)
*Sweeter than the Flowers (1951,
King)
*Seven Nights to Rock (1957, King)
*Ragged But Right (1961, King)

*Seven Nights to Rock, 1946-56
(1981, Rounder/Western)

*Hank Williams, Sr. (1923-53)

*Cold Cold Heart (MGM)
*Hey Good Lookin' (MGM)
*I'll Never Get Out of This World
Alive (MGM)
*I'm So Lonesome I Could Cry
(MGM)
*I Saw the Light (MGM)
*Jambalaya (MGM)
*Honky Tonk Blues (MGM)
*Kawliga (MGM)
*Long Gone Lonesome Blues
(MGM)
*Lovesick Blues (MGM)
*Moaning the Blues (MGM)
*Move It on Over (MGM)
*Ramblin' Man (MGM)
*Settin' the Woods on Fire (MGM)

*Take these Chains from My Heart
(MGM)
*Your Cheatin' Heart (MGM)

*Hank Williams: Country & Western
Classics, Vols. 1-3 (Time-Life)
*Hank Williams Sr.'s Greatest Hits
(MGM)
*The Immortal H. Williams (MGM)
*Very Best of . . . (MGM)
*I Saw the Light (1972, MGM)
*Twenty-four of Hank Williams'
Greatest Hits (1974, MGM)
*Twenty-four Greatest Hits, Vol. 2
(1977, MGM)

*Lefty Frizzell

(William Orville Frizzell, 1928-75)

How Long Will It Take (to Stop
Loving You) (1950, Columbia)
*If You've Got the Money I've Got
the Time (1950, Columbia)
*My Baby's Just Like Money (1950,
Columbia)
Always Late (1951, Columbia)
*Give Me More, More, More (1951,
Columbia)
*I Love You a Thousand Ways
(1951, Columbia)
I Want to Be with You Always
(1951, Columbia)
*Look What Thoughts Will Do
(1951, Columbia)
Mom and Dad's Waltz (1951,
Columbia)
Travelin' Blues (1951, Columbia)
*Long Black Veil (1959, Columbia)
*Saginaw, Michigan (1964,
Columbia)

*Columbia Historic Edition
(Columbia)
*Treasures Untold (Rounder)
*Lefty Frizell's Greatest Hits (1966,
Columbia)
*Remembering Lefty Frizell (1975,
Columbia)

*Hank Snow (1914-)

*I'm Moving On (1950, RCA)
The Golden Rocket (1951, RCA)
Music Makin' Mama from Memphis
(1951, RCA)
(Now and Then, There's) A Fool
Such As I (1951, RCA)
*The Rhumba Boogie (1951, RCA)
I Don't Hurt Anymore (1954,
RCA)
Ninety Miles an Hour (Down a
Dead End Street) (1954, RCA)
I've Been Everywhere (1955, RCA)
Miller's Cave (1955, RCA)

*The Best of . . . (RCA)
Souvenirs (RCA)
This Is My Story (RCA)

Webb Pierce (1926-)

Back Street Affair (1952, Decca)
*Wandering (1952, Decca)
*I'm Walking the Dog (1953, Decca)
That's Me without You (1953,
Decca)
*There Stands the Glass (1953,
Decca)
*More and More (1954, Decca)
*Slowly (1954, Decca)
I Don't Care (1955, Decca)
In the Jailhouse Now (1955, Decca)
Love, Love, Love (1955, Decca)
I Ain't Never (1959, Decca)

*The Best of . . . (MCA)
*Greatest Hits (MCA)

*Ray Price (1926-)

*If You Don't Someone Else Will
(1954, Columbia)
*I'll Be There (1954, Columbia)
*Release Me (1954, Columbia)
*Too Young to Die (1954,
Columbia)
City Lights (1955, Columbia)
*Heartaches by Number (1955,
Columbia)

*Invitation to the Blues (1955,
Columbia)
Same Old Me (1955, Columbia)
*Crazy Arms (1956, Columbia)
My Shoes Keep Walking Back to
You (1956, Columbia)
Make the World Go Away (1960,
Columbia)

*The World of . . . (1970, Columbia)
*Greatest Hits (1971, Columbia)
*The Best of . . . (1976, Columbia)

*George Jones (1931-)

*Why Baby Why (1956, King)
*Color of the Blues (1958, King)
Don't Do This to Me (1958, King)
Eskimo Pie (1958, King)
If I Don't Love You (1958, King)
Long Time to Forget (1958, King)
No Money Down (1958, King)
One is a Lonely Number (1958,
King)
Uh, Uh, No (1958, King)
What Am I Worth? (1958, King)
*All I Have to Offer You Is Me
(1962, Musicor)
*Good Year for the Roses (1962,
Musicor)
*White Lightning (1962, Musicor)
*Window Up Above (1962, Musicor)
*The Race Is On (1965, Musicor)

*Anniversary--Ten Years of Hits
(Epic)
Country & Western Classics: George
Jones (Time-Life)
*Double Gold George Jones
(Musicor)
*George Jones (United Artists)
*The George Jones Stroy (Starday)
*Golden Hits (Starday)
*Sixteen Greates Hits (Trip)
*Still the Same Ole Me (Epic)
*Memories of Us (1975, Epic)
*The Battle (1976, Epic)
*Wine Colored Roses (1987, Epic)

Johnny Horton (1929-60)

*Honky Tonk Man (1956, Columbia)
*I'm Coming Home (1957, Columbia)
Sleepy-Eyed John (1957, Columbia)
*The Battle of New Orleans (1959, Columbia)
Johnny Reb (1959, Columbia)
*When It's Springtime in Alaska (1959, Columbia)
*North to Alaska (1960, Columbia)
*Sink the Bismarck (1960, Columbia)
*The World of Johnny Horton (1971, Columbia)

Maddox Brothers and Rose

*Maddox Brothers and Rose: 1946-51, Vols. 1-2 (Arhoolie)

Harmonica Frank (1908-)

*The Great Original Recordings of . . . (Puritan)

Tennessee Ernie Ford (1919-)

*Best of . . . (Capitol)
*16 Tons (1955, Capitol)

Johnny Paycheck

(Donald Lyttle, 1941-)

*Extra Special (Accord)
*Greatest Hits (Little Darlin')
*The Roots of Rock, Vol. 10: Sun Country (Charly)
*Super Hits Country--The 1940s (Gusto)
*Super Hits Country--The 1950s (Gusto)
*Truck Driver Songs (Gusto)

NASHVILLE SOUND

Eddy Arnold (1918-)

*I'll Hold You in My Heart (1947, Victor)
*I Wouldn't Know Where to Begin (1956, RCA)
*Make the World Go Away (1965, RCA)
*I Want to Go with You (1966, RCA)

*Best of . . ., Vols. 1-2 (RCA)

Kitty Wells (1918-)

*Making Believe
*One by One
*It Wasn't God Who Made Honky Tonk (1952, MCA)
*Day into Night (1960s MCA)

*Kitty Wells Story (1963, MCA)

*Patsy Cline (1932-63)

*Walking After Midnight (1957, Decca)
*Crazy (1961, Decca)
*I Fall to Pieces (1961, Decca)
*She's Got You (1962, Decca)

*The Patsy Cline Story (1968, MCA)

Don Gibson (1928-)

*I Can't Stop Loving You (1958, RCA)
*Oh Lonesome Me (1958, RCA)
*Just One Time (1960, RCA)
*Sea of Heartbreak (1961, RCA)

*The Best of . . . (RCA)
Rockin' Rollin' (Bear Family)

*Conway Twitty (1933-)

*It's Only Make Believe (1958, MGM)
*Story of My Love (1959, MGM)

*Lonely Blue Boy (1960, MGM)
*Next in Line (1968, MGM)
*You've Never Been This Far Before (1973, MGM)

Greatest Hits, Vol. 1 (1972, MCA)
Greatest Hits, Vol. 2 (1976, MCA)

*Loretta Lynn (1935-)

*I'm a Honky Tonk Girl (1953, Zero)
*Success (1962, Decca)
*Don't Come Home Drinkin' (With Lovin' on Your Mind) (1966, Decca)
*Fist City (1968, Decca)
*Woman of the World (1969, Decca)
*Coal Miner's Daughter (1970, Decca)
*The Pill (1975, Decca)

Don't Come Home Drinkin' (1967, MCA)
Greatest Hits, Vol. 1 (1968, MCA)
Loretta Lynn Writes 'em and Sings 'em (1970, MCA)
Coal Miner's Daughter (1971, MCA)
Greatest Hits, Vol. 2 (1974, MCA)
When the Tingle Becomes a Chill (1976, MCA)

Tammy Wynette (1942-)

Apartment No. 9 (1966, Columbia)
*D-I-V-O-R-C-E (1967, Epic)
*I Don't Wanna Play House (1967, Columbia)
*Take Me to Your World (1967, Columbia)
*Stand By Your Man (1968, Epic)

Your Good Girl's Gonna Go Bad (1967, Epic)
D-I-V-O-R-C-E (1968, Epic)
Greatest Hits (1969, Epic)
Stand By Your Man (1969, Epic)

Tom T. Hall (1936-)

*Ballad of Forty Dollars (1968, Mercury)
*A Week in a Country Jail (1968, Mercury)
*It Sure Gets Cold in Des Moines (1971, Mercury)
Kentucky Feb. 27 1971 (1971, Mercury)
*Trip to Hyden (1971, Mercury)
I Love (1974, Mercury)

In Search of a Song (1971, Mercury)
Greatest Hits (1972, Mercury)
Rhymer and Other Five and Dimers (1973, Mercury)

Dolly Parton (1946-)

Dumb Blonde (1967, Monument)
Something Fishy (1967, Monument)
Daddy Come and Get Me (1970, RCA)
Down from Dover (1970, RCA)
How Great Thou Art (1970, RCA)
*Joshua (1970, RCA)
Just the Way I Am (1970, RCA)
*Mule Skinner Blues (1970, RCA)
*Touch Your Woman (1972, RCA)
*Coat of Many Colors (1973, RCA)
*Jolene (1973, RCA)
*Here You Come Again (1977, RCA)
Two Doors Down (1978, RCA)
Baby I'm Burnin' (1979, RCA)
9 to 5 (1980, RCA)

Best of . . . (1970, RCA)
Coat of Many Colors (1971, RCA)
Jolene (1973, RCA)
My Tennessee Mountain Home (1973, RCA)
Love Is Like a Butterfly (1974, RCA)
Bargain Store (1975, RCA)
Best of . . . (1975, RCA)
New Harvest . . . First Gathering (1977, RCA)

Chet Atkins (1924-)

*Canned Heat (1947, RCA)

Country Music (Time-Life)
The Night Atlanta Burned (1975, RCA)
Chester and Lester (1976, RCA)

*Johnny Cash (1932-)

*Cry, Cry, Cry (1955, Sun)
Hey Porter (1955, Sun)
There You Go (1955, Sun)
*Folsom Prison Blues (1956, Sun)
*I Walk the Line (1956, Sun)
Ballad of a Teenage Queen (1957, Sun)
Big River (1957, Sun)
Get Rhythm (1957, Sun)
Luther's Boogie (1957, Sun)
*All Over Again (1958, Columbia)
*Guess Things Happen That Way (1958, Sun)
*The Ways of a Woman in Love (1958, Sun)
*Don't Take Your Guns to Town (1959, Columbia)
Lorraine of Pontchartrain (1960, Columbia)
Another Man Done Gone (1963, Columbia)
Busted (1963, Columbia)
*Ring of Fire (1963, Columbia)
Tell Him I'm Gone (1963, Columbia)
*Understand Your Man (1964, Columbia)
Don't Think Twice (1965, Columbia)
It Ain't Me Babe (1965, Columbia)
Long Black Veil (1965, Columbia)
Mama You Been on My Mind (1965, Columbia)
Orange Blossom Special (1965, Columbia)
Wildwood Flower (1965, Columbia)
*Jackson (1967, Columbia)
Cocaine Blues (1968, Columbia)
Daddy Sang Bass (1968, Columbia)

Give My Love to Rose (1968, Columbia)
Send a Picture of Mother (1968, Columbia)
25 Minutes to Go (1968, Columbia)
*A Boy Named Sue (1969, Columbia)
*What Is Truth (1970, Columbia)
Man in Black (1971, Columbia)
Singin' in Viet Nam Talkin' Blues (1971, Columbia)
A Thing Called Love (1972, Columbia)
Committed to Parkview (1976, Columbia)
Far Side Banks of Jordan (1976, Columbia)
Mountain Lady (1976, Columbia)
*One Piece at a Time (1976, Columbia)
After the Ball (1977, Columbia)
Lady (1977, Columbia)
My Cowboy's Last Ride (1977, Columbia)
No Earthly Good (1977, Columbia)

Now There Was a Song (Columbia)
With His Hot and Blue Guitar (1957, Sun)
Songs That Made Him Famous (1958, Sun)
Fabulous Johnny Cash (1959, Columbia)
At Folsom Prison (1968, Columbia)
The Legend (1970, Sun)
The Rambler (1977, Columbia)
Rockabilly Blues (1980, Columbia)
Johnny Cash Is Coming to Town (1987, Mercury)

Charlie Pride (1938-)

Best of..., Vols. 1-2 (RCA)
Country Charlie Pride (1966, RCA)

Connie Smith (1941-)

Best of..., Vols. 1-2 (RCA)
If It Ain't Love (RCA)

Tanya Tucker (1958-)

Greatest Hits (1975, Columbia)

Porter Wagoner (1927-)

Best of . . ., Vols. 1-2 (RCA)

BAKERSFIELD

Buck Owens (1929-)

*Second Fiddle (1959, Capitol)
*I've Got a Tiger by the Tail (1965, Capitol)

Best of . . ., Vols. 1-3 (Capitol)
Country Music (Time-Life)

*Merle Hagggard (1937-)

Sing a Sad Song (1963, Tally)
Sam Hill (1964, Tally)
*My Friends Are Gonna Be Strangers (1965, Capitol)
The Bottle Let Me Down (1966, Capitol)
*I'm a Lonesome Fugitive (1966, Capitol)
Swinging Doors (1966, Capitol)
*Okie from Muskogee (1969, Capitol)
Hungry Eyes (1971, Capitol)
Mama Tried (1971, Capitol)
Silver Wings (1971, Capitol)
*Today I Started Loving You Again (1971, Capitol)
Workin' Man Blues' (1971, Capitol)
*If We Make It through December (1974, Capitol)
*Footlights (1979, Capitol)
*Heaven Was a Drink of Wine (1979, Capitol)

Someday We'll Look Back (Capitol)
Okie from Muskogee (1969, Capitol)
The Fightin' Side of Me (1970, Capitol)
Best of . . . (1972, Capitol)

Songs I'll Always Sing (1976, Capitol)
Serving 190 Proof (1979, MCA)
Songs for the Mama Who Tried (1981, MCA)

COUNTRYPOLITAN

*Charlie Rich (1934-)

*Lonely Weekend (1958, Sun)
Sittin' and Thinkin' (1958, Sun)
*Mohair Sam (1965, Smash)
Big Boss Man (1967, RCA)
*Life Has Its Little Ups and Downs (1969, RCA)
*Behind Closed Doors (1973, Epic)
*The Most Beautiful Girl (1973, Epic)

So Lonesome I Could Cry (Hi)
Sun's Best of . . . (Sun)
Set Me Free (1968, Epic)
The Fabulous Charlie Rich (1969, Epic)
Lonely Weekends (1969, Sun)
Boss Man (1970, Epic)
A Time for Tears (1970, Sun)
Best of . . . (1972, Epic)
Behind Closed Doors (1973, Epic)
The Early Years (1974, Sun)
Big Boss Man/My Mountain Blues (1977, RCA)

Anne Murray (1946-)

What About Me? (1968, Archives)
*Snowbird (1970, Capitol)
*Danny's Song (1973, Capitol)
He Thinks I Still Care (1974, Capitol)
Walk Right Back (1974, Capitol)
*You Need Me (1974, Capitol)
*You Won't See Me (1974, Capitol)

What About Me? (1968, Archives)
Country (1974, Capitol)
Love Song (1974, Capitol)

Crystal Gayle (1951-)

*Wrong Road Again (1974, Liberty)
I'll Get Over You (1976, Liberty)
You Never Miss a Real Good Thing
(Till He Says Goodbye) (1976,
Liberty)
*Don't It Make My Brown Eyes Blue
(1977, Liberty)
Talking in Your Sleep (1978,
Liberty)

Classic Crystal (Liberty)
Crystal Gayle (1975, Liberty)
We Must Believe in Magic (1977,
Liberty)

Glen Campbell (1938-)

Greatest Hits (1971, Capitol)
Best of . . . (1976, Capitol)

CONTEMPORARY COUNTRY

*Roger Miller (1936-)

*Dang Me (1964, Mercury)
*Kansas City Star (1964, Mercury)
*King of the Road (1964, Mercury)
*You Can't Roller Skate in a Buffalo
Herd (1966, Mercury)

Best of . . . (Mercury)
Dang Me (1964, Mercury)
**Golden Hits* (1965, Smash)
Return of . . . (1965, Smash)

*Willie Nelson (1933-)

*Bloody Mary Morning (1972,
Atlantic)
*Heaven and Hell (1972, Atlantic)
*Pick Up the Tempo (1972, Atlantic)
*Blue Eyes Crying in the Rain (1975,
Columbia)
*Remember Me (1975, Columbia)
*On the Road Again (1980,
Columbia)

*Always on My Mind (1982,
Columbia)

Phases and Stages (1972, Atlantic)
Red Headed Stranger (1975,
Columbia)
Troublemaker (1976, Columbia)
To Lefty from Willie (1977,
Columbia)
Stardust (1978, Columbia)

Waylon Jennings (1937-)

Jole Blon (1959, Brunswick)
Mac Arthur Park (1969, RCA)
*Luckenbach Texas (1977, RCA)
*Goodhearted Woman (1978, RCA)
*Amanda (1979, RCA)

Heartaches by the Number (1965,
RCA)
*The Only Daddy That'll Walk the
Line* (1965, RCA)
Dreamin' My Dreams (1975, RCA)
O'l Waylon (1977, RCA)
Waylon and Willie (1978, RCA)
Greatest Hits (1979, RCA)
It's Only Rock & Roll (1983, RCA)

Gary Stewart (1944-)

Out of Hand (1975, RCA)
Your Place or Mine (1977, RCA)
Cactus and Rose (1980, RCA)
Greatest Hits (1981, RCA)

*Hank Williams, Jr. (1949-)

*Stand in the Shadows (1965, MGM)
*All My Rowdy Friends (Have
Settled Down) (1981, Elecktra)

Living Proof (1973, War.)
Hank Williams Jr. and Friends
(1976, MGM)
The New South (1977, War.)
Whiskey Bent and Hell Bound
(1980, Elektra)
The Pressure Is On (1981, Elektra)
Man of Steel (1983, War.)
Major Moves (1984, War.)

*Jimmy Murphy (1925-)

*Electricity (1978, Sugar Hill)

*Electricity (1978, Sugar Hill)

Joe Ely (1947-)

*Cornbread Moon (1978, MCA)
*Gambler's Wife (1978, MCA)
*I Had My Hopes Up High (1978, MCA)

*Joe Ely (1977, MCA)
*Honky Tonk Masquerade (1978, MCA)
*Live Shots (1981, MCA)

Bobby Bare (1935-)

Greatest Hits (RCA)
The Winner and Other Losers (1976, RCA)
As Is (1981, Columbia)

Carlene Carter

Musical Shapes (1980, War.)

Narvel Felts

*Greatest Hits (1975, MCA)

Kinky Friedman (1944-)

*Sold American (1973, MCA)
*Lasso from El Passo (1976, Epic)

Don Williams (1939-)

*Greatest Hits (1975, MCA)

Johnny Lee

*Lookin' for Love (1980, Asylum)

NEW TRADITIONALISM

*Gram Parsons (1946-73)

Gram Parsons (1973, Reprise)

Grievous Angel (1974, Reprise)
Sleepless Nights (1976, A&M)
*Early Years (1979, Sierra)

*Emmylou Harris (1947-)

*Pieces of the Sky (1975, Warner Bros.)
*Profile--Best of . . . (1978, Warner Bros.)
*Roses in the Snow (1980, Warner Bros.)

Rodney Crowell

*I Ain't Living Long Like This (1978, Warner Bros.)
*Street Language (1986, Warner Bros.)

John Anderson

*John Anderson, Vol. 1 (1980, Warner Bros.)
*I Just Came Home to Count the Memories (1981, Warner Bros.)
*John Anderson, Vol. 2 (1981, Warner Bros.)
*Swinging (1983, Warner Bros.)

*Ricky Skaggs (1954-)

*Waitin' for the Sun to Shine (1981, Epic)
*Family and Friends (1982, Rounder)
*Highways & Heartaches (1983, Epic)
Love's Gonna Get Ya (1986, Epic)

George Strait

Greatest Hits (MCA)
*Strait Country (1981, MCA)
#7 (1986, MCA)
*Ocean Front Property (1987, MCA)

*Randy Travis

*Storms to Life (1986, Warner Bros.)
*Always and Forever (1987, Warner Bros.)

*Steve Earle

Guitar Town (1986, MCA)
Early Tracks (1987, Epic)
Exit O (1987, MCA)

*Dwight Yoakam

Guitars, Cadillacs, Etc., Etc. (1986, Reprise)
Hillbilly Deluxe (1987, Reprise)

*Reba McEntire

What Am I Gonna Do About You (1986, MCA)
Whoever's in New England (1986, MCA)
Greatest Hits (1987, MCA)

Patty Loveless

If My Heart Had Windows (1987, MCA)

Lyle Lovett

Lyle Lovett (1987, MCA)

T. Graham Brown

I Tell It Like It Used to Be (1986, Capitol)
Brilliant Conversationalist (1987, Capitol)

O'Kanes

The O'Kanes (1987, Columbia)

*Judds

(Naomi Judd, 1946- ; Wynonna Judd, 1964-)

Why Not Me (1984, RCA)
Rockin' with Rhythm (1985, RCA)
Heartland (1987, RCA)

Whites

Ain't No Birds (1987, MCA)

Rockabilly and Rock'n'Roll

General Anthologies

Nuggets (Sire)
Oldies But Goodies, Vols., 3-6, 8, 10-12, 14 (Original Sound)
Original Memphis Rock and Roll (Sun)
Original Rock Oldies--Golden Hits, Vols. 1-2 (Specialty)
Rock and Roll Show (Gusto)
*The Roots of Rock'n'Roll (Savoy)
Super Oldies of the Fifties, Vols. 3, 7 (Trip)
Super Oldies of the Sixties, Vols. 3, 6 (Trip)
This Is How It All Began, Vols. 1-2 (Specialty)
*Wild Wild Young Women (Rounder)
*Echoes of a Rock Era: The Early Years (1958, Rounder)
*Echoes of a Rock Era: The Middle Years (1962, Rounder)
*King-Federal Rockabilly (1978, King)
*Beach Beat Classics, Vol. 2 (1980, Ripete)
Rockabilly Stars, Vol. 1, (1981, Epic)
*Sun Records--The Rocking Years (1986, Charly)
*Sun Records--The Blues Years (1986, Charly)

ROCKABILLY/ ROCK'N'ROLL

Roy Hall with His Cohutta Mountains Boys

(Roy Hall, 1922-84)

*Dirty Boogie (1950, Fortune)

Five Years in Prison (1950, Fortune)
My Freckle Face Gal (1950, Fortune)
Never Marry a Tennessee Girl (1950, Fortune)
Okee Doaks (1950, Fortune)
We Never Get Too Big to Cry (1950, Fortune)

Roy Hall solo

*Ain't You Afraid (1950, Bullet)
*Mule Boogie (1950, Bullet)
All by Myself (1955, Decca)
*Whole Lotta Shakin' Goin' On (1955, Decca)
*Diggin' the Boogie (1956, Decca)

Boogie Rockabilly (Decca)

*Bill Haley (1925-81)

We're Recruiting (1944, Vogue)
Candy Kisses (1948, Cowboy)
Tennessee Border (1948, Cowboy)
Too Many Parties, Too Many Pals (1948, Cowboy)
I'm Gonna Dry Ev'ry Tear with a Kiss (1949, Holiday)
Why Do I Cry over You (1949, Holiday)
*I'm Crying (1951, Holiday)
*Pretty Baby (1951, Holiday)
*Rocket 88 (1951, Holiday)
Jukebox Cannonball 1952, (Holiday)

*Bill Haley with the Comets

*Crazy, Man, Crazy (1950, Essex)
Icy Heart (1952, Essex)
*Rock the Joint (1952, Essex)
*(We're Gonna) Rock around the Clock (1952, Decca)
Birth of the Boogie (1954, Decca)
*Dim, Dim the Lights (1954, Decca)
*Shake Rattle and Roll (1954, Decca)
Thirteen Woman (1954, Decca)

*Burn That Candle (1955, Decca)
*Razzle-Dazzle (1955, Decca)
*R-O-C-K (1955, Decca; 1956, Decca)
*See You Later Alligator (1955, Decca)
Skinny Minnie (1958, Decca)

Rock around the Clock (1955, Decca)
Rock around the Clock (1956, Decca)
Rock'n'Roll Stage Show (1956, Decca)
Golden Hits (1972, MCA)

Skeets McDonald (1915-68)

Mean and Evil Blues (1950, Fortune)
The Tattooed Lady (1950, Fortune)
Fuss and Fight (1951, Capitol)
Ridin' with the Blues (1951, Capitol)
Scoot, Git and Begone (1951, Capitol)
Today I'm Moving Out (1951, Capitol)
Don't Let the Stars Get in Your Eyes (1952, Capitol)
Your Love Is Like a Faucet (1954, Capitol)
*Heart-Breakin' Mama (1956, Capitol)
*I Got a New Field to Plow (1956, Capitol)
*You Oughta See Grandma Rock (1956, Capitol)

Goin Steady with the Blues (1958, Capitol)

Jimmie Logsdon (1922-)

It's All Over But the Shouting (1951, Decca)
I Wanna Be Mama'd (1952, Decca)
H. Williams Sings the Blues No More (1953, Decca)
Good Deal Lucille (1954, Decca)

Let's Have a Happy Time (1954, Decca)
Midnight Boogie (1954, Decca)
Midnight Blues (1955, Dot)
I Got Rocket in My Pocket (1957, Roulette)
Mother's Flower Garden (1963, King)

Wanda Jackson (1937-)

Lovin', Country Style (1954, Decca; 1956, Decca)
The Night to Love (1954, Decca; 1956, Decca)
You Can't Have My Love (1954, Decca)
Tears at the Grand Ole Opry (1955, Decca)
*Hot Dog! That Made Him Mad (1956, Capitol)
I Gotta Know (1956, Capitol)
Wasted (1956, Decca)
*Fujiama Mama (1958, Capitol)
*Let's Have a Party (1960, Capitol)
*Mean, Mean, Mean (1960, Capitol)
Right or Wrong (1961, Capitol)
Riot in Cell Block #9 (1961, Capitol)
A Girl Don't Have to Drink to Have Fun (1967, Capitol)
Come on Home to This Lonely Heart (1974, Capitol)

Only Rock'n'Roll (Capitol)
W. Jackson (1958, Capitol)
Rock with Wanda (1960, Capitol)
Right or Wrong (1961, Capitol)

Janis Martin

That Rockin' Gal (1956; 1959)
That Rockin' Gal Rocks On (1956; 1959)

*Carl Perkins (1932-)

Gone, Gone, Gone (1955, Sun)
Honky Tonk Gal (1955, Sun)
Turn Around (1955, Sun)

All Mama's Children (1956, Sun)
*Blue Suede Shoes (1956, Sun)
Boppin' the Blues (1956, Sun)
Perkins Wiggle (1956, Sun)
Put Your Cat Clothes On (1957, Sun)
Everybody's Trying to Be My Baby (1958, Columbia)
Her Love Rubbed Off (1958, Columbia)
Pink Pedal Pushers (1958, Columbia)
Right String Baby (but Wrong Yo-Yo) (1958, Columbia)
Dixie Fried (1959, Columbia)
Only You (1959, Columbia)
Somebody Tell Me (1959, Columbia)

The Sun Years
Whole Lotta Shakin' (1959, Columbia)
Blue Suede Shoes (1969, Sun)
Original Golden Hits (1969, Sun)
Rocking Guitar Man (1975, Charly)
Original Carl Perkins (1976, Charly)

*Jerry Lee Lewis (1935-)

Deep Elm Blues (1954, Sun)
Old Pal of Yesterday (1954, Sun)
Silver Threads (amongst the Gold) (1954, Sun)
You're the Only Star in My Blue Heaven (1954, Sun)
Big Legged Woman (1955, Sun)
Ubangi Stomp (1955, Sun)
*Crazy Arms (1956, Sun)
Little Queenie (1956, Sun)
Matchbox (1956, Sun)
Milkshake Mademoiselle (1956, Sun)
Slipin' Around (1956, Sun)
*Great Balls of Fire (1957, Sun)
When the Saints Go Marchin' In (1957, Sun)
*Whole Lotta Shakin' (1957, Sun)
*Breathless (1958, Sun)

*High School Confidential (1958, Sun)
I'll Sail My Ship Alone (1958, Sun)
I'm the Guilty One (1958, Sun)
*Lewis Boogie (1958, Sun)
Drinkin' Wine Spo-Dee-O-Dee (1973, Mercury)
Rockin' My Life Away (1978, Elektra)

Golden Hits of . . . (1964, Smash)
Jerry Lee Lewis' Original Golden Hits, Vols. 1-2 (1969, Sun); Vol. 3 (1971, Sun)
Best of . . . (1970, Smash)
Monsters (1971, Sun)

Country Hits of Jerry Lee Lewis

Another Place, Another Time (1968, Smash)
To Make Love Sweeter for You (1968, Smash)
What Made Milwaukee Famous (Made a Loser Out of Me) (1968, Smash)
There Must Be More to Love Than This (1971, Mercury)
Would You Take Another Chance on Me (1971, Mercury)
Chantilly Lace (1972, Mercury)
Middle Age Crazy (1977, Mercury)
Thirty-nine and Holding (1981, Mercury)

The Original (Sun)
Live at the Star Club Hamburg (1964, Philips)
Another Place, Another Time (1968, Smash)
Golden Cream of the Country (1969, Sun)
Rockin' Rhythm and Blues (1969, Sun)
A Taste of Country (1969, Sun)
Memphis Country (1970, Sun)
Ole Tyme Country Music (1970, Sun)
Sunday Down South (1970, Sun)
Best of . . ., Vol. 2 (1978, Mercury)

Killer Country (1980, Elektra)
*The Killer 1963-68 (1986, Smash-Bear)

Mickey Gilley

*Gilley's Smokin' (1976, Playboy)
*Mickey Gilley's Greatest Hits, Vol. 1 (1976, Playboy)
*Mickey Gilley's Greatest Hits, Vol. 2 (1977, Playboy)
Lonely Hearts (1981, Epic)

Buddy Holly (1938-59)

Blue Days, Black Nights (1956, Decca)
Cindy Lue [Peggy Sue] (1956, Decca)
Don't Come Back Knockin' (1956, Decca)
Girl on My Mind (1956, Decca)
Love Me (1956, Decca)
Midnight Shift (1956, Decca)
Modern Don Juan (1956, Decca)
Rock around with Ollie Vee (1956, Decca)
*Oh Boy (1957, Coral)
*Peggy Sue (1957, Coral)
*That'll Be the Day (1957, Brunswick)
*Early in the Morning (1958, Coral)
Fool's Paradise (1958, Coral)
Listen to Me (1958, Coral)
Maybe Baby (1958, Coral)
*Rave On (1958, Coral)
Think It Over (1958, Coral)
True Love Ways (1958, Coral)
Well . . . Alright (1958, Coral)
*It Doesn't Matter Anymore (1959, Coral)

*The Complete Buddy Holly (1969, MCA)
*Twenty Golden Greats (1978, MCA)

*Elvis Presley (1935-77)

Don't Cry Daddy (RCA)
My Happiness (1953, Sun)

That's When Your Heartaches Begin (1953, Sun)
Blue Moon (1954, Sun)
*Blue Kentucky Moon (1954, Sun)
Casual Love Affair (1954, Sun)
*Good Rockin' Tonight (1954, Sun)
I Don't Care if the Sun Don't Shine (1954, Sun)
I'll Never Stand in Your Way (1954, Sun)
I Love You Because (1954, Sun)
Milkcow Blues Boogie (1954, Sun)
*That's Alright (1954, Sun)
*You're a Heartbreaker (1954, Sun)
*Baby Let's Play House (1955, Sun)
I Forgot to Remember to Forget (1955, Sun)
I'm Left, You're Right, She's Gone (1955, Sun)
*Mystery Train (1955, Sun)
Anyway You Want Me (That's the Way I'll Be) (1956, RCA)
*Don't Be Cruel (1956, RCA)
*Heartbreak Hotel (1956, RCA)
I Got a Woman (1956, RCA)
I Want You, I Need You (1956, RCA)
I Was the One (1956, RCA)
*Love Me Tender (1956, RCA)
Too Much (1956, RCA)
*All Shook Up (1957, RCA)
Hard Headed Woman (1957, RCA)
*Jailhouse Rock (1957, RCA)
*Teddy Bear (1957, RCA)
That's When Your Heartaches Begin (1957, RCA)
Big Hunk o' Love (1959, RCA)
*Are You Lonesome Tonight (1960, RCA)
It's Now or Never (1960, RCA)
Stuck on You (1960, RCA)
I Feel So Bad (1961, RCA)
Little Sister (1961, RCA)
Surrender (1961, RCA)
Good Luck Charm (1962, RCA)
Return to Sender (1962, RCA)
(You're the) Devil in Disguise (1963, RCA)
If I Can Dream (1968, RCA)

In the Ghetto (1969, RCA)
Kentucky Rain (1969, RCA)
Suspicious Minds (1969, RCA)
Burning Love (1972, RCA)

*Elvis (1956, RCA)
*Elvis Presley (1956, RCA)
*A Date With Elvis (1959, RCA)
*For LP Fans Only (1959, RCA)
Elvis Is Back (1960, RCA)
Girls! Girls! Girls! (1962, RCA)
Spinout (1966, RCA)
*Elvis (1968, RCA)
*From Elvis in Memphis (1969,
  RCA)
*That's the Way It Is (1970, RCA)
I'm 10,000 Years Old (1971, RCA)
Elvis Today (1975, RCA)
Promised Land (1975, RCA)
Elvis Sings the Wonderful World of
  Christmas (1976, RCA)
*The Sun Sessions (1976, RCA)

*Gospel and Inspirational Albums of
Elvis Presley*

*His Hand in Mine (1961, RCA)
*How Great Thou Art (1967, RCA)
You'll Never Walk Alone (1971,
  Camden)
*He Touched Me (1972, RCA)

Elvis Presley Anthologies

*Elvis' Golden Records, Vol. 1 (1958,
  RCA)
*Elvis' Golden Records, Vol. 2 (1960,
  RCA)
*Elvis' Golden Records, Vol. 3 (1963,
  RCA)
*Elvis' Golden Records, Vol. 4 (1968,
  RCA)
*World Wide Fifty Gold Award Hits,
  Vol. 1 (1970)
*C'mon Everbody (1971, Camden)
*World Wide Fifty Gold Award Hits,
  Vol. 2 (1971)
Elvis: A Legendary Performer, Vol. 1
  (1974)

Elvis: A Legendary Performer, Vol. 2
  (1976, RCA)

Ricky Nelson (1940-85)

I'm Walking (1957, Verve)
*Believe What You Say (1958,
  Imperial)
*Poor Little Fool (1958, Imperial)
*Just a Little Too Much (1959,
  Imperial)
*Hello Mary Lou (1961, Imperial)
*Travelin' Man (1961, Imperial)
*Teenage Idol (1962, Imperial)
She Belongs to Me (1969, Decca)
*Garden Party (1972, Decca)

*Ricky (1957, Imperial)
*Song by Ricky (1959, Imperial)
More Songs by Ricky (1960,
  Imperial)
*Legendary Masters Series (1971,
  United Artists)
Playing to Win (1981, Capitol)

*Roy Orbison (1936-)

Blue Angel (1956, Monument)
Domino (1956, Sun)
*Oobie Doobie (1956, Sun)
Rock House (1956, Sun)
Devil Doll (1957, Sun)
*Only the Lonely (1960, Monument)
Candy Man (1961, Monument)
The Crowd (1961, Monument)
*Crying (1961, Monument)
I'm Hurtin (1961, Monument)
Love Hurts (1961, Monument)
*Running Scared (1961, Monument)
*Dream Baby (1962, Monument)
*Leah (1962, Monument)
Blue Bayou (1963, Monument)
Falling (1963, Monument)
In Dreams (1963, Monument)
Mean Woman Blues (1963,
  Monument)
Pretty Paper (1963, Monument)
It's Over (1964, Monument)
Oh Pretty Women (1964,
  Monument)

Goodnight (1965)
Ride Away (1965, MGM)

Greatest Hits (1962, Monument)
Crying (1963, Monument)
In Dreams (1963, Monument)
Lonely and Blue (1963, Monument)
Pretty Woman (1964, Monument)
Very Best of . . . (1966, Monument)
The Original Sound of . . . (1969, Sun)
All-Time Greatest Hits (1972, Monument)

Little Richard

(Richard Penniman, 1932-)

Taxi Blues (1951, Specialty)
Every Hour (1952, Specialty)
Get Rich Quick (1953, Specialty)
*Tutti Frutti (1955, Specialty)
*Long Tall Sally (1956, Specialty)
*Rip It Up (1956, Specialty)
*Jenny Jenny (1957, Specialty)
*Keep a Knockin' (1957, Specialty)
*Lucille (1957, Specialty)
*Good Golly Miss Molly (1958, Specialty)
Bama Lama Bama Loo (1964, Specialty)

Little Richard (1958, Specialty)
The Fabulous L. Richard (1959, Specialty)
Little Richard's Grooviest Seventeen Original Hits (1959, Specialty)
Well Alright (1959, Specialty)
The Explosive Little Richard (1986, Epic)
Greatest Hits--Recorded Live (1986, Epic)

*Chuck Berry (1926-)

*Maybellene (1955, Chess)
Thirty Days (1955, Chess)
Memphis Tennessee (1956, Chess)
No Money Down (1956, Chess)
*Roll Over Beethoven (1956, Chess)

*Lucille (1957, Specialty)
Rock'n'Roll Music (1957, Chess)
Round and Round (1957, Chess)
School Day (1957, Chess)
Brown-Eyed Handsome Man (1958, Chess)
Carol (1958, Chess)
Johnny B. Goode (1958, Chess)
Little Queenie (1958, Chess)
Memphis (1958, Chess)
Sweet Little Sixteen (1958, Chess)
Living in the U.S.A. (1959, Chess)
Nadine (1964, Chess)
No Particular Place to Go (1964, Chess)
My Ding-a-Ling (1972, Chess)
Rockit (1979, Chess)

Chuck Berry Is on Top (Chess)
Rockin' at the Hops (Chess)
More Chuck Berry (1960, Chess)
Chuck Berry's Greatest Hits (1964, Chess)
Chuck Berry's Golden Decade (1967, Chess)
Chuck Berry's Golden Decade, Vol. 2 (1973, Chess)
Rockit (1979, Atco)
Rock'n'Roll Rarities (1986, Chess)

*Bo Diddley (1928-)

*Who Do You Love?
*Bo Diddley (1955, Checker)
*I'm a Man (1955, Checker)
*Mona (1956, Checker)
You Pretty Thing (1958, Checker)
*Say Man (1959, Checker)
*Road Runner (1960, Checker)
You Can't Judge a Book by the Cover (1962, Checker)

Bo Diddley--Sixteen All Time Greatest Hits (1967, Checker)
Got My Own Bag of Tricks (1971, Chess)

Sonny Burgess

Ain't Got A Thing (1955, Sun)

Sadie's Back in Town (1955, Sun)
We Wanna Boogie (1955, Sun)

Legendary Sun Performer (Charly)

Johnny Burnette and the Rock and Roll Trio

(Johnny Burnette, 1934-64)

Rock Therapy (1956, Sun)
Train Kept A-Rollin' (1956, Sun)
You're Undecided (1956, Sun)
*You're Sixteen (1960, Liberty)

Tear It Up (1976, Solid Smoke)

*Eddie Cochran (1938-60)

Cut Across Shorty (1957, Liberty)
*Come On Everybody (1958,
    Liberty)
Pink Pegged Slacks (1958, Liberty)
*Summertime Blues (1958, Liberty)
*Twenty Flight Rock (1958, Liberty)
*Something Else (1959, Liberty)
Three Steps to Heaven (1960,
    Liberty)

Eddie Cochran (1960, Liberty)
The Legendary Masters Series, Vol. 4
    (1972, United Artists)
The Eddie Cochran Singles Album
    (1979, United Artists)

*Everly Brothers

(Don Everly, 1937- ; Phil Everly,
1939-)

Thou Shalt Not Steal (1955,
    Columbia)
Barbara Allen (1956, Cadence)
I'm Here to Get My Baby out of Jail
    (1956, Cadence)
Keep On Lovin Me (1956,
    Columbia)
Kentucky (1956, Cadence)
Who's Gonna Shoe Your Pretty
    Little Feet (1956, Cadence)

*Bye, Bye Love (1957, Cadence)
*Wake Up Little Suzie (1957,
    Cadence)
*All I Have to Do Is Dream (1958,
    Cadence)
*Bird Dog (1958, Cadence)
*Problems (1959, Cadence)
*Till I Kissed You (1959, Cadence)
*Cathy's Clown (1960, Warner Bros.)
*When Will I Be Loved (1960,
    Cadence)
*Walk Right Back (1961, Warner
    Bros.)
Crying in the Rain (1962, Warner
    Bros.)
That's Old Fashioned (1962,
    Warner Bros.)
Gone, Gone, Gone (1964, Warner
    Bros.)
Bowling Green (1967, Warner
    Bros.)

The Everly Bros. Greatest Hits
    (Barnaby)
End of an Era (1957)
The Everly Bros. (1958, Cadence)
Songs Our Daddy Taught Us (1958,
    Cadence)
Roots (1986, Edsel)

*Gary U.S. Bonds (1939-)

*New Orleans (1960, Legrand)
*Not Me (1961, Legrand)
*Quarter to Three (1961, Legrand)
*School Is Out (1961, Legrand)
*Copy Cat (1962, Legrand)
*Dear Lady Twist (1962, Legrand)
Daddy's Come Home (1981, EMI)
This Little Girl (1981, EMI)

Dance Till Quarter to Three (1960,
    Legrand)
Greatest Hits (1963, Legrand; 1981,
    Legrand)
Dedication (1981, EMI)

*Gene Vincent (1935-71)

*Be-Bop-a-Lula (1956, Capitol)

Git It (1956, Capitol)
*Race with the Devil (1956, Capitol)
Who Slapped John? (1956, Capitol)
Woman in Love (1956, Capitol)
*Dance to the Bop (1957, Capitol)
*Lotta Lovin (1957, Capitol)
Bring It On Home to Me (1970,
Capitol)

*Greatest Hits (Capitol)
*Bluejean Bop (1956, Capitol)
*Gene Vincent Rocks and the Blue
Caps Roll (1958, Capitol)
*The Gene Vincent Story, Vols. 1-8
(1973, Capitol)
*The Bop That Just Won't Stop (1974,
Capitol)
*The Capitol Years (1986, Charly)

*Richie Valens (1941-59)

*Come On, Let's Go (1958, Del-Fi)
*Donna (1958, Del-Fi)
*La Bamba (1959, Del-Fi)

*Best of ... (1981, Del-Fi)
History of ... (1981, Del-Fi)

*Etta James (1938-)

*Good Rockin' Daddy (1955,
Modern)
*The Wallflower (1955, Modern)
*All I Could Do Was Cry (1960,
Argo)
My Dearest Darling (1960, Argo)
*At Last (1961, Argo)
Most of All (1961, Argo)
Trust in Me (1961, Argo)
*Something Got a Hold on Me
(1962, Argo)
Stop the Wedding (1962, Argo)
Pay Back (1963, Argo)
*Pushover (1963, Argo)
Two Sides to Every Story (1963,
Argo)
*Baby What You Want Me to Do
(1964, ARgo)
Loving You More Every Day (1964,
Argo)

*Tell Mama (1967, Cadet)
*Security (1968, Cadet)
Almost Persuaded (1969, Cadet)
Losers Weepers (1970, Cadet)

*Chess Masters (Chess)
Tell Mama (1968, Cadet)
*Peaches (1971, Chess)
Deep in the Night (1978, Warner
Bros.)

*Jay Hawkins (1929-)

Screamin' Blues (1953, Gotham)
Baptize Me in Wine (1954, Timely)
She Put the Wamee on Me (1955,
Mercury)
I Is (1956, Grand)
*I Put a Spell on You (1956, Ekeh)
*Alligator Wine (1958, Okeh)

*At Home with Screamin' Jay Hawkins
(1958, Epic)
I Put a Spell on You (1969, Epic)
Screamin' the Blues (1979, Red
Lightnin')

*Huey Smith (1924-)

*Rockin' Pneumonia and the Boogie
Woogie Flu (1957, Ace)
*Don't You Just Know It (1958,
Ace)
Don't You Know Yockomo (1958,
Ace)
Pop-Eye (1962, Ace)

*Rockin' Pneumonia and the Boogie
Woogie Flu (Sue)
*Huey "Piano" Smith and the Clowns
(1979, Vivid-Ace)

Larry Williams (1935-80)

Just Because (1956, Specialty)
*Bony Maronie (1957, Specialty)
*Short Fat Fanny (1957, Specialty)
You Bug Me, Baby (1957,
Specialty)
*Dizzy, Miss Lizzy (1958, Specialty)

Greatest Hits (Okeh)
Here Is . . . (Specialty)
Original Golden Blues Giants
(Liberty)
Original Hits (Sonet)
Slow Down (Specialty)

Esquerita

I Need You (1955, Capitol)
Oh, Baby (1955, Capitol)
Rockin' the Joint (1955, Capitol)
The Green Door (1956, Capitol)
*I'm Battie over Hattie (1956,
Capitol)

Esquerita (1959, Capitol)

Arthur Gunther (1926-76)

*Baby, Let's Play House (1954,
Excello)

Sanford Clark

*The Fool (1956, Dot)

Buddy Knox (1933-)

*Party Doll (1957, Roulette)
Swingin' Daddy (1958, Roulette)
Teasable Pleaseable You (1959,
Roulette)

Jimmy Bowen (1937-)

*I'm Sticking with You (1957,
Roulette)
By the Light of the Silvery Moon
(1958, Roulette)

Charlie Feathers

Defrost Your Heart (1955, Sun)
I Forgot to Remember to Forget
(1955, Sun)
Mound of Clay (1955, Sun)
Uh Huh Honey (1955, Sun)

One Hand Loose
Wide Muddy River, Vol. 2

Rockabilly's Main Man (1955; 1959)

Sony Fisher

Texas Rockabilly

*Dale Hawkins (1938-)

*Suzie Q (1957, Checker)
A House, a Car, and a Wedding
Ring (1958, Checker)
La Do-Dada (1958, Checker)
Class Cutter Yeah Yeah (1959,
Checker)
Liza Jane (1959, Checker)
My Babe (1959, Checker)

Chess Rock'n'Rhythm Series (Chess)
Suzie Q (1958, Chess)
Dale Hawkins (1977, Chess)

*Ronnie Hawkins (1935-)

*Forty Days (1959, Roulette)
*Mary Lou (1959, Roulette)
Who Do You Love? (1963,
Roulette)
Down in the Alley (1970, Cotillion)

Arkansas Rock Pile
Premonition (Roulette)
Rockin' (Pye)
The Best of . . . 1963, (Roulette)

*Billy Lee Riley

*Flying Saucers Rock'n'Roll (1955,
Sun)
*Red Hot (1955, Sun)

Funk Harmonica (Crescendo)
Billy Lee Riley in Action (1966,
Crescendo)
Legendary Sun Performers (1978,
Sun)

*Jack Scott (1936-)

*Leroy (1958, Carlton)
*My True Love (1958, Carlton)
Goodbye Baby (1959, Carlton)

*The Way I Walk (1959, Carlton)
*Burning Bridges (1960, Top Rank)
*What in the World's Come Over
    You (1960, Top Rank)

Jack Scott Rocks (Rock and Roll)
Jack Scott on Groove (RCA)

Warren Smith (1934-)

Red Cadillac and a Black
    Moustache (1955, Sun)
Rock'n'Roll Ruby (1955, Sun)
Tonight Will Be the Last Night
    (1955, Sun)
*Ubangi Stomp (1955, Sun)

Legendary Sun Performers (Sun)

LATER ROCKABILLY

Billy Swan (1944-)

I Can Help (1975, Columbia)
Billy Swan (1976, Columbia)

Joe "King" Carrasco

Joe "King" Carrasco and the Crowns
    (1981, Hannibal)
Party Weekend (1983, Hannibal)

Shakin' Pyramids

Skin 'em Up (1981, Virgin)

Stray Cats

Built for Speed (1982, EMI)
Rant n' Rave with the Stray Cats
    (1983, EMI)

Tail Gators

Swamp Rock (1985, Wrestler)
Mumbo Jumbo (1986, Wrestler)

Georgia Satellites

Keep the Faith (1985, Making
    Waves)

Georgia Satellites (1986, Elektra)

ROCKIN' SOUNDS OF LOUISIANA

Al Ferrier (1935-)

My Baby Done Gone Away (1955,
    Goldband)
*No No Baby (1955, Goldband)
*Hey Baby (1957, Excello)

The Birth of Rockabilly (Goldband)
*Al Ferrier and Warren Storm:
    Boppin' Tonight* (1976, Flyright)

Johnny Jano

*Havin' a Whole Lot of Fun (1956,
    Excello)
Mabel's Gone (1957, Goldband)

I'm Proud to Be a Cajun (Delta of
    Texas)
King of Louisiana Rockabilly
    (Flyright)
Sings Cajun Pure (Goldband)

Gene Terry

*Cindy Lou (1957, Goldband)
*Teardrops in My Eyes (1957,
    Goldband)

Larry Hart

Coffins Have No Pocket (1958,
    Goldband)
*Come On Baby (1958, Goldband)
*Freight Train (1958, Goldband)
*Good Rocking Joe (1958,
    Goldband)
*I'm Just a Mender (1958,
    Goldband)
*Oh Nelly (1958, Goldband)

Bayou Rock (Goldband)

Little Billy Earl

Couple in the Car (1958,
Goldband)
Go Dan Tucker (1958, Goldband)

*Doug Kershaw (1936-)

*So Lovely Baby (1953, Hickory)
*When Will I Learn (1953, Feature)

*Rusty and Doug

(Rusty Kershaw, 1938- ; Doug
Kershaw, 1936-)

*Hey Sheriff (1958, Hickory)
*Louisiana Man (1958, Hickory)
*Diggy Diggy Lo (1961, Hickory)

*Cajun Stripper (1963, RCA)
*Rust . . . Cajun in the Blues Country
(1970)
*Ragin' Cajun (1976, War.)
*Rusty and Doug Kershaw (1981,
Flywright)

Anthologies

*Louisiana Swamp Pop (1977,
Flyright)
*Rockin' Fever--Jay Miller Sessions
(1978, Flyright)
*Bayou Boogie--Jay Miller Sessions
(1980, Flyright)
*Boppin' It!--Jay Miller Sessions
(1980, Flyright)
*Girl on the Right Blue Jeans--Jay
Miller Sessions (1980, Flyright)
*Too Hot to Handle--Jay Miller
Sessions (1981, Flyright)

SWAMP-POP

*Bobby Charles (1938-)

*Laure Lee (1955, Chess)
*On Bended Knee (1955, Chess)
One Eyed Jack (1955, Chess)

*(See You) Later Alligator (1955,
Chess)
Take It Easy Greasy (1955, Chess)
*Why Can't You (1956, Chess)
*Why Did You Leave (1956, Chess)
Four Winds (1957, Imperial)
Bye Bye Baby (1958, Imperial)
I Just Want You (1958, Imperial)
Those Eyes (1959, Imperial)
*(Before I) Grow Too Old (1972,
Bearsville)
*Small Town Talk (1972, Bearsville)

*Bobby Charles (1972, Bearsville)

*Roy Perkins

(Ernie Suarez, 1935-)

Here I Am (1955, Meladee)
*You're on My Mind (1955,
Meladee)
You're Gone (1955, Meladee)
Drop Top (1956, Ram)

*Bobby Page

*Hippy-Ti-Yo (1958, Ram)
*Loneliness (1958, Ram)

*Jimmy Clanton

*Just a Dream (1958, Ace)
My Own True Love (1959, Ace)
Another Sleepless Night (1960,
Ace)
What Am I Gonna Do (1961, Ace)
Venus in Blue Jeans (1962, Ace)
Darkest Street in Town (1963, Ace)
Curly (1969, Laurie)

Big Bopper

(J.P. Richardson, 1931-59)

Big Bopper's Wedding (1958,
Mercury)
*Chantily Lace (1958, Mercury)
Little Red Riding Hood (1958,
Mercury)

*Cookie and the Cupcakes

(Huey Thierry)

Breaking Up Is Hard to Do
Even Though
I Cried
Trouble in My Life
*Mathilda (1959, Lyrics)
*Sea of Love (1959, Lyrics)
*Until Then (1959, Lyrics)
I've Been So Lonely (1960, Lyrics)
*Got You on My Mind (1963, Chess)

*Cookie and the Cupcakes, Vol. 2
(Jin)
*3 Great Rockers (Jin)

*Rod Bernard (1940-)

*This Should Go On Forever (1958,
Jin)
*One More Chance (1959, Mercury)
*Colinda (1962, Hall-Way)
*Fais Do-Do (1962, Hall-Way)
Forgive (1962, Hall-Way)
I Might as Well (1962, Hall-Way)
Loveliness (1962, Hall-Way)

*Boogie Is Black and White (Jin)
*Rod Bernard (Jin)

*Rambling Aces

Madam Sostan (Crazy Cajun)
The Wedding March (Crazy Cajun)
99 Years Waltz (1959, Swallow)
Musicians Waltz (1964, Crazy
Cajun)

*Jivin' Gene

(Gene Bourgeois)

*Breaking Up Is Hard to Do (1959,
Mercury)
Going Out with the Tide (1960,
Mercury)

*Johnnie Allan (1938-)

*Lonely Days and Lonely Nights
(1959, Jin)
*South to Louisiana (1960, Viking)
Your Picture (1960, Viking)
Somewhere on Skid Row (1973, Jin)

*Johnny Allan Sings (Jin)
*South to Louisiana (1982, Jin)
Cajun Country (1983)

*Joe Barry with the Dukes of Rhythm

(Joe Barry, 1939-)

Greatest Moment of My Life (1960,
Jin)
Heartbroken Love (1960, Jin)
I Got a Feeling (1960, Jin)
Little Jewel of the Veaux Carre
(1960, Smash)
Little Papoose (1960, Smash)
Till the End of the World (1960,
Smash)
You Don't Have to Be a Baby to
Cry (1960, Smash)
*For You Sunshine (1961, Jin)
*I'm a Fool to Care (1961, Jin)
*Teardrops in My Heart (1961, Jin)
Chantilly Lace (1968)
*Today I Started Loving You Again
(1968, Nugget)

*Joe Barry (ABC-Dot)

*Barbara Lynn (1942-)

*You'll Lose a Good Thing (1963,
Jamie)
You're Gonna Need Me (1963,
Jamie)
It's Better to Have It (1965, Jamie)
This Is the Thanks I Get (1968,
Atlantic)
(Oh Baby) We Got a Good Thing

(Until Then) I'll Suffer (1971,
    Atlantic)
*Here Is Barbara Lynn (1976, Oval)

*Jimmy Donley (1929-63)

Born to Be a Loser (1961, Jin)
Please Mr. Sandman (1961, Jin)
Think It Over (1961, Jin)
*I'm to Blame (1962, Jin)

Born to Be a Loser (Starflite)

*Rockin' Sidney

(Sidney Simien, 1938-)

Make Me Understand (1957, Carl)
Shed So Many Tears (1961, Jin)
Something Working (1961, Jin;
    1962, Jin)
*If I Could I Would (1962, Jin)
*It Really Is a Hurtin' Thing (1962,
    Jin)
*No Good Woman (1962, Jin)
*You Aint' Nothin' But Fine (1962,
    Jin)
Let's Go to the Fais Do-Do (1974,
    Goldband)
Louisiana Creole Man (1974, Bally
    Hoo)

They Call Me Rockin' (1974,
    Flyright)

*John Fred and His Playboys

(John Fred, 1941-)

*Good Lovin' (1959, Montel)
*Shirley (1959, Montel)
Boogie Children (1965, Paula)
*Judy in Disguise (1967, Paula)
Hey, Hey Bunny (1968, Paula)

John Fred and His Playboys (1965,
    Paula)
34:40 of John Fred and His Playboys
    (1966, Paula)
Agnes English (1967, Paula)

Judy in Disguise with Glasses (1967,
    Paula)
Permanently Stated (1969, Paula)
Love in My Soul* (1970, United
    Artists)

*Dale and Grace

(Dale Houston and Grace
Broussard)

*I'm Leaving It Up to You (1963,
    Montel)
*Stop and Think It Over (1963,
    Montel)
*The Loneliest Night (1964, Montel)

I'm Leaving It Up To You
    (Michelle)

*Freddy Fender

(Baldemar G. Huerta, 1936-)

Holy One (1957, Imperial)
*Wasted Days and Wasted Nights
    (1960, Dot)
Wild Side of Life (1962, Dot)
Roses are Red (1974, Dot)
*Before the Next Teardrop Falls
    (1975, Dot)
Secret Love (1975, Dot)
Since I Met You Baby (1975, GRT)
Living It Down (1976, Dot)
Via Con Dayas (1976, Dot)
You'll Loose a Good Thing (1976,
    Dot)

Swamp Gold (ABC)
Before the Next Teardrop Falls
    (1974, Dot)
Best of . . . (1977, Dot)

*Phil Phillips

(Phillip Baptiste, 1931-)

*Sea of Love (1959, Lyrics)

*Johnnie Preston

*Running Bear (1959, Mercury)

*Elton Anderson

Shed So Many Tears (1959, Vin)
*Secret of Love (1960, Mercury)
*Life Problem (1962, Lanor)

*Cleveland Crochet and His Hillbilly Ramblers

Come Back Little Girl
Coming Home
Hound Dog Baby
Sweet Thing
*Sugar Bee (1961, Goldband)

*Warren Storm (1937-)

*Mama, Mama, Mama (1958, Nasco)
*Prisoner's Song (1958, Nasco)
Birmingham Jail (1959, Nasco)
I Thank You So Much (1959, Rocko)
So Long So Long (1959, Nasco)
Troubles Troubles (Troubles on My Mind) (1959, Nasco)
The Gypsy (1966, Sincere)
Tennessee Waltz (1966, Tear Drop)
Lord I Need Somebody Bad Tonight (1973, Showtime)
My House of Memories (1975, Showtime)

*Family Rules (Crazy Cajun)
*At Last Warren Storm (1973, Showtime)
*Al Ferrier and Warren Storm: Boppin' Tonight (1976, Flyright)

*Joe Carl

*Don't Leave Me Again (1959, Rocko)
Rockin' Fever (1960, Rocko)
You're Too Hot to Handle (1960, Zynn)

*Frankie Ford (1940-)

Alimony (1959, Ace)
*Sea Cruise (1959, Ace)
Time After Time (1960, Ace)
You Talk Too Much (1960, Imperial)
Seventeen (1961, Imperial)

*Best of . . . (Ace)

*? and the Mysterians

*96 Tears (1966, Flint)
*I Need Somebody (1967, Cameo)

Action (1966, Cameo)
*96 Tears (1966, Cameo)

*Doug Sahm (1941-)

*Best of the Sir Douglas Quintet (1965, Tribe)
*1 + 1 + 1 = 4 (1970, Philips)
*Together After Five (1970, Smash)
*Best of . . . (1980, Takoma)
*Border Wave (1981, Takoma)

Lester Robertson and His Upsetters

My Girl Across Town (1960, Montel)
My Heart Forever Yearns (1960, Montel)
Take It Home to Grandma (1960, Montel)

Buck Rogers and His Jets

Crazy Baby (1960, Montel)

Shirley Bergeron (1933-)

J'ai Fait Nom Ede'e' (1960, Lanor)
Chez Tanie (1961, Lanor)
French Rocking Boogie (1961, Lanor)

*The Sound of Cajun Music (1962, Lanor)
Cajun Style Music (1963)

*Charles Mann

*Keep Your Arms around Me (1965, Lanor)
*Red Red Wine (1966, Lanor)

She's Walking towards Me (1980, Lanor)

Jewel and the Rubies

Kidnapper (mid-60s)

Little Bob and the Lollipops

(Camille Bob, 1937-)

*I Got Loaded (1965, La Louisianne)
Nobody But You (1965, La Louisianne)
Harry Hippie (1980, Master-Trak)

Nobody But You (La Louisianne)
Sweet Soul Singer (1967, Jin)

Raful Neal (1936-)

*Change My Way of Living (1967, La Louisianne)
Inflation Time (1980s, Tic Toc)

Aldus Roger (1916-)

Aldus Roger Plays the French Music of South Louisiana (1965, La Louisianne)

T.K. Hulin

(Alton James Hulin, 1943-)

*Graduation Night (1963, L.K.)
*I'm Not a Fool Anymore (1963, L.K.)

*Rockin' Dave Allen (1942-)

*Can't Stand to See You Go (1960, Jin)
Shirley Jean (1960, Jin)

*What's Left for a Fool (1960, Jin)
*Southern Rock'n'Roll of the 60's (1980, Rock-a-Billy)

Phil Bo

(Phil Boudreaux)

Prince Charles and the Rockin' Kings
*Morning Star (1960s, Smash)
Cheryl Ann (1960, Jin)
Don't Take It So Hard (1961, Jin)
*Oh! What a Mistake/Mr. Train (1961, Som)
*My Sea of Tears (1961, L.K.)
*She Wears My Ring (1961, Jin)

Big Sambo

(James Young)

The Rains Came (1962, Eric)

Sunny and the Sunliners

Talk to Me (1962, Tear Drop)

Margo White

Don't Mess with My Man (1963, J
I'm Not Ashamed (1963, Jin)

Tommy McLain (1940-)

(Before I) Grow Too Old (1966, Jin)
Sweet Dreams (1966, Jin)
Sticks and Stones (1967, Jin)
Try to Find Another Man (1967, Jin)

Best of . . . (Jin)

*Clint West

(Maurice Guillory, 1938-)

Mr. Jeweler (1972, Jin)

Shelly's Winter Love (1974, Jin)
Sweet Suzannah (1974, Jin)

*Clint West and the Fabulous Boogie
Kings* (Jin)

Rufus Jagneaux

Downhome Music (1973, Jin)
*Opelousas Sostan (1973, Jin)

Guitar Jeff and the Creoles

Jump and Shout (1958, Rocko)

Skip Morris with Doug Charles and the Boogie Kings

Talk to Your Daughter (1958,
Rocko)

Tommy Strange

Nervous and Shakin' All Over
(1958, Rocko)

Rocket (Rodney) Morgan

This Life I Live (Rocko)
You're Humbuggin' Me (Rocko)
I Know It's a Sin (J. Reed) (1959,
Rocko; 1960, Rocko)
Tag Along (1959, Rocko; 1960,
Rocko)

Henry Clement

Jenny, Jenny, Jenny (1959, Zynn)
Trojan Walla (1959, Spot)
I'm So in Love with You (1960,
Zynn)
What Have I Done Wrong (1960,
Zynn)

Jerry Morris

(Make Me) A Winner in Love
(1959, Zynn)

Lionel Torrence

Rockin' Jole' Blonde (1959, Zynn)
Rooty Tooty (1959, Zynn)

Jerry Star and the Clippers

Side Steppin' (1961, Zynn)

Teen Idols and Teenage Rock

*Bobby Vee (1943-)

Suzie Baby (1959, Liberty)
*Devil or Angel (1960, Liberty)
*Rubber Ball (1960, Liberty)
What Do You Want (1960, Liberty)
*Run to Him (1961, Liberty)
*Take God Care of My Baby (1961, Liberty)
Punish Her (1962, Liberty)
Charms (1963, Liberty)
*The Night Has a Thousand Eyes (1963, Liberty)
*Come Back When You Grow Up (1967, Liberty)

*Legendary Masters Series (Liberty)
*Singles Album (Liberty)
*Devil or Angel (1960)
*Bobby Vee (1961, Liberty)
*Bobby Vee's Golden Greats (1962, Liberty)

Frankie Avalon (1939-)

*DeDe Dinah (1958, Chancellor)
*Ginger Bread (1958, Chancellor)
*Bobby Sox to Stockings (1959, Chancellor)
*A Boy without a Girl (1959, Chancellor)
*Just Ask Your Heart (1959, Chancellor)
*Venus (1959, Chancellor)
*Why (1960, Chancellor)

*Sixteen Greatest Hits (Trip)
*Swingin' on a Rainbow (1959, Chancellor)
*Venus (1959, Chancellor)
*A Whole Lotta Frankie (1961, Chancellor)

*Connie Francis (1938-)

Stupid Cupid (1958, MGM)
*Who's Sorry Now? (1958, MGM)
Frankie (1959, MGM)
If I Didn't Care (1959, MGM)
*Lipstick on Your Collar (1959, MGM)
*My Happiness (1959, MGM)
Among My Souvenirs (1960, MGM)
*Everybody's Somebody's Fool (1960, MGM)
*Mama (1960, MGM)
*Together (1961, MGM)
*Don't Break the Heart That Loves You (1962, MGM)

*Greatest Hits (1960, MGM)
*Very Best of . . . (1963, MGM)
*I'm Me Again (1981, MGM)

Fabian

(Fabian Forte, 1943-)

*Hound Dog Man (1959, Chancellor)
*Tiger (1959, Chancellor)
*Turn Me Loose (1959, Chancellor)

*Sixteen Greatest Hits (Trip/ABC)
*Fabulous Fabian (1959, Chancellor)
*Hold That Tiger (1959, Chancellor)

Freddy Cannon (1940-)

*Tallahassie Lassie (1959, Swan)
*Way Down Yonder in New Orleans (1960, Swan)
*Palisades Park (1962, Swan)
Let's Put the Fun Back in Rock'n'Roll (1981, Buddah)

*The Explosive Freddy Cannon (1961, Swan)

*Neil Sedaka (1939-)

Fallin' (1958, RCA)
Stupid Cupid (1958, RCA)

*The Diary (1959, RCA)
I Go Ape (1959, RCA)
*Oh! Carol (1959, RCA)
*Stairway to Heaven (1960, RCA)
*Calendar Girl (1961, RCA)
*Happy Birthday Sweet Sixteen
   (1961, RCA)
Little Devil (1961, RCA)
*Breaking Up Is Hard to Do (1962,
   RCA)
*Next Door to an Angel (1962,
   RCA)
Bad Blood (1975, Rocket)
Laughter in the Rain (1975,
   Rocket)
Should've Never Let You Go
   (1980, Rocket)

Neil Sedaka Sings His Greatest Hits
   (1962, RCA)
Pure Gold (1976)
Sedaka: The Fifties and Sixties
   (1977, RCA)

*Bobby Rydell (1942-)

Kissin' Time (1959, Cameo)
*We Got Love (1959, Cameo)
Sway (1960, Cameo)
*Swingin' School (1960, Cameo)
Volare (1960, Cameo)
*Wild One (1960, Cameo)
*Forget Him (1964, Cameo)

Bobby's Biggest Hits (1961, Cameo)

*Brenda Lee (1944-)

All You Gotta Do (1960, Decca)
*Dum Dum (1960, Decca)
*I'm Sorry (1960, Decca)
*I Want to be Wanted (1960, Decca)
Rockin' around the Christmas Tree
   (1960, Decca)
*Sweet Nothings (1960, Decca)
If This Is Our Last Time (1971,
   MCA)
Nobody Wins (1973, MCA)

Brenda Lee (1960, Decca)
Ten Golden Years (1966, MCA)

Brenda Lee Story (1967, MCA)

*Del Shannon (1939-)

*Hats Off to Larry (1961, Big Top)
Hey! Little Girl (1961, Big Top)
*Runaway (1961, Big Top)
So Long Baby (1961, Big Top)
Little Town Flirt (1962, Big Top)
From Me to You (1963, Big Top)
*Keep Searching (1965, Amy)
Stranger in Town (1965, Amy)
And the Music Plays On (1974,
   United Artists)
Tell Her No (1975, Island)
Sea of Love (1982, Elecktra)

Drop Down and Get Me (Demon)
Runaway (1961, Big Top)
Little Town Flirt (1963, Big Top)
The Best of . . . (1967, Pickwick)
Tenth Anniversary Album (1971,
   Sunset)
The Vintage Years (1975, Sire)

Bobby Darin (1936-73)

*Queen of the Hop (1958, Atco)
*Splish Splash (1958, Atco)
*Dream Lover (1959, Atco)
*Mack the Knife (1959, Atco)
*Things (1962, Atco)
*You're the Reason I'm Living
   (1963, Capitol)
If I Were a Carpenter (1966,
   Atlantic)

The Best of . . . (Capitol)
That's All (1959, Atco)
The Bobby Darin Story (1961, Atco)
If I Were a Carpenter (1966,
   Atlantic)
Bobby Darin 1936-1973 (1974,
   Motown)

*Gene Pitney (1941-)

(I Wanna) Love My Life Away
   (1961, Musicor)

*(The Man Who Shot) Liberty
    Valance (1962, Musicor)
*Only Love Can Break a Heart
    (1962, Musicor)
  Town Without Pity (1962, Musicor)
  Half Heaven-Half Heartache (1963,
    Musicor)
  Mecca (1963, Musicor)
*I'm Gonna Be Strong (1964,
    Musicor)
*It Hurts to Be in Love (1964,
    Musicor)

Greatest Hits, Vol. 1 (Hallmark)
Just for You (1961, Musicor)
Only Love Can Break a Heart (1962,
    Musicor)
Big Sixteen (1963, Musicor)
World Wide Winners (1963,
    Musicor)
Big Sixteen, Vol. 2 (1964, Musicor)
It Hurts to Be in Love (1964)
Double Gold: The Best of . . . (1968,
    Musicor)

George Hamilton (1937-)

*A Rose and a Baby Ruth (1956,
    ABC-Paramount)
*Why Don't They Understand (1957,
    ABC-Paramont)

Abilene (1963, RCA)

Pat Boone (1934-)

*Ain't That a Shame (1955, Dot)
*I Almost Lost My Mind (1956, Dot)
*Love Letters in the Sand (1957,
    Dot)
  Sugar Moon (1958, Dot)
*Moody River (1961, Dot)
*Speedy Gonzales (1962, Dot)

Pat's Great Hits (1957, Dot)

Paul Anka (1941-)

*Diana (1957, ABC-Paramount)
*You Are My Destiny (1958, ABC-
    Paramount)

*Lonely Boy (1959, ABC-
    Paramount)
*Puppy Love (1960, ABC-Para)
  Dance on Little Girl (1961, ABC-
    Paramount)
  (You're) Having My Baby (1974,
    United Artists)
  Hold Me 'Til the Mornin' Comes
    (1983, Columbia)

Paul Anka Sings His Big 15, Vols. 1-
    2 (1960, ABC)
Vintage Years 1957-61 (1977, Sire)

Lesley Gore (1946-)

*It's My Party (1963, Mercury)
*Judy's Turn to Cry (1963, Mercury)
  She's a Fool (1963, Mercury)
*You Don't Own Me (1964,
    Mercury)

I'll Cry If I Want To (1963,
    Mercury)
*Lesley Gore Sings of Mixed-Up
    Hearts* (1964, Mercury)
The Golden Hits of . . . (1965,
    Mercury)

Instrumental Rock

Bill Doggett (1916-)

*Honky Tonk (1956, King)
*Slow Walk (1956, King)

*Bill Doggett (King)
Everybody Dance to the Honky Tonk (King)
Hot Doggett (King)

*Duane Eddy (1938-)

*Cannonball (1958, Jamie)
*Ramrod (1958, Jamie)
*Rebel Rouser (1958, Jamie)
*Forty Miles of Bad Road (1959, Jamie)
*Peter Gun (1960, Jamie)
The Ballad of Palladin (1962, RCA)
Dance with the Guitar Man (1962, RCA)
Deep in the Heart of Texas (1962, RCA)
Play Me Like You Play Your Guitar (1975, London)
You Are My Sunshine (1977, Asylum)

*Legend of Rock (London)
*The Vintage Years (Sire)
Especially for You (1958, Jamie)
*Have Twangy Guitar Will Travel (1958, Jamie)
Duane Eddy's Sixteen Greatest Hits (1965, Jamie)
Pure Gold (1978, RCA)

*Champs

*Tequila (1958, Challenge)
Too Much Tequila (1960, Challenge)
Limbo Rock (1962, Challenge)
Tequila Twist (1962, Challenge)

*Go Champs Go (Line)
*Everybody's Rockin' (1960, Challenge)

*The Best of the Champs (1977, London)

*Ventures

Ghost Rider in the Sky (1960, Dolton)
Walk Don't Run (1960, Dolton)
Perfidia (1961, Dolton)
Lullaby of the Leaves (1962, Dolton)
Diamond Head (1963, Dolton)
I Walk the Line (1963, Dolton)
Lonely Bull (1963, Dolton)
2,000 Pound Bee (1963, Dolton)
Hawaii Five-O (1969, Dolton)
Surfin' and Spyin' (1981, Liberty)

*Walk Don't Run (1960, Dolton)
Surfing (1963, Dolton)
The Ventures Play Telstar and Lonely Bull (1963, Liberty)
*Golden Greats by the Ventures (1967, Liberty)
Tenth Anniversary Album (1970, Liberty)
Very Best of the Ventures (1975, Liberty)

*Raybeats

*Guitar Beat (1981, Jem)

*Link Wray (1930-)

*Rumbel (1958, Cadence)
*Rawhide (1959, Epic)

*Early Recordings (Chiswick)
*Link Wray and the Waymen (1960, Epic)
Link Wray (1971, Polydor)
Live at the Paradise (1981, Charisma)

Johnny and the Hurricanes

(Johnny Paris, 1904-)

Crossfire (1959, Warwick)
*Red River Rock (1959, Warwick)

Reveille Rock (1959, Warwick)
Beatnik Fly (1960, Warwick)

Johnny and the Hurricanes (1960,
Warwick)
Stormsville (1960, Warwick)

Shadows

Feelin' Fine (1959, Columbia)
*Apache (1960, Columbia)
Atlantis (1961, Columbia)
Shindig (1963, Columbia)
Don't Make My Baby Blue (1965,
Columbia)

The Shadows (1961, Fame)
The Shadows (1962, Columbia)
Greatest Hits (1963, Columbia)

Bill Black Combo

(Bill Black, 1926-65)

White Silver Hands (1960, Hi)
Smokie (Part 2) (1962, Hi)

Greatest Hits (1963, Hi)

Bill Justis (1926-82)

*Raunchy (1957, Philips)
College Man (1958, Philips)

Plays 12 Big Instrumental Hits
(1962, Smash)
Raunchy (1969, Philips)

Wailers

Fabulous Wailers (Allied)

Royaltones

Poor Boy/Wail (1958, Jubille)

Joe Houston

All Night Long (United Artists)

Booker T. and the MGs

(Booker T. Jones, 1944-)

*Green Onions (1962, Stax)
Boot-Leg (1965, Stax)
My Sweet Potato (1966, Stax)
*Hip Hug-Her (1967, Stax)
Time Is Tight (1969, Stax)

Best of . . . (1968, Atlantic)
Green Onions (1968, Atlantic)
Greatest Hits (1974, Stax)

Anthology

Rock'n'Roll Instrumentals Anthology,
Vols. 1-2 (Guitar)

The Twist

*Chubby Checker

(Ernest Evans, 1941-)

The Class (1959, Parkway)
*The Twist (1960, Parkway)
*The Fly (1961, Parkway)
*Let's Twist Again (1961, Parkway)
*Pony Time (1961, Parkway)
*Limbo Rock (1962, Parkway)
 Popeye the Hitchhiker (1962,
　Parkway)
*Slow Twistin' (1962, Parkway)

*Twist with Chubby Checker (1960,
　Parkway)
 Let's Twist Again (1962, Parkway)
*Twist (1962, Columbia)
 Twistin' around the World (1962,
　Parkway)
 All the Hits (1963, Parkway)
*Greatest Hits (1972, Abko)

Bobby Lewis (1933-)

One Track Mind (1961, Beltone)
Tossin' and Turnin' (1961, Beltone)

The Best of . . . (United Artists)

Joey Dee and the Starlighters

(Joey Dee, 1940-)

*Peppermint Twist (1961, Roulette)
*Hey Let's Twist (1962, Roulette)
 Hot Pastrami with Mashed Potatoes
　(1962, Roulette)
*Shout (1962, Roulette)
 What Kind of Love Is This (1962,
　Roulette)

*The Peppermint Twisters (Scepter)
*Doin' the Twist at the Peppermint
　Lounge (1961, Roulette)
 Hey Let's Twist (1962, Roulette)

Little Eva (1945-)

*Keep Your Hands Off My Baby
　(1962, Dimension)
*The Loco-Motion (1962,
　Dimension)
*Let's Turkey Trot (1963,
　Dimension)
 Swingin' on a Star (1963,
　Dimension)

*Loco-motion (1962,
　Dimension/London)

Dee Dee Sharp (1945-)

*Mashed Potato Time (1961,
　Cameo)
 Ride (1961, Cameo)

*It's Mashed Potato Time (1962,
　Cameo)
*Happy 'bout the Whole Thing (1975,
　Philadelphia International)
*What Color Is Love (1977,
　Philadelphia International)

Surf Music

Anthology

Surfin' Roots (1977, Festival)

INSTRUMENTAL

*Dick Dale and the Del-Tones

*Let's Go Tripping (1961, Deltone)
Misirlou (1962, Deltone)
*The Scavenger (1963, Deltone)

Greatest Hits (Crescendo)
Checkered Flag (1963, Capitol)
Surfers' Choice (1963, Deltone)

*Surfaris

*Wipeout (1963, Dot)

Wipe Out (1963, Dot)
Hit City 64 (1964, Decca)

*Challengers

K-39 (1964, Vault)
Tidal Wave (1964, Vault)

Sidewalk Surfin' (GNP)
25 Great Instrumental Hits (GNP)
Surfbeat (1963, Vault)
On the Move (1964, Vault)
Best of . . . (1982, Rhino)

Crossfires

Out of Control (1982, Rhino)

Malibooz

Malibooz Rule! (1982, Rhino)

VOCAL

Sam the Sham and the Pharaohs

(Domingo Samudio)

Haunted House (1964)
*Wooly Bully (1965, MGM)
Juju Hand (1966, MGM)
*Li'l Red Riding Hood (1967, MGM)
Oh That's Good, No That's Bad (1967, MGM)

Wooly Bully (1965, MGM)
Li'l Red Riding Hood (1966, MGM)
Best of . . . (1967, MGM)
Sam, Hard and Heavy (1970, Atlantic)

Association

Along Comes Mary (1966, Valiant)
*Cherish (1966, Warner Bros.)
*Windy (1967, Warner Bros.)
Never My Love (1967, Warner Bros.)
Everything That Touches You (1968, Warner Bros.)

And Then . . . Along Comes Association (1966, Valiant)
Inside Out (1967, Warner Bros.)
Greatest Hits (1968, Warner Bros.)

Jan and Dean

(Jan Berry, 1941- ; Dean Torrence, 1941-)

Jennie Lee (1958, Arwin)
*Baby Talk (1959, Dore-Challenge)
Heart and Soul (1961, Dore-Challenge)
Honolulu Lulu (1963, Dore-Challenge)
Linda (1963, Dore-Challenge)
*Surf City (1963, Dore-Challenge)
*Dead Man's Curve (1964, Liberty)

*Drag City (1964, Dore-Challenge)
*The Little Old Lady (from
    Pasadena) (1964, Liberty)
Ride the Wild Surf (1964, Liberty)
Sidewalk Surfin' (1964, Liberty)
I Found a Girl (1965, Liberty)
You Really Know How to Hurt a
    Guy (1965, Liberty)
Popsicle (1966, Liberty)

Golden Hits, Vol. 1 (1962, Liberty)
Jan and Dean Take Linda Surfin'
    (1963, Liberty)
Surf City and Other Swinging Cities
    (1963, Liberty)
Drag City (1964, Liberty)
Golden Hits, Vol. 2 (1965, Liberty)
Golden Hits, Vol. 3 (1966, Liberty)
Legendary Masters (1971, United
    Artists)
Gotta Take That One Last Ride
    (1974, United Artists)
Dead Man's Curve (1978, United
    Artists)
One Summer Night (1982, Rhino)

Paul Revere and the Raiders

(Paul Revere, 1942-)

Like Long Hair (1961, independent
    release)
*Louie Louie (1963, Columbia)
*Just Like Me (1965, Columbia)
*Kicks (1965, Columbia)
*Steppin' Out (1965, Columbia)
Hungry (1966, Columbia)
*Him or Me-What's It Gonna Be?
    (1967, Columbia)
Ups and Downs (1967, Columbia)
*Indian Reservation (1971,
    Columbia)

Greatest Hits (1967, Columbia)
All-Time Greatest Hits (1972,
    Columbia)

Kingsmen

*Louie Louie (1963, Wand)

15 Greatest Hits (Wand)
The Kingsmen, Vols. 2-3 (Wand)
The Kingsmen In Person (Wand)
The Kingsmen (1980, Piccadilly)

*Beach Boys

Surfin' (1961, Candix)
*Surfin' Safari (1962, Capitol)
In My Room (1963, Capitol)
*Surfer Girl (1963, Capitol)
*Surfin' U.S.A. (1963, Capitol)
*Don't Worry Baby (1964, Capitol)
*Fun, Fun, Fun (1964, Capitol)
*I Get Around (1964, Capitol)
*Wendy (1964, Capitol)
*California Girls (1965, Capitol)
*Help Me, Rhonda (1965, Capitol)
*God Only Knows (1966, Capitol)
*Good Vibrations (1966, Capitol)
*Wouldn't It Be Nice (1966, Capitol)
*Caroline No (1967, Capitol)
*Do It Again (1967, Capitol)
*Heroes and Villains (1967, Capitol)
*Sail on Sailor (1972, Brother)
Rock and Roll Music (1976,
    Brother)
Almost Summer (1978, Brother)
Come Go with Me (1982, Caribou)

Surfer Girl (1962, Capitol)
Surfin' Safari (1962, Capitol)
Little Deuce Coupe (1963, Capitol)
All Summer Long-California Girls
    (1964, Capitol)
Shut Down, Vols. 1-2 (1964,
    Capitol)
Beach Boys Today! (1965, Capitol)
Pet Sounds (1966, Capitol)
20/20-Wild Honey (1967, Reprise)
Endless Summer (1974, Capitol)
Spirit of America (1975, Capitol)

Chicano Music

NORTHERN NEW MEXICO AND COLORADO

ALABADO STYLE

Buenos Dias, Paloma Blanca, Five Alabados of Northern New Mexico (Taos)
New Mexico Alabados (Taos)
Meliton M. Trujillo Sings Taos Spanish Songs (Taos)
Spanish Folksongs of the Americas (Cantemos)
Bahaman Songs, French Ballads and Dance Tunes, Spanish Religious Songs and Game Songs, 1934-1940 (Library of Congress)
Folk Music of New Mexico, 1946-1951 (Folkways)
Folk Music USA, 1946-1951 (Folkways)

POP ARTISTS (1970S)

Al Hurricane

Canciones del alma (Hurricane)
Corridos canta Al Hurricane (Hurricane)
Instrumentales con Al Hurricane (Hurricane)
Mi Saxophone (Hurricane)
Para las madrecitias (Hurricane)
Sigue cantando (Hurricane)

Tiny Morrie

No Hay Amor (1974, Hurricane)

Canciones tristes y alegres (Hurricane)
Exitos de Tiny Morrie (Hurricane)
Lonely Letters (Hurricane)

Mas exitos de Tiny Morrie (Hurricane)
Para las madrecitas (Hurricane)

LOWER TEXAS/ MEXICAN BORDER

NORTENO STYLE AND TEJANO STYLES

Texas-Mexican Border Music, Vol. 1: *An Introduction, 1930-60* (Folk-Lyrics)
Texas-Mexican Border Music, Corridos, Part 2 (Folk-Lyrics)
Texas-Mexican Border Music, Norteno Accordion, 1920-1950 (Folk-Lyrics)
Texas-Mexican Border Music, The String Bands (Folk-Lyrics)

GROUPS

Los Alegres de Teran

Lo mejor de Los Alegres de Teran, Vols. 1-3 (Falcon)

Los Relampagos del Norte
Los Tremendos Gavilanes

VOCALISTS

Lydia Mendoza

Songs of Love, Courtship, and Marriage (Library of Congress)

Jose Morante and Los Conquistadores

Corridos y tragedias de siglo 20, Vols. 1-2 (Norteno)

Johnny Rodriquez

All I Ever Meant to Do Was Sing (Mercury)

Introducing J. Rodriguez (Mercury)
Just Get Up and Close the Door
(Mercury)
My Third Album (Mercury)
Songs about Ladies and Love
(Mercury)

Bobby "El Charro Negro" Butler

El Papalote (1963, Buena Suerte)

AZTLAN AREA

Edward "Lalo" Guerrero

Christmas Songs with Lalo Guerrero
(ca. 1930-50, L&M)

MARIACHI STYLE

Los Camperos de Nati Cano

Puro Mariachi-Los Camperos
(Indigo)

VOCALISTS

Danny Valdez

Mestizo (A&M)

Ray Camacho

*The International Ray Camacho and
the Teardrops* (California
Artists)

Miguel Barragan

Adelante (Bronze)

MEXICAN-BACKGROUND CONTEMPORARY SINGERS

Manuel S. Acuna

Joan Baez

Vicky Carr

Trini Lopez

Andy Russell

Richie Valens

MEXICAN/CHICANO ROCK GROUPS

Santana

Malo (Jorge Santana)

Cannibal and the Headhunters

Tango

Tierra

El Chicano

Sapo

Yaqui

Macondo

*Los Lobos

**How Will the Wolf Survive* (1984,
Slash)
**By the Light of the Moon* (1987,
Slash)

Anthology

East Side Revue (1969, Rampart)

North American Indian Music

*Ed Lee Natay

Ed Lee Natay: Navajo Singer (Canyon)
Traditional Navajo Songs (Canyon)

Robert E. Lee

Navajo Social Songs (Canyon)
Traditional Papago Music (Canyon)

Amos Richards

Amos Richards and His Group: Songs from the Pima (Canyon)
Sioux Favorites (Canyons)

William Horncloud

Great Plains Singers (Canyon)
Sioux Grass Songs and Round Dances (Canyon)

Pat Kennedy and Singers

The Denver Indian Singers (Canyons)
From the Land of the Blackfeet (Canyon)

Patsy Cassadore

I Build the Wickiup (Canyon)

XIT

Plight of the Redman (Canyon)
Silent Warrior (Canyon)

Anthologies

Authentic Music of the American Indian (Everet)
Indian Music of the Canadian Plains (Indian House)

Iroquois Social Dance Songs
(Iroqrafts)
*Music of the American Indians of the
Southwest* (Folkways)
Navajo (Library of Congress)
Northwest-Puget Sound (Library of
Congress)
War Songs of the Ponca (Indian
House)

Folk Music

General Anthologies

*AFS Anthology of American Folk
Music* (AFS)
American Folk Songs for Children
(Atlantic)
Anthology of American Folk Music,
Vols. 1-3 (Folkways)
Anthology of Folk Music, Vol. 2
(Sine)
The Asch Recordings, Vols. 1-4
(Folkways)
Folk Music from Wisconsin, 1940-46
(Library of Congress)
Folk Music U.S.A. (Folkways)
Folk Sound of Iowa (University of
Iowa)
Greatest Folksingers of the Sixties
(Vanguard)
Green Fields of Illinois (Puritan)
Missouri Folk Songs (Folkways)
Roots of America's Music, Vols. 1-2
(Arhoolie)
Songs of the Great Lakes
(Folkways)
Southern Folk Heritage Series
(Atlantic)
*Southern Journey: A Collection of
Field Recordings from the South*
(Prestige International)
Sweet Nebraska Land (Folkways)
Traditional Songs of the Midwest
(Folkways)
Songs of the Michigan Lumberjacks
(1938, Library of Congress)
Old Time Music at Newport (1963,
Vanguard)

Social and Historical Anthologies

Red Allen

*American History in Ballad and
Song,* Vols. 1-2 (Folkways)

Dorsey Dixon

> *Babies in the Mill* (Testament)

Joe Glazer

> *The Songs of Joe Hill* (Folkways)

Tom Glazer

> *The Musical Heritage of America* (CMS)

Harry Jackson

> *The Cowboy: His Songs and Brag Talk* (Folkways)

Kathy Khan

> *The Working Girl: Women's Songs from Mountains, Mines, and Mills* (Voyager)

Rev. F.D. Kirkpatrick

> *Ballads of Black America*

John A. Lomax

> *The Ballad Hunter*, Vols. 1-5 (AFS)

Alan Mills

> *Negro Songs of Protest* (Rounder)

New Lost City Ramblers

> *American Moonshine and Prohibition* (Folkways)
> *Songs from the Depression* (Folkways)

Hermes Nye

> *Railroad Songs and Ballads* (AFS)

Mike Seeger

> *Tipple, Loom and Rail* (Folkways)

Pete Seeger

> *American Industrial Ballads* (Folkways)
> *Frontier Ballads*, Vols. 1-2 (Folkways)
> *Songs of the Civil War* (Folkways)

Studs Terkel

> *Hard Times* (Caedmon)
> *The Traditional Music of Beech Mountain, N.C.*, Vols. 1-2 (Folk-Legacy)

ANGLO-AMERICAN MUSIC/TRADITIONAL STYLES

SOUTHERN TRADITIONAL

*Aunt Molly Jackson (1880-1960)

> *The Library of Congress Recordings* (Rounder)
> *The Songs and Stories of . . .* (Folkways)

*Sarah Ogan Gunning (1910-)

> *Girl of Constant Sorrow* (Folk-Legacy)

*Horton Barker (1889-196?)

> *Horton Barker* (Folkways)

*Dorsey Dixon (1897-)

> *Babies in the Mill* (Testament)

*Dock Boggs (1898-1971)

> *Legendary Singer and Banjo Player*, Vols. 1-3 (Folkways)
> *Excerpts from Interview* (1963, Folkways)
> *Dock Boggs*, Vols. 1-3 (1964-70 Folkways)

Dock Boggs Interviews, 1927-28
(1965, Folkways)

*Fiddlin' John Carson (?-1935)

The Old Hen Cackled (ca. 1920,
Rounder)

*Blind Alfred Reed (1921-)

*How Can a Poor Man Stand Such
Times and Live?* (ca. 1927-29,
Rounder)

*Rosco Holcomb (1913-)

The High Lonesome Sound (1965,
Folkways)
*The Music of Rosco Holcomb and
Wade Ward* (ca. 1960,
Folkways)

*Hobart Smith (1897-1965)

Hobart Smith (Folk-Legacy)

*Almeda Riddle

Ballads and Hymns from the Ozarks
(1972, Rounder)

*Texas Gladden

Library of Congress Recordings

*Emma Dusenberry

Library of Congress Recordings

*John Jacob Niles

The Ballads of . . . (Tradition)
An Evening with . . . (Tradition)
Folk Balladeer (RCA)
Folk Songs (Folkways)
John Jacob Niles Sings Folk Songs
(1964, Folkways)

SOUTHERN INTERPRETIVE

*Bascom Lamar Lunsford (1882-)

Appalachian Minstrel
Smokey Mountain Ballads (1947,
Folkways)
Music from South Turkey Creek
(1976, Rounder)

*Jean Ritchie (1922-)

*British Traditional Ballads in the
Southern Mountains*, Vols. 1-2
(Folkways)
Carols of All Seasons (Tradition)
Clear Waters Remembered
(Geordie-Sire)
Precious Memories (Folkways)
The Ritchie Family of Kentucky
(Folkways)
Singing Family of the Cumberlands
(Riverside)

*Hedy West (1938-)

Hedy West, Vols. 1-2 (Vanguard)
Old Times and Hard Times (1967,
Folk-Legacy)

*Frank Proffitt (1913-69)

Folk Songs (Folkways)
Frank Proffitt (Folk-Legacy)
Memorial Album (Folk-Legacy)
Frank Proffitt Sings Folk Songs
(1962, Folkways)
Reese, North Carolina (1962, Folk-
Legacy)

*Obray Ramsey

Folksongs from the Three Laurels
(ca. 1960, Prestige)

*Doc Watson (1923-)

Deep River Blues (1965, Vanguard)
Little Darling Pal of Mine (1965,
Vanguard)

Tennessee Stud (1965 Vanguard)

Doc Watson (Vanguard)
Doc and Merle Watson: Ballads from Deep Gap (Vanguard)
The Essential (Vanguard)
Watson Family (1961, Folkways)
Doc Watson and Son (1965, Vanguard)
Southbound (1967, Vanguard)
Memories (1975, United Artists)

OTHER ARTISTS

John Abbott

Moses Ash

Clarence Ashley

Phillips Barry

Doc Hopkins

Max Hunter

Bessie Jones

Chad Mitchele

Lawrence Older

Cecil Sharp

Virgil Sturgill

WESTERN, SOUTHWESTERN, AND NORTHWESTERN TRADITIONAL

*Woody Guthrie (1912-67)

*Deportee (1930, Library of Congress)
*Pastures of Plenty (1930, Library of Congress)

*Pretty Boy Floyd (1930, Library of Congress)
*So Long, It's Been Good to Know You (1930, Library of Congress)
*This Land Is Your Land (1930, Library of Congress)
*Tom Joad (1930, Library of Congress)

Bound for Glory (Folkways)
Early Years (Tradition)
Immortal Woody Guthrie (Olympic)
Legendary Woody Guthrie (Tradition)
Woody Guthrie (Everest)
Woody Guthrie: Library of Congress Recordings (1940, Electra)
*Cowboy Songs (1944, Stinson)
Folk Songs by Woody Guthrie and Cisco Houston (1944, Stinson)
*Songs to Grow On (1951, Folkways)
*Songs to Grow On, Vol. 2 (1958, Folkways)
*Songs to Grow On, Vol. 3 (1961, Folkways)
*Woody Guthrie Sings Folk Songs (1962, Folkways)
*Dust Bowl Ballads (1964, Folkways)
*This Land Is Your Land (1967, Folkways)
*A Legendary Performer (1977, RCA)

*Pete Seeger (1919-)

*We Shall Overcome (1940, Folkways)
If I Had a Hammer (1957, Folkways)
Little Boxes (1957, Folkways)
Where Have All the Flowers Gone (1957, Folkways)
A Hard Rain's A-Gonna Fall (1962, Columbia)
Turn! Turn! Turn! (1962, Columbia)

*American Favorite Ballads, Vols. 1-5 (Folkways)
*American Industrial Ballads (Folkways)

*Broadside (Folkways)
*Darling Corey (Folkways)
*Frontier Ballads, Vol. 1: *The Track* (Folkways)
*Frontier Ballads, Vol. 2: *The Settlers* (Folkways)
*Pete Seeger and the Almanac Singers: Talking Union and Other Union Songs (Folkways)
*Songs of Struggle and Protest, 1930-50 (Folkways)
*Songs of the Civil War (Folkways)
*Songs of the Railroad, 1924-34 (Vetco)
*Three Saints, Four Sinners and Six Other People (Odyssey)
*Songs and Ballads of the Bituminous Miners (1940, Library of Congress)
*Songs and Ballads of the Anthracite Miners (1946, Library of Congress)
*Pete Seeger Sings American Ballads (1957, Folkways)
*We Shall Overcome (1963, Columbia)
*Waist-Deep in the Big Muddy and Other Love Songs (1967, Columbia)

*Almanac Singers

**Mr. President (1941, Victor)
**Talking Union (1941, Victor)

*Talking Union (1942, Victor)
Union Maid (1943, Victor)
*Union Train a Comin' (1943, Victor)

*Weavers

**Goodnight Irene (1950, Decca)
**On Top of Old Smokey (1950, Decca)
Kisses Sweeter Than Wine (1955, Vanguard)
When the Saints Go Marching In (1955, Vanguard)

*Best of . . . (Decca)
Greatest Hits (Vanguard)
*The Weavers at Carnegie Hall (1961, Vanguard)

*Cisco Houston (1932-)

American Folksongs (Folkways)
*Cowboy Songs (1944, Stinson)
Cowboy Ballads (1952, Folkways)
Railroad Ballads (1953, Folkways)
Hard Travelin' (1954, Folkways)
I Ain't Got No Home (1967, Vanguard)

*Ramblin' Jack Elliott (1931-)

Country Style (Prestige)
Hard Travelin' (Fantasy)
Muleskinner (Topic)
Ramblin' Jack Elliott (Everest Archives)
Ramblin' Jack Elliott (Prestige)
Ramblin' Jack Elliott (Vanguard)
*Songs to Grow On (Folkways)
Ramblin' Jack Elliott Sings Woody Guthrie and Jimmy Rodgers (1962, MTR)
*Essential Ramblin' Jack Elliott (1976, Vanguard)

*Burl Ives (1909-)

Call Me Mr. In-Between (1962, Decca)
Funny Way of Laughin' (1962, Decca)
A Little Bitty Tear (1962, Decca)
Mary Ann Regrets (1962, Decca)

Animal Folk (Disneyland)
Songs of the West (Decca)
*The Best of . . . (1965, MCA)

*Earl Robinson (1910-)

Black and White
The House I Live In
Joe Hill

Ballad for Americans (1957,
Folkways)
The Lonesome Train (1957,
Folkways)
*A Walk in the Sun (1957, Folkways)
E. Robinson Sings (1960, Folkways)

WESTERN, SOUTHWESTERN, AND NORTHWESTERN INTERPRETIVE

*Mike Seeger (1933-)

Music from Tru Vine (Mercury)
The Second Annual Farewell Reunion (Mercury)
American Folk Songs (1957, Folkways)
Old Time Country Music (1962, Folkways)
Tipple, Loom and Rail (1966, Folkways)

*Peggy Seeger (1935-)

American Folksongs for Banjo (Folk-Lyric)
Folksongs of Courting and Complaint (Folkways)
Peggy Seeger and Ewan MacColl: The Amorous Muse (Argo)
Peggy Seeger and Ewan MacColl: The Angry Muse (Argo)
Peggy Seeger and Ewan MacColl: The Long Harvest (Argo)
Peggy Seeger and Ewan MacColl: At the Present Moment (1973, Rounder)
Peggy Seeger and Ewan MacColl: Folkways of Contemporary Songs (1973, Folkways)

NORTHEASTERN TRADITIONAL AND INTERPRETIVE

John Allison (1914-)

Witches and War Whoops (Folkways)

*Paul Clayton

Bay State Ballads (Folkways)
Cumberland Mountain Folksongs (Folkways)
Folksongs and Ballads of Virginia (Folkways)
Whaling and Sailing Songs (Tradition)

Harold Harrington

Songs of Old Vermont (Droll Yankee)

Sandy Ives

Folksongs of Maine (Folkways)

Margaret MacArthur

Folksongs of Vermont (Folkways)

Milt Okun (1923-)

Adirondack Folk Ballads (Stinson)

Grant Rogers

Songmaker of the Catskills (Folk-Legacy)

MIDWESTERN TRADITIONAL AND INTERPRETIVE

Gene Bluestein

Songs of the North Star State (Folkways)

Bob Gibson

Folksongs of Ohio (Stinson)

Joan O'Bryant

Folksongs and Ballads of Kansas (Folkways)

BRITISH, SCOTTISH, AND IRISH TRADITIONAL AND INTERPRETIVE

*Jeannie Robertson

The Great Scots Traditional Ballad Singer (Topic)

Margaret Barry

Folksongs of Britain (Caedmon)

*Ewan MacColl (1915-)

Chorus from the Gallows (Topic)
The English and Scottish Popular Ballads, Vols. 1-3 (Folkways)
Ewan MacColl and Peggy Seeger: Classic Scot Ballads (Tradition)
Four Pence a Day (Stinson)
The Singing Streets (Folkways)

*Jean Redpath

Jean Redpath (Folk-Legacy)
Scottish Ballad Book (Folk-Legacy)
Frae My Ain Countrie (1973, Folk-Legacy)

Boys of the Lough

The Boys of . . . (Trailer)
Second Album (Rounder)

*Chieftains

The Chieftains, Vols. 1-4 (Claddagh)

Fili Na

Farewell to Connaught (Outlet)
An Ghaoth Aniar (Mercier)
Three (Outlet)

*Planxty

The Well Below the Valley (Polydor)
Cold Blow and the Rainy Night (1979, Shanachie)

Peg Clancy Power

Peg Clancy Power (Folk-Legacy)

Sarah and Rita Keane

Once I Loved: Songs from the West of Ireland (Claddagh)

*Clancy Brothers

Jug of Punch (1967, Columbia)
The Leaving of Liverpool (1967, Columbia)
The Patriot Game (1967, Columbia)
Red-Haired Mary (1967, Columbia)
The Rising of the Moon (1967, Columbia)

The Best of the Clancy Brothers and Tommy Makem
In Person at Carnegie Hall (1963, Columbia)
Freedom's Sons (1967, Columbia)
Greatest Hits (1974, Vanguard)

*Clannad

Clannad Two (1979, Shanachie)
Dulaman (1979, Shanachie)
Clannad in Concert (1980, Shanachie)
Crann Ull (1980, Tara)

*De Danann

My Irish Molly (1981, Shanachie)

Selected Jigs and Reels (1980,
Shanachie)
The Star-Spangled Molly (1981,
Shanachie)

FOLK REVIVAL, PROFESSIONAL AND STRAIGHT FOLK

*Bob Dylan (1941-)

Highway 61 (1961, Columbia)
See That My Grave Is Kept Clean
(1961, Columbia)
*Song to Woody (1961, Columbia)
*Talking New York (1961,
Columbia)
*Blowin' in the Wind (1962,
Columbia)
*Don't Think Twice, It's All Right
(1962, Columbia)
*Girl from the North Country (1962,
Columbia)
*I Shall Be Free (1962, Columbia)
*Masters of War (1962, Columbia)
*Talking World War Three Blues
(1962, Columbia)
Boots of Spanish Leather (1964,
Columbia)
*Chimes of Freedom (1964,
Columbia)
I Don't Believe You (1964,
Columbia)
*I Shall Be Free No. 10 (1964,
Columbia)
*The Lonesome Death of Hattie
Carroll (1964, Columbia)
*My Back Pages (1964, Columbia)
North Country Blues (1964,
Columbia)
*One Too Many Mornings (1964,
Columbia)
*Only a Pawn in Their Game (1964,
Columbia)
*Restless Farewell (1964, Columbia)
Spanish Harlem Incident (1964,
Columbia)

*When the Ship Comes In (1964,
Columbia)
*Ballad of a Thin Man (1965,
Columbia)
*Don't Look Back (1965, Columbia)
*Just Like Tom Thumb's Blues
(1965, Columbia)
*Like a Rolling Stone (1965,
Columbia)
*Love Minus Zero/No Limit (1965,
Columbia)
Maggie's Farm (1965, Columbia)
*Mr. Tambourine Man (1965,
Columbia)
*Positively 4th Street (1965,
Columbia)
*Rainy Day Women #12 & 35,
(1965, Columbia)
*She Belongs to Me (1965,
Columbia)
*Subterranean Homesick Blues
(1965, Columbia)
*I Want You (1966, Columbia)
Just Like a Woman (1966,
Columbia)
*Odds and Ends (1966, Columbia)
Please Mrs. Henry (1966,
Columbia)
*Tears of Rage (1966, Columbia)
*This Wheel's on Fire (1966,
Columbia)
*Too Much of Nothing (1966,
Columbia)
*Visions of Johanna (1966,
Columbia)
All Along the Watchtower (1968,
Columbia)
I Dreamed I Saw St. Augustine
(1968, Columbia)
*J.W. Harding (1968, Columbia)
Pretty Boy Floyd (1968, Columbia)
*Lay Lady Lay (1969, Columbia)
Final Theme (1973, Columbia)
*Knockin' on Heaven's Door (1973,
Columbia)
Forever Young (1974, Asylum)
Wedding Song (1974, Asylum)
You Angel You (1974, Asylum)
Hurricane (1975, Columbia)

Joey (1975, Columbia)
Mozambique (1975, Columbia)
Sara (1975, Columbia)
Simple Twist of Fate (1975,
  Columbia)
Tangled Up in Blue (1975,
  Columbia)
Gotta Serve Somebody (1979,
  Columbia)
Every Grain of Sand (1981,
  Columbia)
It's All Over Now, Baby Blue (1981,
  Columbia)

Bob Dylan (1961, Columbia)
The Freewheelin' Bob Dylan (1962,
  Columbia)
Another Side of Bob Dylan (1964,
  Columbia)
The Times They Are a-Changing
  (1964, Columbia)
Bringing It All Back Home (1965,
  Columbia)
Highway 61 Revisited (1965,
  Columbia)
Blonde on Blonde (1966, Columbia)
Bob Dylan's Greatest Hits (1967,
  Columbia)
John Wesley Harding (1968,
  Columbia)
Nashville Skyline (1969, Columbia)
Bob Dylan's Greatest Hits, Vol. 2
  (1971, Columbia)
Pat Garrett and Billy the Kid (1973,
  Columbia)
Before the Flood (1974, Asylum)
Planet Waves (1974, Asylum)
The Basement Tapes (1975,
  Columbia)
Blood on the Tracks (1975,
  Columbia)
Desire (1975, Columbia)
Shot of Love (1981, Columbia)
Infidels (1983, Columbia)
Knocked Out Loaded (1986,
  Columbia)

*Koerner, Ray, and Glover

*Blues, Rags and Hollers (Elektra)
*Lots More Blues, Rags and Hollers
  (Elektra)
Return of Koerner, Ray, and Glover
  (Elektra)

John Koerner (1938-) solo

Running, Jumping, Standing Still
  (Elektra)
Spider Blues (Elektra)

*Joan Baez (1941-)

Joan Baez (1960, Vanguard)
In Concert, Part 1 (1962, Vanguard)
In Concert, Part 2 (1963, Vanguard)
Joan Baez (1963, Vanguard)
Joan Baez (1964, Vanguard)
Farewell, Angelina (1965,
  Vanguard)
Noel (1966, Vanguard)
First Ten Years (1970, Vanguard)
Ballad Book (1972, Vanguard)

*Judy Collins (1939-)

*I Know Where I'm Going (1962,
  Elektra)
Wild Mountain Thyme (1962,
  Elektra)
*Lonesome Death of Hattie Carrol
  (1964, Elektra)
*Pack Up Your Sorrows (1965,
  Elektra)
Tomorrow Is a Long Time (1965,
  Elektra)
*Both Sides Now (1968, Elektra)
My Father (1968, Elektra)
Since You Asked (1968, Elektra)
*Amazing Grace (1971, Elektra)
Famous Blue Raincoat (1972,
  Elektra)
Joan of Arc (1972, Elektra)
Cook with Honey (1973, Elektra)
Secret Gardens (1973, Elektra)
Send in the Clowns (1975, Elektra)

A Maid of Constant Sorrow (1962, Elektra)
*Golden Apples of the Sun (1963, Elektra)
Judy Collins #3 (1963, Elektra)
The Judy Collins Concert (1964, Elektra)
Judy Collins Fifth Album (1965, Elektra)
In My Life (1967, Elektra)
*Who Knows Where the Time Goes (1968, Elektra)
Wildflowers (1968, Elektra)
*Colors of the Day/The Best of . . . (1972, Elektra)
The First Fifteen Years (1977, Elektra)
So Early in the Spring (1977, Elektra)
*Times of Our Lives (1982, Elektra)

*Ian and Sylvia

(Ian Tyson, 1933- ; Sylvia Tyson, 1940-)

Four Strong Winds (1963, Vanguard)
Tomorrow Is a Long Time (1963, Vanguard)
You Were on My Mind (1964, Vanguard)
For Lovin' Me (1965, Vanguard), G. Lightfoot comp.

*Ian and Sylvia (1962, Vanguard)
Four Strong Winds (1963, Vanguard)
Northern Journey (1964, Vanguard)
Ian and Sylvia: Early Morning Rain (1965, Vanguard)
The Best of . . . (1968, Vanguard)
*Greatest Hits, Vol. 1 (1970, Vanguard)
*Greatest Hits, Vol. 2 (1971, Vanguard)

Kate and Anna McGarrigle

(Kate McGarrigle, 1946- ; Anna McGarrigle, 1944-)

*Kate and Anna McGarrigle (1975, Warner Bros.)
*Dancer with Bruised Knees (1977, Warner Bros.)
Pronto Monto (1978, Warner Bros.)
*Love Over and Over (1982, Polydor)

*Odetta

(Odetta Holmes, 1930-)

Odetta at Carnegie Hall (Vanguard)
*Ballads and Blues (1957, Tradition), *Best of . . .* (1958, Tradition)
At the Gate of Horn (1959, Tradition)
*The Essential Odetta (1973, Vanguard)

Bonnie Dobson

Dear Companion (1962, Prestige)

*Phil Ochs (1940-76)

The Bells (1964, Elektra)
*The Power and the Glory (1964, Elektra)
*Draft Dodger Rag (1965, Elektra)
Here's to the State of Mississippi (1965, Elektra)
*I Ain't a'Marchin' Anymore (1965, Elektra)
In the Heat of the Summer (1965, Elektra)
There But for Fortune (1965, Elektra)
*Canons of Christianity (1966, Elektra)
*The Ringing of Revolution (1966, Elektra)
Santo Domingo (1966, Elektra)
*Crucifixion (1967, A&M)
Miranda (1967, A&M)

The Party (1967, A&M)
*Small Circle of Friends (1967, A&M)
Joe Hill (1968, A&M)
*The War Is Over (1968, A&M)
When in Rome (1968, A&M)
*My Life (1969, A&M)
Where Were You in Chicago (1969, A&M)
*Here's to the State of Richard Nixon (1974, A&M)

*All the News That's Fit to Sing (1964, Elektra)
*A Toast to Those Who Are Gone (1964, Elektra)
I Ain't a'Marchin' Anymore (1965, Elektra)
*Phil Ochs in Concert (1966, Elektra)
Pleasures of the Harbor (1967, A&M)
Tape from California (1968, A&M)
*Rehearsals for Retirement (1969, A&M)
*Chords of Fame (1976, A&M)

*Tom Paxton (1937-)

Forest Lawn
Going to the Zoo
*Talking Watergate
Whose Garden Was This?
*Last Thing on My Mind (1964, Elektra)
*What Did You Learn in School Today (1964, Elektra)
*Talking Vietnam Pot Luck Blues (1965, Elektra)

Ramblin' Boy (1964, Elektra)
Ain't That News (1964, Elektra)
*The Complete Tom Paxton (1971, Elektra)

*Richard and Mimi Farina

(Richard Farina, 1937-66; Mimi Farina, 1945-)

*Pack Up Your Sorrows (1965, Vanguard)

*Celebration for a Grey Day (1965, Vanguard)
*Reflections in a Crystal Wind (1966, Vanguard)
Memories (1968, Vanguard)
Best of . . . (1971, Vanguard)

*Tom Rush (1941-)

Mind Rambling (1963, Prestige)
*Blues, Songs, Ballads (1965, Prestige)
Tom Rush (1965, Elektra)
*Tom Rush-Take a Little Walk with Me (1966, Elektra)
*The Circle Game (1968, Elektra)
Tom Rush (1970, Columbia)
*Classic Rush (1971, Elektra)

*Arlo Guthrie (1947-)

*Alice's Restaurant (1963, Reprise)
Try Me One More Time (1968, Reprise)
Coming into Los Angeles (1969, Reprise)
City of New Orleans (1972, Reprise)
Lightning Bar Blues (1972, Reprise)
Children of Abraham (1974, Reprise)
Presidential Rag (1974, Reprise)
Connection (1976, Reprise)
Manzanillo Bay (1976, Reprise)
Massachusetts (1976, Reprise)

*Alice's Restaurant (1967, Reprise)
Arlo (1968, Reprise)
*Running Down the Road (1969, Reprise)
*Hobo's Lullaby (1972, Reprise)

Last of the Brooklyn Cowboys (1973, Reprise)
Arlo Guthrie (1974, Reprise)
Amigo (1976, Reprise)
Outlasting the Blues (1979, Reprise)

*Joni Mitchell (1943-)

Marcie (1968, Reprise)
*Michael from Mountain (1968, Reprise)
Night in the City (1968, Reprise)
I Don't Know Where I Stand (1969, Reprise)
That Song about the Midway (1969, Reprise)
Big Yellow Taxi (1970, Reprise)
All I Want (1971, Reprise)
Carey (1971, Reprise)
Last Time I Saw Richard (1971, Reprise)
My Old Man (1971, Reprise)
*Cold Blue Steel and Sweet Fire (1972, Asylum)
Judgment of the Moon and Stars (1972, Asylum)
You Turn Me On, I'm a Radio (1972, Asylum)
Cactus Tree (1974, Asylum)
*Help Me (1974, Asylum)
Jericho (1974, Asylum; 1977 Asylum)
Rainy Night House (1974, Asylum)
The Same Situation (1974, Asylum)
The Hissing of Summer Lawns (1975, Asylum)
Refuge of the Road (1976, Asylum)
Chinese Cafe (1982, Geffen)
You Dream Flat Tire (1982, Geffen)

Joni Mitchell (1968, Reprise)
Clouds (1969, Reprise)
Ladies of the Canyon (1970, Reprise)
Blue (1971, Reprise)
For the Roses (1972, Asylum)
Court and Spark (1974, Asylum)
Hejiro (1976, Asylum)

Wild Things Run Fast (1982, Geffen)

*Tim Hardin (1941-)

This Is Tim Hardin (1962, Atco)
Tim Hardin 1 (1966, MGM)
Tim Hardin 2 (1967, MGM)
Tim Hardin 3 Live in Concert (1968, Verve)
Tim Hardin 4 (1969, Verve)

*Eric Andersen (1943-)

Today Is the Highway (1965, Vanguard)
'Bout Changes and Things (1966, Vanguard)
'Bout Changes and Things, Take 2 (1968, Vanguard)
Blue River (1972, Columbia)

*Hazel Dickens

Come All Ye Coal Miner (1975, Rounder)
Hard-Hitting Songs for Hard-Hit People (1981, Rounder)

*Hazel Dickens and Alice Gerrard

Won't You Come and Sing for Me? (1967, Folkways)
Hazel and Alice (1973, Rounder)
Hazel Dickens and Alice Gerrard (1976, Rounder)

*Barbara Dane (1927-)

Barbara Dane and the Chamber Bros. (1964, Folkways)
Barbara Dane Sings the Blues (1965, Folkways)

*Richie Havens (1941-)

Richie Havens Record (1963, Douglas)
Mixed Bag (1968, MGM)

*Gordon Bok

Peter Kagan and the Wind (1972, Folk-Legacy)
**Bay of Fundy* (1976, Folk-Legacy)

*Michael Cooney

**The Cheese Stands Alone* (1969, Folk-Legacy)

*Bruce (U. Utah) Phillips

**Good Though* (1973, Philo)
El Capitan (1975, Philo)

*Carl Sandburg (1878-)

**American Songbag* (Caedmon)
C. Sandburg Sings American (Everest)
Flat Rock Ballads (Columbia)
The Great Carl Sandburg (Lyrichord)

*Tony and Irene Saletan

Tony and Irene Saletan (Folk-Legacy)

*Helen Schneyer

Ballads, Broadsides, and Hymns (Folk-Legacy)

*Frank Hamilton (1934-)

Sings Folk Songs (Folkways)

*Tom Paley

Folk-Songs from the Southern Appalachian Mountains (1953, Elektra)

*Willis Alan Ramsey (1951-)

Willis Alan Ramsey (Shelter)

*Suzanne Vega

**Suzanne Vega* (1985, A&M)

**Solitude Standing* (1987, A&M)

Nanci Griffith

**Last of the True Believers* (1986, Rounder)
**Lone Star State of Mind* (1987, A&M)

*Buffy Sainte-Marie (1941-)

*Universal Soldier (1964, Vanguard)
*Many a Mile (1965, Vanguard)
*Until It's Time for You to Go (1965, Vanguard)
Mister Can't You See (1972, Vanguard)

FOLK POP

*Kingston Trio

*Tom Dooley (1958, Capitol)
The Tiguano Jail (1959, Capitol))
El Matador (1960, Capitol)
Where Have All the Flowers Gone (1962, Capitol)
Reverend Mr. Black (1963, Capitol)

From the Hungry I (Capitol)
Scarlet Ribbons (Capitol)
Tom Dooley (Capitol)
**The Best of . . .*, Vol. 1 (1962, Capitol)

*Peter, Paul, and Mary

(Peter Yarrow, 1938- ; Paul Stookey, 1937- ; Mary Travers, 1937-)

*If I Had a Hammer (1962, Warner Bros.)
*Lemon Tree (1962, Warner Bros.)
Blowin' in the Wind (1963, Warner Bros.)
Don't Think Twice, It's All Right (1963, Warner Bros.)

*Puff the Magic Dragon (1963, Warner Bros.)
*Tell It on the Mountain (1964, Warner Bros.)
Cuckoo (1965, Warner Bros.)
Motherless Child (1965, Warner Bros.)
San Francisco Bay Blues (1965, Warner Bros.)
*I Dig Rock and Roll Music (1967, Warner Bros.)
*Leaving on a Jet Plane (1969, Warner Bros.)

Peter, Paul, and Mary (1962, Warner Bros.)
Peter, Paul, and Mary in the Wind (1963, Warner Bros.)
Peter, Paul, and Mary Moving (1963, Warner Bros.)
A Song Will Rise (1965, Warner Bros.)
Album 1700 (1967, Warner Bros.)

Chad Mitchell Trio

Mighty Day on Campus (1962, Kapp)
Best of . . . (1963, Kapp)

*New Christy Minstrels

Green, Green (1963, Columbia)
Saturday Night (1963, Columbia)
Today (1964, Columbia)

Brothers Four

Greenfields (1960, Columbia)
Frogg (1961, Columbia)

Best Music On-Off Campus (1961, Columbia)

Limelighters

Tonight: In Person (1961, RCA)
Slightly Fabulous Limelighters (1961, RCA)

*Richard Dyer-Bennett

Richard Dyer-Bennett, Vol. 4 (1957, Dyer-Bennett)
Richard Dyer-Bennett, Vol. 5 (1958, Dyer-Bennett)

*Alfred Deller and the Deller Consort

The Wraggle Taggle Gypsies: English Ballads and Folk Songs

*Simon and Garfunkel

(Paul Simon, 1942- ; Art Garfunkel, 1942-)

*Sounds of Silence (1965, Columbia)
The Dangling Conversation (1966, Columbia)
59th Street Bridge Song (1966, Columbia)
For Emily Whenever I May Find Her (1966, Columbia)
A Hazy Shade of Winter (1966, Columbia)
*Homeward Bound (1966, Columbia)
*I Am a Rock (1966, Columbia)
At the Zoo (1967, Columbia)
Fakin' It (1967, Columbia)
*Mrs. Robinson (1967, Columbia)
Scarborough Fair/Canticle (1968, Columbia)
*The Boxer (1969, Columbia)
*Bridge over Troubled Water (1970, Columbia)
*Cecilia (1970, Columbia)
El Condor Pasa (1970, Columbia)
*My Little Town (1975, Columbia)

Wednesday Morning, 3 A.M. (1965, Columbia)
Parsley, Sage, Rosemary and Thyme (1966, Columbia)
Sounds of Silence (1966, Columbia)
Bookends (1968, Columbia)
Bridge over Troubled Water (1970, Columbia)

*Simon and Garfunkel's Greatest Hits
  (1972, Columbia)
The Concert in Central Park (1982,
  Warner Bros.)

Paul Simon solo

Me and Julio Down by the
  Schoolyard (1972, Columbia)
*Mother and Child Reunion (1972,
  Columbia)
*Kodachrome (1973, Columbia)
*Loves Me Like a Rock (1973,
  Columbia)
American Tune (1974, Columbia)
*50 Ways to Leave Your Lover
  (1976, Columbia)
Still Crazy After All These Years
  (1976, Columbia)
*Slip Slidin' Away (1977, Columbia)
*Late in the Evening (1980, War.)
One Trick Pony (1980, War.)

*Paul Simon (1972, Columbia)
*There Goes Rhymin' Simon (1973,
  Columbia)
*Still Crazy After All These Years
  (1975, Columbia)
Greatest Hits (1977, Columbia)
One Trick Pony (1980, War.)
*Graceland (1986, War.)

Art Garfunkel solo

Breakaway (1975, Columbia)
Watermark (1977, Columbia)

*James Taylor (1948-)

Brighten Your Mind with My Day
  (1967)
Night Owl (1967)
*Carolina on My Mind (1970, War.)
*Fire and Rain (1970, War.)
Country Road (1971, War.)
Long Ago and Far Away (1971,
  War.)
*You've Got a Friend (1971, War.)
Don't Let Me Be Lonely Tonight
  (1972, War.)

*How Sweet It Is (To Be Loved By
  You) (1975, War.)
Shower the People (1976, War.)
*Handy Man (1977, War.)
Your Smiling Face (1977, War.)
Up on the Roof (1979, War.)

James Taylor (1968, Apple)
*Sweet Baby James (1970, Warner
  Bros.)
Mud Slide Slim and the Blue
  Horizon (1971, Warner Bros.)
*Gorilla (1975, Warner Bros.)
*Greatest Hits (1976, Warner Bros.)
*J.T. (1977, Columbia)

*Cat Stevens (1947-)

I Love My Dog (1966, Deram)
Matthew and Son (1967, Deram)
I'm Gonna Get Me a Gun (1968,
  Deram)
Lady D'Arbanville (1970, A&M)
*Wild World (1971, A&M)
Moon Shadow (1971, A&M)
*Peace Train (1971, A&M)
*Morning Has Broken (1972, A&M)
Sitting (1972, A&M)
The Hurt (1973, A&M)
*Another Saturday Night (1974,
  A&M)
*Oh Very Young (1974, A&M)
Ready (1975, A&M)
Two Fine People (1975, A&M)
(Remember the Days of the) Old
  Schoolyard (1977, A&M)

Matthew and Son (1967, Deram)
New Masters (1968, Deram)
Cats Cradle (1970, London)
Mona Bone Jakon (1970, A&M)
The World of Cat Stevens (1970,
  Decca)
*Tea for the Tillerman (1971, A&M)
Catch Bull at Four (1972, A&M)
Teaser and the Firecat (1972, A&M)
*Greatest Hits (1975, A&M)

*Carly Simon (1945-)

Winken, Blinken and Nod (1964,
  Kapp)
*Anticipation (1971, Elektra)
Dan, My Fling (1971, Elektra)
Legend in Your Own Time (1971,
  Elektra)
Reunions (1971, Elektra)
Share the End (1971, Elektra)
*That's the Way I've Always Heard It
  Should Be (1971, Elektra)
*You're So Vain (1972, Elektra)
The Right Thing to Do (1973,
  Elektra)
Haven't Got Time for the Pain
  (1974, Elektra)
Attitude Dancing (1975, Elektra)
*Nobody Does It Better (1977,
  Elektra)
*You Belong to Me (1978, Elektra)
Jesse (1980, Warner Bros.)

Carly Simon (1970, Elektra)
Anticipation (1971, Elektra)
*No Secrets (1972, Elektra)
**The Best of . . .* (1975, Elektra)
Another Passenger (1976, Elektra)
Boys in the Trees (1978, Elektra)

*Roches

**Seductive Reasoning* (1975,
  Columbia)
*The Roches (1979, War.)
Nurds (1980, War.)
Keep On Doing (1982, War.)

*Melanie

(Melanie Safka, 1947-)

Beautiful People (1967, Columbia)
Look What They've Done to My
  Song, Ma (1969, Buddah)
*Lay Down (Candles in the Rain)
  (1970, Buddah)
Peace Will Come (According to
  Plan) (1970, Buddah)

*Brand New Key (1971,
  Neighborhood)
The Nickel Song (1972, Buddah)
Ring the Living Bell (1972,
  Neighborhood)
Bitter Bad (1973, Neighborhood)

*Born to Be (1969, Buddah)
*Melanie (1969, Buddah)
**Candles in the Rain* (1970, Buddah)
Leftover Wine (1970, Buddah)
Gather Me (1971, Neighborhood)
The Good Book (1971, Buddah)
Four Sides of . . . (1972, Buddah)
Stoneground Words (1972,
  Neighborhood)
At Carnegie Hall (1973,
  Neighborhood)
As I See It Now (1974,
  Neighborhood)
Mad Rugada (1974, Neighborhood)
Sunset and Other Beginnings (1975,
  Neighborhood)
*Photograph (1976, Atlantic)
**Best of . . .* (1978, Buddah)
**Photogenic--Not Just Another Pretty
  Face* (1978, Midsong)
*Ballroom Streets (1979, RCA)

*Loggins and Messina

(Kenny Loggins, 1948- ; Jim
Messina, 1947-)

*Your Mama Don't Dance (1972,
  Columbia)
My Music (1973, Columbia)
Thinking of You (1973, Columbia)

**Loggins and Messina* (1972,
  Columbia)
**Loggins and Messina Sittin'* (1972,
  Columbia)
On Stage (1974, Columbia)
**The Best of . . .* (1976, Columbia)

*Don McLean (1945-)

*American Pie (1971, United Artists)

*Castles in the Air (1972, United
   Artists)
Vincent (1972, United Artists)
Dreidel (1973, Millenium)
Since I Don't Have You (1981,
   Millenium)

Tapestry (1970, United Artists)
American Pie (1971, United Artists)
Don McLean (1972, United Artists)

*Seals and Crofts

(Jim Seals, 1940- ; Dash Crofts,
1940-)

*Summer Breeze (1972, Warner
   Bros.)
*Diamond Girl (1973, Warner Bros.)
Hummingbird (1973, Warner Bros.)
We May Never Pass This Way
   Again (1973, Warner Bros.)
I'll Play for You (1975, Warner
   Bros.)
*Get Closer (1976, Warner Bros.)
My Fair Share (1977, Warner
   Bros.)
You're the Love (1978, Warner
   Bros.)

Down Home (1970, TA)
Seals and Crofts (1970, TA)
Year of Sunday (1971, Warner
   Bros.)
Summer Breeze (1972, Warner
   Bros.)
Diamond Girl (1973, Warner Bros.)
Greatest Hits (1975, Warner Bros.)

*America

*A Horse with No Name (1972,
   Warner Bros.)
*I Need You (1972, Warner Bros.)
*Ventura Highway (1972, Warner
   Bros.)
Don't Cross the River (1973,
   Warner Bros.)
*Tin Man (1974, Warner Bros.)
Daisy Jane (1975, Warner Bros.)

*Lonely People (1975, Warner Bros.)
*Sister Golden Hair (1975, Warner
   Bros.)
Today's the Day (1976, Warner
   Bros.)
*You Can Do Magic (1982, Capitol)
The Border (1983, Capitol)

America (1972, Warner Bros.)
Homecoming (1972, Warner Bros.)
Hat Trick (1973, Warner Bros.)
Holiday (1974, Warner Bros.)
History: America's Greatest Hits
   (1975, Warner Bros.)

*Michael Hurley

Long Journey (1976, Rounder)
Snockgrass (1980, Rounder)

PARODY FOLK

*Erik Darling

Eric Darling (Elektra)
Train Time (Vanguard)
True Religion (Vanguard)
The Possible Dream (1975,
   Vanguard)

*Smothers Brothers

Think Ethnic

FOLK ROCK

*Dillards

Back Porch Bluegrass (1963,
   Elektra)
Live . . . Almost (1964, Elektra)
Pickin' and Fiddlin' (1965, Elektra)
Copperfields (1970, Elektra)
Tribute to the American Duck (1973,
   Poppy)
*The Dillards/Incredible Flying L.A.
   Time Machine* (1977, Flying
   Fish)

Glitter Grass from the Nashwood
  Hollyville Strings (1977, Flying
  Fish)
Homecoming and Family Reunion
  (1981, Flying Fish)

*Dillard and Clark

(Doug Dillard, 1942- ; Gene Clark,
1941-)

*The Fantastic Expedition of Dillard
  and Clark (1968, A&M)
*Through the Morning through the
  Night (1969, A&M)

*Byrds

*All I Really Want to Do (1965,
  Columbia)
He Was a Friend of Mine (1965,
  Columbia)
*Mr. Tambourine Man (1965,
  Columbia)
Satisfied Mind (1965, Columbia)
*Turn, Turn, Turn (1965, Columbia)
*Eight Miles High (1966, Columbia)
I'll Feel a Whole Lot Better (1966,
  Columbia)
John Riley (1966, Columbia)
*Mr. Spaceman (1966, Columbia)
We'll Meet Again (1966, Columbia)
Wild Mountain Thyme (1966,
  Columbia)
The World Turns All Around Her
  (1966, Columbia)
Girl with No Name (1967,
  Columbia)
*My Back Pages (1967, Columbia)
*So You Want to Be a Rock'n'Roll
  Star (1967, Columbia)
Time Between (1967, Columbia)
Goin' Back (1968, Columbia)
Hickory Wind (1968, Columbia)
One Hundred Years from Now
  (1968, Columbia)
You Showed Me (1973, Columbia)
You Won't Have to Cry (1973,
  Columbia)

*Mr. Tambourine Man (1965,
  Columbia)
*Fifth Dimension (1966, Columbia)
*Turn, Turn, Turn (1966, Columbia)
*Byrds' Greatest Hits (1967,
  Columbia)
*Younger Than Yesterday (1967,
  Columbia)
*The Notorious Byrd Bros. (1968,
  Columbia)
*Sweetheart of the Rodeo (1968,
  Columbia)
*Preflyte (1973, Columbia)
*The Byrds Play Dylan (1980,
  ' Columbia)

*Turtles

*It Ain't Me Babe (1965, White
  Whale)
Let Me Be (1965, White Whale)
You Baby (1966, White Whale)
*Happy Together (1967, White
  Whale)
*She'd Rather Be with You (1967,
  White Whale)
She's My Girl (1967, White Whale)
You Know What I Mean (1967,
  White Whale)
*Elenore (1968, White Whale)
*You Showed Me (1969, White
  Whale)

*It Ain't Me Babe (1965, White
  Whale)
*You Baby (1966, White Whale)
*Happy Together (1967, White
  Whale)
*Greatest Hits (1974, Sire)
Best of . . . (1987, Rhino)
Chalon Road (1987, Rhino)
Shell Shock (1987, Rhino)

*Mamas and the Papas

*California Dreamin' (1966, Dunhill)
*I Saw Her Again (1966, Dunhill)
Look through My Window (1966,
  Dunhill)

Monday, Monday (1966, Dunhill)
*Words of Love (1966, Dun)
*Creque Alley (1967, Dunhill)
*Dedicated to the One I Love (1967, Dunhill)
Glad to Be Unhappy (1967, Dunhill)
Twelve Thirty (1967, Dunhill)

If You Can Believe Your Eyes and Ears (1966, Dunhill)
The Mamas and the Papas (1966, Dunhill)
Deliver (1967, Dunhill)
Farewell to the First Golden Era (1967, Dunhill)
The Mamas and the Papas (1968, Dunhill)
Sixteen of Their Greatest Hits (1969, Dunhill)
Twenty Golden Hits (1973, Dunhill)

*Lovin' Spoonful

*Do You Believe in Magic (1965, Kama Sutra)
*You Didn't Have to Be So Nice (1965, Kama Sutra)
*Daydream (1966, Kama Sutra)
*Did You Ever Have to Make Up Your Mind? (1966, Kama Sutra)
*Nashville Cats (1966, Kama Sutra)
*Rain on the Roof (1966, Kama Sutra)
*Summer in the City (1966, Kama Sutra)
Darling Be Home Soon (1967, Kama Sutra)
She Is Still a Mystery (1967, Kama Sutra)
Six O'Clock (1967, Kama Sutra)

Hums of the Lovin' Spoonful (1965, Kama Sutra)
Daydream (1966, Kama Sutra)
Best of... (1967, Kama Sutra)
Everything Playing (1967, Kama Sutra)
Revelation: Revolution (1969, Kama Sutra)

CONTEMPORARY FOLK BANDS

*New Lost City Ramblers

Old-Timey Songs for Children (Folkways)
Depression Songs (1958, Folkways)
New Lost City Ramblers, Vols. 1-5 (1958-64 Folkways)
American Moonshine and Prohibition (1962, Folkways)
Modern Times (1968, Folkways)
The "New" N.L.C.R. (1972, Folkways)
Remembrance of Things to Come (1973, Folkways)
On the Great Divine (1975, Folkways)

*Holy Modal Rounders

Indian War Whoop (1967, ESP)
Holy Modal Rounders, Vol. 1 (1968, Prestige)
Stampfel and Weber (1972, Fantasy)
Alleged in Their Own Time (1976, Round)
Going Nowhere Fast (1981, Adelphi)

*Mother Earth and Tracy Nelson

(Tracy Nelson, 1944-)

Bring Me Home (Reprise)
Tracy Nelson (Atlantic)
Tracy Nelson (Reprise)
Deep Are the Roots (1965, Prestige)
Living with the Animals (1968, Mercury)
Make a Joyful Noise (1969, Mercury)
Poor Man's Paradise (1975, Columbia)

*Jim Kweskin Jug Band

Jim Kweskin and the Jug Band
(1963, Vanguard)
Jug Band Music (1965, Vanguard)
Relax Your Mind (1966, Vanguard)
Best of . . . (1968, Vanguard)
Greatest Hits (1970, Vanguard)

*Pentangle

The Pentangle (1969, Reprise)
Sweet Child (1969, Reprise)
Basket of Light (1970, Reprise)
Cruel Sister (1971, Reprise)

*Bert Jansch

Jack Orion (1970, Vanguard)

*10,000 Maniacs

Secrets of the I Ching (1983,
Christian Burial Music)
The Wishing Chair (1986, Christian
Burial Music)
In My Tribe (1987, Elektra)

*Fairport Convention

Fairport Convention (1969, A&M)
Unhalfbricking (1969, A&M)
Liege and Lief (1970, A&M)
Fairport Chronicles (1976, A&M)

*Steeleye Span

Gaudete (1972, Chrysalis)
Thomas the Rhymer (1974,
Chrysalis)
All around My Hat (1976,
Chrysalis)

Hark! The Village Wait (1970,
Chrysalis)
Please to See the King (1971,
Chrysalis)
*Ten Man Mop or Mr. Reservoir
Butler Rides Again* (1971,
Chrysalis)

Below the Salt (1972, Chrysalis)
Now We Are Six (1974, Chrysalis)
All around My Hat (1975, Chrysalis)
Commoner's Crown (1976,
Chrysalis)
*The Steeleye Span Story--Original
Masters* (1977, Chrysalis)

Incredible String Band

*The 5000 Spirits or the Layers of the
Onion* (1967, Elektra)
The Hangman's Beautiful Daughter
(1968, Elektra)
Relics (1970, Elektra)

FOLK BLUES

*Ry Cooder (1947-)

Ry Cooder (1970, Reprise)
Boomer's Story (1972, Reprise)
Into the Purple Valley (1972,
Reprise)
Paradise and Lunch (1974, Reprise)
Chicken Skin Music (1976, Reprise)
Bop Till You Drop (1979, Warner
Bros.)

*Little Feat

Little Feat (1971, Warner Bros.)
Sailin' Shoes (1972, Warner Bros.)
Dixie Chicken (1973, Warner Bros.)
Feats Don't Fail Me Now (1974,
Warner Bros.)
The Last Record Album (1975,
Warner Bros.)
Waiting for Columbus (1978,
Warner Bros.)
Hoy Hoy (1981, Warner Bros.)

*Bonnie Raitt (1949-)

Bonnie Raitt (1971, Warner Bros.)
Give It Up (1972, Warner Bros.)
Takin' My Time (1973, Warner
Bros.)
Nine Lives (1986, Warner Bros.)

Woodentops

Giant (1986, Columbia)

Anthologies

Blues Project (Elektra)
The Border (1982, MCA)

FOLK GUITAR
VIRTUOSOS

*John Fahey (1939-)

*Death Chants, Breakdowns and
Military Waltzes* (1962, Takoma)
*Dances of Death and Other
Plantation Favorites* (1964,
Takoma)
Blind Joe Death (1967, Takoma)
The New Possibility (Xmas Album)
(1969, Takoma)
Fare Forward Voyagers (1973,
Takoma)
John Fahey/Leo Kottke/Peter Lang
(1974, Takoma)
Best of . . ., 1959-77 (1977, Takoma)

*Leo Kottke (1945-)

Circle round the Sun (1969,
Symposium)
Mudlark (1971, Capitol)
Six and Twelve-String Guitar (1972,
Takoma)
Greenhouse (1973, Capitol)
My Feet Are Smiling (1973, Capitol)
L. Kottke (1976, Chrysalis)
L. Kottke--The Best (1978, Capitol)
Guitar Music (1981, Chrysalis)

BLUEGRASS NEW WAVE

*David Grisman (1945-)

Hot Dawg (1976, A&M)
David Grisman Quintet (1979,
Kaleidoscope)

David Grisman (1980, Rounder)
David Grisman Quintet (1980,
Warner Bros.)
Mondo Mando (1981, Warner
Bros.)

*Tony Rice (1950-)

Tony Rice (1976, Rounder)
Manzanita (1978, Rounder)
The Bluegrass Album (1980,
Rounder)
Mar West (1980, Rounder)

*Mark O'Connor (1961-)

Mark O'Connor (1974, Rounder)
Markology (1978, Rounder)
On the Rampage (1979, Rounder)

Soul Music

General Anthologies

Brunswick's Greatest Hits
(Brunswick)
Golden Soul (Atlantic)
Soul Years (Atlantic)
Fifteen Original Big Hits, Vol. 1
(1981, Stax)
Soul Deep, Vol. 1 (1981, Atlantic)
Okeh Soul (1982, Epic)
Solar's Greatest Hits (1982, Solar)

MEMPHIS AND SOUTHWEST

*Bobby Bland (1930-)

*Drifting from Town to Town (1952, Duke)
It's My Life Baby (1955, Duke)
*Farther On up the Road (1957, Duke)
I'll Take Care of You (1959, Duke)
*Cry Cry Cry (1960, Duke)
*Don't Cry No More (1961, Duke)
*I Pity the Fool (1961, Duke)
*Turn on Your Lovelight (1961, Duke)
*Stormy Monday (1962, Duke)
Yield Not to Temptation (1962, Duke)
Call On Me (1963, Duke)
That's the Way Love Is (1963, Duke)

The Best of . . ., Vol. 2 (Duke)
Two Steps from the Blue (Duke)
Call On Me (1963, Duke)
Ain't Nothing You Can Do (1964, Duke)
The Best of . . . (1973, Duke)
California Album (1973, ABC)
Dreamer (1974, ABC)
Introspective of the Early Years (1982, ABC)

*Junior Parker (1927-71)

Feelin' Good (1953, Sun)
*Mystery Train (1953, Sun)
Mother-in-Law Blues (1954, Duke)
Sweet Home Chicago (1954, Duke)
Yonders Wall (1954, Duke)
Barefoot Rock (1955, Duke)
*Next Time You See Me (1957, Duke)
*Driving Wheel (1961, Duke)
In the Dark (1961, Duke)
*Annie Get Your Yo-Yo (1962, Duke)
*Ain't Gon' Be No Cutting Loose (1971, Capitol)
Drowning on Dry Land (1971, Capitol)

Baby Please (Mercury)
Driving Wheel (1960, Duke)
The Best of Little Junior Parker (1962, Duke)
The ABC Collection
You Don't Have to Be Black . . . (1973, Groove People)
Junior Parker and Billy Love (1977, Charly)
I Wanna Ramble (1982, Ace)

*Little Johnnie Taylor (1937-)

*Part Time Love (1963, Galaxy)
Since I Found a New Love (1964, Galaxy)
*I Got to Love Somebody's Baby (1966, Stax)
*I Had a Dream (1966, Stax)
Somebody's Sleeping in My Bed (1967, Stax)
*Who's Making Love 1968, (Stax)
I Could Never Be President (1969, Stax)
Love Bones (1969, Stax)
Take Care of Your Homework (1969, Stax)
Testify (I Wanna) (1969, Stax)
*I Am Somebody, Part 2 (1970, Stax)
Steal Away (1970, Stax)

Jody's Got Your Girl and Gone
(1971, Stax)
Hi-Jackin' Love (1971, Stax)
Cheaper to Keep Her (1973, Stax)
*I Believe in You (You Believe in
Me) (1973, Stax)
*I've Been Born Again (1974, Stax)
Disco Lady (1975, Columbia)

Eargasm (1976, Columbia)
The Johnnie Taylor Chronicle (1977,
Stax)
Part Time Love (1980, Charly)
I Shoulda Been a Preacher (1981,
Red Lightnin')

*James Brown (1928-)

Please Please Please (1956,
Federal)
*Try Me (1958, Federal)
*Baby, You're Right (1961, King)
*I Don't Mind (1961, King)
*Mashed Potatoes (1961)
*Night Train (1961, King)
*Think (1961, King)
*Prisoner of Love (1962, King)
*Out of Sight (1964, Smash)
*I Got You (1965, King)
Cold Sweat (1965, King)
*Papa's Got a Brand New Bag (1965,
King)
I Got the Feelin' (1966, King)
*It's a Man's, Man's World (1966,
King)
America Is My Home (1968, King)
Don't Be a Drop-Out (1968, King)
Give It Up or Turn It Loose (1968,
King)
I Don't Want Nobody to Give Me
Nothing (1968, King)
Say It Loud, I'm Black and I'm
Proud (1968, King)
King Heroin (1969, King)
Mother Popcorn (1969, King)
Get Up I Feel Like Being a Sex
Machine (1970, King)
Superbad (1970, King)
Hot Pants (1971, Polydor)

Make It Funky (1971, Polydor)
Talking Loud and Saying Nothing
(1971, Polydor)
Get on the Good Foot (1972,
Polydor)
I Got Ants in My Pants (1973,
Polydor)
The Payback (1974, Polydor)
My Thang (1974, Polydor)
Papa Don't Take No Mess (1974,
Polydor)
It's Too Funky in Here (1979,
Polydor)

*The James Brown Show--Live at the
Apollo*, Vol. 1 (1963, King)
Pure Dynamite! (1964, King)
Unbeatable (1964, King)
Papa's Got a Brand New Bag (1965,
King)
I Got You (I Feel Good) (1966,
King)
It's a Man's World (1966, King)
Soul Classics, Vol. 1 (1972, Polydor)
The Payback (1974, Polydor)
Live/Hot on the One (1980,
Polydor)

Jimmy Jones (1937-)

*Good Timin' (1960, Cub)
*Handy Man (1960, Cub)

Oldies But Goodies, Vol. 7
(Original Sound)

Gene Daniels (1935-)

*A Hundred Pounds of Clay (1961,
Liberty)
*Tower of Strength (1961, Liberty)
*Chip Chip (1962, Liberty)

The Facts of Life (Sunset)

Rufus Thomas (1917-)

Bear Cat (1953, Sun)
*The Dog (1963, Stax)
Do the Funky Penguin (1963, Stax)
*Walking the Dog (1963, Stax)

Do the Funky Chicken (1970, Stax)
Do the Push and Pull (1970, Stax)
The Breakdown (1971, Stax)

May I Have Your Ticket, Please?
    (1964, Stax)
Walking the Dog (1964, Stax)
Funky Chicken (1970, Stax)
Rufus Thomas (1980, Gusto)

*Wilson Pickett (1941-)

I Found Love (1962)
*If You Need Me (1963, Double L)
*It's Too Late (1963, Double L)
*In the Midnight Hour (1964,
    Atlantic)
*Don't Fight It (1965, Atlantic)
*Land of 1,000 Dances (1966,
    Atlantic)
*Mustang Sally (1966, Atlantic)
*634-5789 (1966, Atlantic)
*Funky Broadway (1967, Atlantic)
I'm a Midnight Mover (1968,
    Atlantic)
Cole, Cooke and Redding (1970,
    Atlantic)
Call My Name, I'll Be There (1971,
    Atlantic)
Don't Knock My Love (1971,
    Atlantic)
Don't Let the Green Grass Fool
    You (1971, Atlantic)
Engine Number 9 (1971, Atlantic)
Fire and Water (1971, Atlantic)

The Sound of . . . (Atlantic)
In the Midnight Hour (1965,
    Atlantic)
The Exciting W. Pickett (1966,
    Atlantic)
The Best of . . . (1967, Atlantic)
Wilson Pickett's Greatest Hits (1973,
    Atlantic)

*Otis Redding (1941-67)

*I've Been Loving You Too Long
    (1965, Stax)
*Mr. Pitiful (1965, Stax)

*Respect (1965, Stax)
*Satisfaction (1965, Stax)
Fa-Fa-Fa-Fa-Fa (Sad Song) (1966,
    Stax)
*I Can't Turn You Loose (1966,
    Stax)
*My Lover's Prayer (1966, Stax)
*Try a Little Tenderness (1966, Stax)
*Tramp (1967, Stax)
*(Sitting on) the Dock of the Bay
    (1968, Stax)

Otis Redding Sings Soul (Atlantic)
*The Great Otis Redding Sings Soul
    Ballads* (1965, Volt)
Pain in My Heart (1965, Atlantic)
Dictionary of Soul (1966, Volt)
Otis Blue (1966, Atlantic)
Otis Redding Live in Europe (1966,
    Atco)
The Soul Album (1966, Volt)
History of . . . (1967, Atco)
The Immortal Otis Redding (1968,
    Atco)
*Jimmy Hendrix and Otis Redding at
    Monterey* (1970, Reprise)
Best of . . . (1972, Atco)

*Joe Tex (1933-82)

*Hold What You've Got (1964,
    Atlantic)
*I Want to (Do Everything for You)
    (1965, Atlantic)
*The Love You Save (1965, Atlantic)
*A Sweet Woman Like You (1965,
    Atlantic)
*You Got What It Takes (1965,
    Atlantic)
Skinny Legs and All (1967,
    Atlantic)
I Gotcha (1972, Atlantic)
Ain't Gonna Bump No More (with
    No Big Fat Woman) (1977,
    Epic)

The Best of . . . (1965, Parrot)
Hold On to What You've Got (1965,
    Atlantic)
New Boss (1965, Atlantic)

The Love You Save (1966, Atlantic)

*Sam and Dave

(Sam Moore, 1935- ; Dave Prater, 1937-)

*Hold On! I'm Coming (1966, Stax)
*Said I Wasn't Gonna Tell Nobody (1966, Stax)
*You Don't Know Like I Know (1966, Stax)
*You Got Me Hummin' (1966, Stax)
*Soul Man (1967, Stax)
*When Something Is Wrong with My Baby (1967, Stax)
*I Thank You (1968, Stax)

Double Dynamite (1966, Stax)
Hold On I'm Coming! (1966, Stax)
Soul Men (1967, Stax)
The Best of . . . (1969, Atlantic)
Can't Stand Up for Falling Down (1985, Edsel)

*Percy Sledge (1941-)

*It Tears Me Up (1966, Atlantic)
*Warm and Tender Love (1966, Atlantic)
*When a Man Loves a Woman (1966, Atlantic)
*Out of Left Field (1967, Atlantic)
Sudden Stop (1968, Atlantic)
*Take Time to Know Her (1968, Atlantic)
Any Day Now (1969, Atlantic)
Sunshine (1973, Atlantic)
I'll Be Your Everything (1974, Atlantic)

Warm and Tender Soul (1966, Atlantic)
When a Man Loves a Woman (1966, Atlantic)
The Percy Sledge Way (1967, Atlantic)
Take Time to Know Her (1968, Atlantic)
The Best of . . . (1969, Atlantic)

Two Originals of Percy Sledge (1975, Atlantic)
Percy! (1983, Monument)

Staple Singers

*Heavy Makes You Happy (1971, Stax)
I'll Take You There (1972, Stax)
*Respect Yourself (1972, Stax)
If You're Ready (Come with Me) (1973, Stax)
Let's Do It Again (1974, Stax)

City in the Sky (Stax)
Pray On (Epic)
Uncloudy Day (Vee Jay)
Soul Folk in Action (1968, Stax)
We'll Get Over (1968, Stax)
Heavy Makes You Happy (1971, Stax)
Beatitude: Respect Yourself (1972, Stax)
Be What You Are (1973, Stax)
Great Day (1975, Milestone)

*Isaac Hayes (1938-)

By The Time I Get to Phoenix (1969, Enterprise)
Walk on By (1969, Enterprise)
Never Can Say Goodbye (1971, Enterprise)
*The Theme from Shaft (1971, Stax/Enterprise)
Zeke the Freak (1978, Polydor)
Don't Let Go (1979, Polydor)
Do You Wanna Make Love (1979, Polydor)

Hot Buttered Soul (1969, Enterprise)
Shaft (1971, Enterprise)
Chocolate Chip (1975, ABC)
Enterprise--His Greatest Hits (1980, Stax)

*O.V. Wright

(Overton Vertis Wright, 1939-)

*Ace of Spade (1970,
Backbeat/MCA)

*Eight Men and Four Women (1967,
MCA)
*A Nickel and a Nail/Ace of Spade
(1970, MCA)
*Memphis Unlimited (1973, MCA)

*Ann Peebles (1947-)

Walk Away (1969, Hi)
*I Feel Like Breaking Up
Somebody's Home Tonight
(1971, Hi)
I Pity the Fool (1971, Hi)
99 Pounds (1971, Hi)
*Part Time Love (1971, Hi)
*I'm Gonna Tear Your Playhouse
Down (1972, Hi)
*I Can't Stand the Rain (1974, Hi)

*Part Time Love (1971, Hi)
*Straight from the Heart (1972, Hi)
*I Can't Stand the Rain (1974, Hi)
The Handwriting Is on the Wall
(1975, Hi)

*Sly Johnson (1937-)

Is It Because I'm Black? (1970, Hi)
*Back for a Taste (1973, Hi)
The Love You Left Behind (1973,
Hi)
We Did It (1973, Hi)
*Take Me to the River (1975, Hi)
*I Only Have Your Love (1976, Hi)

*Back for a Taste of Your Love
(1973, Hi)
*Total Explosion (1976, Hi)

*Denise LaSalle

*Trapped by a Thing Called Love
(1971, Westbound)
*Man-Sized Job (1972, Westbound)

*Trapped by a Thing Called Love
(1971, Westbound)
Here I Am Again (1975,
Westbound)

Eddie Floyd (1935-)

*Big Bird (1967, Stax)
*Knock on Wood (1967, Stax)
*Raise Your Hand (1967, Stax)
*Bring It on Home to Me (1968,
Stax)
*I've Never Found a Girl (1968,
Stax)
*California Girl (1970, Stax)

*Knock on Wood (1967, Stax)
*I've Never Found a Girl (1968, Stax)
California Girl (1970, Stax)
*Chronicle (1978, Stax))

*Joe South (1942-)

*Games People Play (1968, Capitol)
*Walk a Mile in My Shoes (1970,
Capitol)

*Introspect/Games People Play (1968,
Capitol)
**Don't It Make You Want to Go
Home* (1969, Capitol)
*Joe South's Greatest Hits (1970,
Capitol)
*So the Seeds are Growing (1971,
Capitol)

CHICAGO

Dee Clark (1938-)

*Just Keep It Up (1959, Abner)
Raindrops (1961, Vee Jay)
Your Friends (1961, Vee Jay)

*14 Golden Recordings from the
Historical Vaults of Vee Jay
Records* (ABC)
Graffiti Gold, Vol. 2 (Vee Jay)
Rock'n'Soul, Vols. 5, 7 (ABC)

*Sam Cooke (1935-64)

*Lovable (1956, Specialty)
*You Send Me (1957, Keen)
Everybody Likes to Cha Cha (1959, Keen)
*Only Sixteen (1959, Keen)
*Chain Gang (1960, ABC)
*Wonderful World (1960, ABC)
*Cupid (1961, RCA)
*Sad Mood (1961, RCA)
*Bring It On Home to Me (1962, RCA)
*Having a Party (1962, RCA)
*Nothing Can Change This Love (1962, RCA)
*Twistin' the Night Away (1962, RCA)
*Another Saturday Night (1963, RCA)
*Frankie and Johnny (1963, RCA)
*Little Red Rooster (1963, RCA)
*Send Me Some Lovin' (1963, RCA)
A Change Is Gonna Come (1964, RCA)
Ain't That Good News (1964, RCA)
Good Times (1964, RCA)
*Shake (1964, RCA)
Somebody Ease My Troubling Mind (1964, RCA)

Golden Sounds of . . . (Trip)
The Gospel Soul of Sam Cook (Speciality)
The Gospel Soul of Sam Cook, Vol. 2 (Speciality)
Songs by . . . (Keene)
That's Heaven to Me (Speciality)
Two Sides of Sam Cooke (Speciality)
The Best of Sam Cooke (1962, RCA)
Live at the Harlem Square Club (1963, RCA)
Ain't That Good News (1964, Speciality)
This Is Sam Cooke (1970, RCA)

The Man and His Music (1986, RCA)

*Brook Benton (1931-)

Rainy Night in Georgia (Cotillion)
A Million Miles from Nowhere (1956, Vik)
Endlessly (1959, Mercury)
*It's Just a Matter of Time (1959, Mercury)
*So Many Ways (1959, Mercury)
Thank You Pretty Baby (1959, Mercury)
Baby (You've Got What It Takes) (1960, Mercury)
A Rockin' Good Way (1960, Mercury)
The Boll Weevil Song (1961, Mercury)
Frankie and Johnny (1961, Mercury)
Lie to Me (1961, Mercury)
Revenge (1961, Mercury)
Think Twice (1961, Mercury)
Shadrack (1962, Mercury)
Hotel Happiness (1963, Mercury)

Golden Hits (1961, Mercury)

*Dinah Washington (1924-63)

Evil Gal Blues (1943, Keynote)
Salty Papa Blues (1943, Keynote)
Baby Get Lost (1949, Mercury)
Trouble in Mind (1952, Mercury)
*What a Diff'rence a Day Makes (1959, Mercury)
*Baby (You've Got What It Takes) (1960, Mercury)
*A Rockin' Good Way (1960, Mercury)
*This Bitter Earth (1960, Mercury)

What a Diff'rence (Mercury)
Dinah Washington Sings Fats Waller (1957, Mercury)
Dinah Washington Sings Bessie Smith (1958, Mercury)
The Two of Us (1960, Mercury)

The Dinah Washington Story (1963, Roulette)

*Al Green (1946-)

Back Up Train (1967, Hot Line Music Journal)
*I Can't Get Next To You (1970, Hi)
*Right Now, Right Now (1970, Hi)
*You Say It (1970, Hi)
*Tired of Being Alone (1971, Hi)
*I'm Still in Love with You (1972, Hi)
It Ain't No Fun for Me (1972, Hi)
*Let's Stay Together (1972, Hi)
*Look What You Done for Me (1972, Hi)
*Old Time Lovin' (1972, Hi)
*You Ought to Be with Me (1972, Hi)
Call Me (Come Back Home) (1973, Hi)
*Sweet Sixteen (1973, Hi)
*Take Me to the River (1973, Hi)
Here I Am (Come and Take Me) (1974, Hi)
Sha La La (Make Me Happy) (1974, Hi)
*L-O-V-E (1975, Hi)
*Love Ritual (1975, Hi)
Love Sermon (1975, Hi)
*Belle (1977, Hi)

Al Green Gets Next to You (1970, Hi)
Green Is Blues (1970, Hi)
I'm Still in Love with You (1972, Hi)
Let's Stay Together (1972, Hi)
Call Me (1973, Hi)
Livin' for You (1973, Hi)
Al Green Explores Your Mind (1974, Hi)
Al Green Is Love (1975, Hi)
Greatest Hits (1975, Hi)
Full of Fire (1976, Hi)
The Belle Album (1977, Hi)
Greatest Hits (1978, Hi)
Truth'n'Time (1978, Hi)

Tokyo . . . Live (1981, Cream)

*Impressions

*For Your Precious Love (1958, VeeJay)
*Gypsy Woman (1961, ABC)
*It's All Right (1963, ABC)
*I'm So Proud (1964, ABC)
*Keep on Pushin' (1964, ABC)
*Talking About My Baby (1964, ABC)
*Amen (1965, ABC)
*People Get Ready (1965, ABC)
*We're a Winner (1968, ABC)
Check Out Your Mind (1971, Curtom)
Ain't Got Time (1972, Curtom)
(Baby) Turn On to Me (1972, Curtom)

The ABC Collection--Curtis Mayfield and the Impressions (ABC)
The Impressions (1964, ABC)
People Get Ready (1965, ABC)
Best of . . . (1968, ABC)
Impressions Sixteen Greatest Hits (1971, ABC)
Vintage Years--The Impressions featuring Jerry Butler and Curtis Mayfield (1976, Sire)

*Curtis Mayfield (1942-) solo

*Freddie's Dead (1972, Curtom)
*Superfly (1972, Curtom)
She Don't Let Nobody (But Me) (1981, Boardwalk)
Toot'n' Toot'n' Toot (1981, Boardwalk)

Curtis Mayfield (Curtom)
Root (Curtom)
Superfly (1972, Curtom)
Let's Do It Again (1975, Curtom)
Love Is the Place (1981, Brunswick)

*Jerry Butler (1939-) solo

*Giving Up Love (1960, Vee Jay)

*He Will Break Your Heart (1960, Vee Jay)
*Hey, Western Union Man (1968, Mercury)
*Never Give You Up (1968, Mercury)
*Lost (1969, Mercury)
*Moody Woman (1969, Mercury)
*Only the Strong Survive (1969, Mercury)
*What's the Use of Breaking Up (1969, Mercury)

All-Time Jerry Butler Hits (Trip)
Sixteen Greatest Hits (Trip)
*Mr. Dream Merchant (1967, Mercury)
*The Ice Man Cometh (1969, Mercury)
*Ice on Ice (1969, Mercury)
*The Best of ... (1970, Mercury)
Ice and Hot (1982, Fountain)

*Betty Everett (1939-)

*Getting Mighty Crowded (1964, Vee Jay)
I Can't Hear You (1964, Vee Jay)
*Let It Be Me (1964, Vee Jay)
*The Shoop Shoop Song (1964, Vee Jay)
*You're No Good (1964, Vee Jay)
I Can't Say No to You (1969, Unicorn)
It's Been a Long Time (1969, Unicorn)
There'll Come a Time (1969, Unicorn)
I Got to Tell Somebody (1971, Fantasy)

Betty Everett Starring ... (Tradition)
*Love Rhymes (1974, Fantasy)
There'll Come a Time (1974, MCA)
Happy Endings (1975, Fantasy)

Billy Stewart (?-1970)

Billy's Blues, Parts 1 and 2 (1957, Chess)

Baby, You're My Only Life (1960, Okeh)
*I Do Love You (1965, Chess); (1969 Chess)
*Fat Boy (1966, Chess)
*Secret Love (1966, Chess)
*Sitting in the Park (1966, Chess)
*Summertime (1966, Chess)
*Every Day I Have the Blues (1967, Chess)

I Do Love You (1965, Chess)
Summertime (1966, Chess)
*Billy Stewart Remembered (1970, Chess)
*The Greatest Sides (1982, Chess)

*Fontella Bass (1940-)

*Rescue Me (1966, Chess)

The "New" Look (1966, Checker)

*Major Lance (1944-)

Delilah (1962, Okeh)
*The Monkey Time (1963, Okeh)
*Um, Um, Um, Um, Um, Um (1964, Okeh)

Rhythm of ... (Okeh)
*The Monkey Time (1963, Okeh)
*Best of ... (1964, Okeh)
*Major's Greatest Hits (1965, Okeh)
*Greatest Hits (1973, Con-Tempo)
Best of ... (1976, Epic)

*Gene Chandler (1940-)

The Girl Is a Devil (1961)
*Duke of Earl (1962, Vee Jay)
*Just Be True (1964, Constellation)
*Good Times (1965, Constellation)
*Nothing Ca Stop Me (1965, Constellation)
*You Can't Hurt Me No More (1965, Constellation)
From the Teacher to the Preacher (1968, Constellation)

*The Two Sides of ... (Brunswick)

Duke of Earl (1962, Vee Jay)
Just Be True (1964, Constellation)
The Duke of Soul (1966, Checker)
The Girl Don't Care (1967, Brunswick)
I'll Make the Living If You Make the Loving Worthwhile (1982, Chi-Sound)

*Tyrone Davis (1938-)

*Can I Change My Mind? (1968, Tangerine)
*Is It Something You've Got? (1969, Dakar)
*Turn Back the Hands of Time (1970, Dakar)
I'll Be Right Here (1971, Dakar)
Let Me Back In (1972, Dakar)
Could I Forget You? (1972, Dakar)

*Can I Change My Mind? (1969, Dakar)
*Turn Back the Hands of Time (1970, Dakar)
*Tyrone Davis' Greatest Hits (1972, Dakar)

*Chi-Lites

*Have You Seen Her? (1971, Brunswick)
*Coldest Days of My Life (1972, Brunswick)
*Oh Girl (1972, Brunswick)
Hot on a Thing (1982, 20th Century)

Half a Love (1961, Brunswick)
*Give It Away (1969, Brunswick)
*Give More Power to the People (1971, Brunswick)
*Greatest Hits/Chi-Lites (1972, Brunswick)
*Lonely Man (1972, Brunswick)
*Greatest Hits, Vol. 2 (1976, Brunswick)
*Happy Being Lonely (1976, Mercury)
Bottom's Up (1983, Larc)

*Otis Clay

*Tryin' to Live My Life without You (1965, One-Der-Ful)

Got to Find a Way (P-Vine)
I Can't Take It (1977, Hi)

*Barbara Acklin (1943-)

*Am I the Same Girl? (1968, Brunswick)
From the Teacher to the Preacher (1968, Brunswick)
*Just Ain't No Love (1968, Brunswick)
*Love Makes a Woman (1968, Brunswick)
*I Did It (1970, Brunswick)

*Great Soul Hits of . . . (Brunswick)
*Love Makes a Woman (1968, Brunswick)
Seven Days of Night (1969, Brunswick)
I Did It (1970, Brunswick)
Someone Else's Arms (1970, Brunswick)

DETROIT

*Jackie Wilson (1934-84)

*Relet Petite (1956, Brunswick)
*Lonely Teardrops (1958, Brunswick)
*To Be Loved (1958, Brunswick)
Talk That Talk (1959, Brunswick)
That's Why (1959, Brunswick)
You Better Know It (1959, Brunswick)
All My Love (1960, Brunswick)
Am I the Man (1960, Brunswick)
Alone at Last (1960, Brunswick)
*Doggin' Around (1960, Brunswick)
*Night (1960, Brunswick)
*A Woman, a Lover, a Friend (1960, Brunswick)
*My Empty Arms (1961, Brunswick)

*Baby Workout (1963, Brunswick)
*Whispers (1966, Brunswick)
(Your Love Keeps Lifting Me)
  Higher and Higher (1966,
  Brunswick)

Higher and Higher (Brunswick)
Nostalgia (Brunswick)
Jackie Wilson Sings the Blues (1960,
  Brunswick)
My Golden Favorites (1960,
  Brunswick)
My Golden Favorites, Vol. 2 (1960,
  Brunswick)
Jackie Wilson's Greatest Hits (1972,
  Brunswick)
The Jackie Wilson Story (1983,
  Brunswick)

Marv Johnson (1938-)

*You Got What It Takes (1959,
  United Artists)
*I Love the Way You Love (1960,
  United Artists)

*Della Reese (1932-)

Don't You Know (1959)

Amen!, (Jubilee)
Classic Della (RCA)

MOTOWN

*Marvelettes

*Please Mr. Postman (1961, Tamla)
*Beechwood 4-5789 (1962, Tamla)
*Someday, Someway (1963, Tamla)
*Strange I Know (1963, Tamla)
*Playboy (1964, Tamla)
*Danger Heartbreak Dead Ahead
  (1965, Tamla)
*I'll Keep Holding On (1965, Tamla)
*Too Many Fish in the Sea (1965,
  Tamla)
*Don't Mess with Bill (1966, Tamla)

*The Hunter Gets Captured by the
  Game (1967, Tamla)
*My Baby Must Be a Magician
  (1967, Tamla)
*Destination: Anywhere (1968,
  Tamla)
*Here I Am Baby (1968, Tamla)

Greatest Hits (1966, Tamla)
Marvelettes (1967, Tamla)
Anthology (1975, Tamla)

*Contours

*Whole Lotta Woman (1961, Gordy)
*Do You Love Me? (1962, Gordy)
Shake Sherry (1963, Gordy)
Can You Jerk Like Me? (1965,
  Gordy)
The Day When She Needed Me
  (1965, Gordy)
First I Look at the Purse (1965,
  Gordy)
Just a Little Misunderstanding
  (1966, Gordy)
It's So Hard Being a Loser (1967,
  Gordy)

Do You Love Me? (1981, Gordy)
The Contours (1981, Gordy)

*Smokey Robinson and the Miracles

(Smokey Robinson, 1940-)

*Got a Job (1958, Motown)
Bad Girl (1959, Motown)
*I've Been Good to You (1959,
  Tamla)
*You Can Depend on Me (1959,
  Tamla)
*Shop Around (1960, Tamla)
*I'll Try Something New (1962,
  Tamla)
*What's So Good About Goodbye?
  (1962, Tamla)
*Mickey's Monkey (1963, Tamla)
*You Really Got a Hold On Me
  (1963, Tamla)

*Come On and Do the Jerk (1964, Tamla)
*Ooo Baby Baby (1965, Tamla)
*The Tracks of My Tears (1965, Tamla)
*Going to a Go-Go (1966, Tamla)
*I Second That Emotion (1967, Tamla)
*More Love (1967, Tamla)
*Baby Baby Don't Cry (1969, Tamla)
*The Tears of a Clown (1970, Tamla)

*Greatest Hits from the Beginning (1965, Tamla)
*Greatest Hits, Vol. 2 (1968, Tamla)
*Anthology (1974, Motown)
*Away We A-Go-Go (1981, Motown)
*Doing Mickey's Monkey (1981, Motown)

*Smokey Robinson solo

*Baby, That's Backatcha (1974, Tamla)
*Virgin Man (1974, Tamla)
*Cruisin (1979, Tamla)
*Heavy on Pride (Light on Love) (1980, Tamla)
*Into Each Rain Some Life Must Fall (1980, Tamla)
*Let Me Be the Clock (1980, Tamla)
*Melody Man (1980, Tamla)
*Wine, Woman and Song (1980, Tamla)
*Being with You (1981, Tamla)

Pure Smokey (1974, Tamla)
A Quiet Storm (1974, Tamla)
Where There's Smoke (1979, Tamla)
Being with You (1981, Tamla)
*One Heartbeat (1987, Motown)

*Miracles

*Do It Baby (1974, Tamla)
*Don't Cha Love It (1974, Tamla)
*Love Machine, Part 1 (1976, Tamla)

Renaissance (1973, Tamla)
Don't Cha Love It (1975, Tamla)

Love Crazy (1977, Tamla)
Miracles Greatest Hits (1977, Tamla)

*Barrett Strong (1941-)

*Money (1960, Motown)

Live and Love (1976, Capitol)

*Marvin Gaye (1939-84)

Mama Loocie (1959, Chess)
*Stubborn Kind of Fellow (1962, Tamla)
*Can I Get a Witness (1963, Tamla)
*Hitch Hike (1963, Tamla)
*Pride and Joy (1963, Tamla)
*You're a Wonderful One (1963, Tamla)
*Baby Don't You Do It (1964, Tamla)
Once Upon a Time (1964, Tamla)
What's the Matter with You (1964, Tamla)
*Ain't That Peculiar (1965, Tamla)
*I'll Be Doggone (1965, Tamla)
*Ain't No Mountain High Enough (1967, Tamla)
It Takes Two (1967, Tamla)
*Your Precious Love (1967, Tamla)
*Ain't Nothing Like the Real Thing (1968, Tamla)
*I Heard It through the Grapevine (1968, Tamla)
*You're All I Need to Get By (1968, Tamla)
*Mercy Mercy Me [Ecology] (1971, Tamla)
*What's Going On? (1971, Tamla)
*Let's Get It On (1973, Tamla)
Trouble Man (1973, Tamla)
You're a Special Part of Me (1973, Tamla)
Don't Knock My Love (1974, Tamla)
My Mistake (Was to Love You) (1974, Tamla)
*Got to Give It Up, Part 1 (1977, Tamla)

*Sexual Healing (1982, Columbia)

*Soulful Mood (1961, Tamla)

*Marvin Gaye's Greatest Hits (1964, Tamla)

*Super Hits (1970, Tamla)

*What's Going On? (1971, Tamla)

*Let's Get It On (1973, Tamla)

*Anthology (1974, Tamla)

Greatest Hits (1976, Tamla)

Here My Dear (1978, Tamla)

*Motown Superstar Series, Vol. 15 (1981, Tamla)

M.P.G. (1981, Tamla)

*Midnight Love (1982, Columbia)

*Dream of a Lifetime (1985, Columbia)

Marvin Gaye with Tammi Terrell (Tammi Terrell, 1946-1970)

*Motown Superstar Series, Vol. 2: Marvin Gaye and Tammi Terrell (1980, Tamla)

Greatest Hits (1981, Tamla)

United (1981, Tamla)

You're All I Need (1981, Tamla)

Temptations

*Temptations with David Ruffin (David Ruffin, 1941-)

Dream Come True (1962, Gordy)

*The Way You Do the Things You Do (1964, Gordy)

*Don't Look Back (1965, Gordy)

*It's Growing (1965, Gordy)

*My Girl (1965, Gordy)

*Since I Lost My Baby (1965, Gordy)

*Ain't Too Proud to Beg (1966, Gordy)

*Beauty's Only Skin Deep (1966, Gordy)

*Get Ready (1966, Gordy)

*(I Know) I'm Losing You (1966, Gordy)

*All I Need (1967, Gordy)

*You're My Everything (1967, Gordy)

*Loneliness Made Me Realize It's That I Need (1967, Gordy)

Temptations with Dennis Edwards (Dennis Edwards, 1943-)

*Cloud Nine (1968, Gordy)

*I Could Never Love Another (After Loving You) (1968, Gordy)

*I Wish It Would Rain (1968, Gordy)

*Please Return Your Love to Me (1968, Gordy)

*Don't Let the Loneliness Get You Down (1969, Gordy)

*Psychedelic Shack (1969, Gordy)

*Run Away Child, Running Wild (1969, Gordy)

*Ball of Confusion (1970, Gordy)

*Just My Imagination (Running Away with Me) (1971, Gordy)

Temptations

Hey Girl (I Like Your Style) (Gordy)

*Papa Was a Rollin' Stone (1972, Gordy)

Masterpiece (1973, Gordy)

The Plastic Man (1973, Gordy)

Power (1980, Gordy)

Standing on the Top (1982, Gordy)

*Meet the Temptations (1964, Gordy)

*Temptations' Greatest Hits, Vol. 1 (1966, Gordy)

*In a Mellow Mood (1967, Gordy)

Anthology with Diana Ross and the Supremes (1968, Motown)

*Temptations' Greatest Hits, Vol. 2 (1970, Gordy)

*Masterpiece (1973, Gordy)

*Anthology (1977, Motown)

*The Temptations Sing Smokey (1979, Gordy)

David Ruffin solo

I'm So Glad I Feel You (1969, Motown)

I've Lost Everything I've Ever Loved (1969, Motown)

*My Whole World Ended (The Moment You Left Me) (1969, Motown)

Everything's Come Up Love (1976, Motown)

Heavy Love (1976, Motown)

Walk Away from Love (1976, Motown)

Break My Heart (1979, Motown)

David Ruffin at His Best (1978, Motown)

My Whole World Ended (1981, Motown)

Eddie Kendricks (1939-) solo

Can I (1971, Tamla)

It's So Hard for Me to Say Goodbye (1971, Tamla)

Eddie's Love (1972, Tamla)

If You Let Me (1972, Tamla)

Darling Come Back Home (1973, Tamla)

Girl You Need a Change of Mind (1973, Tamla)

*Keep On Truckin' (1973, Tamla)

*Boogie Down (1974, Tamla)

One Tear (1974, Tamla)

Son of Sagittarius (1974, Tamla)

Tell Her Love Has Felt the Need (1974, Tamla)

Get the Cream off the Top (1975, Tamla)

Happy (1975, Tamla)

Shoeshine Boy (1975, Tamla)

He's a Friend (1976, Tamla)

Ain't No Smoke without Fire (1978, Arista)

Intimate Friends (1978, Tamla)

Eddie Kendricks at His Best (1978, Tamla)

Motown Superstar Series, Vol. 19 (1981, Motown)

*Mary Wells (1943-)**

*Bye Bye Baby (1961, Motown)

*The One Who Really Loves You (1962, Motown)

*Two Lovers (1962, Motown)

*You Beat Me to the Punch (1962, Motown)

*Laughing Boy (1963, Motown)

*What's Easy for Two Is So Hard for One (1963, Motown)

*You Lost the Sweetest Boy (1963, Motown)

*Your Old Stand By (1963, Motown)

*My Guy (1964, Motown)

*Once Upon a Time (1964, Motown)

*What's the Matter with You Baby (1964, Motown)

*Dear Lover (1966, Atco)

Dig the Way I Feel (1969, Jubilee)

Bye Bye Baby (1961, Motown)

One Who Really Loves You (1962, Motown)

Mary Well's Greatest Hits (1963, Motown)

Lamont Dozier (1941-)

Bigger Than Life (1985, Demon)

Four Tops

Kiss Me Baby (1956, Chess)

*Baby I Need Your Loving (1964, Motown)

*Ask the Lonely (1965, Motown)

*I Can't Help Myself (Sugar Pie, Honey Bunch) (1965, Motown)

*Same Old Song (1965, Motown)

Without the One You Love (1965, Motown)

*Reach Out I'll Be There (1966, Motown)

*Bernadette (1967, Motown)

*Seven Rooms of Gloom (1967, Motown)

*Standing in the Shadows of Love (1967, Motown)

Love Child (1968, Motown)

I'm Living in Shame (1969,
  Motown)
*Still Waters (Love) (1970, Motown)
*Keeper of the Castle (1972, ABC)
*Ain't No Woman Like the One I've
  Got (1973, ABC)
*When She was My Girl (1981,
  ABC)

Four Tops Greatest Hits (1967,
  Motown)
Reach Out (1967, Motown)
Anthology (1974, Motown)
Motown Superstar Series, Vol. 14
  (1981, Motown)
  The Four Tops (1982, Motown)

*Supremes

(Diana Ross, 1944-)

Let Me Go the Right Way (1962,
  Motown)
When the Lovelight Starts Shining
  through His Eyes (1963,
  Motown)
*Baby Love (1964, Motown)
*Come See About Me (1964,
  Motown)
*Where Did Our Love Go? (1964,
  Motown)
*Back in My Arms Again (1965,
  Motown)
*I Hear a Symphony (1965, Motown)
*Stop! In the Name of Love (1965,
  Motown)
*You Can't Hurry Love (1966,
  Motown)
*You Keep Me Hangin' On (1966,
  Motown)
*The Happening (1967, Motown)
*Love Is Here and Now You're Gone
  (1967, Motown)
*Reflections (1967, Motown)
*I'm Gonna Make You Love Me
  (1968, Motown)
*Love Child (1968, Motown)
  I'll Try Something New (1969,
  Motown)

I'm Living in Shame (1969,
  Motown)
*Someday We'll Be Together (1969,
  Motown)

*Anthology: Diana Ross and the
  Supremes* (1974, Motown)

Supremes without Diana Ross

Stoned Love (1970, Motown)
Up the Ladder to the Roof (1970,
  Motown)
Nathan Jones (1971, Motown)
Floy Joy (1972, Motown)
You're My Drivin Wheel (1976,
  Motown)

Meet the Supremes (1966, Motown)
Supremes A Go-Go (1966, Motown)
*Supremes Sing Holland-Dozier-
  Holland* (1967, Motown)
Motown Superstar Series, Vol. 1
  (1981, Motown)

*Martha and the Vandellas

(Martha Reeves, 1941-)

I'll Have to Let Him Go (1960,
  Gordy)
*Come and Get These Memories
  (1963, Gordy)
*Heat Wave (1963, Gordy)
*Quicksand (1963, Gordy)
*Dance Party (1964, Gordy)
*Dancing in the Streets (1964,
  Gordy)
*Nowhere to Run (1965, Gordy)
*I'm Ready for Love (1966, Gordy)
Watch Out (1966, Gordy)
*Honey Chile (1967, Gordy)
*Jimmy Mack (1967, Gordy)

Come and Get These Memories
  (1963, Gordy)
Heat Wave (1963, Gordy)
Anthology (1974, Gordy)
Motown Superstar Series, Vol. 2
  (1981, Gordy)

*Gladys Knight and the Pips

(Gladys Knight, 1944-)

Every Beat of My Heat (1961,
  Fury)
Letter Full of Tears (1961, Fury)
*Everybody Needs Love (1967,
  Motown)
*Heard It Though the Grapevine
  (1967, Motown)
*The End of Our Road (1968,
  Motown)
*Nitty Gritty (1968, Motown)
*Friendship Train (1969, Motown)
*I Don't Want to Do Wrong (1970,
  Motown)
*If I Were Your Woman (1970,
  Motown)
*Neither One of Us (Wants to Be the
  First to Say Goodbye) (1970,
  Motown)
*Midnight Train to Georgia (1973,
  Buddah)
*Best Thing That Ever Happened to
  Me (1974, Buddah)
*I've Got to Use My Imagination
  (1974, Buddah)
On and On (1974, Buddah)
Landlord (1980, Columbia)
Save the Overtime (1983,
  Columbia)

Early Hits (Springboard)
Gladys Knight and the Pips (Trip)
Gladys Knight and the Pips (Up
  Front)
How Do You Say Goodbye
  (Springboard)
Everybody Needs Love (1967, Soul)
Feelin' Bluesy (1968, Soul)
Nitty Gritty (1969, Soul)
If I Were Your Woman (1970, Soul)
Neither One of Us (1972, Soul)
Anthology (1974, Buddah)
Imagination (1974, Buddah)
*Gladys Knight and the Pip's Greatest
  Hits* (1976, Buddah)

Motown Superstar Series, Vol. 13
  (1980, Motown)

*Junior Walker (1942-)

*Do the Boomerang (1965, Soul)
*Shake and Fingerpop (1965, Soul)
*Shotgun (1965, Soul)
*How Sweet It Is (To be Loved by
  You) (1966, Soul)
*I'm a Road Runner (1966, Soul)
*Come See About Me (1967, Soul)
*Pucker Up Buttercup (1967, Soul)
*Hip City, Part 2 (1968, Soul)
*These Eyes (1969, Soul)
*What Does It Take (To Win Your
  Love) (1969, Soul)
*Do You See My Love (for You
  Growing) (1970, Soul)
*Gotta Hold on to This Feeling
  (1970, Soul)
*Walk in the Night (1972, Soul)

Shotgun (1965, Pickwick)
Road Runner (1966, Soul)
Home Cooking (1967, Soul)
Greatest Hits (1969, Soul)
These Eyes (1969, Soul)
A Gassss (1970, Soul)
Rainbow Funk (1971, Soul)
Anthology (1974, Soul)
Motown Superstar Series, Vol. 5
  (1981, Motown)

*Stevie Wonder (1950-)

*Castles in the Sand (1963, Tamla)
*Fingertrips Pt.2 (1963, Tamla)
*Up-Tight (1965, Tamla)
*Blowin' in the Wind (1966, Tamla)
*I Was Made to Love Her (1967,
  Tamla)
*For Once in My Life (1968, Tamla)
*A Place in the Sun (1968, Tamla)
*Shoo-Be-Doo-Be-Doo-Da-Day
  (1968, Tamla)
*My Cherie Amour (1969, Tamla)
*Yester-Me, Yester-You, Yesterday
  (1969, Tamla)
*Heaven Help Us All (1970, Tamla)

*If You Really Love Me (1970, Tamla)
*Signed, Sealed, Delivered I'm Yours (1970, Tamla)
*Higher Ground (1973, Tamla)
*Living for the City (1973, Tamla)
*Superstition (1973, Tamla)
*You Are the Sunshine of My Life (1973, Tamla)
*Boogie On Reggae Woman (1974, Tamla)
*You Haven't Done Nothin' (1974, Tamla)
*I Wish (1976, Tamla)
*Sir Duke (1976, Tamla)
*Happy Birthday (1980, Tamla)
*Master Blaster (1980, Tamla)
*Do I Do (1982, Tamla)
*Ebony and Ivory (1982, Tamla)
*That Girl (1982, Tamla)
*I Just Called to Say I Love You (1985, Tamla)

*The Twelve-Year-Old Genius (1966, Tamla)
*Uptight (1966, Tamla)
*Down to Earth (1967, Tamla)
*I Was Made to Love Her (1967, Tamla)
*For Once in My Life (1968, Tamla)
*Stevie Wonder's Greatest Hits (1968, Tamla)
*Signed, Sealed, and Delivered (1970, Tamla)
*Stevie Wonder's Greatest Hits, Vol. 2 (1971, Tamla)
*Music on My Mind (1972, Tamla)
*Talking Book (1972, Tamla)
*Innervisions (1973, Tamla)
*Fulfillingness' First Finale (1974, Tamla)
*Songs in the Key of Life (1976, Tamla)
*Looking Back (1977, Tamla)
Journey through the Secret Life of Planets (1979, Tamla)
*Hotter Than July (1980, Tamla)
*Stevie Wonder's Original Musiquarium 1 (1982, Tamla)

The Woman in Red (1985, Tamla)

*Jackson Five

*ABC (1969, Motown)
 Big Boy (1969
*I Want You Back (1969, Motown)
*I'll Be There (1970, Motown)
*The Love You Save (1970, Motown)
*Mama's Pearl (1971, Motown)
*Maybe Tomorrow (1971, Motown)
*Never Can Say Goodbye (1971, Motown)
*Sugar Daddy (1971, Motown)
*Corner of the Sky (1972, Motown)
*Little Bitty Pretty One (1972, Motown)
*Lookin' through the Windows (1972, Motown)
*Dancing Machine (1974, Motown)
*I Am Love (1975, Motown)

*I Want You Back (1969, Motown)
*Third Album (1970, Motown)
*ABC (1971, Motown)
Motown Superstar Series, Vol. 12 (1980, Motown)
*Anthology (1981, Motown)
*Greatest Hits (1981, Motown)
Victory Tour (1985, Epic)

*Jacksons

*Enjoy Yourself (1976, Epic)
*Show You the Way to Go (1977, Epic)
*Shake Your Body (Down to the Ground) (1979, Epic)
*Heartbreak Hotel (1980, Epic)
*Lovely One (1980, Epic)

*Destiny (1978, Epic)
*Triumph (1980, Epic)

*Michael Jackson (1958-)

*Got to Be There (1971, Epic)
*I Wanna Be Where You Are (1971, Epic)

*Ben (1972, Epic)
*Rockin' Robin (1972, Epic)
*Don't Stop Till You Get Enough
  (1979, Epic)
*Rock with You (1979, Epic)
*She's Out of My Life (1979, Epic)
*Off the Wall (1980, Epic)
*The Girl Is Mine (1982, Epic)
*Beat It (1983, Epic)
*Billie Jean (1983, Epic)

*The Best of ... (1975, Motown)
Off the Wall (1979, Epic)
Motown Superstar Series, Vol. 7
  (1980, Motown)
*Ben (1981, Motown)
*Got to Be There (1981, Motown)
*E.T. Narrated by Michael Jackson
  (1982, MCA)
*Thriller (1982, Epic)
*Bad (1987, Epic)

Jermaine Jackson (1954-)

Daddy's Home (1973, Motown)
Let's Get Serious (1980, Motown)

*My Name Is Jermaine (1976,
  Motown)
*Feel the Fire (1977, Motown)
Frontiers (1978, Motown)
Jermaine (1980, Motown)
Let's Get Serious (1980, Motown)
I Like Your Style (1981, Motown)
Let Me Tickle Your Fancy (1982,
  Motown)
Jermaine Jackson (1984, Arista)

Anthology

*Motown Story (Motown)

NEW YORK

*Clyde McPhatter (1933-72)

Seven Days (1956, Atlantic)
*Treasure of Love (1956, Atlantic)

Just to Hold My Hand (1957,
  Atlantic)
*Long Lonely Nights (1957, Atlantic)
Without Love (There Is Nothing)
  (1957, Atlantic)
*A Lover's Question (1958, Atlantic)
Ta Ta (1960, MGM)
Lover Please (1962, Mercury)
Little Bitty Retty (1963, Mercury)

*Welcome Home (Decca)
*Treasure of Love (1980, Atlantic)

*Roy Hamilton (1929-69)

You'll Never Walk Alone (1954,
  Epic)
*Everybody's Got a Home (1955,
  Epic)
*Unchained Melody (1955, Epic)
*Without a Song (1955, Epic)
*Don't Let Go (1958, Epic)
*Pledging My Love (1958, Epic)
*I Need Your Lovin (1959, Epic)
You Can Have Her (1961, Epic)

*Solomon Burke (1936-)

*Just Out of Reach (1961, Atlantic)
*Cry to Me (1962, Atlantic)
*If You Need Me (1963, Atlantic)
Everybody Needs Somebody to
  Love (1964, Atlantic)
Cry to Me (1964, Atlantic)
You Can Make It If You Try (1964,
  Atlantic)
Got to Get You off My Mind
  (1965, Atlantic)
Tonight's the Night (1965, Atlantic)

*Rock'n'Soul (1964, Atlantic)
*The Best of ... (1965, Atlantic)
*Sidewalks, Fences and Walls (1979,
  Infinity)
*From the Heart (1980, Charly)

Aretha Franklin (1942-)

*Today I Sing the Blues (1960, Col.)
*Operation Heartbreak (1961, Col.)

*Rock-a-bye Your Baby with a Dixie
  Melody (1961, Col.)
*Won't Be Long (1961, Col.)
*Baby I Love You (1967, Atlantic)
*I Never Loved a Man (the Way I
  Love You) (1967, Atlantic)
*Respect (1967, Atlantic)
*Chain of Fools (1968, Atlantic)
*The House That Jack Built (1968,
  Atlantic)
*Say a Little Prayer (1968, Atlantic)
*See Saw (1968, Atlantic)
*Since You've Been Gone (Sweet
  Sweet Baby) (1968, Atlantic)
*Think (1968, Atlantic)
  Don't Play That Song (1970,
  Atlantic)
  Bridge over Troubled Water (1971,
  Atlantic)
  Rock Steady (1971, Atlantic)
  Spanish Harlem (1971, Atlantic)
  Day Dreaming (1972, Atlantic)
  Until You Come Back to Me
  (That's What I'm Gonna Do)
  (1974, Atlantic)
  Love All the Hurt Away (1981,
  Arista)
  Jump to It (1982, Arista)

Aretha (1961, Columbia)
The Electrifying A. Franklin (1962,
  Columbia)
Laughing on the Outside (1963,
  Columbia)
The Great Aretha Franklin (1964,
  Columbia)
Unforgettable (1964, Columbia)
*I Never Loved a Man (the Way I
  Love You)* (1967, Atlantic)
Aretha's Gold (1969, Atlantic)
  Spirit in the Dark (1970, Atlantic)
Aretha's Greatest Hits (1971,
  Atlantic)
Amazing Grace (1972, Atlantic)
Young, Gifted and Black (1972,
  Atlantic)
  Best of . . . (1973, Atlantic)
  Ten Years of Gold (1977, Atlantic)

Love All the Hurt Away (1981,
  Arista)
Jump to It (1982, Arista)
Who's Zoomin' Who? (1985, Arista)
30 Greatest Hits (1987, Atlantic)

*Isley Brothers

*Shout (1959, RCA)
*Twist and Shout (1962, Wand)
  Testify (1964, T-Neck)
*This Old Heart of Mine (1966,
  Tamla)
*It's Your Thing (1969, T-Neck)
  I Turned You On (1969, T-Neck)
  Pop That Thang (1972, T-Neck)
*That Lady, Part 1 (1973, T-Neck)
*Fight the Power, Part 1 (1975, T-
  Neck)

In the Beginning (1971, T-Neck)
Forever Gold (1972, T-Neck)
3 Plus 3 (1973, T-Neck)
The Heat Is On (1975, T-Neck)
  Rock around the Clock (1975,
  Camden)
  The Very Best of . . . (1975, United
  Artists)
The Best of . . . (1978, Buddah)
Motown Superstar Series, Vol. 6
  (1981, Motown)

*Nina Simone (1933-)

*I Love You Porgy (1959,
  Bethlehem)
*Put a Spell on You (1964, Philips)
*Four Women (1969, Philips)

The Finest of . . . (Bethlehem)
Nina at Newport (1961, Colpix)
The Best of . . . (1969, Philips)
The Best of . . . (1970, RCA)
Here Comes the Sun (1971, RCA)
  Baltimore (1978, CTI)

*Jackie Moore (1945-)

*Precious Precious (1971, Atlantic)

Make Me Feel Like a Woman
(Kayvette)

*Dyke and the Blazers

*Funky Broadway (1967, Original
   Sound)

Dyke's Greatest Hits (Original
   Sound)
Funky Broadway (1967, Original
   Sound)

Chairman of the Board

It Will Stand (1961, Minit)
*Give Me Just a Little More Time
   (1970, Invictus)
*Pay to the Piper (1970, Invictus)

Give Me Just a Little More Time
   (1970, Invictus)
Greatest Hits (1973, Invictus)

Freda Payne (1945-)

*Band of Gold (1970, Hot Wax)
Deeper and Deeper (1970, Hot
   Wax)
*Bring the Boys Home (1971, Hot
   Wax)
Cherish What Is Dear to You
   (While It's Near to You) (1971,
   Hot Wax)
You Brought the Joy (1971, Hot
   Wax)

Band of Gold (1970, Invictus)
The Best of . . . (1972, Invictus)

NEW ORLEANS

*King Floyd (1945-)

*Groove Me (1971, Chimneyville)
*King Floyd (1971, Cotillion)
*I Feel Like Dynamite (1977,
   Chimneyville)

King Floyd (1971, Cotillion)
Well Done (1977, Chimneyville)

LOS ANGELES

*Bobby Day (1934-)

Buzz Buzz Buzz (1957, Class)
Little Bitty Pretty One (1957, Class)
*Over and Over (1958, Class)

Rockin' Robin (1958, Class)
Oldies But Goodies, Vols. 5, 9
   (Original Sound)

*Ed Townsend

For Your Love (1958, Capitol)

*Ted Taylor (1917-75)

*Keep Walking On (1958, Ebb)
Be Ever Wonderful (1961, Okeh)
*Rambling Rose (1961, Okeh)
Days Are Dark (1968, Ronn)
*Strangest Feeling (1968, Ronn)
*Legendary Sun Performers (1978,
   Charly)

Keep Walkin' On (Charly)
Shades of Blue (1969, Ronn)
You Can Dig It (1970, Ronn)
Taylor Made (1973, Ronn)
Keepin' My Head above Water
   (1978, MCA)

*Etta James (1938-)

*At Last (1961, Chess)
Trust in Me (1961, Chess)
*Something's Got a Hold on Me
   (1962, Chess)
Stop the Wedding (1962, Chess)
Pay Back (1963, Chess)
*Pushover (1963, Chess)
Two Sides to Every Story (1963,
   Chess)
Would It Make Any Difference to
   You (1963, Chess)
*Baby What You Want Me to Do?
   (1964, Chess)
Loving You More Every Day (1964,
   Chess)

*Tell Mama (1967, Chess)
*Losers and Weepers (1970, Chess)
*I've Found a Love (1972, Chess)

At Last (1961, Cadet)
Tell Mama (1968, Cadet)
Peaches (1971, Chess)
Deep in the Night (1978, Warner
  Bros.)

Honey Cone

Girls It Ain't Easy (1969, Hot Wax)
While You're Out Looking for
  Sugar (1969, Hot Wax)
One Monkey Don't Stop No Show,
  Part 1 (1971, Hot Wax)
Stick Up (1971, Hot Wax)
*Want Ads (1971, Hot Wax)
The Day I Found Myself (1972, Hot
  Wax)
Sittin' on a Time Bomb (Waitin' for
  the Hurt to Come (1972, Hot
  Wax)

Soulful Tapestry (1971, Hot Wax)
Sweet Replies (1971, Hot Wax)

MIAMI

*Betty Wright (1953-)

Paralyzed (1964, Alston)
*Girls Can't Do What the Guys Do
  (1966, T.K.)
*Clean Up Woman (1971, Alston)
Where Is the Love (1975, Alston)

My First Time Around (1968, Atco)
I Love the Way You Love Me (1971,
  Alston)
Danger: High Voltage (1974,
  Alston)

PHILADELPHIA

*Garnet Mimms and the Enchanters

(Garnet Mimms, 1937-)

*Baby Don't You Weep (1963,
  United Artists)
*Cry Baby (1963, United Artists)
*For Your Precious Love (1963,
  United Artists)
A Quiet Place (1964, United
  Artists)

Garnet Mimms solo

Look Away (1964, United Artists)
One Girl (1964, United Artists)
Tell Me Baby (1964, United
  Artists)
A Little Bit of Soap (1965, United
  Artists)
I'll Take Good Care of You (1966,
  United Artists)

Mimms and the Truckin' Co.

What Is It (1977, Arista)

*Intruders

All the Time (1964, Musicor)
*Devil With Angel's Smile (1966,
  Gamble)
*We'll Be United (1966, Gamble)
*Baby, I'm Lonely (1967, Gamble)
*A Love That's Real (1967, Gamble)
*Together (1967, Gamble)
*Cowboys to Girls (1968, Gamble)
*Love Is Like a Baseball Game
  (1968, Gamble)
*Slow Drag (1969, Gamble)
*Sad Girl (1970, Gamble)
*When We Get Married (1972,
  Gamble)
*(Win, Place, or Show) She's a
  Winner (1972, Gamble)
*I'll Always Love My Mama (1975,
  Gamble)

Intruders Super Hits (1973, Gamble)
Save the Children (1973, TSOP)

*Delfonics

He Don't Really Love You (1967)
*La La Means I Love You (1968, Philly Groove)
Break Your Promise (1969, Philly Groove)
I'm Sorry (1969, Philly Groove)
Ready or Not, Here I Come (1969, Philly Groove)
You Get Yours and I'll Get Mine (1969, Philly Groove)
*Didn't I Blow Your Mind (This Time) (1970, Philly Groove)

La La Means I Love You (1968, Philly Groove)
The Sound of Sexy Soul (1969, Philly Groove)
The Delfonics (1971, Philly Groove)

*O'Jays

Lipstick Traces (1965, Imperial)
*Stand in for Love (1966, Imperial)
*I'll Be Sweeter Tomorrow (1967, Minit)
*One Night Affair (1969, Neptune)
*Looky Looky (Look at Me, Girl) (1970, Neptune)
*Back Stabbers (1972, Philadelphia International)
*Love Train (1973, Philadelphia International)
*Give the People What They Want (1975, Phil)
*Darlin' Darlin' Baby (1976, Philadelphia International)
*Livin' for the Weekend (1976, Philadelphia International)
*Message in Our Music (1976, Philadelphia International)
*Stairway to Heaven (1976, Philadelphia International)
*Used to Be My Girl (1978, Philadelphia International)

Comin' Through (1965, Imperial)
Soul Sounds (1967, Minit)
Back Stabbers (1972, Philadelphia International)
Ship Ahoy (1973, Philadelphia International)
Family Reunion (1975, Philadelphia International)
I Love Music, Part 1 (1975, Philadelphia International)

*Harold Melvin and The Blue Notes

If You Love Me (1960s, Josie)
*If You Don't Know Me By Now (1972, Philadelphia International)
*I Miss You (1972, Philadelphia International)
*The Love I Lost (1973, Philadelphia International)
*Satisfaction Guaranteed (1974, Philadelphia International)
*Where Are All My Friends (1974, Philadelphia International)
*Bad Luck (1975, Philadelphia International)
*Hope That We Can Be Together Soon (1975, Philadelphia International)
*Tell the World How I Feel About 'Cha Baby (1976, Philadelphia International)
*Wake Up Everybody (1976, Philadelphia International)

Blue Notes without Teddy Pendergrass

Reaching for the World (1977, ABC)
Prayin' (1979, Source)

Harold Melvin and the Blue Notes (1972, Philadelphia International)
Black and Blue (1973, Philadelphia International)

To Be True (1975, Philadelphia
International)
Wake Up Everybody (1975,
Philadelphia International)
Collector's Item (1976, Philadelphia
International)

*Teddy Pendergrass (1950-)

*I Don't Love You Anymore (1977,
Philadelphia International)
*Close the Door (1978, Philadelphia
International)
*Turn Off the Lights (1979,
Philadelphia International)
*Feel the Fire (1980, Philadelphia
International)
*Love TKO (1980, Philadelphia
International)
*Two Hearts (1980, Philadelphia
International)
*You're My Latest, My Greatest
Inspiration (1982, Philadelphia
International)

Teddy Pendergrass (1977,
Philadelphia International)
Life Is a Song Worth Singing (1978,
Philadelphia International)

*Billy Paul (1934-)

*Me and Mrs. Jones (1972,
Philadelphia International)
*Am I Black Enough for You (1973,
Philadelphia International)
*Thanks for Saving My Life (1974,
Philadelphia International)
*Let's Make a Baby (1976,
Philadelphia International)

Going East (1971, Philadelphia
International)
360 Degrees of . . . (1972,
Philadelphia International)

*Stylistics

*You're a Big Girl Now (1968,
Sebring)

*Stop, Look, Listen (to Your Heart)
(1971, Avco)
*You Are Everything (1971, Avco)
*Betcha By Gooly Wow (1972, Avco)
*I'm Stone In Love with You (1972,
Avco)
*People Make the World Go Around
(1972, Avco)
*Break Up to Make Up (1973, Avco)
*Rock'n Roll Baby (1973, Avco)
*You'll Never Get to Heaven (1973,
Avco)
*You Make Me Feel Brand New
(1974, Avco)

The Fabulous Stylistics (H&L)
The Stylistics (1971, H&L)
Round 2 (1972, H&L)
Rockin' Roll Baby (1973, H&L)
Let's Put It All Together (1974,
H&L)
Best of . . . (1975, H&L)

*Spinners

That's What Girls Are Made For
(1961, Tri-Phi)
I'll Always Love You (1965,
Motown)
Truly Yours (1966, Motown)
It's a Shame (1970, Motown)
We'll Have It Made (1971,
Motown)
*Could It Be I'm Falling in Love
(1972, Atlantic)
*I'll Be Around (1972, Atlantic)
*Ghetto Child (1973, Atlantic)
*One of a Kind (Love Affair) (1973,
Atlantic)
*I'm Coming Home (1974, Atlantic)
*Mighty Love, Part 1 (1974, Atlantic)
*Then Came You (1974, Atlantic)
*Sadie (1975, Atlantic)
*They Just Can't Stop (the Games
People Play) (1975, Atlantic)
*The Rubberband Man (1976,
Atlantic)
*Wake Up Susan (1976, Atlantic)

*You're Throwing a Good Love
   Away (1977, Atlantic)
*If You Wanna Do a Dance (1978,
   Atlantic)

*Spinners (1973, Atlantic)
*Mighty Love (1974, Atlantic)
*Pick of the Litter (1975, Atlantic)
Spinners Live (1975, Atlantic)
The Best of . . . (1978, Atlantic)

*Lou Rawls (1935-)

Love Is a Hurtin' Thing (1966,
   Capitol)
*Dead End Street (1967, Capitol)
*Tobacco Road (1967, Capitol)
*A Natural Man (1971, MGM)
*Groovy People (1976, Philadelphia
   International)
*You'll Never Find Another Love
   Like Mine (1976, Philadelphia
   International)
*Lady Love (1977, Philadelphia
   International)
*See You When I Git There (1977,
   Philadelphia International)
*Let Me Be Good to You (1979,
   Philadelphia International)

*Best of . . . (1968, Capitol)
*All Things in Time (1976,
   Philadelphia International)
*The Best of . . . (1976, Capitol)
*Unmistakably Lou (1977,
   Philadelphia International)
*When You Hear Lou, You've Heard
   It All (1977, Philadelphia
   International)

Anthology

Philadelphia Classics (1977,
   Philadelphia)

Early Rock and Soul Producers

Jerry Leiber (1933-) and Mike Stoller (1933-)

*Only in America (Atlantic)

Drifters
   SEE ALSO UNDER **Doo-Wop**

Ben E. King (1938-) lead vocal

Dance with Me (1959, Atlantic)
*There Goes My Baby (1959,
   Atlantic)
Save the Last Dance for Me (1960,
   Atlantic)
*This Magic Moment (1960,
   Atlantic)

Ben E. King solo

Spanish Harlem (1960, Atco)
I (Who Have Nothing) (1962, Atco)
Don't Play That Song (1962, Atco)
*Stand by Me (1962, Atco)
*Supernatural Thing, Part 1 (1975,
   Atlantic)
Music Trance (1980, Atco)

*Ben E. King's Greatest Hits (1964,
   Atco)
*Supernatural (1975, Atco)
Benny and Us (1977, Atco)
Let Me Live in Your Life (1978,
   Atco)
*Stand By Me (1981, Atlantic)
*What Is Soul (1981, Atlantic)
*Here Comes the Night (1985, Edsel)

Rudy Lewis lead vocal

Sweets for My Sweet (1961,
   Atlantic)
*Up on the Roof (1962, Atlantic)
*On Broadway (1963, Atlantic)

Rat Race (1963, Atlantic)

Coasters

Down in Mexico (1956, Atco)
*Searchin' (1957, Atco)
*Young Blood (1957, Atco)
*Yakety Yak (1958, Atco)
*Along Came Jones (1959, Atco)
*Charlie Brown (1959, Atco)
*Poison Ivy (1959, Atco)
*Little Egypt (1961, Atco)

Greatest Hits (Atco)
The Coasters (1956, Atlantic)
One By One (1959, Atco)
Coast Along (1960, Atco)
Greatest Recordings (1962, Atco)
On Broadway (1974, King)
Wake Me, Shake Me (1980,
    Atlantic)
Thumbin' a Ride (1985, Edsel)

*Other Productions by Leiber and
Stoller*

Elvis Presley

Elkie Brooks

Procol Harum

Stealer's Wheel

Bert Berns (1929-67)

Drifters
SEE ALSO UNDER **Doo-Wop**

I've Got Sand in My Shoes (1964,
    Atlantic)
Saturday Night at the Movies (1964,
    Atlantic)
*Under the Boardwalk (1964,
    Atlantic)

McCoys

SEE ALSO **Garnet Mimms; Irma
Thomas**

*Hang on Sloopy (1965, Bang)
SF Sorrow Is Born (1965, Bang)
*Stormy Monday (1965, Bang)

Hang On Sloopy (1965, Bang)
You Make Me Feel So Good (1966
    Bang)
Infinite McCoys (1968, Mercury)
Human Ball (1969, Mercury)

Roger Cook and Roger Greenaway

Drifters
SEE ALSO UNDER **Doo-Wop**

Like Sister and Brother (1973, Bell)
Down on the Beach Tonight (1974,
    Bell)
Kissin' in the Back Row of the
    Movies (1974, Bell)

Drifter' Golden Hits (1968, Atlantic)
The Early Years (1971, Atco)
Twenty-four Original Hits (1975,
    WEA)

*Luther Dixon

Shirelles

I Met Him on a Sunday (1958,
    Decca)
*Dedicated to the One I Love (1959,
    Scepter)
Tonight's the Night (1960, Scepter)
*Will You Still Love Me Tomorrow?
    (1960, Scepter)
Mama Said (1961, Scepter)
*Baby, It's You (1962, Scepter)
Soldier Boy (1962, Scepter)

Remember When (Scepter)
The Shirelles Sing Their Very Best
  (Springboard)
The Very Best of the Shirelles (United
  Artists)
Tonight's the Night (1961, Scepter)
Baby It's You (1962, Scepter)
The Shirelles (1981, Everest)

Chuck Jackson (1937-)

*Any Day Now (1962, Scepter)
*I Don't Want to Cry (1962, Scepter)

I Wanna Give You Some Love
  (EMI)
Patty (1976, Stang)

Dionne Warwick (1941-)

Don't Make Me Over (1962,
  Scepter)
*Anyone Who Had a Heart (1963,
  Scepter)
*Walk On By (1964, Scepter)
Who Can I Turn To? (1964,
  Scepter)
You'll Never Get to Heaven (1964,
  Scepter)
I Just Don't Know What to Do with
  Myself (1966, Scepter)
Message to Michael (1966, Scepter)
Trains and Boats and Planes (1966,
  Scepter)
Alfie (1967, Scepter)
Do You Know the Way to San Jose?
  (1968, Scepter)
Valley of the Dolls (1968, Scepter)
I'll Never Fall in Love Again (1969,
  Scepter)
This Girl's in Love with You (1969,
  Scepter)
Make It Easy on Yourself (1971,
  Scepter)

Dionne Warwick: More Greatest Hits
  (Scepter)
Dionne Warwick Sings Her Very Best
  (Scepter)

Dionne Warwick Sings One Hit After
  Another (Scepter)
The Golden Voice of D. Warwick
  (Scepter)

Other Productions of Dionne Warwick

Then Came You (1974, Warner
  Bros.)
Once You Hit the Road (1975,
  Warner Bros.)
Deja Vu (1979, Warner Bros.)
I'll Never Love This Way Again
  (1979, Warner Bros.)
Take the Short Way Home (1982,
  Warner Bros.)

*Phil Spector (1940-)

Christmas LP (Spector)
Greatest Hits (Spector)
Phil Spector Wall of Sound (1981,
  Phil Spector International)

Crystals

Oh Yeah Maybe Baby (1961,
  Philles)
*There's No Other (Like My Baby)
  (1961, Philles)
*He Hit Me (And It Felt Like a Kiss)
  (1962, Philles)
*He's a Rebel (1962, Philles)
*Uptown (1962, Philles)
*Da Doo Ron Ron (1963, Philles)
*Then He Kissed Me (1963, Philles)
*All Grown Up (1964, Philles)
Little Boy (1964, Philles)

Ronettes

Baby I Love You (1963, Philles)
*Be My Baby (1963, Philles)
(The Best Part of) Breakin' Up
  (1964, Philles)
Do I Love You? (1964, Philles)
*Walking in the Rain (1964, Philles)
*Is This What I Get for Loving You?
  (1965, Philles)

I Can Hear Music (1966, Philles)

The Ronettes (Philles)
*The Fabulous Ronettes Featuring
Veronica* (1964, Philles)

Righteous Brothers

Little Latin Lupe Lu (1963,
Moonglow)
*You've Lost That Lovin' Feelin'
(1964, Philles)
*Ebb Tide (1965, Philles)
*Go Ahead and Cry (1965, Verve)
Just Once in My Life (1965, Philles)
Unchained Melody (1965, Philles)
*(You're My) Soul and Inspiration
(1965, Verve)

You've Lost That Lovin' Feelin'
(1965, Philles)
Soul and Inspiration (1966, Philles)
The Righteous Bros. Greatest Hits,
Vol. 1 (1967, Verve)
Rock and Roll Heaven (1974,
Haven)

Bill Medley (1940-) solo

Brown Eyed Woman (1968, MGM)
Peace Brother Peace (1968, MGM)

Barbara Lewis (1944-)

*Hello Stranger (1963, Atlantic)
*Baby, I'm Yours (1965, Atlantic)
Make Me Your Baby (1965,
Atlantic)

Baby, I'm Yours (1965, Atlantic)
Hello Stranger (1981, Solid Smoke)

Chiffons

*He's So Fine (1963, Laurie)
*One Fine Day (1963, Laurie)
*Sweet Talkin' Guy (1966, Laurie)

He's So Fine (1963, Laurie)
Sweet Talking Guy (1966, Laurie)

*Everything You Always Wanted to
Hear by the Chiffons But
Couldn't Get* (1973, Laurie)

Ike and Tina Turner

(Ike Turner, 1931- ; Tina Turner,
1938-)
SEE ALSO UNDER **Rhythm and
Blues: Club Blues**

From the Beginning (Kent)
Goodbye So Long (Kent)
Greatest Hits (War.)
*A Fool in Love (1960, Sue)
*I Idolize You (1961, Sue)
*It's Gonna Work Out Fine (1961,
Sue)
*Poor Fool (1962, Sue)
*Tra La la la la (1962, Sue)
River Deep, Mountain High (1966,
Philles)
The Hunter (1969, Blue Thumb)
Her Man, His Woman (1970,
Capitol)
I Want to Take You Higher (1970,
Liberty)
Nuff Said (1971, United Artists)
Proud Mary (1971, Liberty)
Feel Good (1972, United Artists)
Nutbush City Limits (1973, United
Artists)
Very Best of . . . (1976, United
Artists)
Delilah's Power (1977, United
Artists)

*Ike and Tina Turner's Festival of
Live Performers* (Kent)
Too Hot to Hold (Springboard)
River Deep, Mountain High (1966,
Philles)
Please,Please,Please (1970, Kent)
The Soul of . . . (1973, Kent)
The World of . . . (1973, United
Artists)
Ike and Tina Turner's Greatest Hits
(1976, United Artists)

Tina Turner solo

> The Queen (Sp.)
> Acid Queen (1975, United Artists)
> Rough (1979, United Artists)
> *Private Dancer (1984, Capitol)
> *Break Every Rule (1986, Capitol)

Other Productions of Phil Spector

Dion (Dion DiMucci)

Beatles

George Harrison

John Lennon

Ramones

Shadow Morton (1942-)

Anthology of Shadow Morton Productions

> *Red Bird Story*, Vol. 1: *The Hit Factory* (Charly)

Shangri-Las

> Give Him a Great Big Kiss (1964, Red Bird)
> *The Leader of the Pack (1964, Red Bird)
> *May (1964, Red Bird)
> *Remember (Walking in the Sand) (1964, Red Bird)
> Give Us Your Blessings (1965, Red Bird)
> *I Can Never Go Home Anymore (1965, Red Bird)
> *Out in the Streets (1965, Red Bird)
> Right Now and Not Later (1965, Red Bird)
> He Cried (1966, Red Bird)
> *Long Live Our Love (1966, Red Bird)

> *Past, Present, and Future (1966, Red Bird)

> *Leader of the Pack* (1964, Red Bird)
> *Shangri-Las* (1965, Red Bird)
> *Golden Hits* (1966, Mercury)
> *I Can Never Go Home Anymore* (1966, Red Bird)
> *Remember (Walking in the Sand)* (1976, Charly)

Bob Crewe

Four Seasons

> *Big Girls Don't Cry (1962, Vee Jay)
> *Sherry (1962, Vee Jay)
> Ain't That a Shame (1963, Vee Jay)
> *Candy Girl (1963, Vee Jay)
> *Walk Like a Man (1963, Vee Jay)
> Alone (1964, Vee Jay)
> Big Man in Town (1964, Vee Jay)
> Bye Bye Baby (1965, Philips)
> *Dawn (1964, Vee Jay)
> *Rag Doll (1964, Vee Jay)
> Ronnie (1964, Vee Jay)
> *Save It For Me (1964, Vee Jay)
> Stay (1964, Vee Jay)
> Girl Come Running (1965, Philips)
> *Let's Hang On (1965, Philips)
> Working My Way Back to You (1965, Philips)
> I've Got You Under My Skin (1966, Philips)
> Opus 17 (Don't Worry 'bout Me) (1966, Philips)
> *Tell It to the Rain (1966, Philips)
> Beggin' (1967, Philips)
> *C'mon Marianne (1967, Philips)
> Watch the Flowers Grow (1967, Philips)
> Who Loves You (1975, Private Stock)
> December 1963 (Oh What a Night) (1976, Private Stock)
> Grease (1980, Private Stock)

> *Big Girls Don't Cry* (1963, Vee Jay)
> *Sherry* (1963, Vee Jay)

Dawn (1964, Philips)
Rag Doll (1964, Philips)
Four Seasons Story (1975, Private
    Stock)

Frankie Valli (1937-) solo

*My Eyes Adored You (1975, Private
    Stock)
Our Day Will Come (1975, Private
    Stock)
Swearin' to God (1975, Private
    Stock)

Berry Gordy (1929-)

Contours

Marvelettes

Smokey Robinson

Supremes

Temptations

Jr. Walker

Mary Wells

Stevie Wonder

Jerry Wexler (1917-)

Solomon Burke

Ray Charles

Clyde McPhatter

Jerry Ragavoy (1930-)

Garnet Mimms

Howard Tate

Steve Cropper (1941-)

Otis Redding

George Martin (1926-)

America

Beatles

Jeff Beck

Cheap Trick

Jerry and the Pacemakers

Billy J. Kramer

Jimmy Webb

Tom Dowd (1925-)

Allman Brothers

Ray Charles

Eric Clapton

Cream

Aretha Franklin

Otis Redding

Lynyrd Skynyrd

Dusty Springfield

Rod Stewart

Young Rascals

Mickie Most (1938-)

Animals

Jeff Beck

Donovan

Herman's Hermits

Hot Chocolate

Lulu

Richard Perry (1942-)

Captain Beefheart

Nilsson

Pointer Sisters

Leo Sayer

Carly Simon

Ringo Starr (Richard Starkey)

Barbra Streisand

Bill Szymczyk (1943-)

Eagles

James Gang

J. Geils Band

Jo Jo Gunne

B.B. King

Joe Walsh

Who

Glyn Johns (1942-)

Joan Armatrading

Beatles

Eric Clapton

Eagles

Faces

Led Zeppelin

Steve Miller

Rolling Stones

Boz Scaggs

Who

Tony Visconti (1944-)

Boomtown Rats

David Bowie

Osibisa

Iggy Pop

T. Rex

Thin Lizzy

Chris Thomas (1947-)

Climax Blues Band

Bryan Ferry

Elton John

Pink Floyd

Pretenders

Procol Harum

Roxy Music

Sex Pistols

Pete Townshend

Wings

Todd Rundgren (1948-)

Nazz

Utopia

Grand Funk

Meatloaf

New York Dolls

Patti Smith

Nicky Chinnh (1945-) and Mike Chapman (1947-)

Blondie

Knack

Suzi Quatro

Sweet

Roy Thomas Baker (1946-)

Cars

Foreigner

Journey

Queen

Leslie Kong (1933-71)

Jimmy Cliff

Desmond Dekker

Maytals

Melodians
The "King" Kong Collection '81
(Island)

Eric Morris

Wailers

British Rhythm and Blues and Traditional Jazz (1950s and Early 1960s)

*Humphrey Lyttleton

21 Years On (1969, Polydor)
Best of Hump, 1949-56 (1972, Parlophone)

*Ken Colyer

The Early Days (1953, Storyville)

*Chris Barber (1930-)

*Petite Fleur (Little Flower) (1952, Laurie)

Chris Barber Jubilee Album, vols. 1-6 (1949-74, Black Lion)

*Kenny Ball and His Jazzman

(Kenny Ball, 1937-)

*Midnight in Moscow (1962, Kapp)

*Mr. Acker Bilk (1929-)

*Stranger on the Shore (1962, Atco)

*Lonnie Donegan and His Skiffle Group

(Lonnie Donegan, 1931-)

*Rock Island Line/John Henry (1954, Decca)
*Does Your Chewing Gum Lose It's Flavor (On the Bedpost Over Night) (1961, Dot)
*My Old Man's a Dustman (1962, Dot)

New Orleans Joys (1954, Decca)
Rock Island Line (1954, Decca)
Lost John (1956, Decca)
More Tops with Lonnie (1961, Pye)
Golden Age of Donegan (1962, Golden Guinea)
Showcase (1968, Marble Arch)
Lonnie Donegan Rides Again (1969, Marble Arch)
Puttin' on the Style (1978, United Artists)

*Alexis Korner's Blues Incorporated

(Alexis Korner, 1928-)

*Alexis Korner's All Stars Inc. (1969, Transatlantic)

*Graham Bond (1937-74)

A Bond Between Us (Columbia)
Long Tall Shorty (Decca)
Tammy (Columbia)
The Sound of . . . (1965, Columbia)

British Pop Music (1950s and Early 1960s)

*Tommy Steele (1936-)

Rock with the Cave Man (1958, Decca)

Focus On Tommy Steele (Decca)

*Billy Fury (1941-)

*Maybe Tomorrow (1959, Decca)
*Colette (1960, Decca)
*That's Love (1960, Decca)
Halfway to Paradise (1961, Decca)
I'd Never Find Another You (1964, Decca)
Jealousy (1964, Decca)

Billy Fury (1960, Ace of Clubs)
The Sound of Fury (1960, Decca)
Halfway to Paradise (1961, Ace of CLubs)
Billy (1963, Decca)
We Want Billy (1963, Decca)
Best of . . . (1967, Ace of Clubs)
The Billy Fury Story (1977, Decca)

*Laurie London (1945-)

*He's Got the Whole World (In His Hands) (1958, Capitol)

*Adam Faith (1940-)

*What Do You Want (1959, Parlophone)
*Lonely Pup (1960, Parlophone)
*Poor Me (1960, Parlophone)
*Someone Else's Baby (1960, Parlophone)
It's Allright (1965, Amy)

The Best of . . . (Starline)
I Survive (1974, Warner Bros.)

*Cliff Richard and the Shadows

(Cliff Richard, 1940-)

*Move It (1958, Columbia)
*Livin' Doll (1959, ABC)
*Travellin' Light (1959, Columbia)
*Please Don't Tease (1960, Columbia)
The Next Time (1962, Columbia)
Summer Holiday (1963, Columbia)
*It's All in the Game (1964, Epic)
The Minute You're Gone (1965, Columbia)
Congratulations (1968, Columbia)
Goodbye Sam, Hello Samantha (1970, Columbia)
I Ain't Got the Time Anymore (1970, Columbia)
Jesus (1972, Columbia)
Silver Rain (1972, Columbia)
Sing a Song of Freedom (1972, Columbia)
Sunny Honey Girl (1972, Columbia)
Devil Woman (1976, Rocket)
I'm Nearly Famous (1976, Rocket)
We Don't Talk Anymore (1976, EMI)
Dreaming (1980, EMI)
Daddy's Home (1982, EMI)

*Cliff (1959, Columbia)
*Cliff Sings (1959, Columbia)
*Me and My Shadows (1960, Columbia)
*Listen to Cliff (1961, Columbia)
*Hit Album (1963, Columbia)
I'm Nearly Famous (1976, EMI)
Every Face Tells a Story (1978, EMI)

*Shadows

*Feelin' Fine (1959, Columbia)
*Apache (1960, Columbia)
*Atlantis (1961, Columbia)
*F.B.I. (1961, Columbia)
*Frightened City (1961, Columbia)
*Kon Tiki (1961, Columbia)

Shindig (1963, Columbia)
Don't Make My Baby Blue (1965, Columbia)

*The Shadows (1962, Columbia)
*Greatest Hits (1963, Columbia)
More Hits (1965, Columbia)
The Best of . . . (1977, EMI)
20 Golden Greats (1977, EMI)

*Johnny Kidd and the Pirates

(Johnny Kidd, 1939-66)

*Please Don't Touch (1959, EMI)
*Shakin' All Over (1960, EMI)
*You Got What It Takes (1960, EMI)
*Restless (1960, EMI)
*I'll Never Get Over You (1963, EMI)
*Hungry for Love (1963, EMI)

*Shakin' All Over (1971, Starline)
Best of . . . (1978, EMI)
*Johnny Kidd, Rocker (1978, EMI)

*Tornados

*Telstar (1962, London)

*Telstar (1963, London)

Elkie Brooks (1945-)

*Pearl's a Singer (1977, A&M)
*Sunshine after the Rain (1977, A&M)

Rich Man's Woman (1975, A&M)
*Two Days Away (1977, A&M)

First British Invasion

LIVERPOOL

Beatles

Besame Mucho
Hippy, Hippy Shake
Long Tall Sally
·Red Sails in the Sunset
Roll Over Beethoven
*Love Me Do/P.S. I Love You (1962, Parlophone)
*All I've Got to Do (1963, Parlophone)
*Baby It's You (1963, Parlophone)
*From Me to You (1963, Parlophone)
*It Won't Be Long (1963, Parlophone)
*Please Please Me (1963, Parlophone)
*She Loves You (1963, Parlophone)
*You Really Got a Hold on Me (1963, Parlophone)
Anytime at All (1964, Capitol)
Boys (1964, Capitol)
*Can't Buy Me Love (1964, Capitol)
*A Hard Day's Night (1964, Capitol)
*I Feel Fine/She's A Woman (1964, Capitol)
*I Want to Hold Your Hand (1964, Capitol)
*Matchbox/Slow Down (1964, Capitol)
Things We Said Today (1964, Capitol)
*Twist and Shout (1964, Tollie)
Drive My Car (1965, Capitol)
Dr. Robert (1965, Capitol)
*Help! (1965, Capitol)
I'm a Loser (1965, Capitol)
I've Just Seen a Face (1965, Capitol)
No Reply (1965, Capitol)
Norwegian Wood (1965, Capitol)
Run for Your Life (1965, Capitol)
*Ticket to Ride (1965, Capitol)
Wait (1965, Capitol)
*We Can Work It Out/Day Tripper (1965, Capitol)
The Word (1965, Capitol)
*Yesterday (1965, Capitol)
Eleanor Rigby (1966, Capitol)
I Want to Tell You (1966, Capitol)
Love You Too (1966, Capitol)
*Nowhere Man (1966, Capitol)
*Paperback Writer (1966, Capitol)
Rain (1966, Capitol)
Taxman (1966, Capitol)
Tomorrow Never Knows (1966, Capitol)
*Yellow Submarine (1966, Capitol)
*All You Need Is Love (1967, Capitol)
*Baby You're a Rich Man (1967, Capitol)
A Day in the Life (1967, Capitol)
The Fool on the Hill (1967, Capitol)
*Hello Goodbye (1967, Capitol)
I Am the Walrus (1967, Capitol)
Lucy in the Sky with Diamonds (1967, Capitol)
*Penny Lane (1967, Capitol)
She's Leaving Home (1967, Capitol)
*Strawberry Fields Forever (1967, Capitol)
When I'm Sixty-Four (1967, Capitol)
Back in the U.S.S.R. (1968, Capitol)
Blackbird (1968, Capitol)
Everybody's Got Something to Hide Except Me and My Monkey (1968, Capitol)
Good Night (1968, Capitol)
*Hey Jude/Revolution (1968, Apple)
Julia (1968, Capitol)
*Lady Madonna (1968, Capitol)
Mother Nature's Sun (1968, Capitol)

Ob-La-Di Ob-La-Da (1968,
    Capitol)
Piggies (1968, Capitol)
Rocky Raccoon (1968, Capitol)
While My Guitar Gently Weeps
    (1968, Capitol)
Yer Blues (1968, Capitol)
All Together Now (1969, Capitol)
*The Ballad of John and Yoko
    (1969, Apple)
Carry That Weight (1969, Capitol)
*Come Together (1969, Apple)
*Get Back/Don't Let Me Down
    (1969, Apple)
Golden Slumbers (1969, Capitol)
Hey Bulldog (1969, Capitol)
It's All Too Much (1969, Capitol)
It's Only a Northern Song (1969,
    Capitol)
I Want You (She's So Heavy)
    (1969, Capitol)
Mean Mr. Mustard (1969, Capitol)
Polythene Pam (1969, Capitol)
She Came In through the Bathroom
    Window (1969, Capitol)
*Something (1969, Apple)
Sun King (1969, Capitol)
*Let It Be (1970, Apple)
*The Long and Winding Road (1970,
    Apple)

Please Please Me (1963,
    Parlophone)
With the Beatles (1963, Parlophone)
Beatles '65 (1964, Capitol)
The Beatles' Second Album (1964,
    Capitol)
A Hard Day's Night (1964, United
    Artists)
Meet the Beatles (1964, Capitol)
Something New (1964, Capitol)
Beatles VI (1965, Capitol)
The Early Beatles (1965, Capitol)
Help! (1965, Capitol)
Rubber Soul (1965, Capitol)
Revolver (1966, Capitol)
Yesterday ... and Today (1966,
    Capitol)

Magical Mystery Tour (1967,
    Capitol)
*Sgt. Pepper's Lonely Hearts Club
    Band* (1967, Capitol)
The Beatles (1968, Capitol)
Abbey Road (1969, Capitol)
Hey Jude (1970, Capitol)
Let It Be (1970, Apple)
The Beatles, 1962-66 (1973, Capitol)
The Beatles, 1967-70 (1973, Capitol)
Rock'n'Roll Music (1976, Capitol)
*Live! At the Star-Club in Hamburg,
    Germany, 1962* (1977, Atlantic)
Live at the Hollywood Bowl (1977,
    Capitol)
Love Songs (1977, Capitol)
Rock'n'Roll Music, Vol. 2 (1980,
    Capitol)

John Lennon (1940-80) solo

John Lennon/Plastic Ono Band
    (1970, Apple)
Imagine (1971, Apple)
Live in New York City (1986,
    Capitol)
Menlove Ave. (1986, Capitol)

John Lennon with Yoko Ono

*Unfinished Music No. 1: Two
    Virgins* (1968, Apple)
*Unfinished Music No. 2: Life with
    the Lions* (1969, Apple)
Wedding Album (1969, Apple)
Double Fantasy (1980, Geffen)

Paul McCartney (1942-) solo

Ram (1971, Capitol)
Band on the Run (1973, Apple)
Venus and Mars (1973, Capitol)
Wings Over America (1977, Capitol)
Tug of War (1982, Columbia)
Press to Play (1986, Capitol)

George Harrison (1943-) solo

All Things Must Pass (1970, Apple)
The Concert for Bangladesh (1972,
    Apple)
Cloud Nine (1987, Park Horse)

Ringo Starr (Richard Starkey, 1940-)
solo

*Ringo (1973, Capitol)

Yoko Ono (1933)

Fly (1971, Apple)
Approximately Infinite Universe
(1973, Apple)
Feeling the Space (1973, Apple)
It's All Right (1982, Polydor)
Season of Glass (1982, Geffen)
*Starpeace (1985, Polydor)

*Billy J. Kramer and the Dakotas

(Billy J. Kramer, 1943-)

*Do You Want to Know a Secret?
(1963, Capitol)
*I'll Keep You Satisfied (1963,
Capitol)
*From a Window (1964, Imperial)
*Little Children/Bad to Me (1964,
Imperial)
*Trains and Boats and Planes (1965,
Capitol)

Listen to Billy J. Kramer (1963,
Parlophone)
The Best of . . . (1979, Capitol)

*Gerry and the Pacemakers

(Gerry Marsden, 1942-)

*How Do You Do It? (1963,
Capitol)
*I Like It (1963, Capitol)
*You'll Never Walk Alone (1963,
Capitol)
*Don't Let the Sun Catch You
Crying (1964, Laurie)
*Ferry Cross the Mersey (1965,
Laurie)
*Girl On a Swing (1966, Laurie)

*Gerry and the Pacemakers' Second
Album* (1963, Laurie)

How Do You Do It? (1963,
Columbia)
*Gerry and the Pacemakers' Greatest
Hits* (1964, Laurie)
The Best of . . . (1979, Capitol)

Merseybeats

It's Love That Really Counts (1963,
Fontana)
Don't Turn Around (1964,
Fontana)
*I Think of You (1964, Fontana)
Last Night (1964, Fontana)
Wishin' and Hopin' (1964,
Fontana)

England's Best Sellers (1964,
Archives International)
The Merseybeats (1964, Fontana)

as Merseys

I Love You, Yes I Do (1965,
Fontana)
I Stand Accused (1966, Fontana)
*Sorrow (1966, Fontana)

*Searchers

*Sugar and Spice (1963, Pye)
*Sweets for My Sweet (1963, Pye)
*Don't Throw Your Love Away
(1964, Kapp)
*Love Potion Number Nine (1964,
Kapp)
*Needles and Pinns (1964, Kapp)
Some Day We're Gonna Love
Again (1964, Kapp)
When You Walk in the Room
(1964, Kapp)
Bumble Bee (1965, Kapp)
What Have They Done to the Rain?
(1965, Kapp)
Take Me for What I'm Worth
(1966, Kapp)
Desdemona (1971, Hallmark)

Meet the Searchers (1963, Pye)
Hear! Hear! (1964, Kapp)

Needles and Pins (1964, Kapp)
This Is Us (1964, Kapp)
The New Searchers (1965)
The Searchers (1979, Sire)
Love Melodies (1981, Sire)

*Swingin' Blue Jeans

Hippy Hippy Shake (1963, Regal Zonophone)
Good Golly Miss Molly (1964, HMV)
You're No Good (1964, HMV)

Blue Jeans a-Swingin' (1964, HMV)
Hippy Hippy Hippy Shake (1964, Imperial)
Shaking Time (1964, Electrola)
Tutti Frutti (1964, Regal Zonophone)
The Swinging Blue Jeans (1966, MFP)
Brand New and Faded (1974, Dart)
Swinging Blue Jeans (1978, EMI)

TOTTENHAM

*Dave Clark Five (1942-)

*Do You Love Me? (1963, Columbia)
*Because (1964, Epic)
*Bits and Pieces (1964, Epic)
*Can't You See that She's Mine (1964, Epic)
*Glad All Over (1964, Epic,)
*Catch Us If You Can (1965, Epic)
*I Like It Like That (1965, Epic)
*Over and Over (1965, Epic)
*At the Scene (1966, Epic)
*You Got What It Takes (1967, Epic)
*Everybody Knows (1968, Epic)
*Good Old Rock'n'Roll (1969, Epic)
*Everybody Get Together (1970, Epic)

A Session with the Dave Clark Five (1963, Columbia)

American Tour (1964, Epic)
Glad All Over (1964, Epic)
Coast to Coast (1965, Epic)
Dave Clark Five's Greatest Hits (1966, Epic)
5 by 5 (1967, Epic)
Everybody Knows (1968, Columbia)
Good Old Rock'n'Roll (1971, Epic)

MANCHESTER

*Wayne Fontana and the Mindbenders (1945-)

*Um, Um, Um, Um, Um, Um (1964, Fontana)
*Game of Love (1965, Fontana)
It's Just a Little Bit Too Late (1965, Fontana)

The Mindbenders without Fontana

*A Groovey Kind of Love (1966, Fontana)
Ashes to Ashes (1967, Fontana)

Wayne Fontana and the Mindbenders (1965, Fontana)
Eric, Rick, Wayne, Bob (1966, Fontana)
The Mindbenders (1966, Fontana)
A Groovy Kind of Love (1967, Fontana)

*Freddie and the Dreamers

(Freddie Garrity, 1940-)

*If You've Gotta Make a Fool of Somebody (1963, Columbia)
*I'm Telling You Now (1963, Columbia)
*You Were Made for Me (1963, Columbia
*I Understand (Just How You Feel) (1964, Columbia)
Do the Freddie (1965, Mercury)

Freddie and the Dreamers (1963, Columbia)

You Were Made for Me (1964, Columbia)
Do the Freddie (1965, Mercury)
I'm Telling You Now (1965, Tower)
**The Best of . . .* (1979, Capitol)

*Hollies

*Searchin' (1963, Imperial)
*Stay (1963, Imperial)
*Here I Go Again (1964, Imperial)
*Just One Look (1964, Imperial)
*We're Through (1964, Imperial)
*I'm Alive (1965, Imperial)
*Look through Any Window (1965, Imperial)
*Yes I Will (1965, Imperial)
*Bus Stop (1966, Imperial)
*Stop Stop Stop (1966, Imperial)
*Carrie-Anne (1967, Epic)
On a Carousel (1967, Imperial)
Pay You Back with Interest (1967, Imperial)
Jennifer Eccles (1968, Epic)
Sorry Suzanne (1969, Epic)
*He Ain't Heavy, He's My Brother (1970, Epic)
*Long Cool Woman (In a Black Dress) (1972, Epic)
Magic Woman Touch (1973, Epic)
*The Air That I Breath (1974, Epic)
Another Night (1975, Epic)
Stop In the Name of Love (1983, Atlantic)

*Hear Here (1965, Imperial)
*Here I Go (1965, Imperial)
The Hollies (1965, Imperial)
Bus Stop (1966, Imperial)
Evolution (1967, Epic)
Stop, Stop, Stop (1967, Imperial)
*Hollies Greatest (1968, Epic)
Words and Music by Bob Dylan (1969, Epic)
He Ain't Heavy, He's My Brother (1970, Epic)
Moving Finger (1971, Epic)
Distant Light (1972, Epic)
Romany (1972, Epic)

Greatest Hits (1973, Epic)
Hollies (1974, Epic)
Another Night (1975, Epic)
Write On (1976, Epic)
The Hollies (1977, Epic)
A Crazy Steal (1978, Epic)
Double Seven O Four (1979, Epic)
Buddy Holly (1980, Epic)
What Goes Around (1983, Atlantic)

*Herman's Hermits

*I'm into Something Good (1964, MGM)
*Can't You Hear My Heartbeat (1965, MGM)
*I'm Henry VIII, I Am (1965, MGM)
*Just a Little Bit Better (1965, MGM)
*Mrs. Brown You've Got a Lovely Daughter (1965, MGM)
*Silhouettes (1965, MGM)
*Wonderful World (1965, MGM)
*Dandy (1966, MGM)
*No Milk Today (1967, MGM)
*There's a Kind of Hush (1967, MGM)
I Can Take or Leave You Loving (1968, MGM)
My Sentimental Friend (1969, MGM)
Years May Come, Years May Go (1970, MGM)

**The Best of . . .* (1965, MGM)
**Introducing Herman's Hermits* (1965, MGM)
*On Tour (1965, MGM)
The Best of . . ., Vol. 2 (1966, MGM)
Hold On! (1966, MGM)
**There's a Kind of Hush All Over the World* (1967, MGM)
The Best of . . ., Vol. 3 (1968, MGM)
Herman's Hermits XX (Their Greatest Hits) (1973, Abkco)

OTHER

*Zombies

Leave Me Be (1964, Parrot)
*She's Not There (1964, Parrot)
*Tell Her No (1965, Parrot)
*Time of the Season (1969, Date)

The Zombies (1965, Parrot)
Early Days (1969, London)
Odessey and Oracle (1969, Date)
Time of the Zombies (1973, Date)
Odessey and Oracle (1985, Edsel)

*Tremeloes

*Do You Love Me? (1964)
*Even the Bad Times Are Good
(1967, Epic)
*Here Comes My Baby (1967, Epic)
*Silence Is Golden (1967, Epic)

Even the Bad Times Are Good
(1967, Columbia)
Here Comes My Baby (1967,
Columbia)
Suddenly You Love Me (1967,
Columbia)
58/68 World Explosion (1968,
Columbia)
Shiner (1974, DMJ)

Peter and Gordon

(Peter Asher, 1944- ; Gordon
Waller, 1945-)

*I Don't Want to See You Again
(1964, Capitol)
Nobody I Know (1964, Capitol)
*A World Without Love (1964,
Capitol)
*I Go to Pieces (1965, Capitol)
To Know You Is to Love You
(1965, Capitol)
True Love Ways (1965, Capitol)
*Lady Godiva (1966, Capitol)
Woman (1966, Capitol)

Knight in Rusty Armour (1967,
Capitol)
Sunday for Tea (1967, Capitol)

I Don't Want to See You Again
(1964, Capitol)
A World without Love (1964,
Capitol)
Peter and Gordon--I Go to Pieces
(1965, Capitol)
True Love Ways (1965, Capitol)
The Best of . . . (1966, Capitol)
Woman (1966, Capitol)
Lady Godiva (1967, Capitol)
Hot, Cold, and Custard (1968,
Capitol)

Chad and Jeremy

(Chad Stuart, 1945- ; Jeremy
Clyde, 1945-)

*A Summer Song (1964, World Art)
*Willow Weep for Me (1964, World
Art)
Yesterday's Gone (1964, World
Art)
Before and After (1965, Columbia)
I Don't Wanna Lose You Baby
(1965, Columbia)
If I Loved You (1965, World Art)
*Distant Shores (1966, Columbia)

The Ark (Columbia)
Before and After (Columbia)
The Best of . . . (1966, Capitol)
Of Cabbages and Kings (1967,
Columbia)
Yesterday's Gone (1967, World Art)

Nashville Teens

*Tobacco Road (1964, London)

Nashville Teens (1974, New World)

Honeycombs

*Have I the Right (1964,
Interphone)
*I Can't Stop (1965, Interphone)

Here Are the Honeycombs (1965, Interphone)

Unit Four Plus Two

*Concrete and Clay (1965, London)

Fortunes

Here It Comes Again (1965, Press)
*You've Got Your Troubles (1965, Press)

Here Comes That Rainy Day Feeling Again (1971, Capitol)

*Walker Brothers

*Love Her (1965, Philips)
*Make It Easy On Yourself (1965, Smash)
*The Sun Ain't Gonna Shine (Anymore) (1966, Smash)

The Walker Brothers (1965, Star Club)
Portrait (1966, Philips)

*Bachelors

*Diane (1964, London)
I Believe (1964, London)
No Arms Can Ever Hold You (1965, London)
Marie (1965, London)
Love Me with All of Your Heart (1966, London)

Presenting: The Bachelors (1964, London)

R&B-Influenced British Groups and Singers

*Rolling Stones

*Come On (1963, Decca)
*I Wanna Be Your Man (1963, Decca)
Empty Heart (1964, Decca)
*It's All Over Now (1964, London)
Little Red Rooster (1964, Decca)
*Not Fade Away (1964, Decca)
*Tell Me (You're Coming Back) (1964, London))
*Time Is On My Side (1964, London)
Everybody Needs Somebody to Love (1965, London)
*Get Off of My Cloud (1965, London)
Heart of Stone (1965, London)
*(I Can't Get No) Satisfaction (1965, London)
*The Last Time (1965, London)
Mona (1965, London)
Play With Fire (1965, London)
That's How Strong My Love Is (1965, London)
The Under Assistant West Coast Promotion Man (1965, London)
*As Tears Go By (1966, London)
Flight 505 (1966, London)
Goin' Home (1966, London)
*Have You Seen Your Mother, Baby, Standing In the Shadow? (1966, London)
Lady Jane (1966, London)
*Mother's Little Helper (1966, London)
*19th Nervous Breakdown (1966, London)
*Paint It Black (1966, London)
Stupid Girl (1966, London)
Under My Thumb (1966, London)
All Sold Out (1967, London)

Complicated (1967, London)
Connection (1967, London)
*Dandelion (1967, London)
In Another Land (1967, London)
*Let's Spend the Night Together (1967, London)
My Obsession (1967, London)
*Ruby Tuesday (1967, London)
*She's a Rainbow (1967, London)
2000 Man (1967, London)
*Jumpin' Jack Flash (1968, London)
Salt of the Earth (1968, London)
Street Fighting Man (1968, London)
Sympathy for the Devil (1968, London)
*Gimme Shelter (1969, London)
*Honky Tonk Woman (1969, London)
Let It Bleed (1969, London)
Midnight Rambler (1969, London)
*You Can't Always Get What You Want (1969, London)
Bitch (1971, Rolling Stone)
*Brown Sugar (1971, Rolling Stone)
Moonlight Mile (1971, Rolling Stone)
*Wild Horses (1971, Rolling Stone)
*Happy (1972, Rolling Stone)
*Tumbling Dice (1972, Rolling Stone)
*Angie (1973, Rolling Stone)
*Ain't Too Proud to Beg (1974, Rolling Stone)
*Heartbreaker (1974, Rolling Stone)
If You Really Want to Be My Friend (1974, Rolling Stone)
*It's Only Rock'n'Roll (1974, Rolling Stone)
Luxury (1974, Rolling Stone)
Crazy Mama (1976, Rolling Stone)
*Fool to Cry (1976, Rolling Stone)
Hand of Fate (1976, Rolling Stone)
Melody (1976, Rolling Stone)
Memory Motel (1976, Rolling Stone)
*Beast of Burden (1978, Rolling Stone)
*Miss You (1978, Rolling Stone)

*Emotional Rescue (1980, Rolling Stone)
*Start Me Up (1981, Rolling Stone)
Waiting On a Friend (1981, Rolling Stone)
*Undercover of the Night (1983, Rolling Stone)
*Harlem Shuffle (1986, Rolling Stone)

Around and Around (Decca)
The Rolling Stones (1964, London)
Out of Our Heads (1965, London)
The Rolling Stones Now! (1965, London)
12 by 5 (1965, London)
Aftermath (1966, London)
Big Hits (High Tide and Green Grass) (1966, London)
Between the Buttons (1967, London)
Flowers (1967, London)
Their Satanic Majesties Request (1967, London)
Beggar's Banquet (1968, London)
Let It Bleed (1969, London)
'Get Yer Ya-Ya's Out!/Rolling Stones in Concert (1970, London)
Sticky Fingers (1971, Rolling Stone)
Exile on Main Street (1972, Rolling Stone)
Hot Rocks, 1964-71 (1972, London)
More Hot Rocks/Big Hits and Fazed Cookies (1972, London)
It's Only Rock'n'Roll (1974, Rolling Stone)
Black and Blue (1976, Rolling Stone)
Love You Give (1977, Rolling Stone)
Some Girls (1978, Rolling Stone)
Tatto You (1981, Rolling Stone)
Undercover (1983, Rolling Stone)
Dirty Work (1986, Rolling Stone)

Bill Wyman (1936-) solo

In Another Land (1967, London)

Monkey Grip (1974, London)
Stone Alone (1976, London)

Live at Fulham Town Hall (1986, London)

Mick Jagger (1943-) solo

Memo from Turner (1970, London)

She's the Boss (1985, Columbia)

Ron Wood (1947-) solo

*I've Got My Own Album to Do (1974, Warner Bros.)
*Now Look (1975, Warner Bros.)
Mahoney's Last Stand (1976, Atco)
Gimme Some Neck (1979, Columbia)
1234 (1981, Columbia)

*Animals

Inside--Looking Out
*Baby Let Me Take You Home (1964, EMI)
*The House of the Rising Sun (1964, MGM)
*I'm Crying (1964, MGM)
Bring It On Home to Me (1965, MGM)
*Don't Let Me Be Misunderstood (1965, MGM)
*It's My Life (1965, MGM)
*We Gotta Get Out Of This Place (1965, MGM)
Don't Bring Me Down (1966, MGM)
*A Girl Named Sandoz (1966, MGM)
See See Rider (1966, MGM)
*When I Was Young (1966, MGM)
Monterey (1967, MGM)
*San Franciscan Nights (1967, MGM)
Sky Pilot (1968, MGM)

The Animals (1964, MGM)
Animal Tracks (1965, MGM)
On Tour (1965, MGM)
The Best of . . . (1966, MGM)
Best of Eric Burdon and the Animals, Vol. 2 (1967, MGM)

Winds of Change (1967, MGM)
The Twain Shall Meet (1968, MGM)
Love Is (1969, MGM)
Best of . . . (1973, Abkco)
Before We Were So Rudely Interrupted (1977, United Artists)

*Manfred Mann (1940-)

*Cock-a-Hoop (1963, HMV)
*Why Should We Not? (1963, HMV)
*Do Wah Diddy Diddy (1964, Ascot)
*5-4-3-2-1 (1964, HMV)
*Sha La La (1964, Ascot)
*Come Tomorrow (1965, Ascot)
*If You Gotta Go Go Now (1965, HMV)
*Pretty Flamingo (1966, United Artists)
Semi-Detached Suburban Mr. James (1966, HMV)
Ha Ha Said the Clown (1967, HMV)
Fox on the Run (1968, Mercury)
*Mighty Quinn (1968, Mercury)
My Name Is Jack (1968, HMV)
Ragamuffin Man (1969, HMV)
Living without You (1972, Polydor)
Joybringer (1973, HMV)
*Blinded by the Light (1976, Warner)
Spirit in the Night (1977, Warner)
Davy's on the Road Again (1978, HMV)
Don't Kill It Carol (1979, HMV)
You Angle You (1979, Warner)
*Runner (1984, Arista)

The Manfred Mann Album (1964, Ascot)
The Five Faces Of Manfred Mann (1965, Ascot)
Mann Made (1965, Ascot)
Mann Made Hits (1965, Ascot)
My Little Red Book of Winners (1965, Ascot)

Pretty Flamingo (1966, United
  Artists)
Up the Junction (1967, Fontana)
The Mighty Quinn (1968, Mercury)
Manfred Mann's Earth Band (1972,
  Polydor)
The Best of . . . (1974, Janus; 1977,
  Capitol)
The Roaring Silence (1976, Warner)

*Spencer Davis Group

(Spencer Davis, 1942-)

Gimme Some Lovin' (1965, Sonet)
Keep On Running (1965, Sonet)
Somebody Help Me (1965, Son)

Every Little Bit Hurts (1965, Wing)
1st Album (1965, Sonet)
Autumn (1966, Fontana)
Second Album (1966, Fontana)
Gimme Some Lovin' (1967, United
  Artists)
I'm a Man (1967, United Artists)
*The Spencer Davis Group featuring
  Stevie Winwood* (1981, Island)

Who

as High Numbers

I'm the Face (1964, Fontana)
Zoot Suit (1964, Fontana)

as Who

*Anyway, Anyhow, Anywhere (1965,
  Brunswick)
*Bald Headed Woman (1965,
  Brunswick)
*I Can't Explain (1965, Brunswick)
*My Generation (1965, Brunswick)
*The Kids Are Alright (1966,
  Brunswick)
*A Legal Matter (1966, Decca)
*The Ox (1966, Brunswick)
*Substitute (1966, Brunswick)
*Armenia City in the Sky (1967,
  Decca)

Boris the Spider (1967, MCA)
*Happy Jack (1967, Decca)
*I Can See for Miles (1967, Decca)
A Quick One While He's Away
  (1967, MCA)
Real (1967, MCA)
Whiskey Man (1967, MCA)
*Call Me Lighting (1968, Decca)
*Magic Bus (1968, MCA)
*Pictures of Lily (1968, MCA)
Acid Queen (1969, Decca)
Eyesight to the Blind (1969, Decca)
*I'm Free (1969, Decca)
*Pinball Wizard (1969, Decca)
Sensation (1969, Decca)
*See Me, Feel Me (1970, Decca)
Shakin' All Over (1970, MCA)
Summertime Blues (1970, MCA)
Young Man Blues (1970, MCA)
Baba O'Riley (1971, MCA)
Bargain (1971, MCA)
*Behind Blue Eyes (1971, Decca)
Goin' Mobile (1971, MCA)
I'm a Boy (1971, MCA)
Long Live Rock (1971, MCA)
My Wife (1971, MCA)
Naked Eye (1971, MCA)
Pure and Easy (1971, MCA)
The Seeker (1971, MCA)
Song Is Over (1971, MCA)
*Won't Get Fooled Again (1971,
  Decca)
Drowned (1973, MCA)
5:15 (1973, MCA)
I'm One (1973, MCA)
Is It in My Head (1973, MCA)
*Join Together (1972, Decca)
Love, Reign O'er Me (1973, MCA)
The Punk Meets the Godfather
  (1973, MCA)
The Real Me (1973, MCA)
*The Relay (1973, Track)
Glow Girl (1974, MCA)
Little Billy (1974, MCA)
Postcard (1974, MCA)
Blue Red and Grey (1975, MCA)
Dreaming from the Waist (1975,
  MCA)

However Much I Booze (1975, MCA)
How Many Friends (1975, MCA)
In a Hand or a Face (1975, MCA)
Slip Kid (1975, MCA)
*Squeeze Box (1975, MCA)
Guitar and Pen (1978, MCA)
Love Is Coming Down (1978, MCA)
Music Must Change (1978, MCA)
Trick of the Light (1978, MCA)
*Who Are You? (1978, MCA)
Another Tricky Day (1981, Warner Bros.)
Don't Let Go the Coat (1981, Warner Bros.)
The Quiet One (1981, Warner Bros.)
You (1981, Warner Bros.)
*You Better You Bet (1981, Warner Bros.)
*Anthena (1982, Warner Bros.)
Cry If You Want (1982, Warner Bros.)
Eminence Front (1982, Warner Bros.)

The Who Sings My Generation (1966, MCA)
Happy Jack (1967, MCA)
The Who Sell Out (1967, MCA)
Magic Bus--The Who On Tour (1968, MCA)
Tommy (1969, MCA)
The Who Live at Leeds (1970, MCA)
Meaty, Beaty, Big and Bouncy (1971, MCA)
Who's Next (1971, MCA)
Quadrophenia (1973, MCA)
Odds and Sods (1974, MCA)
The Who by Numbers (1975, MCA)
Who Are You (1978, MCA)
The Kids Are Alright (1979, MCA)
Quadrophenia (1979, Polydor)
Face Dances (1981, Warner Bros.)
Hooligans (1981, MCA)
It's Hard (1982, Warner Bros.)

Pete Townsend (1945-) solo

*Face to Face (1986, Atco)
*Give Blood (1986, Atco)

Who Came First (1972, Decca)
Rough Mix (1977, MCA)
Empty Glass (1980, Atco)
All the Best Cowboys Have Chinese Eyes (1982, Atco)
Scoop (1983, Atco)
Deep End Live! (1986, Atco)
White City a Novel (1986, Atco)
Another Scoop (1987, Atco)

John Entwistle (1944-) solo

Smash Your Head Against the Wall (1971, Decca)
Whistle Rymes (1972, Decca)
John Entwistle's Rigor Mortis Sets In (1973, MCA)
John Entwistle's Ox (1975, MCA)
Mad Dog (1975, MCA)
Too Late the Hero (1981, Atco)

Roger Daltrey (1944-) solo

Walking in My Sleep (1984, Atlantic)
After the Fire (1985, Atlantic)
Let Me Down Easy (1986, Atlantic)
Quicksilver Lightning (1986, Atlantic)

Daltrey (1973, MCA)
Ride a Rock Horse (1975, MCA)
One of the Boys (1977, MCA)
McVicar (1980, Polydor)
Best Bits (1982, MCA)
Parting Should Be Painless (1984, Atlantic)
Under the Raging Moon (1986, Atlantic)

Keith Moon (1948-78) solo

Two Sides of the Moon (1975, MCA)

Who as Baba Society

Happy Birthday (1970, MCA)

I Am (1972, MCA)
With Love (1976, MCA)

Kinks

*You Really Got Me (1964, Reprise)
*You Still Want Me (1964, Pye)
*All Day and All of the Night (1965, Reprise)
*See My Friends (1965, Reprise)
*Set Me Free (1965, Reprise)
*Tired of Waiting for You (1965, Reprise)
*Who'll Be the Next in Line (1965, Reprise)
*A Well Respected Man (1965, Reprise)
*Dead End Street (1966, Reprise)
*Dedicated Follower of Fashion (1966, Reprise)
*Sunny Afternoon (1966, Reprise)
*Mr. Pleasant (1967, Reprise)
 Village Green (1968, Reprise)
 Wonderboy (1968, Reprise)
 Australia (1969, Reprise)
 Mr. Churchill Says (1969, Reprise)
 Victorica (1969, Reprise)
 Apeman (1970, Reprise)
*Lola (1970, Reprise)
 This Time Tomorrow (1970, Reprise)
 Acute Schizophrenia (1971, RCA)
 Here Come the People in Grey (1971, RCA)
 Holloway Jail (1971, RCA)
 Skin and Bones (1971, RCA)
 Twentieth Century Man (1971, RCA)
*Supersonic Rocket Ship (1972, Reprise)
*Mirror of Love (1974, RCA)
*Sleepwalker (1977, Arista)
*Rock'n'Roll Fantasy (1978, Arista)
*(Wish I Could Fly Like) Superman (1979, Arista)
*Come Dancing (1983, Arista)
*Don't Forget to Dance (1983, Arista)

You Really Got Me (Reprise)
Kinks (1964, Pye)
 Kinks-Size (1965, Reprise)
Greatest Hits (1966, Reprise)
The Live Kinks (1967, Reprise)
Something Else (1968, Reprise)
Arthur/Decline and Fall of the British Empire (1969, Reprise)
The Kinks Are the Village Green Preservation Society (1969, Reprise)
Lola Versus Powerman and the Moneygoround (1970, Reprise)
 Kinks Part Two: Continuing Saga of Lola . . . (1971, Reprise)
 Everybody's in Show-Biz (1972, RCA)
Kink Kronicles (1972, Reprise)
 Preservation, Act One (1973, RCA)
 Preservation, Act Two (1974, RCA)
 Schoolboys in Disgrace (1975, RCA)
 Greatest Hits--Celluloid Heroes (1976, RCA)
 Sleepwalker (1977, Arista)
 Misfits (1978, Arista)
Low Budget (1979, Arista)
 One for the Road (1980, Arista)
 Give the People What They Want (1981, Arista)
 State of Confusion (1983, Arista)
Good Day (1985, Arista)
Sold Me Out (1985, Arista)
Word of Mouth (1985, Arista)
 Think Visual (1986, MCA)

Dave Davies (1947-) solo

Death of a Clown (1967, Reprise)
Hold My Hand (1967, Reprise)
Lincoln County (1967, Reprise)
Susannah's Still Alive (1967, Reprise)

*Small Faces

*Whatcha Gonna Do About It? (1965, Decca)
*All or Nothing (1966, Decca)
*Hey Girl (1966, Decca)

*My Mind's Eye (1966, Decca)
*Sha La La La Lee (1966, Decca)
*Here Comes the Nice (1967, Decca)
*I Can't Make It (1967, Decca)
*Itchycoo Park (1967, Decca)
*Tin Soldier (1967, Decca)
*Lazy Sunday (1968, Decca)
*Universal (1968, Decca)
*Afterglow of Your Love (1969,
    Decca)

The Small Faces (1966, Decca)
From the Beginning (1967, Decca)
There Are but Four Small Faces
    (1967, Immediate)
Ogden's Nut Gone Flake (1968,
    Immediate)
Autumn Stone (1969, Immediate)
In Memoriam (1970, Immediate)
The Vintage Years (1975, Sire)

*Faces

*Stay with Me (1972, Warner Bros.)

First Step (1970, Warner Bros.)
Long Player (1971, Warner Bros.)
*A Nod Is as Good as a Wink . . . To
    a Blind Horse* (1971, Warner
    Bros.)
Snakes and Ladders: The Best of . . .
    (1976, Warner Bros.)

Ronnie Lane (1948-) solo

Any More for Any More (1974, GM)
Ronnie Lane's Slim Chance (1975,
    A&M)
One for the Road (1976, Island)

*Troggs

*I Can't Control Myself (1966,
    Fontana)
*Wild Thing (1966, Fontana)
*With a Girl Like You (1966,
    Fontana)
*Give It to Me (1967, Fontana)
Hi Hi Hazel (1967, Fontana)
Night of the Long Grass (1967,
    Fontana)

Cousin Jane (1968, Fontana)
Girl in Black (1968, Fontana)
*Little Girl (1968, Fontana)
*Love Is All Around (1968, Fontana)
Maybe the Madman (1969,
    Fontana)
Strange Movies (1973, Pye)

Wild Thing (1966, Fontana)
Love Is All Around (1968, Fontana)
The Original Troggs Tapes (1976,
    Private Stock)
The Troggs (1976, Pye)
Vintage Years (1976, Sire)

*Dusty Springfield (1939-)

Island of Dreams (1962, Philips)
Say I Won't Be There (1962,
    Philips)
*Silver Threads and Golden Needles
    (1962, Philips)
*I Only Want to Be with You (1964,
    Philips)
*Stay Awhile (1964, Philips)
*Wishin' and Hopin' (1964, Philips)
*You Don't Have to Say You Love
    Me (1966, Philips)
*Son-Of-A Preacher Man (1968,
    Atlantic)

The Dusty Springfield Album (1964,
    Philips)
Dusty Springfield's Golden Hits
    (1966, Philips)
You Don't Have to Say You Love Me
    (1966, Philips)
Look of Love (1967, Philips)
Stay Awhile (1968, Mercury)
Dusty in Memphis (1969, Atlantic)
White Heat (1982, Casablanca)

*Georgie Fame and the Blue
    Flames

(Georgie Fame, 1943-)

*Yeh Yeh (1965, Imperial)
*Get Away (1967, Imperial)

Get Away (1966, Imperial)
Yeh, Yeh (1966, Imperial)
Sound Venture (1967, Columbia)

Georgie Fame solo

*The Ballad of Bonnie and Clyde
(1968, Epic)

**The Ballad of Bonnie and Clyde*
(1968, Epic)

*Tom Jones (1940-)

*It's Not Unusual (1965, Parrot)
*What's New, Pussycat? (1965,
Parrot)
*Thunderball (1966, Parrot)
*Detroit City (1967, Parrot)
*Green Green Grass of Home (1967,
Parrot)
*Delilah (1968, Parrot)
*Help Yourself (1968, Parrot)
*Love Me Tonight (1969, Parrot)

Thirteen Smash Hits (1967, Parrot)
Fever Zone (1968, Parrot)
This Is Tom Jones (1969, Parrot)
**Tom Jones' Greatest Hits* (1973,
London)

British Pop Vocalists

*Lulu (1948-)

*Here Comes the Night (1964,
Decca)
*Shout (1964, Decca)
Leave a Little Love (1965, Decca)
The Boat That I Row (1967, Decca)
*To Sir with Love (1967, Epic)
Best of Both Worlds (1968, Epic)
Boom Bang-a-Bang (1969, Decca)
Oh Me Oh My (I'm a Fool for You
Baby) (1970, Atco)
The Man Who Sold the World
(1974, Decca)
I Could Never Miss You (More
Than I Do) (1981, Alfa)

*To Sir with Love (1967, Epic)
New Routes (1970, Epic)
Lulu (1981, Alfa)

*Millie

*My Boy Lollipop (1964, Philips)

*Petula Clark (1933-)

*The Little Shoemaker (1954, Pye)
Majorca (1955, Pye)
Casanova (1961, Pye/Reprise)
Chariot (1961, Pye)
Monsieur (1961, Pye)
My Friend the Sea (1961,
Pye/Reprise)
*Romeo (1961, Pye)
*Sailor (1961, Pye)
Ya Ya Twist (1961, Pye)
*Downtown (1965, Warner Bros.)
*I Know a Place (1965, Warner
Bros.)
*I Couldn't Live without Your Love
(1966, Warner Bros.)
*My Love (1966, Warner Bros.)
*Don't Sleep in the Subway (1967,
Warner Bros.)

*This Is My Song (1967, Warner
  Bros.)
Kiss Me Goodbye (1968, Warner
  Bros.)

Downtown (1965, Warner Bros.)
Greatest Hits, Vol. 1 (1965, Warner
  Bros.)

*Sandie Shaw (1947-)

Sandie Shaw (1965, Reprise)

*Donovan

(Donovan Leitch, 1946-)

*Catch the Wind (1965, Hickory)
*Colours (1965, Pye)
*Sunshine Superman (1966, Epic)
*Universal Soldier (1965, Pye)
*Mellow Yello (1966, Epic)
 Epistle to Dippy (1967, Epic)
 There Is a Mountain (1967, Epic)
 Wear Your Love Like Heaven
  (1967, Epic)
*Hurdy Gurdy Man (1968, Epic)
 Jennifer Juniper (1968, Epic)
 Atlantis (1969, Epic)
 Goo Goo Barabajagal (Love Is Hot)
  (1969, Epic)
 Riki Tiki Tavi (1970, Epic)
 Celia of the Seals (1971, Epic)
 I Like You (1973, Epic)

Catch the Wind (1965, Hickory)
Sunshine Superman (1966, Epic)
Mellow Yellow (1967, Epic)
Donovan in Concert (1968, Epic)
A Gift from a Flower to a Garden
  (1968, Epic)
Hurdy Gurdy Man (1968, Epic)
Barabajagal (1969, Epic)
Donovan's Greatest Hits (1969,
  Epic)

American Mop-Top Groups

*Rascals/Young Rascals

I Ain't Gonna Eat Out My Heart
  Anymore (1965, Atlantic)
*Good Lovin' (1966, Atlantic)
You Better Run (1966, Atlantic)
*A Girl Like You (1967, Atlantic)
*Groovin' (1967, Atlantic)
*How Can I Be Sure (1967, Atlantic)
It's Wonderful (1967, Atlantic)
I've Been Lonely Too Long (1967,
  Atlantic)
*A Beautiful Morning (1968,
  Atlantic)
*People Got to Be Free (1968,
  Atlantic)
A Ray of Hope (1968, Atlantic)
Carry Me Back (1969, Atlantic)
Heaven (1969, Atlantic)
See (1969, Atlantic)

The Young Rascals (1966, Atlantic)
Collections (1967, Atlantic)
Groovin' (1967, Atlantic)
Freedom Suite (1968, Atlantic)
Once upon a Dream (1968,
  Atlantic)
*The Rascals' Greatest Hits/Time
  Peace* (1968, Atlantic)
Time Peace (1968, Atlantic)
See (1969, Atlantic)
Search and Nearness (1970,
  Atlantic)

*Mitch Ryder and the Detroit Wheels

(Mitch Ryder, 1945-)

*Devil with a Blue Dress On/Good
  Golly Miss Molly Medley (1966,
  New Voice)
*Jenny Take a Ride (1966, New
  Voice)

Little Latin Lupe Lu (1966, New
Voice)
*Sock It To Me, Baby (1967, New
Voice)
Too Many Fish in the Sea/Three
Little Fishes Medley (1967, New
Voice)

Mitch Ryder solo

What Now My Love (1967,
DynoVoice)

Breakout (1966, New Voice)
Jenny Take a Ride (1966, New
Voice)
Sock It to Me (1967, New Voice)
What Now My Love (1967,
DynoVoice)
Mitch Ryder Sings the Hits (1968,
New Voice)
The Detroit Memphis Experience
(1969, Dot)

*Paul Revere and the Raiders

(Paul Revere, 1942-)

*Like, Long Hair (1961, Gardena)
Louie Louie (1963, Columbia)
Just Like Me (1965, Columbia)
*Steppin' Out (1965, Columbia)
The Airplane Strike (1966,
Columbia)
*Good Thing (1966, Columbia)
*Hungry (1966, Columbia)
*Kicks (1966, Columbia)
*Him or Me--What's It Gonna Be?
(1967, Columbia)
I Had a Dream (1967, Columbia)
Ups and Downs (1967, Columbia)
Don't Take It So Hard (1968,
Columbia)
Mr. Sun. Mr. Moon (1969,
Columbia)
Too Much Talk (1968, Columbia)
Let Me (1969, Columbia)
Birds of a Feather (1971,
Columbia)

*Indian Reservation (1971,
Columbia)

All-Time Greatest Hits (1972,
Columbia)

*Tommy James and the Shondells

(Tommy James, 1947-)

*Hanky Panky (1962, Roulette)
It's Only Love (1966, Roulette)
Say I Am (What I Am) (1966,
Roulette)
Gettin' Together (1967, Roulette)
I Like the Way (1967, Roulette)
*I Think We're Alone Now (1967,
Roulette)
*Mirage (1967, Roulette)
*Crimson and Clover (1968,
Roulette)
Do Something to Me (1968,
Roulette)
*Mony Mony (1968, Roulette)
Ball of Fire (1969, Roulette)
*Crystal Blue Persuasion (1969,
Roulette)
She (1969, Roulette)
*Sweet Cherry Wine (1969,
Roulette)

Hanky Panky (1966, Roulette)
Mony Mony (1968, Roulette)
Cellophane Symphony (1969,
Roulette)
Crimson and Clover (1969,
Roulette)
The Best of Tommy James (1971,
Roulette)

Tommy James solo

*Draggin' the Line (1971, Roulette)
I'm Comin' Home (1971, Roulette)
Three Times in Love (1980,
Millennium)

*Sir Douglas Quintet

(Doug Sahm, 1941-)

She's About a Mover (1965, Tribe)
The Rains Came (1966, Tribe)
Mendocino (1969, Smash)

Best of . . . (1965, Tribe)
Honkey Blues (1968, Smash)
Mendocino (1969, Smash)
Border Wave (1981, Takoma)

*Gary Lewis and the Playboys

(Gary Lewis, 1946-)

*Count Me In (1965, Liberty)
*Everybody Loves a Clown (1965, Liberty)
*Save Your Heart for Me (1965, Liberty)
*She's Just My Style (1965, Liberty)
*This Diamond Ring (1965, Liberty)
*Green Grass (1966, Liberty)
My Heart's Symphony (1966, Liberty)
*Sure Gonna Miss Her (1966, Liberty)
(You Don't Have to) Paint Me a Picture (1966, Liberty)
Girls in Love (1967, Liberty)
Where Will the Words Come From? (1967, Liberty)
Sealed with a Kiss (1968, Libery)

This Diamond Ring (1965, Liberty)
Golden Greats (1966, Liberty)
The Greatest Hits of . . . (1978, Power)

*Jay and the Americans

(John "Jay" Traynor, 1943-)

*She Cried (1962, United Artists)
Only in America (1963, United Artists)
*Come a Little Bit Closer (1964, United Artists)

*Cara, Mia (1965, United Artists)
Let's Lock the Door (and Throw Away the Key) (1965, United Artists)
Some Enchanted Evening (1965, United Artists)
Sunday and Me (1965, United Artists)
Crying (1966, United Artists)
*This Magic Moment (1969, United Artists)
Walkin' in the Rain (1970, United Artists)

Jay and the Americans Greatest Hits, Vol. 1 (1965, United Artists)
Jay and the Americans Greatest Hits, Vol. 2 (1967, United Artists)

*Bobby Fuller Four

(Bobby Fuller, 1943-66)

Let Her Dance (1965, Mustang)
*I Fought the Law (1966, Mustang)
*Love's Made a Fool of You (1966, Mustang)

I Fought the Law (1965, Mustang)
KRLA King of the Wheels (1966, Mustang)
The Best of . . . (1981, Rhino)

*Left Banke

*Walk Away Renee (1966, Smash)
*Pretty Ballerina (1967, Smash)
Queen of Paradise/And One Day (1980, Camerica)

Walk Away Renee/Pretty Ballerina (1967, Smash)
The Left Banke Too (1969, Smash)

Remains

The Remains (1978, Spoonfed)
Diddy Wah Diddy (1982, Eva)

Anthology

The American Dream: The London-American Legend (1975, London)

Bubblegum and Instant Groups

Monkees

*I'm a Believer (1966, Colgems)
*(I'm Not Your) Steppin' Stone (1966, Colgems)
*Last Train to Clarksville (1966, Colgems)
*Daydream Believer (1967, Colgems)
The Girl I Knew Somewhere (1967, Colgems)
*A Little Bit Me, a Little Bit You (1967, Colgems)
*Pleasant Valley Sunday (1967, Colgems)
Words (1967, Colgems)
D.W. Washburn (1968, Colgems)
Tapioca Tundra (1968, Colgems)
*Valleri (1968, Colgems)

*The Monkees (1966, Colgems)
Headquarters (1967, Colgems)
More of . . . (1967, Colgems)
Pisces, Aquarius, Capricorn, and Jones (1967, Colgems)
The Birds, the Bees, and the Monkees (1968, Colgems)
*The Monkees' Greatest Hits (1969, Arista)

*Archies

Bang-Shang-a-Lang (1968, Calender)
*Jingle Jangle (1969, Kirshner)
*Sugar Sugar (1969, Calender)
Who's Your Baby? (1970, Kirshner)

Everything's Archie (1969, RCA)
Jingle Jangle (1969, RCA)
Greatest Hits (1970, Kirshner)
Sunshine (1970, Kirshner)

170

*Partridge Family

*I Think I Love You (1970, Bell)
*Doesn't Somebody Want to Be
  Wanted? (1971, Bell)
*I'll Meet You Half Way (1971, Bell)
I Woke Up in Love This Morning
  (1971, Bell)
Breaking Up Is Hard to Do (1972,
  Bell)
It's One of Those Nights (Yes Love)
  (1972, Bell)
Looking through the Eyes of Love
  (1973, Bell)

The Partridge Family Album (1971,
  Bell)

*1910 Fruitgum Company

Goody Goody Gumdrops (1968,
  Buddah)
*1, 2, 3 Red Light (1968, Buddah)
*Simon Says (1968, Buddah)
*Indian Giver (1969, Buddah)
Special Delivery (1969, Buddah)
The Train (1969, Buddah)

1, 2, 3 Red Light (1968, Buddah)
Simon Says (1968, Buddah)
Indian Giver (1969, Buddah)

*Ohio Express

Beg, Borrow, and Steal (1967,
  Cameo)
Chewy Chewy (1968, Buddah)
Down at Lulu's (1968, Buddah)
*Yummy Yummy Yummy (1968,
  Buddah)
Mercy (1969, Buddah)

Beg, Borrow, and Steal (1968,
  Cameo)
Chewy Chewy (1968, Buddah)
Ohio Express (1968, Buddah)
Salt Water Taffy (1968, Buddah)
Mercy (1969, Buddah)
Very Best of . . . (1969, Buddah)

San Francisco Bay Area, 1967

*Jefferson Airplane

The Ballad of You, Me and Pooneil
  (1967, RCA)
Plastic Fantastic Lover (1967,
  RCA)
*Somebody to Love (1967, RCA)
3/5 of a Mile in Ten Seconds (1967,
  RCA)
*White Rabbit (1967, RCA)
Won't You Try/Saturday Afternoon
  (1967, RCA)
Greasy Heart (1968, RCA)
Lather (1968, RCA)
Triad (1968, RCA)
Good Shepherd (1969, RCA)
Volunteers (1969, RCA)
We Can Be Together (1969, RCA)
Wooden Ships (1969, RCA)

After Bathing at Baxter's (1967,
  RCA)
Jefferson Airplane Takes Off (1966,
  RCA)
Surrealistic Pillow (1967, RCA)
Crown of Creation (1968, RCA)
Bless Its Pointed Little Head (1969,
  RCA)
Volunteers (1969, RCA)
Bark (1971, Grunt)
Long John Silver (1972, Grunt)
Thirty Seconds over Winterland
  (1973, Grunt)
Flight Log, 1966-76 (1977, Grunt)
2400 Fulton Street--An Anthology
  (1987, RCA)

*Jefferson Starship

Caroline (1974, Grunt)
Ride the Tiger (1974, Grunt)
That's for Sure (1974, Grunt)
Fast Buck Freddie (1975, Grunt)
*Miracles (1975, Grunt)
Play on Love (1975, Grunt)

With Your Love (1976, Grunt)
*Count on Me (1978, Grunt)
Runaway (1978, Grunt)
Jane (1979, Grunt)
Find Your Way Back (1981, Grunt)
Be My Lady (1982, Grunt)
Winds of Change (1983, Grunt)
No Way Out (1984, Grunt)

Blows Against the Empire (1970, RCA)
Dragon Fly (1974, Grunt)
Red Octopus (1975, Grunt)
Gold (1979, Grunt)
Nuclear Furniture (1984, Grunt)

KBC Band

Their Initial Album (1986, Arista)

Hot Tuna

Hot Tuna (1970, RCA)
Hoppkorv (1976, Grunt)

*Beau Brummels

Don't Talk to Strangers (1965, Autumn)
Good Time Music (1965, Autumn)
*Just a Little (1965, Autumn)
*Laugh Laugh (1965, Autumn)
*You Tell Me Why (1965, Autumn)
One Too Many Mornings (1966, Autumn)

Introducing the Beau Brummels (1965, Autumn)
Beau Brummels (1966, Pye)
Beau Brummels, '66 (1966, Warner Bros.)
Best of . . . (1967, Vault)
Triangle (1967, Warner Bros.)
Bradley's Barn (1968, Warner Bros.)
The Beau Brummels (1975, Warner Bros.)
Autumn in San Francisco (1985, Edsel)

*Grateful Dead

Grateful Dead (1967, Warner Bros.)
Anthem of the Sun (1968, Warner Bros.)
Aoxomoxoa (1969, Warner Bros.)
American Beauty (1970, Warner Bros.)
Live Dead (1970, Warner Bros.)
Workingman's Dead (1970, Warner Bros.)
Europe, '72 (1972, Warner Bros.)

*Moby Grape

Moby Grape (1967, Columbia)
Moby Grape, 1969 (1969, Columbia)
Truly Fine Citizen (1970, Columbia)
Great Grape (1971, Columbia)
20 Granite Creek (1971, Reprise)

*Youngbloods

*Get Together (1967, RCA)
Grizzly Bear (1967, RCA)
Darkness Darkness (1968, RCA)

Earth Music (1967, RCA)
Youngbloods (1967, RCA)
Elephant Mountain (1969, RCA)
Best of . . . (1970, RCA)
Rock Festival (1970, Racoon)
This Is the Youngbloods (1972, RCA)

*Country Joe and the Fish

Feel Like I'm Fixin' to Die (1967, Vanguard)
F-I-S-H (1967, Vanguard)
Flying High (1967, Vanguard)
Janis (1967, Vanguard)
Not So Sweet Martha Lorraine (1967, Vanguard)
Super Bird (1967, Vanguard)
Who Am I? (1967, Vanguard)
Good Guys/Bad Guys Cheer (1968, Vanguard)
Rockin' Round the World (1970, Vanguard)

172

Electric Music for the Mind and Body (1967, Vanguard)
Feel Like I'm Fixin' to Die (1967, Vanguard)
Together (1968, Vanguard)
Country Joe and the Fish (1970, Vanguard)
Greatest Hits (1970, Vanguard)
The Life and Times of . . . (1971, Vanguard)

*Creedence Clearwater Revival

Brown-Eyed Girl (1965, Fantasy)
I Put a Spell on You (1968, Fantasy)
Suzie Q (1968, Fantasy)
*Bad Moon Rising (1969, Fantasy)
*Born on the Bayou (1969, Fantasy)
*Commotion (1969, Fantasy)
*Down on the Corner (1969, Fantasy)
*Fortunate Son (1969, Fantasy)
*Green River (1969, Fantasy)
*Lodi (1969, Fantasy)
*Proud Mary (1969, Fantasy)
*I Heard It through the Grapevine (1970, Fantasy)
*Lookin' Out My Back Door (1970, Fantasy)
*Travelin' Band (1970, Fantasy)
*Up around the Bend (1970, Fantasy)
*Who'll Stop the Rain? (1970, Fantasy)
*Have You Ever Seen the Rain? (1971, Fantasy)
*Sweet Hitch-Hiker (1971, Fantasy)
Someday Never Comes (1972, Fantasy)

Creedence Clearwater Revival (1968, Fantasy)
Bayou Country (1969, Fantasy)
Green River (1969, Fantasy)
Willy and the Poor Boys (1969, Fantasy)
Cosmo's Factory (1970, Fantasy)
Pendulum (1970, Fantasy)

Creedence Gold (1972, Fantasy)
Mardi Gras (1972, Fantasy)
More Creedence Gold (1973, Fantasy)
Golliwogs Pre-Creedence (1975, Fantasy)
Chronicle (1976, Fantasy)
Creedence 1969 (1978, Fantasy)
Creedence 1970 (1978, Fantasy)
Creedence Country (1981, Fantasy)
Royal Albert Hall Concert (1981, Fantasy)

John Fogerty (1945-) solo

The Blue Ridge Rangers (1973, Fantasy)
John Fogerty (1975, Asylum)
Centerfield (1985, Warner Bros.)
Eye of the Zombie (1986, Warner Bros.)

Tom Fogerty (1941-) solo

Excalibur (1972, Fantasy)
Deal It Out (1981, Fantasy)

*Steve Miller Band

(Steve Miller, 1943-)

Baby's Calling Me Home (1968, Capitol)
Living in the U.S.A. (1968, Capitol)
Brave New World (1969, Capitol)
Space Cowboy (1969, Capitol)
Your Saving Grace (1971, Capitol)
*The Joker (1973, Capitol)
*Rock'n Me (1976, Capitol)
Take the Money and Run (1976, Capitol)
*Fly Like an Eagle (1977, Capitol)
*Jet Airliner (1977, Capitol)
Jungle Love (1977, Capitol)
Swingtown (1977, Capitol)
Heart Like a Wheel (1981, Capitol)
*Abracadabra (1982, Capitol)

Children of the Future (1968, Capitol)
Brave New World (1969, Capitol)

Sailor (1969, Capitol)
Living in the U.S.A. (1971, Capitol)
Anthology (1972, Capitol)
Recall the Beginning (1972, Capitol)
The Joker (1973, Capitol)
Fly Like an Eagle (1976, Capitol)
Book of Dreams (1977, Capitol)
Abracadabra (1982, Capitol)
Live (1983, Capitol)
Living in the 20th Century (1987, Capitol)

*Quicksilver Messenger Service

Dino's Song (1968, Capitol)
The Fool (1968, Capitol)
Fresh Air (1970, Capitol)

Quicksilver Messenger Service (1968, Capitol)
Happy Trails (1969, Capitol)
Shady Grove (1970, Capitol)
Anthology (1973, Capitol)

*Electric Flag

A Long Time Comin' (1968, Columbia)

*Blue Cheer

Summertime Blues (1968, Philips)

Outside Inside (1968, Philips)
Vincebus Eruptum (1968, Philips)
New! Improved! (1969, Philips)

*Santana

Soul Sacrifice (1969, Columbia)
*Black Magic Woman (1970, Columbia)
*Evil Ways (1970, Columbia)
Everybody's Everything (1971, Columbia)
Oye Como Va (1971, Columbia)
No One to Depend On (1972, Columbia)
Dance Sister Dance (1976, Columbia)
She's Not There (1977, Columbia)

Stormy (1979, Columbia)
You Know That I Love You (1980, Columbia)
Winning (1981, Columbia)
Hold On (1982, Columbia)

Santana (1969, Columbia)
Santana: Abraxas (1970, Columbia)
Santana 3 (1971, Columbia)
Caravanserai (1972, Columbia)
Welcome (1973, Columbia)
Borboletta (1974, Columbia)
Greatest Hits (1974, Columbia)
Amigos (1976, Columbia)
Festival (1977, Columbia)
Moonflower (1977, Columbia)
Zebop (1981, Columbia)
Havana Moon (1983, Columbia)
Freedom (1987, Columbia)

Carlos Santana (1947-) solo

Love, Devotion, Surrender (1973, Columbia)
Illumination (1974, Columbia)
Lotus (1979, Columbia)
Oneness; Silver Dreams-Golden Reality (1979, Columbia)
The Swing of Delight (1980, Columbia)

*Janis Joplin (1943-70)

Piece of My Heart (1968, Columbia)
Kozmic Blues (1969, Columbia)
Maybe (1969, Columbia)
Try (Just a Little Bit Harder) (1969, Columbia)
*Me and Bobby McGee (1971, Columbia)
My Baby (1971, Columbia)
A Woman Left Lonely (1971, Columbia)

Big Brother and the Holding Company (1967, Mainstream)
Cheap Thrills (1968, Columbia)
I Got Dem Ol' Kozmic Blues Again, Mama (1969, Columbia)
Pearl (1971, Columbia)

174

In Concert (1972, Columbia)
Greatest Hits (1973, Columbia)
Janis (1974, Columbia)
Anthology (1980, Columbia)
*Farewell Song (1982, Columbia)

*It's a Beautiful Day

White Bird (1969, Columbia)

It's a Beautiful Day (1969,
    Columbia)
Marrying Maiden (1970, Columbia)

*Dan Hicks and His Hot Licks

Where's the Money? (1971, Blue
    Thumb)
Striking It Rich (1972, Blue Thumb)
*Last Train to Hicksville (1973, Blue
    Thumb)
*It Happened One Bite (1978, Warner
    Bros.)

Los Angeles, 1967

*Frank Zappa and the Mothers of Invention

(Frank Zappa, 1940-)

Help (1966, Verve)
How Could I Be Such a Fool (1966,
    Verve)
I'm a Rock (1966, Verve)
The Return of the Son of Monster
    Magnet (1966, Verve)
Trouble Comin' Everyday (1966,
    Verve)
You Didn't Try to Call Me (1966,
    Verve)
America Drinks and Goes Home
    (1967, Verve)
Brown Shoes Don't Make It (1967,
    Verve)
Plastic People (1967, Verve)
The Chrome Plated Megaphone of
    Destiny (1968, Verve)
Mother People (1968, Verve)

*Freak Out (1966, Verve)
*Absolutely Free (1967, Verve)
Cruising with Ruben and the Jets
    (1968, Verve)
*We're Only in It for the Money
    (1968, Verve)
Mother Mania (1969, Bizarre)
*Uncle Meat (1969, Bizarre)
*Burnt Weeny Sandwich (1970,
    Bizarre)
*Weasels Ripped My Flesh (1970,
    Bizarre)
The Grand Wazoo (1973, Reprise)
Over-Nite Sensation (1973,
    Discreet)
One Size Fits All (1974, Discreet)

*Frank Zappa solo

The Gumbo Variations (1969,
    Bizarre)
Peaches en Regalia (1969, Bizarre)
Willie the Wimp (1969, Bizarre)

Big Swifty (1972, Bizarre)
Don't Eat the Yellow Snow (1976, Discreet)
Broken Hearts Are for Assholes (1979, Zappa)
Dancing Fool (1979, Zappa)
I Have Been in You (1979, Zappa)
Jewish Princes (1979, Zappa)
Catholic Girls (1980, Zappa)
Crew Slut (1980, Zappa)
I Don't Wanna Get Drafted (1980, Mercury)
Outside Now (1980, Zappa)
A Token of My Extreme (1980, Zappa)
Wet T-Shirt Nite (1980, Zappa)
Bamboozled by Live (1981, Barking Pumpkin)
The Blue Light (1981, Barking Pumpkin)
Canard du Jour (1981, Barking Pumpkin)
Conehead (1981, Barking Pumpkin)
Doreen (1981, Barking Pumpkin)
Dumb All Over (1981, Barking Pumpkin)
Easy Meat (1981, Barking Pumpkin)
Fine Girl (1981, Barking Pumpkin)
Goblin Girl (1981, Barking Pumpkin)
Harder Than Your Husband (1981, Barking Pumpkin)
Heavenly Bank Account (1981, Barking Pumpkin)
The Meek Shall Inherit Nothing (1981, Barking Pumpkin)
Mudd Club (1981, Barking Pumpkin)
Teenage Wind (1981, Barking Pumpkin)
Valley Girl (1982, Barking Pumpkin)

Lumpy Gravy (1968, Verve)
Hot Rats (1969, Bizarre)
Chunga's Revenge (1970, Bizarre)
Waka Jawaka--Hot Rats (1972, Bizarre)

Apostrophe (1974, Discreet)
Studio Tan (1978, Warner Bros.)
Orchestral Favorites (1979, Warner Bros.)
*Sheik Yerbouti (1979, Zappa)
Sleep Dirt (1979, Warner Bros.)
*Joe's Garage Act 1, 2, 3 (1980, Zappa)
*Return of the Son of Shut Up'n Play Yer Guitar (1981, Barking Pumpkin)
*Shut Up'n Play Yer Guitar (1981, Barking Pumpkin)
*Shut Up'n Play Yer Guitar Some More (1981, Barking Pumpkin)
*Tinseltown Rebellion (1981, Barking Pumpkin)
*You Are What You Is (1981, Barking Pumpkin)

*Captain Beefheart and His Magic Band

(Don Van Vliet, 1941-)

*Safe As Milk (1967, Buddah)
Mirror Man (1968, Buddah)
Strictly Personal (1968, Blue Thumb)
Lick My Decals Off, Baby (1970, Reprise)
*Trout Mask Replica (1970, Reprise)
*The Spotlight Kid (1971, Reprise)
*Clear Spot (1972, Reprise)
Bluejeans and Moonbeams (1974, Mercury)
Unconditionally Guaranteed (1974, Mercury)
Shiny Beast (Bat Chain Puller) (1978, Warner Bros.)
*Doc at the Radar Station (1980, Virgin)
*Ice Cream for Crow (1982, Virgin)

*Spirit

Animal Zoo (1967, Epic)
Mr. Skin (1967, Epic)
Nature's Way (1967, Epic)

Nothin' to Hide (1967, Epic)
*I Got Line on You (1969, Epic)
*Jo Jo Gunne: Run Run Run (1972,
Asylum)

Twelve Dreams of Dr. Sardonicus
(1967, Epic)
Spirit (1968, Epic)
Clear Spirit (1969, Epic)
The Family That Plays Together
(1969, Epic)
Feedback (1972, Epic)
Jo Jo Gunne (1972, Asylum)
Best of . . . (1973, Epic)
Bite Down Hard (1973, Asylum)
Jumping the Gunne (1973, Asylum)
So . . . Where's the Show? (1974,
Asylum)

*Doors

The End
Five to One
Running Blue
*Light My Fire (1967, Elektra)
Love Me Two Times (1967,
Elektra)
People Are Strange (1967, Elektra)
*Hello, I Love You (1968, Elektra)
The Unknown Soldier (1968,
Elektra)
*Touch Me (1969, Elektra)
Love Her Madly (1971, Elektra)
Riders on the Storm (1971,
Elektra)

The Doors (1967, Elektra)
Strange Days (1967, Elektra)
Waiting for the Sun (1968, Elektra)
The Soft Parade (1969, Elektra)
Morrison Hotel (1970, Elektra)
The Doors Greatest Hits (1980,
Elektra)

*Steppenwolf

*Born to Be Wild (1968, Dunhill)
*Magic Carpet Ride (1968, Dunhill)
Move Over (1969, Dunhill)
*Rock Me (1969, Dunhill)

Hey Lawdy Mama (1970, Dunhill)
Monster (1970, Dunhill)
Straight Shootin' Woman (1974,
Dunhill)

Steppenwolf (1968, Dunhill)
Steppenwolf the Second (1968,
Dunhill)
16 Greatest Hits (1973, Dunhill)
16 Great Performances (1975, ABC)
ABC Collection (1976, ABC)
Wolf Tracks (1982, Nautilus)

*Canned Heat

Going up the Country (1968,
Liberty)
On the Road Again (1968, Liberty)
Let's Work Together (1970,
Liberty)

The Very Best of . . . (United
Artists)
Canned Heat (1967, Liberty)
Boogie with Canned Heat (1968,
Liberty)
Living the Blues (1968, Liberty)
Hallelujah (1969, Liberty)
Vintage Heat (1970, Janus)

*Iron Butterfly

In-a-Gadda-Da-Vida (1968, Atco)

Heavy (1968, Atco)
In-a-Gadda-Da-Vida (1968, Atco)
Ball (1969, Atco)
Live (1970, Atco)
Evolution (1971, Atco)

*Love

The Ninth Wave (1965, Capitol)
Hey Joe (1966, Elektra)
*My Little Red Book (1966, Elektra)
*Seven and Seven Is (1966, Elektra)
Bummer in the Summer (1968,
Elektra)
Everlasting First (1968, Blue
Thumb)

The Good Humor Man He Sees
Everything Like This (1968,
Elektra)
A House Is Not a Motel (1968,
Elektra)
You Set the Scene (1968, Elektra)

*Love (1966, Elektra)
Da Capo (1967, Elektra)
*Forever Changes (1968, Elektra)
Four Sail (1969, Elektra)
Out Here (1969, Blue Thumb)
False Start (1970, Blue Thumb)
*Best of... (1980, Rhino)

*Music Machine

*Talk Talk (1966, Original Sound)

*Standells

*Dirty Water (1966, Tower)

*Electric Prunes

*Get Me to the World on Time
(1967, Reprise)
*I Had Too Much to Dream (Last
Night) (1967, Reprise)

*Electric Prunes (1967, Reprise)
Mass in F Minor (1967, Reprise)
Underground (1967, Reprise)
Release of an Oath: The Kol Nidre
(1968, Reprise)
Just Good Old Rock'n'Roll (1969,
Reprise)

*Count Five

*Psychotic Reaction (1966, Double
Shot)

Psychotic Reaction (1966, Double
Shot)

Anthology

Nuggets: Original Artyfacts from the
First Psychedelic Era, 1965-68
(1972, Elektra)

Second British Invasion

General Anthology

History of British Rock, Vols. 1-3
(1974, Sire)

BLUES-INFLUENCED GROUPS

*Yardbirds

*Good Morning Little Schoolgirl
(1964, EMI)
*For Your Love (1965, Epic)
*Heart Full of Soul (1965, Epic)
*I'm a Man (1965, Epic)
*Happenings Ten Years Time Ago
(1966, Epic)
*Over Under Sideways Down (1966,
Epic)
*Shapes of Things (1966, Epic)
*Stroll On (1966, Epic)

*Eric Clapton and the Yardbirds
(Specialty)
*For Your Love (1965, Epic)
Having a Rave Up with the Yardbirds
(1965, Epic)
*Sonny Boy Williamson and the
Yardbirds (1965, Fontana)
Over Under Sideways Down (1966,
Epic)
Shapes of Things (1966, Specialty)
Little Games (1967, Epic)
*The Yardbirds Greatest Hits (1967,
Epic)

John Mayall and the Bluesbreakers

(John Mayall, 1943-)

*Don't Waste My Time (1969,
London)

John Mayall Plays John Mayall
(1964, London)
Bluesbreakers (1965, London)
*Bluesbreakers--John Mayall with Eric
Clapton* (1965, London)
A Hard Road (1966, London)
Crusade (1967, London)
Blues from Laurel Canyon (1969,
London)

*Cream

*Toad (1967, RSO)
*Sunshine of Your Love (1968,
Atco)
*White Room (1968, Atco)
*Badge (1969, RSO)
*Crossroads (1969, Atco)

Disraeli Gears (1967, RSO)
Fresh Cream (1967, RSO)
Wheels of Fire (1968, RSO)
The Best of ... (1969, Atco)
Goodbye (1969, RSO)
Heavy Cream (1973, Polydor)

*Blind Faith

*Can't Find My Way Home (1969,
Atco)
*Presence of the Lord (1969, Atco)
*Well All Right (1969, Atco)

Blind Faith (1969, Atco)

Derek and the Dominoes

*Layla (1970, Atco)
*Why Does Love Got to Be So Sad?
(1970, RSO)

Layla (1970, RSO)

Eric Clapton (1945-) solo

*After Midnight (1970, Atco)
*I Can't Hold Out (1974, RSO)
*I Shot the Sheriff (1974, RSO)
Willie and the Handjive (1974,
RSO)
*Lay Down Sally (1978, RSO)
*Promises (1978, RSO)

*Cocaine (1980, RSO)
*I Can't Stand It (1981, RSO)

461 Ocean Boulevard (1972, Atco)
History of ... (1972, Atco)
Slowhand (1977, RSO)
Backless (1978, RSO)
Just One Night (1980, RSO)
Another Ticket (1981, RSO)
August (1986, Warner Bros.)

Jeff Beck (1944-)

*Beck's Bolero (1967, Epic)
*Love Is Blue (1967 , Epic)
*I Ain't Superstitious (1968, Epic)
*I've Been Drinking (1968, Epic)
*Rock My Plimsoul (1968, Epic)
*You Shook Me (1968, Epic)
*Plynth (1969, Epic)
*Rice Pudding (1969, Epic)
*Raynes Park Blues (1971, Epic)
*Situation (1971, Epic)

Truth (1968, Epic)
Beck-Ola (1969, Epic)
Jeff Beck Group/Rough and Ready
(1971, Epic)
Blow By Blow (1975, Epic)
Wired (1976, Epic)
There and Back (1980, Epic)

*Them

*Baby Please Don't Go (1964,
Decca)
*Don't Start Crying Now (1964,
Decca)
*Gloria (1965, Parrot)
*Here Comes the Night (1965,
Parrot)
*Mystic Eyes (1965, Parrot)
It's All Over Now Baby Blue (1966,
Parrot)
Out of Sight (1966, Parrot)

Angry Young Them (1964, Decca)
Them (1965, Parrot)
Them Again (1966, Parrot)
Them Featuring Van Morrison
(1972, Parrot)

Van Morrison (1945-)

*Brown Eyed Girl (1967, Bang)
He Ain't Give You None (1967, Bang)
Ro Ro Rosey (1967, Bang)
T.B. Sheets (1967, Bang)
Blue Money (1970, Warner Bros.)
Call Me Up in the Dreamland (1970, Warner Bros.)
*Come Running (1970, Warner Bros.)
Crazy Love (1970, Warner Bros.)
*Domino (1970, Warner Bros.)
*Moondance (1970, Warner Bros.)
Stoned Me (1970, Warner Bros.)
*Wild Night (1971, Warner Bros.)
Almost Independence Day (1972, Warner Bros.)
Listen to the Lion (1972, Warner Bros.)
St. Dominic's Preview (1972, Warner Bros.)
Heavy Connection (1977, Warner Bros.)
It Fills You Up (1977, Warner Bros.)
Angelou (1978, Warner Bros.)
It's All in the Game (1978, Warner Bros.)

*Blowin' Your Mind (1967, Bang)
*Astral Weeks (1968, Warner Bros.)
Best of . . . (1970, Bang)
*Moondance (1970, Warner Bros.)
*Van Morrison, His Band and Streetchoir (1970, Warner Bros.)
*Tupelo Honey (1971, Warner Bros.)
*St. Dominic's Preview (1972, Warner Bros.)
*Veedon Fleece (1974, Warner Bros.)
*Into the Music (1979, Warner Bros.)
*Common One (1981, Warner Bros.)
*Beautiful Vision (1982, Warner Bros.)
*Inarticulate Speech of the Heart (1983, Warner Bros.)
*Sense of Wonder (1984, Warner Bros.)

*No Guru, No Method, No Teacher (1986, Mercury)

*Pretty Things

Don't Bring Me Down (1964, Fontana)
Rosalyn (1964, Fontana)
Cry to Me (1965, Fontana)
Honey I Need (1965, Fontana)
Come See Me (1966, Fontana)
A House in the Country (1966, Fontana)
Midnight to Six Man (1966, Fontana)
Deflecting Grey (1967, De Wolf)

Get the Picture (1965, Fontana)
The Pretty Things (1965, Fontana)
Electric Banana (1967, De Wolf)
Emotions (1967, De Wolf)
We Want Your Love (1967, De Wolf)
More Electric Banana (1968, De Wolf)
Even More Electric Banana (1969, De Wolf)
S.F. Sorrow (1969, Rare Earth)
Parachute (1970, Rare Earth)
Silk Torpedo (1974, Swan Song)
*Attention! The Pretty Things! (1975, Fontana)
Greatest Hits (1975, Philips)
Savage Eyes (1975, Swan Song)
The Vintage Years (1976, Sire)
The Singles (1977, Harvest)
Live (1978, Jade)
Real Pretty (1979, Rare Earth)

Jimi Hendrix (1942-1970)

Fire (1967, Reprise)
*Hey Joe (1967, Reprise)
I Don't Live Today (1967, Reprise)
Manic Depression (1967, Reprise)
*Purple Haze (1967, Reprise)
*All Along the Watchtower (1968, Reprise)
Castles Made of Sand (1968, Reprise)

Little Wing (1968, Reprise)
Voodoo Chile (1968, Reprise)
Machine Gun (1970, Capitol)

Are You Experienced? (1967, Reprise)
Axis: Bold as Love (1967, Reprise)
Electric Ladyland (1968, Reprise)
Smash Hits (1969, Reprise)
Band of Gypsies (1970, Capitol)
Jimi Hendrix and Otis Redding Live at the Monterey International Pop Festival (1970, Reprise)

*Led Zeppelin

*Dazed and Confused (1969, Atlantic)
*Good Times Bad Times (1969, Atlantic)
*Whole Lotta Love (1969, Atlantic)
Hangman (1970, Atlantic)
*Immigrant Song (1970, Atlantic)
Living Loving Maid (1970, Atlantic)
Out on the Tiles (1970, Atlantic)
Tangerine (1970, Atlantic)
That's the Way (1970, Atlantic)
*Stairway to Heaven (1971, Atlantic)
*Black Dog (1972, Atlantic)
Going to California (1972, Atlantic)
Rock and Roll (1972, Atlantic)
When the Levee Breaks (1972, Atlantic)
The Crunge (1973, Atlantic)
Dancing Days (1973, Atlantic)
*D'yer Mak'er (1973, Atlantic)
No Quarter (1973, Atlantic)
Over the Hills and Far Away (1973, Atlantic)
*Kashmir (1975, Swan)
*Trampled Underfoot (1975, Swan)
Achilles Last Stand (1976, Swan)
Candy Store Rock (1976, Swan)
Hots on for Nowhere (1976, Swan)
Royal Orleans (1976, Swan)
*Fool in the Rain (1980, Swan)

Led Zeppelin (1969, Atlantic)
Led Zeppelin 2 (1969, Atlantic)

Led Zeppelin 3 (1970, Atlantic)
Untitled (1971, Atlantic)
Houses of the Holy (1973, Atlantic)
Physical Graffiti (1975, Swan)
Presence (1976, Swan)
The Song Remains the Same (1976, Swan)
In Through the Out Door (1979, Swan)

Jimmy Page (1944-) solo

Death Wish 2 (1982, Swan Song)

Robert Plant (1948-) solo

Pictures at Eleven (1982, Swan Song)
Principle of Movements (1984, Atlantic)

Robert Plant with Jimmy Page

Honeydrippers, Vol. 1 (1984, Es Paranza)

*Spooky Tooth

*Society's Child (1971, A&M)
*Better by You, Better by Me (1969, Island)
*Evil Woman (1969, Island)
*Hangman Hang My Shell on a Tree (1969, Island)
*Waiting for the Wind (1969, Island)

It's All About . . . (1968, Island)
Spooky Two (1969, A&M)
The Last Puff (1970, A&M)
You Broke My Heart So I Busted Your Jaw (1973, A&M)

*Fleetwood Mac

*Albatross (1968, Blue Horizon)
*Black Magic Woman (1968, Blue Horizon)
*Need Your Love So Bad (1968, Blue Horizon)
*Man of the World (1969, Blue Horizon)

The Green Maharishi (1970,
 Warner Bros.)
*Oh Well (1970, Warner Bros.)
Over My Head (1975, Reprise)
Rhiannon (Will You Ever Win)
 (1976, Reprise)
Say You Love Me (1976, Reprise)
*Don't Stop (1977, Warner Bros.)
*Dreams (1977, Warner Bros.)
*Go Your Own Way (1977, Warner
 Bros.)
*You Make Loving Fun (1977,
 Warner Bros.)
Beautiful Child (1979, Warner
 Bros.)
Not That Funny (1979, Warner
 Bros.)
*Sara (1979, Warner Bros.)
*Tusk (1979, Warner Bros.)
Think About Me (1980, Warner
 Bros.)
Gypsy (1982, Warner Bros.)
*Hold Me (1982, Warner Bros.)
Love in Store (1982, Warner Bros.)

Fleetwood Mac (1968, Blue
 Horizon)
The Original Fleetwood Mac (1968,
 Polydor)
English Rose (1969, Warner Bros.)
Mr. Wonderful (1969, Blue
 Horizon)
Then Play On (1969, Warner Bros.)
Kiln House (1970, Warner Bros.)
Fleetwood Mac in Chicago (1971,
 Sire)
Future Games (1971, Warner Bros.)
Bare Trees (1972, Warner Bros.)
Heroes Are Hard to Find (1974,
 Warner Bros.)
Fleetwood Mac (1975, Warner
 Bros.)
Original Fleetwood Mac (1977,
 Warner Bros.)
Rumors (1977, Warner Bros.)
Vintage Years (1977, Warner Bros.)
Tusk (1979, Sire)
Fleetwood Mac Live (1980, Warner
 Bros.)

Mirage (1982, Warner Bros.)
Tango in the Night (1987, Warner
 Bros.)

Lindsey Buckingham (1947-) solo

Go Insane (1984, Elektra)

Stevie Nicks (1948-) solo

Bella Donna (1981, Modern)
The Wild Heart (1983, Modern)
Rock a Little (1985, Modern)

*Colosseum

*Valentyne Sweet (1969, Dunhill)

*Those Who Are About to Die Salute
 You* (1969, Dunhill)
Valentyne Suite (1969, Dunhill)
Daughter of Time (1970, Dunhill)
Collector's Colosseum (1971,
 Bronze)
Live (1971, Warner Bros.)

Colosseum 2

Strange New Flesh (1976, Warner
 Bros.)
Electric Savage (1977, MCA)
Wardance (1978, MCA)

Garland Jeffreys (1944-)

Ghost Writer (1977, A&M)
One-Eyed Jack (1978, A&M)
American Boy and Girl (1979,
 A&M)
Escape Artist (1981, Epic)
Rock'n'Roll Adult (1981, Epic)

*Ten Years After

*Spoonful (1967, Deram)
*I'm Going Home (1969, Deram)
*Love Like a Man (1970, Deram)
*I'd Love to Change the World
 (1971, Columbia)
*Baby Won't You Let Me
 Rock'n'Roll You (1972,
 Columbia)

*Choo Choo Mama (1973, Columbia)

London Collector: Ten Years After (London)
Ten Years After (1967, Deram)
Undead (1968, Deram)
Sssh (1969, Deram)
Stonehenge (1969, Deram)
Cricklewood Green (1970, Deram)
Watt (1970, Deram)
A Space in Time (1971, Columbia)
Rock and Roll Music to the World (1972, Columbia)
Anthology (1976, Columbia)
Classic Performances (1977, Columbia)
Hear Me Calling (1981, Decca)

Alvin Lee (1944-) solo

In Flight (1974, Columbia)

Savoy Brown

*I'm Tired (1969, Parrot)
Savoy Brown Boogie (1969, Parrot)
Train to Nowhere (1969, Parrot)
*Tell Mama (1971, Parrot)

London Collector--The Best of . . . (London)
Shake Down (1967, Decca)
Getting to the Pint (1968, Parrot)
A Step Further (1969, Parrot)
Looking In (1970, Parrot)
Raw Sienna (1970, Parrot)
Street Corner Talking (1971, Parrot)
Hellbound Train (1972, Parrot)
Lion's Share (1972, Parrot)
Blues Roots (1978, Decca)
Rock'n'Roll Warriors (1981, Town House)

*Family

*No Mule's Fool (1969, Reprise)
*Strange Band/The Weaver's Answer (1970, Reprise)

*In My Own Time (1971, United Artists)
*Burlesque (1972, United Artists)

Music in a Doll's House (1968, Reprise)
Family Entertainment (1969, Reprise)
Anyway (1970, United Artists)
A Song for Me (1970, Reprise)
Fearless (1971, United Artists)
Bandstand (1972, United Artists)
It's Only a Movie (1973, United Artists)
Best of . . . (1974, Reprise)

GOSPEL-INFLUENCED GROUPS

*Procol Harum

*Homburg (1967, A&M)
*A Whiter Shade of Pale (1967, Deram)
*Quite Rightly So (1968, A&M)
*A Salty Dog (1969, A&M)
Conquistador (1972, A&M)
Pandora's Box (1975, A&M)

Procol Harum (1967, Deram)
A Whiter Shade of Pale (1967, A&M)
Shine On Brightly (1968, A&M)
A Salty Dog (1969, A&M)
Home (1970, A&M)
The Best of . . . (1973, A&M)
Grand Hotel (1973, Chrysalis)
Exotic Birds and Fruit (1974, Chrysalis)
Procol's Ninth (1975, Chrysalis)
Something Magic (1977, Chrysalis)

*Traffic

*Here We Go around the Mulberry Bush (1967, United Artists)
*Hole in My Shoe (1967, United Artists)
*Paper Sun (1967, United Artists)

*No Face, No Name, No Number
(1968, United Artists)
*Empty Pages (1970, United Artists)
Gimme Some Lovin', Part One
(1971, United Artists)
Rock & Roll Stew, Part One (1972,
United Artists)

Mr. Fantasy (1967, United Artists)
Feelin' Alright (1968, United
Artists)
Traffic (1968, United Artists)
*Who Knows What Tomorrow May
Bring* (1968, United Artists)
You Can All Join In (1968, United
Artists)
Last Exit (1969, United Artists)
The Best of . . . (1970, United
Artists)
Freedom Rider (1970, United
Artists)
John Barleycorn Must Die (1970,
United Artists)
The Low Spark of High Heeled Boys
(1971, Island)
Welcome to the Canteen (1971,
United Artists)
Shoot Out at the Fantasy Factory
(1973, Island)
When the Eagle Flies (1974,
Asylum)
Heavy Traffic (1975, United Artists)

Steve Winwood (1948-) solo

*Hold On (1977, Island)
*Let Me Make Something in Your
Life (1977, Island)
*Time Is Running Out (1977, Island)
*Vacant Chair (1977, Island)
*Arc of a Diver (1980, Island)
*While You See a Chance (1980,
Island)
*The Height Love (1986, Island)

Steve Winwood (1977, Island)
Arc of a Diver (1980, Island)
Talking Back to the Night (1982,
Island)
Back in the High Life (1986, Island)

Joe Cocker (1944-)

*I'll Cry Instead (1964, Decca)
*Marjorine (1968, A&M)
*With a Little Help From My Friends
(1968, A&M)
*Delta Lady (1969, A&M)
*Feeling Alright (1969, A&M)
*Cry Me a River (1970, A&M)
*Hitchcock Railway (1970, A&M)
*The Letter (1970, A&M)
*She Came In through the Bathroom
Window (1970, A&M)
Black-Eyed Blues (1971, A&M)
*High Time We Went (1971, A&M)
*Midnight Rider (1972, A&M)
Woman to Woman (1972, A&M)
*Pardon Me Sir (1973, A&M)
*Put Out the Light (1974, A&M)
*You Are So Beautiful (1975, A&M)
Catfish (1976, A&M)
Fun Time (1978, A&M)
Up Where We Belong (1982,
Island)

Joe Cocker! (1969, A&M)
With a Little Help from My Friends
(1969, A&M)
Mad Dogs and Englishmen (1970,
A&M)
Joe Cocker (1972, A&M)
Jamaica Say You Will (1975, A&M)
Stingray (1976, A&M)
Joe Cocker's Greatest Hits (1977,
A&M)
Luxury You Can Afford (1978,
Asylum)
Sheffield Steel (1982, Island)
Cocker (1986, Capitol)

FOLK-INFLUENCED
GROUPS

*Pink Floyd

*Arnold Layne/Candy and a Currant
Bun (Let's Roll Another One)
(1967, EMI)

*Astronomy Domine (1967, EMI)
*Bike (1967, EMI)
*Flaming (1967, EMI)
*Interstellar Overdrive (1967, EMI)
*See Emily Play (1967, EMI)
 It Would Be So Nice (1968, EMI)
*Let There Be More Light (1968,
 Capitol)
 Point Me at the Sky (1968, Capitol)
*Remember a Day (1968, Capitol)
*See Saw (1968, Capitol)
*Set the Controls for the Heart of the
 Sun (1968, Capitol)
*Grantchester Meadows (1969,
 Harvest)
*Echoes (1971, Harvest)
*Breathe (1973, Harvest)
*Eclipse (1973, Harvest)
*Money (1973, Harvest)
*On the Run (1973, Harvest)
*Time (1973, Harvest)
*Have a Cigar (1975, Columbia)
*Shine On You Crazy Diamond
 (1975, Columbia)
*Welcome to the Machine (1975,
 Columbia)
*Raving a Drooling Sheep (1977,
 Columbia)
*You've Gotta Be Crazy (Dogs)
 (1977, Columbia)
*Another Brick in the Wall (Part 2)
 (1980, Columbia)

*Masters of Rock/Best of . . . (1967,
 EMI)
 *The Piper at the Gates of Dawn
 (1967, Tower)
*A Saucer Full of Secrets (1968,
 Capitol)
 *Tonight Let's All Make Love in
 London (1968, Instant Analysis)
 *More '69, Capitol)
 *Atom Heart Mother (1970, Harvest)
 *Zabriskie Point (1970, MGM)
*Meddle (1971, Harvest)
 *Obscured by Clouds (1972, Harvest)
*The Dark Side of the Moon (1973,
 Harvest)
*Animals (1975, Columbia)

*Wish You Were Here (1975,
 Columbia)
*The Wall (1979, Columbia)
 *A Collection of Great Dance Songs
 (1981, Columbia)
 *The Final Cut (1983, Columbia)
 *A Momentary Lapse of Reason
 (1987, Columbia)

*Incredible String Band

*The First Girl I Loved (1967,
 Elektra)
*I Was a Young Man Way Back in
 the 1960s (1967, Elektra)
*A Very Cellular Song (1968,
 Elektra)
*You Get Brighter (1968, Elektra)
*Greatest Friend (1969, Elektra)
*Sleepers, Awake! (1969, Elektra)

 *The Incredible String Band (1966,
 Elektra)
 *The 5000 Spirits or the Layers of the
 Onion (1967, Elektra)
*The Hangman's Beautiful Daughter
 (1968, Elektra)
 *Wee Tam (1968, Elektra)
 *The Big Huge (1969, Elektra)
 *Changing Horses (1969, Elektra)
 *Relics (1970, Elektra)

*Pentangle

 *The Pentangle (1968, Reprise)
 *Sweet Child (1969, Reprise)
 *Basket of Light (1970, Reprise)
 *Cruel Sister (1971, Reprise)
 *Reflections (1971, Reprise)
 *History Book (1972, Transatlantic)
 *Solomon's Seal (1972, Reprise)
 *Collection (1975, Transatlantic)
*Anthology (1978, Transatlantic)

*Jethro Tull

 Bourree (1969, Reprise)
 Fat Man (1969, Reprise)
 For a Thousand Mothers (1969,
 Reprise)

*Living in the Past (1969, Reprise)
*Love Story (1969, Reprise)
 A New Day Yesterday (1969,
   Reprise)
*Sweet Dreams (1969, Reprise)
*The Witch's Promise/The Teacher
   (1970, Reprise)
*Cross-Eyed Mary (1971, Chrysalis)
*Hymn 43 (1971, Chrysalis)
*Life's Long Song (1971, Reprise)
*Locomotive Breath (1971,
   Chrysalis)
*A Passion Play (1973, Chrysalis)
*Bungle in the Jungle (1974,
   Chrysalis)
*Minstrel in the Gallery (1975,
   Chrysalis)
*The Whistler (1977, Chrysalis)

*Stand Up (1969, Chrysalis)
*This Was (1969, Chrysalis)
 Benefit (1970, Chrysalis)
 Aqualung (1971, Chrysalis)
*Living in the Past (1972, Chrysalis)
 Thick as a Brick (1972, Chrysalis)
 Passion Play (1973, Chrysalis)
 War Child (1974, Chrysalis)
 Minstrel in the Gallery (1975,
   Chrysalis)
 MU--The Best of . . . (1976,
   Chrysalis)
 Repeat (1977, Chrysalis)
 Songs from the Wood (1977,
   Chrysalis)
 Bursting Out (1978, Chrysalis)
 Heavy Horses (1978, Chrysalis)
 Stormwatch (1979, Chrysalis)
*A (1980, Chrysalis)
 The Broadsword and the Beast
   (1982, Chrysalis)

*Fairport Convention

 A Sailor's Life (1969, Island)
*Si Tu Dois Partir (If You Gotta Go,
   Go Now) (1969, Polydor)

*Fairport Convention (1969, A&M)
*Unhalfbricking (1969, A&M)

What We Did on Our Holiday
   (1969, Island)
Full House (1970, A&M)
Liege and Lief (1970, A&M)
Babbacombe Lee (1972, Island)
The History of . . . (1972, Island)
Rising for the Moon (1975, Island)
Fairport Chronicles (1976, A&M)

Richard and Linda Thompson

*Wall of Death (1982, Hannibal)

*Richard Thompson Starring as Henry
   the Human Fly* (1972, Island)
Hokey Pokey (1974, Island)
*I Want to See the Bright Lights
   Tonight* (1974, Island)
Pour Down Like Silver (1975,
   Island)
Richard Thompson (1976, Island)
Live (More or Less) (1977, Island)
First Light (1978, Chrysalis)
Sunnyvista (1979, Chrysalis)
Strict Tempo! (1981, Elixir)
Shoot Out the Lights (1982,
   Hannibal)
Hand of Kindness (1983, Hannibal)

Richard Thompson (1949-) solo

Across a Crowded Room (1985 ,
   Polydor)
Daring Adventures (1986, Polydor)

Linda Thompson solo

One Clear Moment (1985, Warner
   Bros.)

Rod Stewart (1945-)

*(I Know) I'm Losing You (1971,
   Mercury)
*Maggie May (1971, Mercury)
*Reason to Believe (1971, Mercury)
 Angle (1972, Mercury)
 Handbags and Gladrags (1972,
   Mercury)
 Stay with Me (1972, Mercury)
 You Wear It Well (1972, Mercury)

Cindy Incidentally (1973, Mercury)
Oh! No Not My Baby (1973,
Mercury)
Farewell/Bring It On Home to
Me/You Send Me (1974,
Mercury)
Mine for Me (1974, Mercury)
Sailing (1975, Mercury)
This Old Heart of Mine (1976,
Warner Bros.)
*Tonight's the Night (Gonna Be
Alright) (1976, Warner Bros.)
The First Cut Is the Deepest (1977,
Warner Bros.)
The Killing of George, Parts 1 & 2
(1977, Warner Bros.)
*You're in My Heart (The Final
Acclaim) (1977, Warner Bros.)
*Da Ya Think I'm Sexy? (1978,
Warner Bros.)
Hot Legs (1978, Warner Bros.)
I Was Only Joking (1978, Warner
Bros.)
Ain't Love a Bitch (1979, Warner
Bros.)
I Don't Want to Talk About It
(1979, Warner Bros.)
*Passion (1980, Warner Bros.)
*Young Turks (1981, Warner Bros.)
Tonight I'm Yours (1982, Warner
Bros.)
Baby Jane (1983, Warner Bros.)
What Am I Gonna Do (I'm So In
Love With You) (1983, Warner
Bros.)
*Infatuation (1984, Warner Bros.)
*Some Guys Have All the Luck
(1984, Warner Bros.)

Rod Stewart and Steampacket
(Specialty)
Rod Stewart and the Faces
(Specialty)
The Rod Stewart Album (1969,
Mercury)
Gasoline Alley (1970, Mercury)
Every Picture Tells a Story (1971,
Mercury)

Never a Dull Moment (1972,
Mercury)
Sing It Again Rod (1973, Mercury)
Smiler (1974, Mercury)
Atlantic Crossing (1975, Warner
Bros.)
Best of . . ., Vols. 1-2 (1976,
Mercury)
A Night on the Town (1976, Warner
Bros.)
Foot Loose and Fancy Free (1977,
Warner Bros.)
Tonight I'm Yours (1981, Warner
Bros.)
Body Wishes (1983, Warner Bros.)
Camouflage (1984, Warner Bros.)
Rod Stewart (1986, Warner Bros.)

*Blodwyn Pig

Ahead Rings Out (1969, A&M)
Getting to This (1970, A&M)

*Strawbs

Lay Down (1972, A&M)
Part of the Union (1973, A&M)
Shine On Silver Sun (1973, A&M)

Strawbs (1969, A&M)
Dragonfly (1970, A&M)
*Just a Collection of Antiques and
Curios* (1970, A&M)
From the Witchwood (1971, A&M)
Grave New World (1972, A&M)
All Our Own Work (1973,
Hallmark)
Bursting at the Seams (1973, A&M)
By Choice (1974, A&M)
Hero and Heroin (1974, A&M)
Ghost (1975, A&M)
Nomadness (1975, A&M)
Deep Cuts (1976, Oyster)
Burning for You (1977, A&M)
Best of . . . (1978, A&M)
Deadlines (1978, A&M)

Humble Pie

*Natural Born Boogie (1969,
  Immediate)
*I Don't Need No Doctor (1971,
  A&M)

As Safe as Yesterday Is (1969,
  Immediate)
Performance: Rockin' at Fillmore
  (1971, A&M)
On to Victory* (1980, Atco)
Go for the Throat* (1981, Atco)

BRITISH POP

*Elton John (1947-)

*I've Been Loving You (1968, MCA)
*Lady Samantha (1969, MCA)
*Your Song (1970, Unicorn)
Friends (1971, Unicorn)
*Crocodile Rock (1972, MCA)
*Honky Cat (1972, MCA)
Levon (1972, Unicorn)
*Rocket Man (1972, MCA)
*Daniel (1973, MCA)
*Goodbye Yellow Brick Road (1973,
  MCA)
*Bennie and the Jets (1974, MCA)
*The Bitch Is Back (1974, MCA)
*Don't Let the Sun Go Down on Me
  (1974, MCA)
*Lucy in the Sky with Diamonds
  (1974, MCA)
*Island Girl (1975, MCA)
*Philadelphia Freedom (1975, MCA)
*Someone Saved My Life Tonight
  (1975, MCA)
I Feel Like a Bullet (In the Gun of
  Robert Ford) (1976, MCA)
Sorry Seems to Be the Hardest
  Word (1976, MCA)
Mama Can't Buy You Love (1979,
  MCA)
Little Jeannie (1980, MCA)
I Guess That's Why They Call It the
  Blues (1983, Geffen)

Sad Songs (Say So Much) (1984,
  Geffen)

Empty Sky (1969, MCA)
Elton John (1970, MCA)
Madman Across the River (1971,
  MCA)
Tumbleweed Connection (1971,
  MCA)
*Don't Shoot Me, I'm Only the Piano
  Player* (1972, MCA)
Honky Chateau (1972, MCA)
Goodbye Yellow Brick Road (1973,
  MCA)
Greatest Hits (1974, MCA)
*Capt. Fantastic and the Brown Dirt
  Cowboy* (1975, MCA)
Rock of the Westies (1975, MCA)
Greatest Hits, Vol. 2 (1977, MCA)
A Single Man (1978, MCA)

ROCK COMEDY/
THEATRICAL ROCK

*Bonzo Dog

I'm Gonna Bring a Watermelon to
  My Baby Tonight (1966,
  Parlophone)
My Brother Makes the Noise for the
  Talkies (1966, Parlophone)
Death Cab for Cutie (1967,
  Liberty)
Jollity Farm (1967, Liberty)
Mickey's Son and Daughter (1967,
  Liberty)
Piggy Bank Love (1967, Liberty)
I Left My Heart in San Francisco
  (1968, Liberty)
*I'm the Urban Spaceman (1968,
  Liberty)

Urban Spaceman (Imperial)
Gorilla (1967, Liberty)
*The Doughnut in Granny's
  Greenhouse* (1968, Liberty)
Keynsham (1969, Imperial)
Tadpoles (1969, Liberty)

Beast of the Bonzos (1971, United
  Artists)
Let's Make Up and Be Friendly
  (1972, United Artists)
The History of the Bonzos (1974,
  United Artists)

*Arthur Brown (1944-)

*Fire (1968, Atlantic)

The Crazy World of Arthur Brown
  (1968, Atlantic)
Galactic Zoo Dossier (1972,
  Polydor)
The Journey (1973, Polydor)
Kingdom Come (1973, Track)
Dance with Arthur Brown (1975,
  Gull)

ART ROCK

Moody Blues

Lose Your Money (1964, London)
Everyday (1965, London)
*From the Bottom of My Heart
  (1965, London)
*Go Now! (1965, London)
I Don't Want to Go On Without
  You (1965, London)
Stop! (1966, Decca)
*Nights in White Satin (1967,
  Deram)
Om (1968, Deram)
*Ride My See-Saw (1968, Deram)
*Tuesday Afternoon (Forever
  Afternoon) (1968, Deram)
Voices in the Sky (1968, Deram)
Question (1970, Threshold)
The Story in Your Eyes (1971,
  Threshold)
Isn't Life Strange? (1972,
  Threshold)
I'm Just a Singer (In a Rock'n'Roll
  Band) (1973, Threshold)
Steppin' in a Slide Zone (1978,
  London)
Gemini Dream (1981, Threshold)

The Voice (1981, Threshold)
Sitting at the Wheel (1983,
  Threshold)

Go Now! (1965, London)
The Magnificent Moodies (1966,
  Decca)
Days of Future Passed (1967,
  Deram)
In Search of the Lost Chord (1968,
  Deram)
On the Threshold of a Dream (1969,
  Deram)
A Question of Balance (1970,
  Threshold)
*To Our Children's Children's
  Children* (1970, Threshold)
Every Boy Deserves Favour (1971,
  Threshold)
Seventh Sojourn (1972, Threshold)
This Is . . . (1974, Threshold)
Octave (1978, London)
Long Distance Voyager (1981,
  Threshold)
The Other Side of Life (1986,
  Polydor)

Move

*Flowers in the Rain (1967, Regal
  Zonophone)
*I Can Hear the Grass Grow (1967,
  Regal Zonophone)
*Night of Fear (1967, Regal
  Zonophone)
*Blackberry Way (1968, Regal
  Zonophone)
*Fire Brigade (1968, Regal
  Zonophone)
Curly (1969, Regal Zonophone)
Brontosaurus (1970, A&M)
Chinatown (1971, A&M)
Tonight (1971, A&M)
California Man (1972, A&M)
*Do Ya (1972, Elektra)

The Move (1968, Regal
  Zonophone)
The Best of . . . (1970, A&M)
Shazam (1970, A&M)

Fire Brigade (1971, MFP)
Looking On (1971, Capitol)
Message from the Country (1971, Capitol)
California Man (1972, Harvest)
Split Ends (1972, United Artists)
Shines On (1979 , Harvest)

Soft Machine

Feelin' Reelin' Squealin' (1966, Probe)
Love Makes Sweet Music (1966, Probe)
Moon in June (1970, Columbia)

At the Beginning (Probe)
The Soft Machine (1968, Probe)
Volume 2 (1968, Columbia)
Third (1970, Columbia)
Fourth (1971, Columbia)
Fifth (1972, Columbia)
Sixth (1973, Columbia)
Seventh (1973, Columbia)
Bundles (1975, Harvest)
Softs (1976, Harvest)
Triple Echo (1977, Harvest)
Alive and Well in Paris (1978, Harvest)
Land of Cockayne (1981, EMO)

Kevin Ayers (1945-) solo

Joy of a Toy (1970, Harvest)
Shooting at the Moon (1971, Harvest)
Whatevershebringswesing (1972, Harvest)
Bananamour (1973, Harvest)
June 1st 1974 (1974, Island)
Sweet Deceiver (1975, Island)
Old Ditties (1976, Island)
Yes, We Have No Mananas (1977, ABC)
Rainbow Takeaway (1978, Harvest)

Caravan

Caravan (1968, MGM)

If I Could Do It All Over Again, I'd Do It All Over You (1970, London)
In The Land of Grey and Pink (1971, London)
Waterloo Lily (1972, London)
For Girls Who Grow Plump in the Night (1973, London)
Caravan and the New Symphonia (1974, London)
Cunning Stunts (1975, London)
Blind Dog at St. Dunstans (1976, Arista)
Canterbury Tales (1976, Decca)
Better by Far (1977, Arista)
The Album (1980, Kingdom)

King Crimson

In the Court of the Crimson King, Part One (1969, Atlantic)

In the Court of the Crimson King (1969, Atlantic)
In the Wake of Poseidon (1970, Atlantic)
Lizard (1971, Atlantic)
Islands (1972, Atlantic)
Lark's Tongue in Aspic (1973, Atlantic)
Red (1974, Atlantic)
Starless and Bible Black (1974, Atlantic)
USA (1975, Atlantic)
Discipline (1981, Warner Bros.)
Beat (1982, War.)
Three of a Perfect Pair (1984, Warner Bros.)

Ian McDonald (1942-) and Mike Giles (1942-)

McDonald and Giles (1971, Cotillion)

Robert Fripp (1946-) solo

Exposure (1979, Polydor)
God Save the Queen-Under Heavy Manners (1980, Polydor)

The Leaque of Gentlemen (1981, Polydor)
Let the Power Fall (1981, Editions EG)

Robert Fripp and Brian Eno *(Brian Eno, 1948-)*

Evening Star (1981, Editions EG)
No Pussyfooting (1981, Editions EG)

Van Der Graaf Generator

*The Aerosol Grey Machine (1968, Mercury)
The Least We Can Do Is Wave (1969, Charisma)
H to He Who Am the Only One (1970, Charisma)
Pawn Hearts (1970, Charisma)

Genesis

*The Knife (1970, Buddah)
*Know What I Like (In Your Wardrobe) (1974, Atco)
The Musical Box (1974, Atco)
Supper's Ready (1974, Atco)
Watchers of the Sky (1974, Atco)
*Spot the Pigeon (1977, Atco)
*Your Own Special Way (1977, Atco)
*Follow You Follow Me (1978, Atco)
*Many Too Many (1978, Atco)
*Misunderstanding (1980, Atlantic)
*Turn It Out Again (1980, Atlantic)
*No Reply at All (1981, Atlantic)
*Abacab (1982, Atlantic)
*Man on the Corner (1982, Atlantic)
*Paperlate (1982, Atlantic)
*That's All! (1983, Atlantic)

From Genesis to Revelation (1969, London)
Trespass (1970, Buddah)
Nursery Cryme (1971, Buddah)
Foxtrot (1972, Buddah)
Genesis Live (1973, Buddah)

*Selling England by the Pound (1973, Atco)
In the Beginning (1974, London)
The Lamb Lies Down on Broadway (1974, Atco)
A Trick of the Tail (1974, Atco)
*Best of . . . (1976, Buddah)
Seconds Out (1977, Atlantic)
Wind and Wuthering (1977, Atco)
And Then There Were Three . . . (1978, Atlantic)
*Duke (1980, Atlantic)
*Abacab (1981, Atlantic)
Three Sides Live (1982, Atlantic)
*Invisible Touch (1986, Atlantic)

Peter Gabriel (1950-) solo

Here Comes the Flood (1977, Atco)
Modern Love (1977, Atco)
Solsbury Hill (1977, Atco)
D.I.Y. (1978, Atlantic)
Home Sweet Home (1978, Atlantic)
On the Air (1978, Atlantic)
Biko (1980, Mercury)
Games without Frontiers (1980, Mercury)
I Don't Remember (1980, Mercury)
Lead a Normal Life (1980, Mercury)
*Shock the Monkey (1982, Geffen)

Peter Gabriel (1977, Atco)
Peter Gabriel (1978, Atco)
*Peter Gabriel (1980, Mercury)
Security (1982, Geffen)
*So (1986, Geffen)

Phil Collins (1951-) solo

*I Missed Again (1981, Atlantic)
*In the Air Tonight (1981, Atlantic)
*You Can't Hurry Love (1982, Atlantic)
*I Don't Care Anymore (1983, Atlantic)
*Against All Odds (Take a Look at Me Now) (1984, Atlantic)
*Don't Lose My Number (1985, Atlantic)

Face Value (1981, Atlantic)
Hello, I Must Be Going (1983, Atlantic)
*No Jacket Required (1985, Atlantic)

Mike Rutherford (1950-) solo

Mike and the Mechanics (1986, Atlantic)

Supertramp

Supertramp: Supertramp (1970, A&M)
*Crime of the Century (1974, A&M)
Even in the Quietest Moments (1977, A&M)

Gentle Giant

Gentle Giant (1970, Vertigo)
Acquiring the Taste (1971, Vertigo)
Three Friends (1972, Columbia)
In a Glass House (1973, WWA)
The Power and the Glory (1974, Capitol)
*Free Hand (1975, Capitol)
A Giant Step (1975, Vertigo)
Interview (1976, Capitol)
Playing the Fool (1977, Capitol)
Civilian (1980, Columbia)
Official "Live" Gentle Giant (1981, Capitol)

Jade Warrior

Jade Warrior (1971, Vertigo)
Released (1971, Vertigo)
Last Autumn's Dream (1972, Vertigo)
Waves (1975, Island)
Kites (1976, Island)

Gong

Angel's Egg (1973, Virgin)
The Flying Teapot (1973, Virgin)
Camembert Electrique (1974, Caroline)
Continental Circus (1974, Philips)

You (1974, Virgin)
Shamal (1976, Virgin)
Expresso (1977, Virgin)
Gazeuse (1977, Virgin)
Gong Est Mort (1977, Tapioca)
Live (1977, Virgin)
Magick Brother (1977, Affinity)
Expresso 2 (1978, Arista)
Downwind (1979, Arista)
Pierre Moerlen's Gong Live (1979, Arista)
Time Is the Key (1979, Arista)

Emerson, Lake, and Palmer

(Keith Emerson, 1944- ; Greg Lake, 1948- ; Cark Palmer, 1951-)

**Lucky Man (1971, Cotillion)
**From the Beginning (1972, Cotillion)
**Nutrocker (1972, Cotillion)
**Karn Evil Nine (1973, Atlantic)
**Fanfare for the Common Man (1977, Atlantic)

*Emerson, Lake and Palmer (1970, Cotillion-Atlantic)
Tarkus (1971, Cotillion-Atlantic)
*Pictures at an Exhibition (1972, Manticore-Atlantic)
Brain Salad Surgery (1973, Manticore-Atlantic)

Emerson, Lake, and Powell

Emerson, Lake & Powell (1986, Polydor)

Yes

**Your Move (1971, Atlantic)
**America (1972, Atlantic)
**And You and I (1972, Atlantic)
**Roundabout (1972, Atlantic)
Going for the One (1977, Atlantic)
Wonderous Stories (1977, Atlantic)
Don't Kill the Whale (1978, Atlantic)

Owner of a Lonely Heart (1983, Atco)
Cinema/Leave It (1984, Atco)

Yes (1969, Atlantic)
Time and the Word (1970, Atlantic)
Fragile (1971, Atlantic)
The Yes Album (1971, Atlantic)
Close to the Edge (1972, Atlantic)
Tales from Topographic Oceans (1973, Atlantic)
Yessongs (1973, Atlantic)
Relayer (1974, Atlantic)
Yesterdays (1975, Atlantic)
90125 (1984, Atco)

Rick Wakeman (1949-) solo

Six Wives of Henry VIII (1973, A&M)
Journey to the Centre of the Earth (1974, A&M)

Electric Light Orchestra

Mr. Radio (1972, United Artists)
10538 Overture (1972, United Artists)
Kuiama (1973, United Artists)
Roll Over Beethoven (1973, United Artists)
Showdown (1973, United Artists)
Daybreaker (1974, United Artists)
Ma-Ma-Ma-Belle (1974, United Artists)
Can't Get It Out of My Head (1975, United Artists)
Evil Woman (1975, United Artists)
Livin' Thing (1976, United Artists)
Strange Magic (1976, United Artists)
Telephone Line (1977, United Artists)
Don't Bring Me Down (1979, Jet)
Shine a Little Love (1979, Jet)
Hold On Tight (1981, Jet)

No Answer (1972, United Artists)
ELO 2 (1973, United Artists)
Eldorado (1974, United Artists)

The Night the Lights Went On in Long Beach (1974, United Artists)
On the Third Day (1974, United Artists)
Face the Music (1975, United Artists)
Ole ELO (1975, United Artists)
A New World Record (1976, Jet)
Out of the Blue (1977, Jet)
Discovery (1979, Jet)
Time (1981, Jet)

Brian Eno (1948-)

No Pussyfooting (1973, Island)
Here Come Warm Jets (1974, Island)
Taking Tiger Mountain by Strategy (1974, Island)
Evening Star (1975, Island; 1981, Editions EG)
Another Green World (1976, Island)
Discreet Music (1976, Island)
Cluster and Eno (1977, Island)
Before and After Science (1978, Island)
Music for Films (1978, Polydor)
Music for Airports (1979, Editions EG)
The Plateaux of Mirrors (1980)
Possible Music (1980)
Music for Airplay (1981)
My Life in the Bush of Ghosts (1981, Sire)
On Land (1982)

Pete Shelley

Homosapien (1981, Island)

Human League

Reproduction (1979, Virgin)
Travelogue (1980, Virgin)
Dare (1982, A&M)
Love and Dancing (1983, A&M)
Crash (1986, A&M)

Depeche Mode

I Just Can't Get Enough (1982, Sire)

Thomas Dolby (1958-)

*Blinded By Science (1983, Harvest)
The Golden Age of Wireless (1983,
  Capitol)
*Flat Earth (1984, Capitol)

Alan Parsons Project

Tales of Mystery and Imagination
  (1976, 20th Century)
*I, Robot (1977, Arista)
Pyramid (1978, Arista)
*Eye In the Sky (1982, Arista)
Best of . . . (1983, Arista)
Ammonia Avenue (1984, Arista)
Vulture Culture (1985, Arista)

Laurie Anderson (1947-)

Big Science (1982, Warner Bros.)
Mister Heartbreak (1984, Warner
  Bros.)
United States Live (1985, Warner
  Bros.)

Country Rock

*Buffalo Springfield

Bluebird (1967, Atco)
Broken Arrow (1967, Atco)
*For What It's Worth (1967, Atco)
Mr. Soul (1967, Atco)
Rock & Roll Woman (1967, Atco)
Kind Woman (1968, Atco)
On the Way Home (1968, Atco)
Uno Mundo (1968, Atco)

Buffalo Springfield (1966, Atco)
*Buffalo Springfield Again (1967,
  Atco)
Last Time Around (1968, Atco)
Retrospective (1969, Atco)
*Buffalo Springfield (1976, Atco)

*Band

Chest Fever (1968, Capitol)
I Shall Be Released (1968, Capitol)
Lonesome Suzie (1968, Capitol)
Long Black Veil (1968, Capitol)
The Weight (1968, Capitol)
Across the Great Divine (1969,
  Capitol)
Jenima Surrender (1969, Capitol)
Look Out Cleveland (1969,
  Capitol)
The Night They Drove Old Dixie
  Down (1969, Capitol)
*Up On Cripple Creek (1969,
  Capitol)
The Shape I'm In (1970, Capitol)
Stage Fright (1970, Capitol)
Time to Kill (1970, Capitol)
Life Is a Carnival (1971, Capitol)
When I Paint My Masterpiece
  (1971, Capitol)
*Don't Do It (1972, Capitol)

*Music from the Big Pink (1968,
  Capitol)
*The Band (1969, Capitol)
Stage Fright (1970, Capitol)
*Rock of Ages (1972, Capitol)

Islands (1977, Capitol)

Levon Helm (1942-) solo

Levon J. Helm and the RCO All Stars (1977, ABC)
American Son (1980, MCA)

Flying Burrito Brothers

The Gilded Palace of Sin (1969, A&M)
Burrito Deluxe (1970, A&M)
The Flying Burrito Bros. (1971, A&M)
Close Up the Honky Tonks (1972, A&M)
Last of the Red Hot Burritos (1972, A&M)
Sleepless Nights (1976, A&M)

*Nitty Gritty Dirt Band

*Buy Me for the Rain (1967, Liberty)
House at Pooh Corner (1970, Liberty)
*Mr. Bojangles (1970, Liberty)
Some of Shelley's Blues (1970, Liberty)
I Saw the Light (1972, United Artists)
*Jambalaya (1972, United Artists)
Keep on the Sunny Side (1972, United Artists)
Orange Blossom Special (1972, United Artists)
*An American Dream (1980, United Artists)
*Make a Little Magic (1980, United Artists)

Nitty Gritty Dirt Band (1967, Liberty)
Pure Dirt (1968, Liberty)
Rare Junk (1968, Liberty)
Alive (1969, Liberty)
Uncle Charlie and His Dog Teddy (1970, Liberty)

All the Good Times (1972, United Artists)
Will the Circle Be Unbroken (1972, United Artists)
Dirt, Silver, and Gold (1976, United Artists)

*Poco

*Crazy Love (1979, ABC)
*Heart of the Night (1979, MCA)

Pickin' Up the Pieces (1969, Epic)
Poco (1970, Epic)
Deliverin' (1971, Epic)
From the Island (1971, Epic)
A Good Feelin' to Know (1972, Epic)
Cantamos (1974, Epic)
Head Over Heels (1975, ABC)
The Very Best of . . . (1975, Epic)
Blue and Grey (1981, MCA)
Cowboys and Englishmen (1982, MCA)
Ghost Town (1982, Atlantic)

*Crosby, Stills & Nash

(David Crosby, 1941- ; Stephen Stills, 1945- ; Graham Nash, 1942-)

*Marrakesh Express (1969, Atlantic)
*Suite: Judy Blue Eyes (1969, Atlantic)
*Just a Song before I Go (1977, Atlantic)
*Southern Cross (1982, Atlantic)
*Wasted on the Way (1982, Atlantic)

Replay (1980, Atlantic)

*Crosby, Stills, Nash & Young

*Ohio (1970, Atlantic)
*Our House (1970, Atlantic)
*Teach Your Children (1970, Atlantic)
*Woodstock (1970, Atlantic)

Deja Vu (1970, Atlantic)
Four Way Street (1971, Atlantic)

So Far (1974, Atlantic)

Neil Young (1945-) solo

Everybody Knows This Is Nowhere
(1969, Reprise)
After the Gold Rush (1970, Reprise)
Harvest (1972, Reprise)
Tonight's the Night (1975, Reprise)
Zuma (1975, Reprise)
Decade (1978, Reprise)
Rust Never Sleeps (1979, Reprise)
Landing on Water (1986, Geffen)

*Stephen Stills solo

*Love the One You're With (1970,
Atlantic)
Change Partners (1971, Atlantic)
*Sit Yourself Down (1971, Atlantic)
Go Back Home (1976, Atlantic)

Stephen Stills (1970, Atlantic)
Stephen Stills 2 (1971, Atlantic)
Manassas (1972, Atlantic)
Still Stills (1976, Atlantic)

*Crosby & Nash

*Immigration Man (1972, Atlantic)
Southbound Train (1972, Atlantic)

Crosby and Nash (1972, Atlantic)
Wind on the Water (1975, ABC)
Live (1977, ABC)
Best of . . . (1978, MCA)

*Commander Cody and His Lost Planet Airmen

(George Frayne)

*Hot Rod Lincoln (1971,
Paramount)
Lost in the Ozone (1971,
Paramount)
Seeds and Stems (Again) (1971,
Paramount)
Mama Hated Diesels (1972,
Paramount)

Lost in the Ozone (1971,
Paramount)
*Hot Licks, Cold Steel, and Trucker's
Favorites* (1972, Paramount)
Country Casanova (1973,
Paramount)
Live from Deep in the Heart of Texas
(1974, Paramount)

James Gang

The James Gang Rides Again (1970,
ABC)
The Best of James Gang/Joe Walsh
(1973, ABC)

Firefall

You Are the Woman (1976,
Atlantic)
Cinderella (1977, Atlantic)
Just Remember I Love You (1977,
Atlantic)
Strange Way (1978, Atlantic)
Headed for a Fall (1980, Atlantic)
Staying with It (1981, Atlantic)

Firefall (1976, Atlantic)
Best of . . . (1981, Atlantic)
Break of Dawn (1982, Atlantic)

Alabama

My Home's Alabama (1980, RCA)
Feels So Right (1981, RCA)
Mountain Music (1982, RCA)
The Closer You Get . . . (1983,
RCA)
Roll On (1984, RCA)
40 Hour Week (1985, RCA)

Marti Jones

Match Game (1986, A&M)

*New Riders of the Purple Sage

New Riders of the Purple Sage
(1971, Columbia)
Powerglide (1972, Columbia)

Adventures of Panama Red (1973, Columbia)
Gypsy Cowboy (1973, Columbia)

*Eagles

*Take It Easy (1972, Asylum)
*Witchy Woman (1972, Asylum)
Peaceful Easy Feeling (1973, Asylum)
*Already Gone (1974, Asylum)
*Best of My Love (1974, Asylum)
*Lyin' Eyes (1975, Asylum)
*One of These Nights (1975, Asylum)
*New Kid in Town (1976, Asylum)
*Take It to the Limit (1976, Asylum)
*Hotel California (1977, Asylum)
Life in the Fast Lane (1977, Asylum)
Please Come Home for Christmas (1978, Asylum)
*Heartache Tonight (1979, Asylum)
*The Long Run (1979, Asylum)
*I Can't Tell You Why (1980, Asylum)
Seven Bridges Road (1981, Asylum)

Eagles (1972, Asylum)
Desperado (1973, Asylum)
On the Border (1974, Asylum)
One of These Nights (1975, Asylum)
Hotel California (1976, Asylum)
Their Greatest Hits (1976, Asylum)
The Long Run (1979, Asylum)

Don Henley (1947-) solo

I Can't Stand Still (1982, Asylum)
Building the Perfect Beast (1985, Geffen)

Joe Walsh (1947-) solo

The Smoker You Drink, The Player You Get (1973, MCA)
So What? (1974, MCA)
The Best of . . . (1978, MCA)
But Seriously Folks (1978, Asylum)

*Dan Fogelberg (1951-)

*Be on Your Way (1972, Columbia)
*To the Morning (1972, Columbia)
Part of the Plan (1975, Epic)
Heart Hotel (1980, Full Moon)
*Longer (1980, Full Moon)
*Same Old Lang Syne (1980, Full Moon)
*Hard to Say (1981, Full Moon)
*Leader of the Band (1981, Full Moon)
Missing You (1982, Full Moon)
Run for the Roses (1982, Full Moon)
Make Love Stay (1983, Full Moon)
The Language of Love (1984, Full Moon)

Home Free (1972, Columbia)
The Innocent Age (1981, Full Moon)

*Asleep at the Wheel

Comin' Right at Ya (1973, United Artists)
Asleep at the Wheel (1974, Epic)
*Bump Bounce Boogie (1975, Capitol)
Fathers and Sons (1975, Epic)
*Let Me Go Home Whiskey (1975, Capitol)
*The Letter That Johnny Walker Read (1975, Capitol)
Texas Gold (1975, Capitol)
*Miles and Miles of Texas (1976, Capitol)
*Nothin' Takes the Place of You (1976, Capitol)
Wheelin' and Dealin' (1976, Capitol)
*My Baby Thinks She's a Train (1977, Capitol)
*The Wheel (1977, Capitol)
*One O'Clock Jump (1978, Capitol)

Collision Course (1978, Capitol)
Served Live (1979, Capitol)
Framed (1980, MCA)
American Band 3 (1981, Capitol)

Singers/Songwriters

Randy Newman (1944-)

Mama Told Me Not to Come (1970, Reprise)
My Old Kentucky Home (1970, Reprise)
Suzanne (1970, Reprise)
God's Song (1972, Reprise)
Political Science (1972, Reprise)
Sail Away (1972, Reprise)
Louisiana 1927 (1974, Reprise)
Rednecks (1974, Reprise)
Short People (1977, Warner Bros.)
The Blues (1983, Warner Bros.)

Randy Newman (1968, Reprise)
Twelve Songs (1970, Reprise)
Randy Newman Live (1971, Reprise)
Sail Away (1972, Reprise)
Good Old Boys (1974, Reprise)
Little Criminals (1977, Warner Bros.)

Gordon Lightfoot (1938-)

Early Morning Rain (1966, United Artists)
For Lovin' Me (1966, United Artists)
Canadian Railroad Trilogy (1968, United Artists)
*If You Could Read My Mind (1970, Reprise)
Wreck of the Edmund Fitzgerald (1976, Reprise)

Lightfoot (1966, United Artists)
The Way I Feel (1968, United Artists)
If You Could Read My Mind (1970, Reprise)
Summertime Dream (1976, Reprise)

Laura Nyro (1947-)

Stoned Soul Picnic

Sweet Blindness
Wedding Bell Blues
And When I Die (1969)
Eli's Coming (1969)
Save the Country (1969, Columbia)
Time and Love (1969, Columbia)
Stoney End (1971)

Eli and the 13th Confession (1968, Columbia)
New York Tendaberry (1969, Columbia)
Christmas and the Beads of Sweat (1970, Columbia)
Gonna Take a Miracle (1971, Columbia)

*Harry Nilsson (1941-)

Cuddly Toy (1967, RCA)
Everybody's Talkin' (1969, RCA)
I Guess the Lord Must be in New York City (1969, RCA)
One (1969, RCA)
Me and My Arrow (1970, RCA)
Without You (1970, RCA)
Coconut (1972, RCA)

The Pandemonium Shadow Show (1967, RCA)
Nilsson Sings Newman (1970, RCA)
Nilsson Schmilsson (1971, RCA)
Pussy Cats (1974, RCA)
Nilsson/Greatest Hits (1978, RCA)

Leonard Cohen (1934-)

Suzanne (1968, Columbia)
Bird On a Wire (1969, Columbia)

Leonard Cohen (1968, Columbia)
Songs from a Room (1969, Columbia)
Best of . . . (1976, Columbia)
Recent Songs (1979, Columbia)

*Jimmy Webb (1946-)

Honey Come Back (1965)
By the Time I Get to Phoenix (1967)

Up, Up, and Away (1967)
MacArthur Park (1968)
Wichita Lineman (1968)
The Worst That Could Happen (1968)
Galveston (1969)
All I Know (1973)

Jimmy Webb Sings Jimmy Webb (1968, Epic)
Words and Music (1970, Epic)
And So On (1971, Epic)
Letters (1972, Epic)
El Mirage (1977, Atlantic)
Angel Heart (1982, Atlantic)

Fred Neil (1937-)

Cocaine
Dolphins
Everybody's Talking
Other Side of This Life

World of Folk Music (1964, FM)
Fred Neil (1966, Capitol)
Everybody's Talking (1969, Capitol)
The Other Side of this Life (1970, Capitol)

John Sebastian (1944-)

Do You Believe in Magic?
Summer in the City
Welcome Back
I Had a Dream (1970, Reprise)

John Sebastian (1970, Reprise)

Carole King (1942-) and Gerry Goffin (1939-)

Will You Love Me Tomorrow? (1961)
Locomotion (1962)
It Might as Well Rain until Tomorrow (1962, Dimension)
Hi-De-Ho (1968)
You've Got a Friend 1968)
Goin' Back (1970, Ode)
It's Too Late/I Feel the Earth Move (1971, Ode)

Jazzman (1974, Ode)
Only Love Is Real (1976, Ode)
One Fine Day (1980, Capitol)

Carole King, Writer (1970, Ode)
Tapestry (1971, Ode)
Really Rosie (1975, Ode)
Thoroughbred (1976, Ode)
Her Greatest Hits (1978, Capitol)

Roy Harper (1941-)

Stormcock (1971, Chrysalis)
*When an Old Cricketer Leaves the
    Crease* (1976, Chrysalis)
1970-1975 (1978, Chrysalis)

John Denver (1943-)

Poems, Prayers, and Promises (1971,
    RCA)
Greatest Hits, Vol. 1 (1973, RCA)

Harry Chapin (1942-81)

Taxi (1972, Elektra)
W.O.L.D. (1972, Elektra)
Cat's in the Cradle (1974, Elektra)

Heads and Tales (1972, Elektra)
Greatest Stories--Live (1976,
    Elektra)

*Tom Waits (1949-)

Ol' 55 (1972, Asylum)

Closing Time (1973, Asylum)
Foreign Affairs (1977, Asylum)
Blue Valentine (1978, Asylum)
Frank's Wild Years (1987, Island)

Linda Ronstadt (1946-)

Heart Like a Wheel (1974, Capitol)
Round Midnight (1986, Asylum)

Janis Ian (1951-)

Society's Child (Baby I've Been
    Thinking) (1966, Verve)
Jesse (1974, Columbia)

At Seventeen (1975, Columbia)
Watercolors (1975, Columbia)

Janis Ian (1967, Verve)
Between the Lines (1975, Columbia)

*Jackson Browne (1948-)

These Days (1968)
Doctor My Eyes (1972, Asylum)
Rock Me on the Water (1972,
    Asylum)
Song for Adam (1972, Asylum)
Take It Easy (1972)
For Everyman (1973, Asylum)
Ready or Not (1973, Asylum)
These Days (1973, Asylum)
For a Dancer (1974, Asylum)
The Road and the Sky (1974,
    Asylum)
Here Come Those Tears Again
    (1976, Asylum)
Running On Empty (1977, Asylum)
Stay (1977, Asylum)

Jackson Browne (1972, Asylum)
For Everyman (1973, Asylum)
Late for the Sky (1974, Asylum)
The Pretender (1976, Asylum)
Running on Empty (1978, Asylum)
Hold Out (1980, Asylum)
Lives in the Balance (1986, Asylum)

Joan Armatrading (1950-)

Whatever's for Us (1973, A&M)
Joan Armatrading (1976, A&M)

*Bruce Cockburn (1945-)

Bruce Cockburn (1970, Epic)
Sunwheel Dance (1972, Epic)
In the Falling Dark (1976, Island)
Human (1980, Millenium)
Inner City Front (1981, Millenium)
Resume (1981, Millenium)

Garland Jeffreys (1944-)

35 Millimeter Dreams (1973,
    Atlantic)

Wild in the Streets (1973, Atlantic)
R.O.C.K. (1981, Epic)
True Confessions (1981, Epic)

Grinder's Switch (1969, Vanguard)
Garland Jeffreys (1973, Atlantic)
*Ghost Writer (1977, A&M)
*One-Eyed Jack (1978, A&M)
*Escape Artist (1981, Epic)

Otis Blackwell

All Shook Up
Don't Be Cruel
Whola Lotta Shakin' Going On

*These Are My Songs (1978, Inner City)

Ellie Greenwich (1940-)

Ellie Greenwich Composes, Produces, and Sings (1968, United Artists)
*Let It Be Written, Let It Be Sung (1973, Verve)

Wes Farrell (1940-)

Come a Little Bit Closer
Goodbye Baby
Hang on Snoopy

*Billy Joel (1949-)

Piano Man (1973, Columbia)
*The Stranger (1977, Columbia)
*52nd Street (1978, Columbia)
*The Bridge (1986, Columbia)

Corey Hart

Fields of Fire (1986, EMI)

Robert Wyatt

Nothing Can Stop Us (1986, Gramavision)
Old Rottenhat (1986, Gramavision)

Paul Brady

Hard Station (1981, Polydor)
True to You (1981, 21 Records)
Back to the Centre (1986)

Leslie Phillips

The Turning (1987, Myrrh)

Nick Drake (1948-74)

Fruit Tree (1987, Hannibal)

Andy White (1942-)

Rove On (1987, MCA)

*Loudon Wainwright (1946-)

Loudon Wainwright III (1970, Atlantic)
Album 2 (1971, Atlantic)
*Album 3 (1973, Capitol)
Attempted Mustache (1973, Columbia)
*I'm Alright (1985, Rounder)
Live One (1987, Rounder)
*More Love Songs (1987, Rounder)

Tonio K.

(Steve Krikorian, 1950-)

Life in the Foodchain (1979, A&M)
Romeo Unchained (1986, A&M)

Southern Rock

*Allman Brothers Band

Statesboro Blues (1971, Capricorn)
*Little Martha (1972, Capricorn)
*Mountain Jam (1972, Capricorn)
*Ramblin' Man (1973, Capricorn)
Can't Lose What You Never Had
(1975, Capricorn)
*Crazy Love (1979, Capricorn)
*Straight From the Heart (1981,
Arista)

Hourglass (1967, Liberty)
Power of Love (1968, Liberty)
Idlewild South (1969, Capricorn)
The Allman Bros. Band (1970,
Capricorn)
*Allman Brothers Band at Fillmore
East* (1971, Capricorn)
Eat a Peach (1972, Capricorn)
Beginnings (1973, Capricorn)
The Road Goes on Forever (1975,
Capricorn)
Enlightened Rogues (1979,
Capricorn)
The Best of . . . (1981, Polydor)

Duane Allman (1946-1971) solo

An Anthology, Vol. 1 (1972,
Capricorn)
An Anthology, Vol. 2 (1974,
Capricorn
Best of . . . (1981, Polydor)

Greg Allman (1947-) solo

Laid Back (1973, Capricorn)
I'm No Angel (1987, Epic)

*Atlanta Rhythm Section

Another Man's Woman (1972,
Polydor)
Cold Turkey Tennessee (1973,
Polydor)
Redneck (1973, Polydor)
Superman (1973, Polydor)

*Angel (1974, Polydor)
*Doraville (1974, Polydor)
*Sky High (1977, Polydor)
*So In To You (1977, Polydor)
*Imaginary Lover (1978, Polydor)
*I'm Not Gonna Let It Bother Me
Tonight (1978, Polydor)
*Do It or Die (1979, Polydor)
*Spooky (1979, Polydor)
*Alien (1981, Columbia)
Higher (1981, Columbia)
Homesick (1981, Columbia)

Atlanta Rhythm Section (1972,
Polydor/MCA)
Back Up against the Wall (1973,
Polydor)
Third Annual Pipe Dream (1974,
Polydor)
Dog Days (1975, Polydor)
Red Tape (1976, Polydor)
A Rock and Roll Alternative (1977,
Polydor)
Champagne Jam (1978, Polydor)
Quinella (1981, Columbia)

*Elvin Bishop (1942-)

Feel It (1970, Fillmore)
So Fine (1970, Fillmore)
Travelin' Shoes (1974, Capricorn)
Juke Joint Jump (1975, Capricorn)
Sure Feels Good (1975, Capricorn)
*Fooled Around and Fell in Love
(1976, Capricorn)

Elvin Bishop (1969, Fillmore)
Feel It (1970, Epic)
*The Best of Elvin Bishop: Crabshaw
Rising* (1972, Epic)
Rock My Soul (1972, Epic)
Let It Flow (1974, Capricorn)
Struttin' My Stuff (1975, Capricorn)
Hometown Boy Makes Good (1976,
Capricorn)
Juke Joint Jump (1977, Capricorn)
Raisin' Hell (1977, Capricorn)
Hog Haven (1978, Capricorn)

*Lynyrd Skynyrd

*The Needle and the Spoon (1974, MCA)
*Sweet Home Alabama (1974, MCA)
*Workin' 74 (MCA)
*Free Bird (1975, MCA)
*Saturday Night Special (1975, MCA)
That Smell (1977, MCA)
Was I Right or Wrong? (1978, MCA)

Pronounced Leh-Nerd Skin-Nerd (1973, MCA)
Second Helping (1974, MCA)
One More from the Road (1976, MCA)
Street Survivors (1977, MCA)
Skynyrd's First . . . and Last (1978, MCA)
Gold and Platinum (1979, MCA)

*Blackfoot

*Highway Song (1979, Atco)
*Train, Train (1979, Atco)

No Reservations (1975, Island)
Flyin' High (1976, Island)
Strikes (1979, Atco)
Tomcattin' (1980, Atco)
Marauder (1981, Atco)

*Molly Hatchet

Molly Hatchet (1978, Epic)
Flirtin' with Disaster (1979, Epic)
Beatin' the Odds (1980, Epic)
No Guts . . . No Glory (1983, Epic)

*Charlie Daniels Band

(Charlie Daniels, 1937-)

*Uneasy Rider (1973, Kama Sutra)
*The South's Gonna Do It (1975, Kama Sutra)
*The Devil Went down to Georgia (1979, Epic)

*In America (1980, Epic)
*The Legend of Wooley Swamp (1980, Epic)
*Still in Saigon (1982, Epic)

Charlie Daniels (1970, Capitol)
Honey in the Rock (1970, Kama Sutra)
To John, Grease and Wolfman (1970, Kama Sutra)
Fire on the Mountain (1974, Epic)
Way Down Yonder (1974, Kama Sutra)
Uneasy Rider (1976, Epic)
Volunteer Jam VII (1981, Epic)
Windows (1982, Epic)

*Marshall Tucker Band

*Take the Highway (1974, Capricorn)
*24 Hours at a Time (1974, Capricorn)
*Fire on the Mountain (1975, Capricorn)
*Can't You See? (1976, Capricorn)
*Heard It in a Love Song (1977, Capricorn)

The Marshall Tucker Band (1973, Capricorn)
A New Life (1974, Capricorn)
Where We All Belong (1974, Capricorn)
Searchin' for a Rainbow (1975, Capricorn)
Long, Hard Ride (1976, Capricorn)
Carolina Dreams (1977, Capricorn)
Greatest Hits (1978, Capricorn)
Tenth (1980, Warner Bros.)
Dedicated (1981, Warner Bros.)
Tuckerized (1982, Warner Bros.)
Just Us (1983, Warner Bros.)

*Dixie Dregs

Free Fall (1977, Capricorn)
What If (1978, Capricorn)
Night of the Living Dregs (1979, Capricorn)

Dregs of the Earth (1980, Arista)

*Outlaws

*There Goes Another Love Song (1975, Arista)
*Ghost Riders in the Sky (1981, Arista)

Outlaws (1975, Arista)
Lady in Waiting (1976, Arista)
Hurry Sundown (1977, Arista)
Bring It Back Alive (1978, Arista)
Playin' to Win (1978, Arista)
In the Eye of the Storm (1979, Arista)
Ghost Riders (1981, Arista)
Los Hombres Malo (1982, Arista)

*.38 Special

*You Keep Runnin' Away (A&M)
*Robin Hood (1979, A&M)
*Hold On Loosely (1981, A&M)
*Caught Up in You (1982, A&M)
*If I'd Been the One (1983, A&M)
*Back Where You Belong (1984, A&M)
*Teacher, Teacher (1984, A&M)
*Somebody Like You (1986, A&M)

.38 Special (1977, A&M)
Special Delivery (1978, A&M)
Rockin' into the Night (1979, A&M)
Wild-Eyed Southern Boys (1981, A&M)
Caught Up in You (1982, A&M)
Special Forces (1982, A&M)
Tour De Force (1983, A&M)
Strength In Numbers (1986, A&M)

*Doobie Brothers

Jesus Is Just Alright (1972, Warner Bros.)
*Listen to the Music (1972, Warner Bros.)
*China Grove (1973, Warner Bros.)
*Long Train Runnin' (1973, Warner Bros.)

Another Park, Another Sunday (1974, Warner Bros.)
*Black Water (1975, Warner Bros.)
Sweet Maxine (1975, Warner Bros.)
*Take Me in Your Arms (Rock Me) (1975, Warner Bros.)
*Takin' It to the Streets (1976, Warner Bros.)
*It Keeps You Runnin' (1977, Warner Bros.)
Dependin' On You (1979, Warner Bros.)
Minute by Minute (1979, Warner Bros.)
*What a Fool Believes (1979, Warner Bros.)
One Step Closer (1980, Warner Bros.)
*Real Love (1980, Warner Bros.)

The Doobie Bros. (1971, Warner Bros.)
The Captain and Me (1973, Warner Bros.)
Toulouse Street (1973, Warner Bros.)
Stampede (1975, Warner Bros.)
Best of the Doobies (1976, Warner Bros.)
Takin' It to the Street (1976, Warner Bros.)
Livin' on the Fault Line (1977, Warner Bros.)
Minute by Minute (1977, Warner Bros.)
One Step Closer (1980, Warner Bros.)
Best of the Doobies, Vol. 2 (1981, Warner Bros.)

*ZZ Top

*Tush (1975, London)
*I Thank You (1980, Warner Bros.)
*Gimme All Your Lovin' (1983, Warner Bros.)
*Legs (1984, Warner Bros.)

First Album (1970, Warner Bros.)

Rio Grande Mud (1972, Warner Bros.)
Tres Hombres (1973, Warner Bros.)
Fandango (1975, Warner Bros.)
Tejas (1976, Warner Bros.)
*The Best of... (1977, Warner Bros.)
Deguello (1979, Warner Bros.)
El Loco (1981, Warner Bros.)
*Eliminator (1983, Warner Bros.)

*Wet Willie

*Keep On Smilin' (1974, Capricorn)
*Everything That You Do (1976, Capricorn)
*Teaser (1976, Capricorn)

Drippin' Wet (1973, Capricorn)
*Keep on Smilin' (1974, Capricorn)
*The Wetter the Better (1976, Capricorn)
*Manorisms (1978, Epic)

*Swimming Pool Q's

The Deep End (1981, A&M)
*Swimming Pool Q's (1984, A&M)
*Blue Tomorrow (1986, A&M)

Sluggers

*Over the Fence (1986, Arista)

Rubber Rodeo

Heartbreak Highway (1986, Polygram)

R.E.O. Speedwagon

*R.E.O./T.W.O. (1972, Epic)
Life as We Knew It (1987, Epic)

Los Angeles Pop

*Leon Russell (1941-)

*Home Sweet Oklahoma (1971, Shelter)
*Stranger in a Strange Land (1971, Shelter)
*Tight Rope (1972, Shelter)
*Lady Blue (1975, Shelter)

Asylum Choir: Looking Inside (1968, Smash)
*Leon Russell (1970, Shelter)
*Leon Russell and the Shelter People (1971, Shelter)
Carney (1972, Shelter)
Hank Wilson's Back (1973, Shelter)
*Best of... (1976, Shelter)
Make Love to the Music (1977, Paradise)
Americana (1978, Paradise)
Life and Love (1979, Paradise)
Looking Back (1979, Olympic)
Leon Russell and New Grass Revival Live (1981, Warner Bros.)
Live Album (1981, Paradise)

*Three Dog Night

*Nobody (1968, Dunhill)
*Easy to Be Hard (1969, Dunhill)
*Eli's Coming (1969, Dunhill)
*One (1969, Dunhill)
*Try a Little Tenderness (1969, Dunhill)
*Mama Told Me (Not to Come) (1970, Dunhill)
*Joy to the World (1971, Dunhill)
*Liar (1971, Dunhill)
*An Old-Fashioned Love Song (1971, Dunhill)
*Black & White (1972, Dunhill)
*Never Been to Spain (1972, Dunhill)
*Shambala (1973, Dunhill)

*The Show Must Go On (1974, Dunhill)
Til the World Ends (1975, Dunhill)

Suitable for Framing (1969, Dunhill)
Three Dog Night (1969, Dunhill)
Captured Live at the Forum (1970, Dunhill)
Naturally (1971, Dunhill)
Seven Separate Fools (1972, Dunhill)
Around the World (1973, Dunhill)
Around the World--Greatest Hits (1974, Dunhill)
Coming Down Your Way (1975, ABC)
American Pastime (1976, ABC)

*Steely Dan

*Do It Again (1972, ABC)
*Reeling in the Years (1973, ABC)
*Rikki Don't Lose That Number (1974, ABC)
Black Friday (1975, ABC)
Peg (1978, ABC)
*Hey Nineteen (1980, MCA)
Time Out of Mind (1981, MCA)

You Gotta Walk It Like You Talk It (1971, Spark)
Can't Buy a Thrill (1972, MCA)
Countdown to Ecstasy (1973, MCA)
Pretzel Logic (1974, MCA)
Katy Lied (1975, MCA)
The Royal Scam (1976, MCA)
Aja (1977, MCA)
Greatest Hits (1978, MCA)
Gaucho (1980, MCA)

Donald Fagen (1950-) solo

The Nightfly (1982, Warner Bros.)

*Rickie Lee Jones (1954-)

*Chuck E.'s in Love (1979, Warner Bros.)
*Company (1979, Warner Bros.)
*Young Blood (1979, Warner Bros.)

Rickie Lee Jones (1979, Warner Bros.)
Pirates (1981, Warner Bros.)
Girl at Her Volcano (1983, Warner Bros.)

*Toto

*Hold the Line (1978, Columbia)
99 (1980, Columbia)
*Africa (1982, Columbia)
Make Believe (1982, Columbia)
*Rosanna (1982, Columbia)
*I Won't Hold You Back (1983, Columbia)

Toto (1978, Columbia)
Hydra (1979, Columbia)
Turn Back (1981, Columbia)
Toto IV (1982, Columbia)

Nicolette Larson (1952-)

*Lotta Love (1978, Warner Bros.)
Let Me Go Love (1980, Warner Bros.)

Nicolette (1978, Warner Bros.)
In the Nick of Time (1979, Warner Bros.)
Radioland (1980, Warner Bros.)

*Christopher Cross (1951-)

Never Be the Same (1980, Warner Bros.)
*Ride Like the Wind (1980, Warner Bros.)
*Sailing (1980, Warner Bros.)
*Arthur's Theme (1981, Warner Bros.)
Say You'll Be Mine (1981, Warner Bros.)
All Right (1983, Warner Bros.)
No Time for Talk (1983, Warner Bros.)
*Think of Laura (1983, Warner Bros.)

Christopher Cross (1980, Warner Bros.)

Another Page (1983, Warner Bros.)

*Maria Muldaur (1943-)

*Midnight at the Oasis (1974,
   Reprise)
*Rockin' Chair (1976, Reprise)

Maria Muldaur (1973, Reprise)
Sweet Harmony (1976, Reprise)

Disco

George McCrae

*Rock Your Baby (1974, T.K.)
I Get Lifted (1975, T.K.)

Rock Your Baby (1974, T.K.)

*Labelle

Down the Aisle (Wedding Song)
   (1963, Newton)
You'll Never Walk Alone (1964,
   Parkway)
*The Revolution Will Not Be
   Televised (1973, RCA)
*Something in the Air (1973, RCA)
*Lady Marmalade (1975, Epic)

Gonna Take a Miracle (1971,
   Columbia)
Pressure Cookin' (1973, RCA)
Nighbirds (1974, Epic)

Patti Labelle (1944-) solo

*Dan Swit Me (1977, Epic)
*Joy to Have Your Love (1977,
   Epic)

Patti Labelle (1977, Epic)
Best of . . . (1981, Epic)

Nona Hendryx (1945-) solo

Nona Hendryx (1977, Epic)

*Gloria Gaynor (1949-)

*Never Can Say Goodbye (1974,
   MGM)
*I Will Survive (1979, Polydor)

Never Can Say Goodbye (1974,
   MGM)
Love Track (1978, Polydor)

*Donna Summer (1948-)

*Love to Love You Baby (1975,
   Oasis)

*Bad Girls (1979, Casablanca)
*Hot Stuff (1979, Casablanca)
*The Wanderer (1980, Geffen)
*She Works Hard for the Money
  (1983, Mercury)

Love to Love You Baby (1975,
  Oasis)
Bad Girls (1979, Casablanca)
On the Radio: Greatest Hits, Vols. 1-
  2 (1979, Casablanca)
The Wanderer (1980, Geffen)
She Works Hard for the Money
  (1983, Mercury)
Cats Without Claws (1985, Geffen)

Giorgio Moroder (1941-)

From Here to Eternity (1977,
  Casablanca)

*Thelma Houston

*Don't Leave Me This Way (1977,
  Tamla)

Anyway You Like It (1976, Tamla)

*Bee Gees

Massachusetts (1967, Atco)
New York Mining Disaster 1941
  (1967, Atco)
I've Gotta Get a Message to You
  (1968, Atco)
I Started a Joke (1969, Atco)
Lonely Day (1970, Atco)
How Can You Mend a Broken
  Heart? (1971, Atco)
*Jive Talkin' (1975, RSO)
*Nights On Broadway (1975, RSO)
*You Should Be Dancing (1976,
  RSO)
*How Deep Is Your Love? (1977,
  RSO)
*Stayin' Alive (1977, RSO)
*Night Fever (1978, RSO)
*Too Much Heaven (1978, RSO)
*Love You Inside Out (1979, RSO)
*Tragedy (1979, RSO)

Bee Gees First (1967, Atco)
Best of . . . (1969, Atco)
Main Course (1975, RSO)
Bee Gees Gold, Vol. 1 (1976, RSO)
Saturday Night Fever (1977, RSO)
Spirits Having Flown (1979, RSO)

Barry White (1944-)

I'm Gonna Love You Just a Little
  More Baby (1973, 20th Century)
Never, Never Gonna Give Ya Up
  (1973, 20th Century)
Can't Get Enough of Your Love,
  Babe (1974, 20th Century)
You're the First, the Last, My
  Everything (1974, 20th Century)

I've Got So Much to Give (1973,
  20th Century)
Stone Gon' (1973, 20th Century)
*Under the Influence of Love
  Unlimited* (1973, 20th Century)
Can't Get Enough (1974, 20th
  Century)

K.C. and the Sunshine Band

Queen of Clubs (1974, T.K.)
Get Down Tonight (1975, T.K.)
That's the Way (I Like It) (1975,
  T.K.)
(Shake, Shake, Shake) Shake Your
  Booty (1976, T.K.)
I'm Your Boogie Man (1977, T.K.)
Please Don't Go (1979, T.K.)

Do It Good (1974, T.K.)
KC and the Sunshine Band (1975,
  T.K.)
Part 3 (1976, T.K.)

Van McCoy

Disco Kid (1975, Avco)
The Hustle (1975, Avco)

Disco Baby (1975, Avco)
The Hustle (1976, H&L)

Hues Corp.

Rockin' Soul (1974, RCA)
Rock the Boat (1974, RCA)

Freedom for the Stallion (1974, RCA)
Love Corporation (1975, RCA)

Silver Convention

Fly, Robin Fly (1975, Midland Int.)
Save Me (1975, Midland Int.)
Get Up and Boogie (That's Right) (1976, Midland Int.)
Silver Convention (1976, Midland Int.)

Sylvester

(Sylvester James)

Dance (Disco Heat) (1978, Fantasy)
You Make Me Feel (Mighty Real) (1979, Fantasy)

Step Two (1978, Fantasy)
Stars (1979, Fantasy)
Too Hot to Sleep (1981, Fantasy)

Village People

Macho Man (1978, Casablanca)
Y.M.C.A. (1978, Casablanca)
In the Navy (1979, Casablanca)

Cruisin (1978, Casablanca)
Macho Man (1978, Casablanca)
Go West (1979, Casablanca)

*Dr. Buzzard's Original "Savannah" Band

*Cherchez la Femme (1976, RCA)
*I'll Play the Fool (1976, RCA)

Dr. Buzzard's Original "Savannah" Band (1976, RCA)

*Chic

*Dance, Dance, Dance (1977, Atlantic)
C'est Chic (1978, Atlantic)
*Le Freak (1978, Atlantic)
*Good Times (1979, Atlantic)
*I Want Your Love (1979, Atlantic)

Risque (1978, Atlantic)
Les Plus Grands Succes de Chic / Chic's Greatest Hits (1979, Atlantic)

Anthologies

Car Wash (1976, MCA)
Saturday Night Fever (1977, RSO)

Hard Rock, U.K.

*Deep Purple

*Hush (1968, Tetragrammatron)
*Kentucky Woman (1968, Tetragrammatron)
*Highway Star (1973, Warner Bros.)
*Smoke on the Water (1973, Warner Bros.)
*Space Truckin' (1973, Warner Bros.)
*Woman from Tokyo (1973, Warner Bros.)

Book of Taliesyn (1968, Tetragrammatron)
Shades of Deep Purple (1968, Tetragrammatron)
Deep Purple (1969, Tetragrammatron)
Deep Purple and the Royal Philharmonic (1970, Warner Bros.)
Deep Purple in Rock (1970, Warner Bros.)
Fireball (1971, Warner Bros.)
Machine Head (1972, Warner Bros.)
Purple Passages (1972, Warner Bros.)
Made in Japan (1973, Warner Bros.)
Who Do We Think We Are (1973, Warner Bros.)
When We Rock, We Rock and When We Roll, We Roll (1978, Warner Bros.)
Deepest Purple (1980, Warner Bros.)
Perfect Strangers (1984, Mercury)
House of Blue Light (1987, Mercury)

*Mott the Hoople

*At the Crossroads (1969, Atlantic)
*Laugh at Me (1969, Atlantic)
*Rock and Roll Queen (1969, Atlantic)
*All the Young Dudes (1972, Columbia)
*Death May Be Your Santa Claus (1972, Atlantic)
*Sweet Jane (1972, Columbia)
*All the Way from Memphis (1973, Columbia)
*The Ballad of Mott the Hoople (1973, Columbia)
*I Wish I Was Your Mother (1973, Columbia)

Mott the Hoople (1969, Atlantic)
Mad Shadows (1970, Atlantic)
All the Young Dudes (1972, Atlantic)
Brain Capers (1972, Atlantic)
Rock and Roll Queen (1972, Atlantic)
Mott (1973, Columbia)
The Hoople (1974, Columbia)
Greatest Hits (1976, Columbia)

*Ian Hunter (1946-) solo

*I Get So Excited (1975, Columbia)
*It Ain't Easy When You Fall (1975, Columbia)
*Once Bitten, Twice Shy (1975, Columbia)
*The Truth, The Whole Truth, Nuthin' but the Truth (1975, Columbia)
*Who Do You Love? (1975, Columbia)
*Cleveland Rock (1979, Columbia)
*Just Another Night (1979, Columbia)
*The Outsider (1979, Columbia)
*Ships (1979, Columbia)

Ian Hunter (1975, Columbia)
Shades of . . . (1978, Columbia)
You're Never Alone with a Schizophrenic (1979, Chrysalis)
Live: Welcome to the Club (1980, Chrysalis)
Short Back and Sides (1981, Chrysalis)

*Humble Pie

*Natural Born Boogie (1969,
   Immediate)
*I Don't Need No Doctor (1971,
   A&M)
*Rolling Stone (1971, A&M)

*As Safe as Yesterday Is (1969,
   Immediate/A&M)
Town and Country (1969, A&M)
Humble Pie (1970, A&M)
*Performance: Rockin' at the Fillmore
   (1971, A&M)
Rock On (1971, A&M)
Eat It (1973, A&M)
Lost and Found (1973, A&M)
Thunderbox (1974, A&M)
Street Rats (1975, A&M)
On the Victory (1980, Atco)
Go for the Throat (1981, Atco)
The Best (1982, Atco)

*Peter Frampton (1950-) solo

*All I Want to Be (1972, A&M)
*Fig Tree Bay (1972, A&M)
*It's a Plain Shame (1972, A&M)
*The Lodger (1972, A&M)
*Do You Feel Like We Do? (1973,
   A&M)
*Lines on My Face (1973, A&M)
*White Sugar (1973, A&M)
*Baby I Love Your Way (1976,
   A&M)
*Show Me the Way (1976, A&M)
*I'm in You (1977, A&M)
*I Can't Stand It No More (1979,
   A&M)
*Lying (1986, Atlantic)

*Wind of Change (1972, A&M)
Frampton's Camel (1973, A&M)
Frampton Comes Alive (1975,
   A&M)
Frampton's (1975, A&M)
Where I Should Be (1979, A&M)
Breaking All the Rules (1981, A&M)
The Art of Control (1982, A&M)
Premonition (1986, Atlantic)

*Free

*All Right Now (1970, A&M)
*Stealer (1970, A&M)
*My Brother Jake (1971, A&M)
*Little Bit of Love (1972, A&M)
Bodie (1973, A&M)
The Highway Song (1973, A&M)
*Wishing Well (1973, A&M)

Tons of Sobs (1969, A&M)
*Fire and Water (1970, A&M)
Free (1970, A&M)
*Highway (1973, A&M)
*Best of ... (1975, A&M)

*Savoy Brown

*I'm Tired (1969, Parrot)
Train to Nowhere (1969, Parrot)
*Tell Mama (1971, Parrot)

*London Collection--The Best of ...
   (London)
Shake Down (1967, Decca)
Getting to the Point (1968, Parrot)
*Blue Matter (1969, Parrot)
A Step Further (1969, Parrot)
Looking In (1970, Parrot)
Raw Sienna (1970, Parrot)
Street Corner Talking (1971, Parrot)
*Hellbound Train (1972, Parrot)
Lion's Share (1972, Parrot)
Rock'N'Roll Warriors (1981, Town
   House)

*Status Quo

*Pictures of Matchstick Men (1968,
   Cadet Concept)
*Don't Waste My Time (1973,
   A&M)
*Oh Baby (1973, A&M)
*Down Down (1975, A&M)

*Picturesque Matchstickable (1968,
   Pye)
Spare Parts (1968, Pye)
Status Quotation (1969, Marble
   Arch)

Ma Kelly's Greasy Spoon (1970, Pye)
Dog of Two Heads (1971, Pye)
Best of . . . (1972, Pye)
Pile Driver (1973, A&M)
Hello (1974, A&M)
On the Level (1975, Capitol)
Status Quo (1976, Capitol)
Live (1977, Capitol)
Rockin' All Over the World (1978, Capitol)
In My Chair (1979, Mode)
Just for the Record (1979, Pye)
Whatever You Want (1979, Vertigo)
Just Supposin' (1980, Vertigo)
Never Too Late (1981, Vertigo)
Rock'n'Roll (1982, Vertigo)

*Slade

*Coz I Love You (1971, Cotillion)
*Get Down and Get With It (1971, Cotillion)
*Mama Weer All Crazee Now (1972, Polydor)
*Take Me Back 'ome (1972, Polydor)
*Cum On Feel the Noize (1973, Reprise)
*Gudbuy T' Jane (1973, Reprise)
*Merry Xmas Everybody (1973, Reprise)
*Skweeze Me Pleeze Me (1973, Reprise)
*Far Far Away (1974, Polydor)
*Thanks for the Memory (1975, Warner Bros.)
*Let's Call It Quits (1976, Warner Bros.)
*My Baby Left Me--That's All Right (1977, Warner Bros.)
*Lock Up Your Daughters (1981, Polydor)
*My Oh My (1984, CBS)
*Run Runaway (1984, CBS)

Beginnings (1969, Fontana)
Play It Loud (1970, Cotillion)
Slayed (1972, Polydor)
Slade Alive (1972, Polydor)

Sladest (1973, Rep.)
Old, New, Borrowed, and Blue (1974, Polydor)
In Flame (1975, Warner Bros.)
Nobody's Fool (1976, Warner Bros.)
Whatever Happened to Slade (1977, Polydor)

*Badfinger

Maybe Tomorrow (1968, Apple)
*Come and Get It (1970, Apple)
*No Matter What (1970, Apple)
*Day After Day (1971, Apple)
*Baby Blue (1972, Apple)
Love Is Gonna Come at Last (1979, Elektra)

Magic Christian Music (1970, Apple)
No Dice (1970, Apple)
Straight Up (1971, Apple)
Ass (1973, Apple)
Badfinger (1974, Warner Bros.)
Wish You Were Here (1974, Warner Bros.)
Airwaves (1979, Elektra)
Say No More (1981, Radio)

*Wishbone Ash

Wishbone Ash (1970, MCA)
Pilgrimage (1971, MCA)
Argus (1972, MCA)
Live Dates (1973, MCA)
Wishbone Four (1973, MCA)
Locked In (1976, Atlantic)
New England (1976, MCA)
Front Page News (1977, MCA)
No Smoke without Fire (1978, MCA)
Just Testing (1979, MCA)
Number the Brave (1981, MCA)

*Black Sabbath

*Paranoid (1970, Warner Bros.)
*Iron Man (1972, Warner Bros.)

Never Say Die (1978, Warner
    Bros.)
Hard Road (1978, Warner Bros.)

Black Sabbath (1970, Warner Bros.)
Masters of Reality (1971, Warner
    Bros.)
Paranoid (1971, Warner Bros.)
Black Sabbath, Vol. 4 (1972,
    Warner Bros.)
Sabbath, Bloody Sabbath (1973,
    Warner Bros.)
Sabotage (1975, Warner Bros.)
Technical Ecstasy (1976, Warner
    Bros.)
We Sold Our Soul for Rock'n'Roll
    (1976, Warner Bros.)
Never Say Die (1978, Warner Bros.)
Heaven and Hell (1980, Warner
    Bros.)
Mob Rules (1981, Warner Bros.)
Black Sabbath (1983, Warner Bros.)

Ozzy Osbourne (1948-) solo

*You Can't Kill Rock'n'Roll (1981,
    Jet)

Blizzard of Ozz (1980, Jet)
Diary of a Madman (1981, Jet)
Speak of the Devil (1982, Jet)
Bark at the Moon (1983, CBS)
*Ozzy Osbourne and Randy Rhoads:
    Tribute* (1987, CBS)

Uriah Heep

*Easy Livin' (1972, Mercury)
*Stealin' (1972, Mercury)
*Blind Eye/Sweet Lorraine (1973,
    Mercury)

Uriah Heep (1970, Mercury)
Very 'eavy, Very 'umble (1970,
    Mercury)
Look at Yourself (1971, Mercury)
Salisbury (1971, Mercury)
Demons and Wizards (1972,
    Mercury)
Magician's Birthday (1972,
    Mercury)

Best of . . . (1976, Mercury)
Fallen Angel (1978, Mercury)

*Nazareth

*Bad Bad Boy (1973, A&M)
*The Ballad of Hollis Brown (1973,
    A&M)
*Broken Down Angel (1973, A&M)
*This Flight Tonight (1973, A&M)
*Love Hurts (1976, A&M)
*My White Bicycle (1976, A&M)

Nazareth (1971, Warner Bros.)
Exercises (1972, A&M)
Razamanaz (1973, A&M)
Loud 'n Proud (1974, A&M)
Rampant (1974, A&M)
Hair of the Dog (1975, A&M)
Fool Circle (1981, A&M)

*Foghat

*I Just Want to Make Love to You
    (1972, Bearsville
*What a Shame (1973, Bearsville)
*Drivin' Wheel (1976, Bearsville)
*Fool for the City (1976, Bearsville)
*Slow Ride (1976, Bearsville)
*I'll Be Standing By (1977,
    Bearsville)
*Stone Blue (1978, Bearsville)
*Third Time Lucky (First Time I Was
    a Fool) (1979, Bearsville)
*Stranger in My Home Town (1980,
    Bearsville)

Foghat (1972, Bearsville)
Foghat (1973, Bearsville)
Rock and Roll (1973, Bearsville)
Energize (1974, Bearsville)
Rock and Roll Outlaws (1974,
    Bearsville)
Fool for the City (1975, Bearsville)
Night Shift (1976, Bearsville)
Foghat Live (1977, Bearsville)
Stone Blue (1978, Bearsville)
Boogie Motel (1979, Bearsville)
Tight Shoes (1980, Bearsville)

Girls to Chat and Boys to Bounce
(1981, Bearsville)
In the Mood for Something Rude
(1982, Bearsville)

Robin Trower (1945-)

Twice Removed from Yesterday
(1973, Chrysalis)
Bridge of Sighs (1974, Chrysalis)
For Earth Below (1975, Chrysalis)
Long Misty Days (1976, Chrysalis)
In City Dreams (1977, Chrysalis)
Robin Trower--Live (1977,
Chrysalis)
Caravan to Midnight (1978,
Chrysalis)
Victims of the Fury (1980, Chrysalis)
BLT (1981, Chrysalis)
Truce (1982, Chrysalis)

UFO

*C'mon Everybody (1972, Beacon)
*Back into My Life (1982, Chrysalis)

UFO Land in Tokyo (1972, Beacon)
UFO/Flying (1973, Beacon)
Phenomenon (1974, Chrysalis)
Force It (1975, Chrysalis)
No Heavy Petting (1976, Chrysalis)
Lights Out (1977, Chrysalis)
Obsessions (1978, Chrysalis)
Strangers in the Night (1978,
Chrysalis)
No Place to Run (1979, Chrysalis)
The Wild, the Willing, and the
Innocent (1981, Chrysalis)
Mechanix (1982, Chrysalis)

*Queen

*Seven Seas of Rhye (1974, Elektra)
*Killer Queen (1975, Elektra)
*Now I'm Here (1975, Elektra)
*Bohemian Rhapsody (1976,
Elektra)
*Somebody to Love (1976, Elektra)
*You're My Best Friend (1976,
Elektra)

Tie Your Mother Down (1977,
Elektra)
*We Are the Champions/We Will
Rock You (1977, Elektra)
*Fat Bottomed Girls/Bicycle Race
(1978, Elektra)
It's Late (1978, Elektra)
*Crazy Little Thing Called Love
(1979, Elektra)
Don't Stop Me Now (1979, Elektra)
*Another One Bites the Dust (1980,
Elektra)
Need Your Loving Tonight (1980,
Elektra)
Play the Game (1980, Elektra)
*Body Language (1984, Elektra)
*Radio Ga-Ga (1984, Capitol)

Queen (1973, Elektra)
Queen II (1974, Elektra)
Sheer Heart Attack (1974, Elektra)
*A Night at the Opera (1975, Elektra)
A Day at the Races (1977, Elektra)
News of the World (1977, Elektra)
The Game (1980, Elektra)
*Greatest Hits (1981, Elektra)
Hot Space (1982, Elektra)
The Works (1984, Capitol)
A Kind of Magic (1986, Capitol)

Bad Company

*Can't Get Enough (1974, Swan
Song)
*Feel Like Makin' Love (1975, Swan
Song)
*Good Lovin' Gone Bad (1975,
Swan Song)
*Movin' On (1975, Swan Song)
Honey Child (1976, Swan Song)
*Young Blood (1976, Swan Song)
Burnin' Sky (1977, Swan Song)
Gone Gone Gone (1979, Swan
Song)
*Rock'n'Roll Fantasy (1979, Swan
Song)

*Bad Company (1974, Swan Song)
Straight Shooter (1975, Swan Song)

Run with the Pack (1976, Swan Song)
Burnin' Sky (1977, Swan Song)
Desolation Angels (1979, Swan Song)
Rough Diamonds (1982, Swan Song)

*Thin Lizzy

*Whisky in a Jar (1973, Decca)
*The Boys Are Back in Town (1976, Mercury)
Cowboy Song (1976, Mercury)
Don't Believe a Word (1977, Mercury)
Rosalie (1978, Mercury)
Waiting for an Alibi (1979, Warner Bros.)
Killer on the Loose (1980, Warner Bros.)

Thin Lizzy (1971, Decca)
Shades of a Blue Orphanage (1972, Decca)
Vagabonds of the Western World (1973, London)
Night Life (1974, Mercury)
Fighting (1975, Mercury)
Jailbreak (1976, Mercury)
Johnny the Fox (1976, Mercury)
Bad Reputation (1977, Mercury)
Black Rose--A Rock Legend (1979, Warner Bros.)
Chinatown (1980, Warner Bros.)
Renegade (1982, Warner Bros.)
Thunder and Lighting (1983, Warner Bros.)

*U.K.

U.K. (1978, Polydor)
Danger Money (1979, Polydor)
Night after Night (1979, Polydor)

*Motorhead

Motorhead (1977, Chiswick)
Bomber (1979, Bronze)
Overkill (1979, Bronze)

Ace of Spaces (1980, Bronze)
On Parole (1980, Liberty)
No Sleep Till Hammersmith (1981, Bronze)
Iron Fist (1982, Bronze)

*Bay City Rollers

*Keep On Dancing (1971)
*Shang-A-Lang (1974)
*Bye Bye Baby (1975, Arista)
*Give a Little Love (1975, Arista)
*Saturday Night (1975, Arista)
*I Only Want to Be with You (1976, Arista)
*Love Like I Love You (1976, Arista)
*Money Honey (1976, Arista)
*Rock and Roll Love Letter (1976, Arista)
*You Made Me Believe in Magic (1977, Arista)

Bay City Rollers (1975, Arista)
Rock'n'Roll Love Letter (1975, Arista)
Dedication (1976, Arista)
Greatest Hits (1977, Arista)
It's a Game (1977, Arista)
Strangers in the Wind (1978, Arista)

*Dire Straits

Down along the Water Line (1979, Warner Bros.)
In the Gallery (1979, Warner Bros.)
*Sultans of Swing (1979, Warner Bros.)
*Tunnel of Love (1979, Warner Bros.)
Water of Love (1979, Warner Bros.)
*Romeo and Juliet (1980, Warner Bros.)
*Ride across the River (1985, Warner Bros.)
*So Far Away (1986, Warner Bros.)
*Walk of Life (1986, Warner Bros.)

Dire Straits (1978, Warner Bros.)

Communique (1979, Warner Bros.)
Making Movies (1980, Warner Bros.)
Love Over Gold (1982, Warner Bros.)
Twisting by the Pool (1983, Warner Bros.)
Alchemy (1984, Warner Bros.)
Brothers in Arms (1985, Warner Bros.)

Cult

Love (1985, Sire)
Electric (1987, Sire)

Love and the Rockets

Express (1987)

Julian Cope

Saint Julian (1987)

Hard Rock, U.S.

*Blue Cheer

*Summertime Blues (1968, Philips)

New! Improved! (1968, Philips)
Outside Inside (1968, Philips)
Vincebus Eruptum (1968, Philips)
Blue Cheer (1969, Philips)
Oh Pleasant Hope (1970, Philips)
The Original Human Beings (1970, Philips)

*Ted Nugent (1948-)

*Baby Please Don't Go (1967, Mainstream)
*Journey to the Centre of the Mind (1968, Mainstream)
*Cat Scratch Fever (1977, Epic)

Ted Nugent and the Amboy Dukes (1968, Mainstream)
Survival of the Fittest (1971, Poly)
Call of the Wild (1974, Discreet)
Journeys/Migrations (1975, Mainstream)
Ted Nugent (1975, Epic)
Tooth, Fang, and Claw (1975, Discreet)
Free-for-All (1976, Epic))
Cat Scratch Fever (1977, Epic)
Double Live Gonzo! (1978, Epic)
Great Gonzos: The Best of Ted Nugent (1978, Epic)
Weekend Warriors (1978, Epic)
State of Shock (1979, Epic)
Scream Dream (1980, Epic))
Intensities in Ten Cities (1981, Epic)

*Bob Seger (1945-)

*Ballad of the Yellow Beret (1966, Are You Kidding Me Records)
*East Side Story (1966, Cameo)
*Heavy Music (1967, Cameo)
*Nutbush City Limits (1967, Cameo)

*Ramblin' Gamblin' Man (1969, Capitol)
*Get Out of Denver (1973, Capitol)
*Katmandu (1975, Capitol)
*Night Moves (1977, Capitol)
*Still the Same (1978, Capitol)
*Old Time Rock & Roll (1979, Capitol)
*Against the Wind (1980, Capitol)
*Fire Lake (1980, Capitol)
*Tryin' to Live My Life without You (1981, Capitol)
*Shame on the Moon (1982, Capitol)
*Even Now (1983, Capitol)
*Little Victories (1983, Capitol)
*Makin' Thunderbirds (1983, Capitol)
*Roll Me Away (1983, Capitol)

Noah (1969, Capitol)
Ramblin' Gamblin' Man (1969, Capitol)
Mongrel (1970, Capitol)
Brand New Morning (1971, Capitol)
Back In (1972, Reprise)
*Smokin' OP's (1972, Reprise)
*Seven (1974, Reprise)
Beautiful Loser (1975, Capitol)
*Live Bullet (1976, Capitol)
Get Out of Denver (1977, Reprise)
*Night Moves (1977, Capitol)
*Stranger in Town (1978, Capitol)
Against the Wind (1980, Capitol)
Nine Tonight (1981, Capitol)
*The Distance (1983, Capitol)
Like a Rock (1986, Capitol)

*Mountain

*Mississippi Queen (1970, Windfall)
*Theme from the Imaginary Western (1971, Windfall)

Leslie West-Mountain (1969, Windfall)
Mountain Climbing (1970, Windfall)
Flowers of Evil (1971, Windfall)
Nantucket Sleighride (1971, Windfall)

Mountain Live (1972, Windfall)
The Road Goes On Forever (1972, Windfall)
The Best of . . . (1973, Columbia)
Avalanche (1974, Columbia)
Twin Peaks (1974, Columbia)

*Roy Buchanan (1939-)

Roy Buchanan (1972, Polydor)
Live Stock (1975, Polydor)
A Street Called Straight (1976, Atlantic)
Loading Zone (1977, Atlantic)
You're Not Alone (1978, Atlantic)
My Babe (1980, Atlantic)

Little Feat

*Little Feat (1971, Warner Bros.)
*Sailin' Shoes (1972, Warner Bros.)
*Dixie Chicken (1973, Warner Bros.)
*Feats Don't Fail Me Now (1974, Warner Bros.)
*The Last Record Album (1975, Warner Bros.)
*Waiting for Columbus (1978, Warner Bros.)
*Hoy Hoy (1981, Warner Bros.)

*Johnny Winter (1941-)

Austin, Texas (United Artists)
Before the Storm (Janus)
*Johnny Winter (1969, Columbia)
Progressive Blues Experiment (1969, Liberty)
*Second Winter (1969, Columbia)
*Johnny Winter And (1970, Columbia)
Story (1970, GRT)
About Blues (1971, Janus)
Early Times (1971, Janus)
Live (1971, Columbia)
*Still Alive and Well (1973, Columbia)
John Dawson Winter III (1974, Blue Sky)
Saint and Sinners (1974, Columbia)
Captured Live (1976, Blue Sky)

Nothin' But the Blues (1978, Blue Sky)
White Hot and Blue (1978, Blue Sky)
Johnny Winter Story (1980, Blue Sky)
Raisin' Cain (1980, Blue Sky)

*Edgar Winter (1946-)

*Keep Playin' That Rock and Roll (1971, Epic)
*Frankenstein I (1973, Epic)
*Free Ride (1973, Epic)
*River's Risin' (1974, Epic)

Entrance (1970, Epic)
*Edgar Winter's White Trash (1971, Epic)
*Roadwork (1972, Epic)
*They Only Come Out at Night (1973, Epic)
Shock Treatment (1974, Epic)
Edgar Winter Group with Rick Derringer (1975, Blue Sky)
Recycled (1979, Blue Sky)

*Grand Funk Railroad

*I'm Your Captain (1970, Capitol)
*Closer to Home (1970, Capitol)
*Footstompin' Music (1972, Capitol)
*We're an American Band (1973, Capitol)
*The Loco-Motion (1974, Capitol)
*Bad Time (1975, Capitol)

On Time (1969, Capitol)
Closer to Home (1970, Capitol)
Live Album (1970, Capitol)
*Survival (1970, Capitol)
*We're an American Band (1973, Capitol)
Grand Funk (1975, Capitol)
Grand Funk Hits (1976, Capitol)

*J. Geils Band (1946-)

*Give It to Me (1972, Atlantic)
*Looking for Love (1972, Atlantic)

*Must of Got Lost (1974, Atlantic)
*One Last Kiss (1979, EMI)
*Come Back (1980, EMI)
*Love Stinks (1980, EMI)
*Centerfold (1981, EMI)
*Angel in Blue (1982, EMI)
*Freeze-Frame (1982, EMI)
*I Do (1982, EMI)

*The J. Geils Band (1970, Atlantic)
Full House (1972, Atlantic)
The Morning After (1972, Atlantic)
Bloodshot (1973, Atlantic)
Ladies Invited (1973, Atlantic)
*Nightmares (and Other Tales from the Vinyl Jungle) (1974, Atlantic)
Hot Line (1975, Atlantic)
Blow Your Face Out (1976, Atlantic)
*Monkey Island (1977, Atlantic)
*Sanctuary (1978, EMI)
The Best of . . . (1979, Atlantic)
*Love Stinks (1980, EMI)
The Best of . . ., Vol. 2 (1981, Atlantic)
*Freeze-Frame (1981, EMI)
Showtime (1982, Atlantic)
You're Getting Even While I'm Getting Odd (1984, EMI)

*Peter Wolf (1945-) solo

Lights Out (1984, EMI)
*Come as You Are (1986, EMI)

*Alice Cooper

(Vincent Furnier, 1948-)

*Eighteen (1971, Warner Bros.)
*Elected (1972, Warner Bros.)
*School's Out (1972, Warner Bros.)
*Hello Hurray (1973, Warner Bros.)
*No More Mr. Nice Guy (1973, Warner Bros.)
*Only Women Bleed (1975, Warner Bros.)
*I Never Cry (1976, Warner Bros.)
*You and Me (1977, Warner Bros.)

*How You Gonna See Me Now
(1978, Warner Bros.)
*Clones (We're All) (1980, Warner
Bros.)

Pretties for You (1969, Straight)
Easy Action (1970, Straight)
Killer (1971, Warner Bros.)
Love It to Death (1971, Warner
Bros.)
School's Out (1972, Warner Bros.)
Billion Dollar Babies (1973, Warner
Bros.)
Alice Cooper's Greatest Hits (1974,
Warner Bros.)
Welcome to My Nightmare (1975,
Atco)
Zipper Catches Skin (1982, Warner
Bros.)

Nazz/Utopia

(*Todd Rundgren, 1948-)

*Hello It's Me (1969, SGC)
*We Gotta Get You a Woman
(1971, Ampex)
Black Maria (1972, Bearsville)
*I Saw the Light (1972, Bearsville)
Wolfman Jack (1972, Bearsville)
International Feel (1973,
Bearsville)
Just One Victory (1973, Bearsville)
Sometimes I Don't Know What to
Feel (1973, Bearsville)
*Good Vibrations (1976, Bearsville)
*Can We Still Be Friends? (1978,
Bearsville)
*Set Me Free (1980, Bearsville)

Nazz (1968, SGC)
Nazz Nazz (1969, SGC)
Nazz 3 (1970, SGC)
Runt (1970, Ampex)
The Ballad of Todd Rundgren
(1971, Ampex)
Something/Anything (1972,
Bearsville)
A Wizard, a True Star (1973,
Bearsville)

Todd (1974, Bearsville)
Todd Rundgren's Utopia (1974,
Bearsville)
Another Live LP (1975, Bearsville)
Faithful (1976, Bearsville)
RA (1977, Bearsville)
Back to the Bars (1978, Bearsville)
Adventures in Utopia (1979,
Bearsville)
Deface the Music (1980, Bearsville)
Healing (1981, Bearsville)
Swing to the Right (1982, Bearsville)
Utopia (1982, Network)
*The Ever-Popular Tortured Artist
Effect* (1983, Bearsville)

*Blue Oyster Cult

Debbie Denise (1976, Columbia)
*(Don't Fear) The Reaper (1976,
Columbia)
Revenge of Vera Gemini (1976,
Columbia)
True Confessions (1976, Columbia)
Death Valley Nights (1977,
Columbia)
I Love the Night (1977, Columbia)
*Burnin' for You (1981, Columbia)
*Take Me Away (1983, Columbia)
*Dancing in the Ruins (1986,
Columbia)

Blue Oyster Cult (1972, Columbia)
Tyranny and Mutation (1973,
Columbia)
Secret Treaties (1974, Columbia)
Agents of Fortune (1976, Columbia)
Spectres (1977, Columbia)
Mirrors (1979, Columbia)
Cultosaurus Erectus (1980,
Columbia)
Fire of Unknown Origin (1981,
Columbia)
Extraterrestrial Live (1982,
Columbia)
The Revolution by Night (1983,
Columbia)
Club Ninja (1986, Columbia)

*Styx

*Lady (1975, Wooden Nickel)
Lorelei (1976, A&M)
*Come Sail Away (1977, A&M)
*Babe (1979, A&M)
*The Best of Times (1981, A&M)
*Too Much Time on My Hands
  (1981, A&M)
*Don't Let It End (1983, A&M)
*Mr. Roboto (1983, A&M)
*Music Time (1984, A&M)

Lady (RCA)
Styx (1972, Wooden Nickel)
Styx 2 (1973, Wooden Nickel)
**Equinox* (1974, A&M)
Miracles (1974, Wooden Nickel)
Serpent (1974, RCA)
**Crystal Ball* (1976, A&M)
Grand Illusion (1977, A&M)
Pieces of Eight (1978, A&M)
Cornerstone (1979, A&M)
Paradise Theater (1980, A&M)
Kilroy Was Here (1983, A&M)

*Bruce Springsteen (1949-)

*Blinded by the Light (1973,
  Columbia)
*For You (1973, Columbia)
*Growin' Up (1973, Columbia)
*Incident on 57th Street (1973,
  Columbia)
*New York City Serenade (1973,
  Columbia)
*Rosalita (1973, Columbia)
*Backstreets (1975, Columbia)
*Born to Run (1975, Columbia)
*Jungleland (1975, Columbia)
*She's the One (1975, Columbia)
*Tenth Avenue Freezeout (1975,
  Columbia)
*Thunder Road (1975, Columbia)
*Adam Raised a Cain (1978,
  Columbia)
*Badlands (1978, Columbia)
*Darkness on the Edge of Town
  (1978, Columbia)

*The Promised Land (1978,
  Columbia)
*Prove It All Night (1978, Columbia)
*Racing in the Streets (1978,
  Columbia)
*Cadillac Ranch (1980, Columbia)
*Drive All Night (1980, Columbia)
*Hungry Heart (1980, Columbia)
*I Wanna Marry You (1980,
  Columbia)
*Out in the Streets (1980, Columbia)
*The Price You Pay (1980,
  Columbia)
*Ramrod (1980, Columbia)
*Wreck on the Highway (1980,
  Columbia)
*Fade Away (1981, Columbia)
*Born in the U.S.A. (1984,
  Columbia)
*Cover Me (1984, Columbia)
*Dancing in the Dark (1984,
  Columbia)
*I'm on Fire (1984, Columbia)
*My Hometown (1984, Columbia)

*Greetings from Asbury Park, New
  Jersey* (1973, Columbia)
**The Wild, the Innocent, and the E.
  Street Shuffle* (1973, Columbia)
**Born to Run* (1975, Columbia)
**Darkness on the Edge of Town*
  (1978, Columbia)
**The River* (1980, Columbia)
**Nebraska* (1982, Columbia)
**Born in the U.S.A.* (1984, Columbia)
**Bruce Springsteen & E. Street Band
  Live, 1975-85* (1986, Columbia)
Tunnel of Love (1987, Columbia)

Rick Derringer with McCoys

*Fever (1965, Bang)
*Hang on Sloopy (1965, Bang)
SF Sorrow Is Born (1965, Bang)
Stormy Monday (1965, Bang)
*Come On Let's Go (1966, Bang)

Hang On Sloopy (1965, Bang)
You Make Me Feel So Good (1966,
  Bang)

Human Ball (1968, Mercury)
Infinite McCoys (1968, Mercury)

*Rick Derringer (1949-) solo

*All-American Boy (1973, Blue Sky)
The Airport Giveth (1974, Blue Sky)
Jump Jump Jump (1974, Blue Sky)
*Rock and Roll Hoochie Koo (1974, Blue Sky)
Slide on Over Slinky (1974, Blue Sky)
Teenage Love Affair (1974, Blue Sky)
Beyond the Universe (1976, Blue Sky)
Derringer (1976, Blue Sky)
Sailor (1976, Blue Sky)
Derringer Live (1977, Blue Sky)
Face to Face (1980, Blue Sky)

*Aerosmith

*Dream On (1973, Columbia)
*Sweet Emotion (1975, Columbia)
*Last Child (1976, Columbia)
*Walk This Way (1976, Columbia)
*Back in the Saddle (1977, Columbia)
*Come Together (1978, Columbia)

Aerosmith (1973, Columbia)
Get Your Wings (1974, Columbia)
Rocks (1976, Columbia)
Toys in the Attic (1976, Columbia)
Draw the Line (1977, Columbia)
Aerosmith's Greatest Hits (1980, Columbia)
Rock in a Hard Place (1982, Columbia)
Done with Mirrors (1985, Geffen)

*Kiss

*Deuce (1974, Casablanca)
*Nothin' to Lose (1974, Casablanca)
*Strutter (1974, Casablanca)
*Rock and Roll All Night (1975, Casablanca)
*Beth (1976, Casablanca)
*Detroit Rock City (1976, Casablanca)
*Calling Dr. Love (1977, Casablanca)
*Christine Sixteen (1977, Casablanca)
*Hard Luck Woman (1977, Casablanca)
*I Want You (1977, Casablanca)
*Rocket Ride (1978, Casablanca)
*I Was Made for Loving You (1979, Casablanca)
*Mr. Blackwell (1981, Casablanca)
*World without Heroes (1981, Casablanca)

Hotter than Hell (1974, Casablanca)
Kiss (1974, Casablanca)
Alive (1975, Casablanca)
Dressed to Kill (1975, Casablanca)
Destroyer (1976, Casablanca)
Rock and Roll Over (1977, Casablanca)
Double Platinum (1978, Casablanca)
Dynasty (1979, Casablanca)
Music from "The Elder" (1981, Casablanca)
Lick It Up (1983, Mercury)
Animalize (1984, Mercury)
Asylum (1985, Mercury)

*Journey

*Lights (1978, Columbia)
*Wheel in the Sky (1978, Columbia)
*Lovin', Touchin', Squeezin' (1979, Columbia)
*Any Way You Want It (1980, Columbia)
*Who's Crying Now (1981, Columbia)
*Open Arms (1982, Columbia)
*Send Her My Love (1983, Columbia)
*Separate Ways (World Apart) (1983, Columbia)

Journey (1975, Columbia)

Look into the Future (1976, Columbia)
Next (1977, Columbia)
Infinity (1978, Columbia)
Evolution (1979, Columbia)
Departure (1980, Columbia)
Escape (1981, Columbia)
Frontiers (1983, Columbia)

*Warren Zevon (1947-)

*Carmelita (1976, Asylum)
*Desperadoes under the Eaves (1976, Asylum)
*Mohammed's Radio (1976, Asylum)
*Excitable Boy (1978, Asylum)
*Werewolves of London (1978, Asylum)
*Bo Diddley (1980, Asylum)
*Jeannie Needs a Shooter (1980, Asylum)
*Play It All Night Long (1980, Asylum)

Wanted--Dead or Alive (1969, Imperial)
Warren Zevon (1976, Asyl)
Excitable Boy (1978, Asylum)
Bad Luck Streak in Dancing Shool (1980, Asylum)
Stand in the Fire (1980, Asylum)
The Envoy (1982, Asylum)
Sentimental Hygiene (1987, Virgin)

*Iron City House Rockers

Love's So Tough (1979, MCA)
Have a Good Time (But Get Out Alive) (1980, MCA)
Blood on the Bricks (1981, MCA)

*Raybeats

Guitar Beat (1981, Jem)

*Polyrock

Polyrock (1980, RCA)
Changing Hearts (1981, RCA)

Steve Van Zandt (1950-)

Men without Women (1982, EMI)
Voice of America (1983, EMI)
Sun City (1985, EMI)
Freedom--No Compromise (1987, Manhattan)

*Tom Petty and the Heartbreakers

(Tom Petty, 1952-)

*American Girl (1976, Shelter)
*Breakdown (1976, Shelter; 1978, Shelter)
*I Need to Know (1978, Shelter)
*Listen to the Heart (1978, Shelter)
*Century City (1979, Backstreet)
*Don't Do Me Like That (1979, Backstreet)
*Even the Losers (1979, Backstreet)
*Refugee (1980, Backstreet)
*The Insider (1981, Backstreet)
*Kings Road (1981, Backstreet)
*A Thing about You (1981, Backstreet)
*The Waiting (1981, Backstreet)
*You Got Lucky (1982, Backstreet)
*Change of Heart (1983, Backstreet)
Needles and Pins (1986, MCA)
*So You Want to Be A Rock & Roll Star (1986, MCA)

Tom Petty and the Heartbreakers (1976, Shelter)
You're Gonna Get It (1978, Shelter)
Damn the Torpedos (1979, Backstreet)
Hard Promises (1981, Backs)
Long after Dark (1982, Backstreet)
Southern Accents (1985, MCA)
Pack Up the Plantation (1986, MCA)
Let Me Up (I've Had Enough) (1987, MCA)

*Cheap Trick

*Big Eyes (1977, Epic)
*Clock Strikes Ten (1977, Epic)

*Surrender (1978, Epic)
*Ain't That a Shame (1979, Epic)
*Dream Police (1979, Epic)
*I Want You to Want Me (1979, Epic)
*Voices (1980, Epic)
 If You Want My Love (1982, Epic)
 She's Tight (1982, Epic)

 Cheap Trick (1976, Epic)
In Color (1977, Epic)
Heaven Tonight (1978, Epic)
 Dream Police (1979, Epic)
Live at Budokan (1979, Epic)
 All Shook Up (1980, Epic)
 One on One (1982, Epic)
 Standing on the Edge (1985, Epic)

*Southside Johnny (1948-) with the Asbury Jukes

*The Fever (1976, Epic)
*This Time Baby (1978, Epic)

I Don't Want to Go Home (1976, Epic)
This Time It's for Real (1977, Epic)
Hearts of Stone (1978, Epic)
Havin' a Party with ... (1979, Epic)
 The Jukes (1979, Mercury)
 Love Is a Sacrifice (1980, Mercury)
Reach Up and Touch the Sky (1981, Mercury)

*Heart

*Crazy on You (1976, Mushroom)
*Magic Man (1976, Mushroom)
*Barracuda (1977, Protrait)
*Heartless (1978, Mushroom)
*Straight On (1978, Portrait)
*Dog and Butterfly (1979, Portrait)
*Even It Up (1980, Epic)
*Tell It Like It Is (1980, Epic)
*This Man Is Mine (1982, Epic)
*These Dreams (1986, Capitol)

 Dreamboat Annie (1976, Mushroom)
 Little Queen (1977, Portrait)

 Dog and Butterfly (1978, Portrait)
 Bebe Le Strange (1980, Epic)
Greatest Hits Live (1980, Epic)
 Heart (1985, Capitol)
Bad Animals (1987, Capitol)
 Magazine (1987, Mushroom)

*Boston

*More Than a Feeling (1976, Epic)
*Long Time (1977, Epic)
*Peace of Mind (1977, Epic)
*Don't Look Back (1978, Epic)
*A Man I'll Never Be (1978, Epic)

Boston (1976, Epic)
 Don't Look Back (1978, Epic)
 Third Stage (1986, MCA)

*Foreigner

*Cold as Ice (1977, Atlantic)
*Feels Like the First time (1977, Atlantic)
*Double Vision (1978, Atlantic)
*Hot Blooded (1978, Atlantic)
*Long, Long Way from Home (1978, Atlantic)
*Blue Morning, Blue Day (1979, Atlantic)
 Dirty White Boy (1979, Atlantic)
 Head Games (1979, Atlantic)
*Urgent (1981, Atlantic)
*Waiting for a Girl Like You (1981, Atlantic)
 Break It Up (1982, Atlantic)
 Juke Box Hero (1982, Atlantic)

Foreigner (1977, Atlantic)
 Double Vision (1978, Atlantic)
 Head Games (1979, Atlantic)
 4 (1981, Atlantic)
Records (1982, Atlantic)
Agent Provocateur (1985, Atlantic)

Lou Gramm solo

Ready Or Not (1987, Atlantic)

*Van Halen

*You Really Got Me (1978, Warner Bros.)

*Dance the Night Away (1979, Warner Bros.)

*Dancing in the Streets (1982, Warner Bros.)

*(Oh) Pretty Woman (1982, Warner Bros.)

I'll Wait (1984, Warner Bros.)

*Jump (1984, Warner Bros.)

Panama (1984, Warner Bros.)

*Why Can't This Be Love? (1986, Warner Bros.)

Van Halen (1978, Warner Bros.)
Van Halen 2 (1979, Warner Bros.)
Women and Children First (1980, Warner Bros.)
Fair Warning (1981, Warner Bros.)
Diver Down (1982, Warner Bros.)
**1984* (1984, Warner Bros.)
**5150* (1986, Warner Bros.)

David Lee Roth (1955-) solo

Eat 'em and Smile (1986, Warner Bros.)

*Sammy Hagar (1949-) solo

*Flamingos Fly (1976, Capitol)

*Your Love Is Driving Me Crazy (1982, Geffen)

*I Can't Drive 55 (1984, Geffen)

*Two Sides of Love (1984, Geffen)

Nine on a Ten Scale (1976, Capitol)
Musical Chairs (1977, Capitol)
**Sammy Hagar* (1977, Capitol)
**Sammy Hagar Live* (1978, Capitol)
Danger Zone (1979, Capitol)
Harder, Faster (1979, Capitol)
Street Machine (1979, Capitol)
Standing Hampton (1981, Geffen)
**Three Lock Box* (1982, Geffen)

*John Cougar Mellencamp (1951-)

I Need a Lover (1979, Riva)

This Time (1980, Riva)

Ain't Even Done with the Night (1981, Riva)

*Hand to Hold On To (1982, Riva)

*Hurts So Good (1982, Riva)

*Jack & Diane (1982, Riva)

*Crumblin' Down (1983, Riva)

*Pink Houses (1983, Riva)

*Authority Song (1984, Riva)

*Small Town (1985, Riva)

*Minutes to Memories (1986, Riva)

*R.O.C.K. in the U.S.A. (1986, Riva)

*Under the Boardwalk (1986, Riva)

Chestnut Street Incident (1976, Mainman/MCA)
A Biography (1978, Riva)
Johnny Cougar (1979, Riva)
Nothing Matters and What If It Did (1980, Riva)
**American Fool* (1982, Riva)
Uh-Huh (1983, Riva)
**Scarecrow* (1985, Riva)

*Pat Benatar (1953-)

*Heartbreaker (1980, Chrysalis)

*Hit Me with Your Best Shot (1980, Chrysalis)

*We Live for Love (1980, Chrysalis)

*Fire and Ice (1981, Chrysalis)

*Promises in the Dark (1981, Chrysalis)

*Treat Me Right (1981, Chrysalis)

*Shadows of the Night (1982, Chrysalis)

*Little Too Late (1983, Chrysalis)

*Looking for a Stranger (1983, Chrysalis)

*Love Is a Battlefield (1983, Chrysalis)

*We Belong (1984, Chrysalis)

*Le Bel Age (1986, Chrysalis)

In the Heat of the Night (1979, Chrysalis)
Crimes of Passion (1980, Chrysalis)
**Precious Time* (1981, Chrysalis)
Get Nervous (1982, Chrysalis)
Live from Earth (1984, Chrysalis)

Seven the Hard Way (1986,
Chrysalis)

*Joan Jett (1960-)

*Bad Reputation (1981, Boardwalk)
Do You Wanna Touch Me? (1981,
Boardwalk)
*Let Me Go (1981, Boardwalk)
Shout (1981, Boardwalk)
Wooly Bully (1981, Boardwalk)
*Crimson and Clover (1982,
Boardwalk)
*I Love Rock'n'Roll (1982,
Boardwalk)
*Little Drummer Boy (1982,
Boardwalk)
*Everyday People (1983, Blackheart)
*Fake Friends (1983, Blackheart)

Bad Reputation (1981, Boardwalk)
I Love Rock'n'Roll (1981,
Boardwalk)
Album (1983, MCA/Blackheart)
Glorious Results of a Misspent Youth
(1984, Blackheart)
Good Music (1986, CBS)

Survivor

Vital Sign (1985, Epic)
Burning Heart (1986, Epic)
When Second Counts (1986, Scotti
Bros.)

Night Ranger

Dawn Patrol (1982, Boardwalk)
Midnight Madness (1983, MCA)
7 Wishes (1986, MCA)

Del-Lords

Frontier Days (1984, EMI)
Johnny Comes Marching Home
(1986, EMI)

Chris Isaak (1956-)

Silvertone (1985, Warner Bros.)
Chris Isaak (1987, Warner Bros.)

Fire Town

In the Heart of the Heart Country
(1987, Atlantic)

Anthologies

American Graffiti, Vols. 1-2 (1973,
MCA)
More American Graffiti (1975,
MCA)
Spitballs (1978, Beserkley)

Pre-Punk and Glitter Rock, U.K.

*David Bowie (1947-)

*The Laughing Gnome (1967, London)
*Love You Till Tuesday (1967, London)
*Space Oddity (1969, Mercury)
*All the Madmen (1970, Mercury)
Karma Man (1970, Mercury)
The Prettiest Star (1970, Mercury)
*She Shook Me Cold (1970, Mercury)
Unwashed and Somewhat Slightly Dazed (1970, Mercury)
*Andy Warhol (1971, RCA)
*Oh! You Pretty Things (1971, RCA)
*Quicksand (1971, RCA)
Song for Bob Dylan (1971, RCA)
Five Years (1972, RCA)
Lady Stardust (1972, RCA)
Moonage Daydream (1972, RCA)
*Rock'n'Roll Suicide (1972, RCA)
*Starman (1972, RCA)
Ziggy Stardust (1972, RCA)
*Jean Genie (1973, RCA)
*Diamond Dogs (1974, RCA)
*Rebel Rebel (1974, RCA)
Across the Universe (1975, RCA)
*Fame (1975, RCA)
*Young Americans (1975, RCA)
*Golden Years (1976, RCA)
John, I'm Only Dancing (1976, RCA)
*TVC 15 (1976, RCA)
*Heroes (1977, RCA)
*African Night Flight (1979, RCA)
*Boys Keep Swinging (1979, RCA)
*Look Back in Anger (1979, RCA)
*Move On (1979, RCA)
*Repetition (1979, RCA)
*Yassassin (1979, RCA)
*Ashes to Ashes (1980, RCA)

*Because You're Young (1980, RCA)
*Fashion (1980, RCA)
*It's No Game (1980, RCA)
*Scary Monsters (1980, RCA)
*Teenage Wildlife (1980, RCA)
*Up the Hill Backwards (1980, RCA)
*China Girl (1983, EMI)
*Let's Dance (1983, EMI)
Modern Love (1983, EMI)
*Blue Jean (1984, EMI)

The World of David Bowie (1967, London)
Man of Words, Man of Music (1969, Mercury)
**Space Oddity* (1969, Mercury)
**The Man Who Sold the World* (1970, Mercury)
**Hunky Dory* (1971, RCA)
**Rise and Fall of Ziggy Stardust and the Spiders from Mars* (1972, RCA)
**Aladdin Sane* (1973, RCA)
Images, 1966-67 (1973, London)
**Young Americans* (1975, RCA)
**Station to Station* (1976, RCA)
**Heroes* (1977, RCA)
**Low* (1977, RCA)
**Lodger* (1979, RCA)
**Scary Monsters* (1980, RCA)
**Let's Dance* (1983, EMI)
Tonight (1984, EMI)
Never Let Me Down (1987, EMI)

*T-Rex

(Marc Bolan, 1948-77)

Hippy Gumbo (1966, Decca)
The Wizard (1966, Decca)
Desdemona (1967, Decca)
Go Go Girl (1967, Decca)
*Ride a White Swan (1970, Reprise)
*Bang a Gong (Get It On) (1972, Reprise)
*Jeepster (1972, Reprise)
*Telegram Sam (1972, Reprise)

*My People Were Fair and Had Sky in
Their Hair But Now They're
Content to Wear Stars on Their
Brows* (1968, Regal)
*Prophets, Seers and Sages, The
Angels of the Ages* (1968, Regal)
Unicorn (1969, Blue Thumb)
Beard of Stars (1970, Regal)
T-Rex (1970, Reprise)
*Electric Warrior (1971, Reprise)
*The Slider (1972, Reprise)
*Tyrannosaurus Rex (1972, A&M)
Tanx (1973, Reprise)
*Zinc Alloy and the Hidden Riders of
Tomorrow* (1974, Reprise)
Zip Gun Boogie (1975, EMI)
Futuristic Dragon (1976, EMI)
Dandy in the Underworld (1977,
EMI)

Gary Glitter

(Paul Francis Gadd, 1944-)

*Walk On By (1961, Decca)
Do You Wanna Touch Me? (1972,
Epic)
Hello, Hello I'm Back Again (1972,
Epic)
*I Didn't Know I Loved You (Till I
Saw You Rock and Roll) (1972,
Bell)
I'm the Leader of the Gang (1972,
Epic)
*Rock and Roll Part 2 (1972, Bell)
Always Yours (1973, Epic)
I Love You Love Me (1973, Epic)
Oh Yes You're Beautiful (1973,
Epic)
Remember Me This Way (1974,
Epic)

Gary Glitter (1973, Epic)
*Glitter (1973, Bell)
Touch Me (1973, Epic)
Glitter and Gold (1981, Epic)

*Roxy Music

*Virginia Plain (1972, Atco)

*Amazona (1973, Atco)
*Serenade (1973, Atco)
*Street Life (1973, Atco)
*The Thrill of It All (1974, Atco)
*Love Is the Drug (1975, Atco)
*Sentimental Fools (1975, Atco)
*She Sells (1975, Atco)
*More Than This (1982, Warner
Bros.)

Roxy Music (1972, Atco)
For Your Pleasure (1973, Atco)
*Stranded (1973, Atco)
*Country Life (1974, Atco)
*Siren (1975, Atco)
*Viva! Roxy Music (1976, Atco)
*Greatest Hits (1977, Atco)
Manifesto (1979, Atco)
Flesh and Blood (1980, Atco)
Avalon (1982, Warner Bros.)

*Bryan Ferry (1945-) solo

Another Time, Another Place (1974,
Atlantic)
*"These Foolish Things" (1974,
Atlantic)
Let's Stick Together (1976, Atlantic)
The Bride Stripped Bare (1978,
Atlantic)
Boys and Girls (1985, Warner
Bros.)

*Roy Wood (1946-)

*I Wish I Could Be Christmas
Everyday (1974, Harvest)
*See My Baby Jive (1974, Harvest)

Boulders (1973, United Artists)
Wizzard's Brew (1973, Harvest)
Introducing Eddy and the Falcons
(1974, United Artists)
See My Baby Jive (1974, Harvest)
Mustard (1975, Jet)
The Roy Wood Story (1976,
Harvest)
Super Active Wizzo (1977, Warner
Bros.)

*Be-Bop Deluxe

Axe Victim (1974, Harvest)
Modern Music (1976, Harvest)
Sunburst Finish (1976, Harvest)
Live in the Air Age (1977, Harvest)
*Best of Be-Bop Deluxe and the Rest
    of Be-Bop Deluxe* (1979,
    Harvest)

Bill Nelson solo

Northern Dream (1971, JEM)
Flaming Desire and Other Passions
    (1982, PVC)
The Love That Whirls (1982, PVC)

*Sweet

Co-Co (1971, RCA)
Funny funny (1971, RCA)
*Little Willy (1973, Bell)
*Ballroom Blitz (1975, Capitol)
Blockbuster (1975, Capitol)
*Fox on the Run (1975, Capitol)
*Love Is Like Oxygen (1978,
    Capitol)

Funny How Sweet Co-Co Can Be
    (1971, RCA)
Biggest Hits (1972, RCA)
The Sweet (1973, Bell)
Desolation Boulevard (1975,
    Capitol)
Give Us a Wink (1976, Capitol)
Level Headed (1978, Capitol)
Sweet 6 (1980, Capitol)

*Ultravox

Hiroshima Mon Amour (1977,
    Island)
*My Sex (1977, Island)
Passing Strangers (1980, Chrysalis)
Sleepwalk (1980, Chrysalis)
Reap the Wild Wind (1983,
    Chrysalis)

Ha! Ha! Ha! (1977, Island)
Ultravox (1977, Island)
Systems of Romance (1978, Antilles)

Three Into One (1980, Antilles)
Vienna (1980, Chrysalis)
Rage in Eden (1981, Chrysalis)
Quartet (1983, Chrysalis)
Lament (1984, Chrysalis)

Punk, U.K.

*Graham Parker

*Don't Ask Me Questions (1976,
  Mercury)
*Fool's Gold (1976, Mercury)
*Heat Treatment (1976, Mercury)
*Pourin' It All Out (1976, Mercury)
*Clear Head (1977, Mercury)
*Hold Back the Night (1977,
  Mercury)
*New York Shuffle (1977, Mercury)
*Problem Child (1977, Mercury)
*The Raid (1977, Mercury)
*Soul on Ice (1977, Mercury)
*Watch the Moon Come Down
  (1977, Mercury)

*Heat Treatment (1976, Mercury)
*Howlin' Wind (1976, Mercury)
Live at the Marble Arch (1976,
  Vertigo)
The Pink Parker (1977, Vertigo)
*Stick To Me (1977, Mercury)
Parkerilla (1978, Mercury)
*Squeezing Out Sparks (1979, Arista)
The Up Escalator (1980, Arista)
Another Gray Area (1982, Arista)
The Real Macaw (1983, Arista)

*Dave Edmunds (1944-)

*I Hear You Knocking (1970,
  MAM)
*Crawling from the Wreckage (1979,
  Swan)
*Girls Talk (1979, Swan)
*Almost Saturday Night (1981,
  Swan)
*Race Is On (1981, Swan)
*From Small Things (Big Things One
  Day Come) (1982, Columbia)
*Slipping Away (1983, Columbia)

*Rockpile (1972, MAM)
*Dave Edmunds and Love Sculpture:
  One Up (1974, EMI)

*Dave Edmunds and Love Sculpture--
  The Classic Tracks, 1968-1972
  (1974, EMI)
Subtle as a Flying Mallet (1975,
  RCA)
Get It (1977, Swan)
Tracks On Wax 4 (1978, Swan)
*Repeat When Necessary (1979,
  Swan)
Twangin' (1981, Swan)
*Dave Edmunds's 7th (1982,
  Columbia)
Information (1983, Columbia)
Riff Raff (1984, Columbia)

Rockpile

Seconds of Pleasure (1980,
  Columbia)

Brinsley Schwarz (1949-)

Brinsley Schwarz (1970, Capitol)
Despite It All (1970, Liberty)
Nervous On the Road (1972, United
  Artists)
Silver Pistol (1972, United Artists)
*Please Don't Ever Change (1973,
  United Artists)
*New Favorites (1974, United
  Artists)
Original Golden Greats (1974,
  United Artists)
*Fifteen Thoughts of B.Schwarz
  (1978, United Artists)
Brinsley Schwarz (1979, Capitol)

*Clash

*Clash City Rockers (1977,
  Columbia)
*Complete Control (1977,
  Columbia)
Police and Thieves (1977,
  Columbia)
*White Man in Hammersmith Palais
  (1977, Columbia)
*White Riot (1977, Columbia)
*English Civil War (1978, Epic)
*Safe European Home (1978, Epic)

*Stay Free (1978, Epic)
*I Fought the Law (1979, Columbia)
*Clampdown (1980, Epic)
*The Guns of Brixton (1980, Epic)
*London Calling (1980, Epic)
*Lost in the Supermarket (1980, Epic)
*Spanish Bombs (1980, Epic)
*Train in Vain (1980, Epic)
*The Call Up (1981, Epic)
*Charlie Don't Surf (1981, Epic)
*Junco Partner (1981, Epic)
*The Magnificent Seven (1981, Epic)
*Rock the Casbah (1982, Epic)
*Should I Stay or Should I Go (1982, Epic)

*The Clash (1977, Columbia)
*Give 'em Enough Rope (1978, Epic)
*The Clash (1979, Epic)
Black Market Clash (1980, Epic)
*London Calling (1980, Epic)
*Sandinista! (1981, Epic)
*Combat Rock (1982, Epic)

*Sex Pistols

*Anarchy in the U.K. (1976, EMI)
*God Save the Queen (1977, Virgin)
*Pretty Vacant (1977, Virgin)

*Never Mind the Bollocks, Here's the Sex Pistols (1977, Warner Bros.)
The Very Best of . . . (1978, Columbia)
The Great Rock'n'Roll Swindle (1980, Virgin)

*Public Image Ltd.

First Issue (1978, Virgin)
Public Image Ltd. (1978, Virgin)
*Metal Box (1979, Virgin)
Paris au Printemps (1980, Virgin)
Flowers of Romance (1981, Warner Bros.)

Rich Kids

Ghosts of Princes in Towers (1978, EMI)

Malcolm McLaren

Duck Rock (1984, Island)
Fans (1985, Island)

Bow Wow Wow

C-30, C-60, C-90, Go! (1981, RCA)
Work (1981, RCA)

See Jungle! See Jungle! Go Join Your Gang, Yeah! City All Over, Go Ape Crazy (1981, RCA)

Dr. Feelgood

Malpractice (1976, Columbia)
Sneakin' Suspicion (1977, Columbia)

Skids

Scared to Dance (1978, Virgin)
Closer (1980, Virgin)

Joy Division

Closer (1980, Factory)
Still (1981, Factory)

Eddie and the Hot Rods

Life On the Line (1977, Island)
Fish-n-Chips (1980, EMI America)

*Ducks Deluxe

Ducks Deluxe (1974, RCA)
Taxi to the Terminal (1974, RCA)
*Don't Mind Rockin' Tonite (1975, RCA)

*Motors

Dancing the Night Away (1977, Virgin)
Airport (1978, Virgin)

Love and Loneliness (1980, Virgin)

The Motors (1977, Virgin)
Approved by the Motors (1978, Virgin)
Tenement Steps (1980, Virgin)

*Ian Dury (1942-)

Sex and Drugs and Rock and Roll (1977, Stiff)
Hit Me With Your Rhythm Stick (1978, Stiff)
What a Waste (1978, Stiff)
Reason to Be Cheerful, Part 3 (1979, Stiff)
Spasticus Autisticus (1981, Polydor)

Wotabunch (1974, Warner Bros.)
Handsome (1975, Dawn)
Best of Kilburn and the High Roads (1977, Bonaparte)
New Boots and Panties (1977, Stiff)
Do It Yourself (1978, Stiff)
Laughter (1980, Stiff)
Juke Box Dury (1981, Stiff)
Lord Upminster (1981, Polydor)

*Jam

Back in My Arms Again (1977, Polydor)
In the City (1977, Polydor)
Sweet Soul Music (1977, Polydor)
*David Watts (1978, Polydor)
*Down in the Tube Station at Midnight (1978, Polydor)
*In the Crowd (1978, Polydor)
News of the World (1978, Polydor)
*Mr. Clean (1978, Polydor)
*The Place I Love (1978, Polydor)
*Eton Rifles (1980, Polydor)
*Start! (1980, Polydor)
That's Entertainment (1980, Polydor)
*Town Called Malice (1982, Polydor)

In the City (1977, Polydor)
This Is the Modern World (1977, Polydor)

All Mod Cons (1978, Polydor)
Setting Sons (1980, Polydor)
Absolute Beginners (1981, Polydor)
Sound Effects (1981, Polydor)
The Gift (1982, Polydor)

*Boys

The Boys (1977, NEMS)
Alternative Chartbusters (1978, NEMS)
To Hell with Boys (1978, Safari)
Boys Only (1980, Safari)

*Vibrators

Pure Mania (1977, Columbia)
V2 (1978, Columbia)
Batteries Included (1980, CBS)

Psychedelic Furs

We Love You/Pulse (1979, Epic)
*Dumb Waiter (1981, CBS)
*Pretty in Pink (1981, CBS)
*Love My Way (1982, Columbia)

The Psychedelic Furs (1980, Columbia)
Talk Talk Talk (1981, Columbia)
Forever Now (1982, Columbia)
Mirror Moves (1984, Columbia)
Midnight to Midnight (1987, Columbia)

*Wire

Pink Flag (1977, Harvest)
Chairs Missing (1978, Harvest)
154 (1979, Warner Bros.)
Document and Eyewitness (1981, Rough Trade)

Damned

New Rose (1976, Stiff)
Love Song (1979, Stiff)
Smash It Up (1979, Stiff)

Damned, Damned, Damned (1977, Stiff)

Music for Pleasure (1977, Stiff)
Machine Gun Etiquette (1979, Chiswick)
The Black Album (1980, IRS)
The Best of . . . (1981, Big Beat/Ace)

Nick Lowe (1949-)

Rollers Show (1978, Columbia)
So It Goes/Heart of the City (1976, Stiff)
*I Love the Sound of Breaking Glass (1977, Radar)
*Cruel to Be Kind (1979, Columbia)

Jesus of Cool (1978, Radar)
Pure Pop for Now People (1978, Columbia)
Labour of Love (1979, Columbia)
Nick the Knife (1981, Columbia)
The Abominable Showman (1983, Columbia)

*Adverts

*Gary Gilmore's Eyes/Bored Teenagers (1977, Anchor)
*One Chord Wonder/Quickstep (1977, Stiff)

Crossing the Red Sea with the Adverts (1978, Bright)

*Tom Robinson (1951-)

*Grey Cortina (1977, EMI)
*2-4-6-8 Motorway (1977, EMI)
Glad to Be Gay (1978, EMI)
*Power in the Darkness (1978, Harvest)

Power in the Darkness (1978, Harvest)
TRB 2 (1979, Capitol)
North by Northwest (1982, IRS)

*XTC

3-D (1977, Virgin)
Go Two (1978, Virgin)

White Music (1978, Virgin)
Drums and Wires (1979, Virgin)
Go Plus (1979, Virgin)
Black Sea (1980, Virgin)
English Settlement (1982, Epic)
Skylarking (1987, Geffen)

Generation X

*Your Generation (1977, Chrysalis)

Generation X (1978, Chrysalis)
Valley of the Dolls (1979, Chrysalis)
Kiss Me Deadly (1981, Chrysalis)

Billy Idol (1955-) solo

Billy Idol (1983, Chrysalis)
Rebel Yell (1983, Chrysalis)
Whiplash Smile (1986, Chrysalis)

X Ray Spex

Germ Free Adolescents (1978, EMI)

*Buzzcocks

*Orgasm Addict (1977, United Artists)
*Whatever Happened To? (1977, United Artists)
*Ever Fallen In Love (1978, United Artists)

Another Music in a Different Kitchen (1977, IRS)
Spiral Scratch (1977, New Hormones)
Love Bites (1978, IRS)
Singles Going Steady (1979, IRS)
A Different Kind of Tension (1980, IRS)

*Stiff Little Fingers

*Alternative Ulster (1978, Rough Trade)
*Suspect Device (1978, Rigid Digits)
*State of Emergencey (1979, Rough Trade)
*White Noise (1979, Rough Trade)

*Bloody Dub (1980, Chrysalis)
*Fly the Flag (1980, Chrysalis)
*I Don't Like You (1980, Chrysalis)
*Nobody's Hero (1980, Chrysalis)
*Tin Soldiers (1980, Chrysalis)

Inflammable Material (1979, Rough
     Trade)
Hanx! (1980, Chrysalis)
Nobody's Heroes (1980, Chrysalis)
Go For It (1981, Chrysalis)

*Undertones

*Teenage Kicks (1978, Sire)
*Get Over You (1979, Sire)
*Wednesday Week (1980, Sire)
*It's Going to Happen (1981,
     Harvest)
*Beautiful Friend (1982, EMI)

The Undertones (1979, Sire)
Hypnotized (1980, Sire)
Positive Touch (1981, Harvest)

Scritti Politti

Cupid & Psyche (1985, Warner
     Bros.)

Feargal Sharkey

Feargal Sharkey (1986, A&M)

Big Audio Dynamite

No. 10, Upping St. (1986, Columbia)
This Is B.A.D. (1986, Columbia)

Sigue Sigue Sputnik

Flaunt It (1986, Manhattan)

Tesla

Mechanical Resonance (1987,
     Geffen)

Anthologies

The Peel Sessions (Strange Fruit EP
     Series)

Life in the European Theatre (1981,
     Warner Bros.)
Oi! (1981, EMI)
Strength thru Oi, Vol. 2 (1981, Decca)

Punk, U.S.

*Seeds

*Can't Seem to Make You Mine
(1966, GNP Crescendo)
Mr. Farmer (1966, GNP
Crescendo)
*Pushin' Too Hard (1966, GNP
Crescendo)
Rollin' Machine (1966, GNP
Crescendo)
Tripmaker (1966, GNP Crescendo)
*Up in Her Room (1966, GNP
Crescendo)
*900 Million People Daily All
Making Love (1967, GNP
Crescendo)
*Two Fingers Pointing on You
(1967, GNP Crescendo)

*The Seeds (1966, GNP Crescendo)
*A Web of Sound (1966, GNP
Crescendo)
*Future (1967, GNP Crescendo)
*Merlin's Music Box (1967, GNP
Crescendo)
Fallin' Off the Edge (1977, GNP
Crescendo)

*Velvet Underground

All Tomorrow's Parties (1967,
Verve)
Femme Fatale (1967, Verve)
*Heroin (1967, Verve)
*I'll Be Your Mirror (1967, Verve)
Sunday Morning (1967, Verve)
*Venus in Furs (1967, Verve)
*Waiting for the Man (1967, Verve)
*Candy Says (1969, MGM)
*I'm Set Free (1969, MGM)
*Pale Blue Eyes (1969, MGM)
*Head Held High (1970, Cotillion)
*New Age (1970, Cotillion)
*Oh! Sweet Nuthin' (1970, Cotillion)
*Rock'n'Roll (1970, Cotillion)

*The Velvet Underground and Nico
(1967, Verve)
*White Light, White Heat (1967,
Verve)
*The Velvet Underground (1969,
MGM)
*Loaded (1970, Cotillion)
Squeeze (1972, Polydor)
*The Velvet Underground Live at
Max's Kansas City (1972,
Cotillion)
*1969 Velvet Underground Live
(1974, Mercury)
*VU (1985, Verve)

*Lou Reed (1943-) solo

*Walk on the Wild Side (1972, RCA)

Lou Reed (1972, RCA)
*Transformer (1972, RCA)
*Berlin (1973, RCA)
*Rock'n'Roll Animal (1974, RCA)
*Sally Can't Dance (1974, RCA)
Coney Island Baby (1976, RCA)
*Street Hassle (1978, Arista)
Growing Up in Public (1980, Arista)
*Rock'n'Roll Diary (1980, Arista)
New Sensation (1984, RCA)
*Mistrial (1986, RCA)

Nico (Christa Päffgen, 1933-) solo

The Last Mile (1965, Immediate)
The End (1974, Reprise)
Waiting for the Man (1981, ROIR)

Chelsea Girl (1968, MGM)
Desert Shore (1971, Reprise)
The End (1974, Island)
Drama of Exile (1981, ROIR)

Suzi Quatro (1950-)

Rolling Stone (1972, RAK)
*Can the Can (1973, Bell)
Daytona Demon (1973, Bell)
*48 Crash (1973, Bell)
*Devil's Gate Drive (1974, Bell)
*The Wild One (1974, Bell)
*Stumblin' In (1979, RSO)

Suzi Quatro (1973, Bell)
Quatro (1974, Bell)
If You Knew Suzi (1978, RSO)
Rock Hard (1980, Dreamland)
Lipstick (1981, RSO)

Sparks

Sparks (1972, Bearsville)
Kimono My House (1974, Island)
Propaganda (1975, Island)
Big Beat (1976, Columbia)
Sparks In Outer Sauce (1983, Atlantic)

*Iggy Pop and the Stooges

(James Osterberg, 1947-)

*No Fun (1969, Elektra)
*Now I Wanna Be Your Dog (1969, Elektra)
*The Stooges (1969, Elektra)
*Dirt (1970, Elektra)
*Raw Power (1973, Columbia)

*Fun House (1970, Elektra)
*Raw Power (1973, Columbia)

Iggy Pop solo

*The Idiot (1977, RCA)
*Lust for Life (1977, RCA)
New Values (1979, Arista)
Soldier (1980, Arista)
Zombie Birdhouse (1982, Animal)
*Blah-Blah-Blah (1986, A&M)

*MC 5

*Kick Out the Jams (1969, Elektra)

*Kick Out the Jams (1969, Elektra)
*Back in the U.S.A. (1970, Atlantic)
High Time (1971, Atlantic)

Flamin' Groovies

*Sneakers/Supersnazz (1969, Epic)
Flamingo (1970, Kama Sutra)
Teenage Head (1971, Kama Sutra)

Shake Some Action (1976, Sire)
Flamin' Groovies Now (1978, Sire)

Dictators

The Dictators Go Girl Crazy (1975, Epic)
*Manifest Destiny (1977, Asylum)
Bloodbrothers (1978, Asylum)

*New York Dolls

*Looking for a Kiss (1973, Mercury)
*Personality Crisis (1973, Mercury)
*There's Gonna Be a Showdown (1974, Mercury)

Lipstick Killers (1972, ROIR)
*New York Dolls (1973, Mercury)
*Too Much Too Soon (1974, Mercury)

*Sylvain Sylvain solo

*Sylvain Sylvain (1979, RCA)
*Syl Sylvain and the Teardrops (1981, RCA)

*David Johansen (1950-) solo

*Frenchette (1978, Blue Sky)
*Lonely Tenement (1978, Blue Sky)
*Famingo Road (1979, Blue Sky)
*Melody (1979, Blue Sky)
*Swaheto Woman (1979, Blue Sky)
*My Obsession (1981, Blue Sky)
*You Fool You (1981, Blue Sky)
*Animals Medley (1982, Blue Sky)
*Build Me Up Buttercup (1982, Blue Sky)

David Johansen (1978, Blue Sky)
*In Style (1979, Blue Sky)
Here Comes the Night (1981, Blue Sky)
*Live It Up (1982, Blue Sky)

Jobriath

(Jobriath Boone, 1949-)

> *Creatures of the Street* (1973, Elektra)
> *Jobriath* (1973, Elektra)

*Patti Smith (1946-)

*Hey Joe/Piss Factory (1974)
*Gloria (1975, Arista)
*Land (of 1,000 Dances) (1975, Arista)
*Because the Night (1978, Arista)

Horses (1975, Arista)
Easter (1978, Arista)
Wave (1979, Arista)
Never Enough (1987, Columbia)

*Ramones

*Beat on the Brat (1976, Sire)
*Blitzkrieg Bop (1976, Sire)
*Now I Wanna Sniff Some Glue (1976, Sire)
*Here Today, Gone Tomorrow (1977, Sire)
*Sheena Is a Punk Rocker (1977, Sire)
*Don't Come Close (1978, Sire)
*Danny Says (1980, Sire)
*Do You Remember Rock'n'Roll Radio? (1980, Sire)
*Rockaway Beach (1988, Sire)

The Ramones (1976, Sire)
Leave Home (1977, Sire)
Rocket to Russia (1977, Sire)
Road to Ruin (1978, Sire)
End of the Century (1980, Sire)
Subterranean Jungle (1983, Sire)
Too Tough to Die (1984, Sire)

*Modern Lovers

Hospital (1971, Warner Bros.)
*Pablo Picasso (1971, Warner Bros.)
*Road Runner (1971, Warner Bros.)
*Egyptian Reggae (1977, Beserkley)

Modern Lovers (1971, Warner Bros.)
Modern Lover Live (1971, Warner Bros.)
Rock'n'Roll with the Modern Lovers (1977, Beserkley)
Back in Your Life (1978, Beserkley)
Modern Love Songs (1979, Beserkley)

Jonathan Richman (1952-)

> *Rockin' and Romance* (1985, Twin Tone)

*Richard Hell and the Voidoids

(Richard Hell, 1949-)

*Blank Generation (1977, Stiff)
*Love Comes in Spurts (1977, Stiff)
*The Kid with the Replaceable Head (1979, Red Star)

Blank Generation (1977, Sire)
Destiny Street (1982, Red Star)

*Mink DeVille

*Mixed Up Shook Up Girl (1977, Capitol)
*Spanish Stroll (1977, Capitol)
*Soul Twist (1978, Capitol)

Mink DeVille (1977, Capitol)
Return to Magenta (1978, Capitol)
Le Chat Bleu (1980, Capitol)
Coup de Grace (1981, Atlantic)

*Blondie

(Deborah Harry, 1945-)

*X Offender (1975, Private Stock)
Hangin' on the Telephone (1978, Chrysalis)
*Heart of Glass (1978, Chrysalis)
Dreaming (1979, Chrysalis)
One Way or Another (1979, Chrysalis)

Atomic (1980, Chrysalis)
*Call Me (1980, Chrysalis)
*The Tide Is High (1980, Chrysalis)
Faces (1981, Chrysalis)
*Rapture (1981, Chrysalis)
Island of Lost Souls (1982,
  Chrysalis)

Blondie (1977, Private Stock)
*Parallel Lines (1978, Chrysalis)
Plastic Letters (1978, Chrysalis)
Eat to the Beat (1979, Chrysalis)
Autoamerican (1980, Chrysalis)
Best of . . . (1981, Chrysalis)
The Hunter (1982, Chrysalis)
*Rockbird (1986, Geffen)

*Television

*Little Jonny Jewel (1974)

*Marquee Moon (1977, Elektra)
Adventure (1978, Elektra)
The Blow-Up (1982, ROIR)

*Tom Verlaine solo

*Tom Verlaine (1979, Elektra)
*Dreamtime (1981, Warner Bros.)

Stranglers

IV Rattus Norvegicus (1977, A&M)
Black and White (1978, A&M)
Stranglers IV (1979, IRS)
*X Certs (1979, United Artists)

Dead Boys

Young, Loud, and Snotty (1977,
  Sire)
We Have Come for Your Children
  (1978, Sire)

*Germs

*GI (1979, Slash)
What We Do Is Secret (1981, Slash)

*Suicide

Suicide (1977, Red Star)

*Alan Vega/Martin Rev/Suicide
  (1980, Antilles)
Suicide (1980, Red Star)

Wipers

Is This Real? (1980, Park Avenue)
Youth of America (1981, Park
  Avenue)

Shaggs

The Philosophy of the World (1969,
  Red Rooster)
The Shaggs' Own Thing (1982, Red
  Rooster)

Plasmatics

Beyond the Valley of 1984 (1981,
  Stiff)
New Hope for the Wretched (1981,
  Stiff)
Coup d'Etat (1982, Capitol)

*Dead Kennedys

*Drug Me (1981, IRS)
*California uber Alles (1981, IRS)
*Chemical Warfare (1981, IRS)
*Kill the Poor (1981, IRS)
*Stealing People's Mail (1981, IRS)
*Too Drunk to Fuck (1981, IRS)

*Fresh Fruit for Rotting Vegetables
  (1981, IRS)
In God We Trust, Inc. (1981,
  Alternative Tentacles)
Plastic Surgery Disasters (1982,
  Alternative Tentacles)
Frankenchrist (1985, Alternative
  Tentacles)
Bedtime for Democracy (1986,
  Alternative Tentacles)

*Minutemen

*Double Nickles on the Dime (1985,
  SST)
*3-Way Tie/For Last (1986, SST)

*Jesus and Mary Chain

*Psychocandy (1986, Reprise)

Charlie Sexton

Beat's So Lonely (1986, MCA)

Pictures for Pleasure (1986, MCA)

Hüsker Dü

Candy Apple Grey (1986, Warner
Bros.)

Post-Punk/ Underground Rock, U.S.

Feelies

*Crazy Rhythms (1980, Coyote)
*The Good Earth (1986, Coyote)

True Believers

*True Believers (1986, EMI)

Long Ryders

Native Sons (1986, Zippo)
State of Our Union (1986, Island)
Two-Fisted Tales (1987, Island)

Green on Red

Green on Red (1982, Down There)
Gas Food Lodging (1985, Mercury)
No Free Lunch (1986, Mercury)

Dream Syndicate

*The Days of Wine and Roses (1982,
A&M)
*Medicine Show (1983, A&M)
*Out of the Grey (1986, Big Time)

Rain Parade

Emergency Third Rail Power Trip
(1986, Zippo)

True West

Drifters (1986, Zippo)

Get Smart/Embarrassment

*Fresh Sounds from Middle America,
Vols. 1-3 (1981-86, Fresh
Sounds)

Fetchin' Bones

Bad Pumpkin (1986, Capitol)

EIEIO

*Land of Opportunity (1985, Demon)

Lyres

*On Fyre (1984, Ace of Hearts)
*Lyres Lyres (1986, Ace of Hearts)

Mission of Burma

Signals, Calls and Marches (1981, Ace of Heart)

Mekons

The Edge of the World (1985, Twin Tone)
Fear of Whiskey (1985, Twin Tone)
Honky Tonkin' (1987, Twin Tone)

Fleshtones

Fleshtones vs. Reality (1987, Emergo)

Volcano Suns

All Night Lotus Party (1986, Homestead)

Balancing Act

*New Campfire Songs (1986, Type A)

Ben Vaughn Combo

*The Many Moods of . . . (1986, Restless)

Silos

*About Her Steps (1986, Record Collect)

Soul Asylum

*Made to Be Broken (1986, Twin Tones)

Minutemen/Firehose

*Ballot Result (1987, SST)
*Ragin', Full-On (1987, SST)

77's

All Fall Down (1984, Exit)
77's (1987, Exit)

New Wave, U.K.

*Elvis Costello (1955-)

*Alison (1977, Columbia)
*Less Than Zero (1977, Columbia)
*Everyday I Write the Book (1983, Columbia)

*My Aim Is True (1977, Columbia)
*This Year's Model (1978, Columbia)
*Armed Forces (1979, Columbia)
*Get Happy (1979, Columbia)
 Taking Liberties (1980, Columbia)
 Trust (1980, Columbia)
*Imperial Bedroom (1982, Columbia)
*Punch the Clock (1983, Columbia)
*Goodbye Cruel World (1984, Columbia)
*Blood & Chocolate (1986, Columbia)

*Boomtown Rats

*Looking After No. 1 (1977, Mercury)
*She's So Modern (1979, Columbia)
 I Don't Like Mondays (1980, Columbia)
*Banana Republic (1981, Columbia)

 The Boomtown Rats (1977, Mercury)
 The Fine Art of Surfacing (1979, Columbia)
 A Tonic for the Troops (1979, Columbia)
 Mondo Bongo (1980, Columbia)
 Ratrospective (1983, Columbia)

Bob Geldof (1954-) solo

*Deep in the Heart of Nowhere (1986, Atlantic)

*Police

*Fall Out (1978, IRS)
 Message in the Bottle (1979, A&M)
*Roxanne (1979, A&M)

 Walking on the Moon (1979, A&M)
*De Do Do Do, De Da Da Da (1980, A&M)
*Don't Stand So Close to Me (1981, A&M)
*Every Little Thing She Does Is Magic (1981, A&M)
*King of Pain (1983, A&M)
*Wrapped Around Your Finger (1984, A&M)

 Outlandos d'Amour (1978, A&M)
*Regatta de Blanc (1979, A&M)
*Zenyatta Mondatta (1980, A&M)
*Ghost in the Machine (1981, A&M)
*Synchronicity (1983, A&M)
 Every Breath You Take--The Singles (1986, A&M)

*Sting (Gordon Sumner, 1951-) solo

*Fortress Around Your Heart (1985, A&M)
*Russians (1986, A&M)

*The Dream of the Blue Turtle (1985, A&M)
*Bring on the Night (1986, A&M)
 ... Nothing Like the Sun (1987, A&M)

Andy Summers (1942-) solo

 Love is the Strongest Way (1987, MCA)

Magazine

*Shot by Both Sides (1978, Virgin)
*Philadelphia (1980, Virgin)

 Real Life (1978, Virgin)
 Secondhand Daylight (1979, Virgin)
 The Correct Use of Soap (1980, Virgin)
 Magic, Murder, and the Weather (1981, IRS)
 After the Fact (1982, IRS)

*Squeeze

*Take Me I'm Yours (1978, A&M)
*Cool for Cats (1979, A&M)
*If I Didn't Love You (1980, A&M)
*Tempted (1980, A&M)
*Black Coffee in Bed (1982, A&M)

U.K. Squeeze (1978, A&M)
Cool for Cats (1979, A&M)
*Argybargy (1980, A&M)
*East Side Story (1981, A&M)
*Sweets from a Stranger (1982,
   A&M)
Babylon and On (1987, A&M)
*Cosi Fan Tutti Fruitti (1987, A&M)

Siouxsie and the Banshees

*Hong Kong Garden (1978, Polydor)
*Christine (1980, PVC)

The Scream (1978, Polydor)
Join Hands (1979, Polydor)
Kaleidoscope (1980, Polydor)
Greatest Hits (1981, Polydor)
Ju Ju (1981, Polydor)
Hyaena (1984, Geffen)

*Gang of Four

*Damaged Goods (1977, Fast
   Product)
*At Home, He's a Tourist (1980,
   Warner Bros.)
*Man In Uniform (1980, Warner
   Bros.)
*To Hell With Poverty (1981,
   Warner Bros.)

*Damaged (1977, Fast Product)
*Entertainment (1979, Warner Bros.)
Gang of Four (1980, Warner Bros.)
*Another Day, Another Dollar (1981,
   Warner Bros.)
Solid Gold (1981, Warner Bros.)
Songs of the Free (1982, Warner
   Bros.)
Hard (1983, Warner Bros.)

*Joe Jackson (1955-)

*Is She Really Going Out with Him?
   (1979, A&M)
*Steppin' Out (1982, A&M)
*Breaking Us into Two (1983,
   A&M)
*You Can't Get What You Want
   (1984, A&M)

I'm the Man (1979, A&M)
*Look Sharp (1979, A&M)
Beat Crazy (1980, A&M)
Jumpin' Jive (1981, A&M)
*Night and Day (1982, A&M)
Body and Soul (1984, A&M)
*Big World (1986, A&M)

*Madness

*Baggy Trousers (1979, Stiff)
*One Step Beyond (1979, Stiff)
*The Prince (1979, Two-Tone)
*House of Fun (1981, Stiff)
*It Must Be Love (1983, Geffen)
*Our House (1983, Geffen)

*One Step Beyond (1979, Sire)
*Absolutely (1980, Sire)
Madness 7 (1981, Stiff)
The Rise and Fall (1982, Stiff)
Madness (1983, Geffen)
Keep Moving (1984, Geffen)

Adam and the Ants

Ant Music (1980, Epic)
Dog Eat Dog (1980, Epic)

Dirk Wears White Sox (1979, Do-It)
*Kings of the Wild Frontier (1980,
   Epic)
Prince Charming (1981, Columbia)

Adam Ant (Stuart Goddard) solo

*Goody Two Shoes (1982, Epic)

Friend or Foe (1980, Epic)
Strip (1983, Epic)

Simple Minds

Life in a Day (1979, Zoom)
Real to Real Cacophony (1979, Zoom)
Empires and Dance (1980, Zoom)
New Gold Dreams (1981, Stiff)
Sons and Fascination/Sister Feeling Call (1981, Virgin)
Themes for Great Cities (1981, Stiff)
Sparkle in the Rain (1983, Virgin)
Once Upon a Time (1985, Virgin)

*U2

*I Will Follow (1980, Island)
*New Years Day (1981, Island)
*Sunday Bloody Sunday (1982, Island)
*Pride (In the Name of Love) (1984, Island)

Boy (1980, Island)
October (1981, Island)
War (1982, Island)
Under a Blood Red Sky (1984, Island)
The Unforgettable Fire (1984, Island)
Joshua Tree (1987, Island)

*Echo and the Bunnymen

Crocodiles (1980, Sire)
Heaven Up Here (1981, Sire)
Porcupine (1983, Sire)
Echo and the Bunnymen (1984, Sire)
Ocean Rain (1984, Sire)
Echo and the Bunnymen (1987, Sire)

UB40

*Madame Medusa (1980, Deptford Fun City)
*One in Ten (1980, Deptford Fun City)
*The Earth Dies Screaming (1981, Deptford Fun City)

*Rec Red Wine (1984, A&M)

Signing Off (1980, Graduate)
Present Arms (1981, Deptford Fun City)
Present Arms in Dub (1981, Deptford Fun City)
UB44 (1982, Deptford Fun City)
Labour of Love (1983, A&M)
The Singles Album (1983, Deptford Fun City)
Geffery Morgan (1984, A&M)
Rat in the Kitchen (1986, A&M)

*Duran Duran

*Planet Earth (1981, Harvest)
*Hungry Like the Wolf (1982, Harvest)
*Is There Something I Should Know (1983, Capitol)
*Union of the Snake (1983, Capitol)
*Reflex (1984, Capitol)
*The Wild Boys (1984, Capitol)

Duran Duran (1981, Harvest)
Rio (1982, Harvest)
Seven and the Ragged Tiger (1983, Capitol)
Arena (1984, Capitol)
Notorious (1986, Capitol)

Andy Taylor (1961-) solo

Thunder (1987, MCA)

Thompson Twins

Lies (1983, Arista)
Doctor! Doctor! (1984, Arista)
*Hold Me Now (1984, Arista)

A Product of . . . (1981, Arista)
In the Name of Love (1982, Arista)
Side Kicks (1983, Arista)
Into the Gap (1984, Arista)

Spandau Ballet

Gold (1983, Chrysalis)
*True (1983, Chrysalis)

Only When You Leave Me (1984, Chrysalis)

Journeys to Glory (1981, Reformation)
True (1983, Chrysalis)
Parade (1984, Chrysalis)
Through the Barricades (1987, Epic)

Fixx

*One Thing Leads to Another (1983, MCA)
Saved By Zero (1983, MCA)
The Sign of Fire (1983, MCA)
Are We Ourselves? (1984, MCA)

Shuttered Room (1982, MCA)
Reach the Beach (1983, MCA)
Phantoms (1984, MCA)

Culture Club

Do You Really Want to Hurt Me? (1983, Epic)
I'll Tumble for You (1983, Epic)
Karma Chameleon (1983, Virgin)
Time (Clock of the Heart) (1983, Epic)
Miss Me Blind (1984, Virgin)

Colour by Numbers (1983, Epic)
Kissing to be Clever (1983, Epic)
Waking Up with the House on Fire (1984, Virgin)

Boy George (1961-) solo

Sold (1987, Virgin)

Eurythmics

Love Is a Stranger (1983, RCA)
Sweet Dreams (Are Made of This) (1983, RCA)
Here Comes the Rain Again (1984, RCA)
Right By Your Side (1984, RCA)
Who's That Girl? (1984, RCA)

Sweet Dreams (1983, RCA)
Touch (1984, RCA)

Touch Dance (1984, RCA)
Be Yourself Tonight (1985, RCA)
Revenge (1986, RCA)
Savage (1987, RCA)

Waterboys

A Pagan Place (1984, Island)
This Is the Sea (1986, Island)

Big Country

In a Big Country (1983, Mercury)

The Crossing (1983, Mercury)
Steeltown (1984, Mercury)
Wonderland (1984, Mercury)

Smiths

The Smiths (1984, Sire)
Meat Is Murder (1985, Sire)
The Queen Is Dead (1986, Sire)
Louder than Bombs (1987, Sire)
Strangeways, Here We Come (1987, Rough Trade)

Frankie Goes to Hollywood

Welcome to the Pleasure Dome (1985, Island)

Alison Moyet

Alf (1985, Columbia)
Invisible (1985, Columbia)
Love Resurrection (1985, Columbia)
Raindancing (1987, Columbia)

Bronski Beat

Age of Consent (1985, London/MCA)
Truthdare Doubledare (1986, MCA)

Blue Nile

I Love This Life (1985, RSO)
Tinseltown in the Rain (1985, RSO)

Walk Across the Rooftops (1985, RSO)

Katrina and the Waves

Katrina and the Waves (1985, Capitol)
Katrina and the Waves (1986, Capitol)
Waves (1986, Capitol)

Kim Wilde (1960-)

Kim Wilde (1982, EMI America)
Teases & Dares (1985, MCA)

Cactus World News

Urban Beaches (1986, MCA)

Blue in Heaven

Explicit Material (1986, Island)

Screaming Blue Messiahs

**Gun-Shy* (1986, Elektra)

General Public

**Hand to Mouth* (1986, I.R.S.)

Simply Red

**Picture Book* (1986, Elektra)
**Men and Women* (1987, Elektra)

Easterhouse

Contenders (CBS)
In Your Own Hands (1985, Rough Trade)
Inspiration (1986, Rough Trade)

China Crisis

**Different Shapes & Passive Rhythm* (1982, A&M)
Flaunt the Imperfection (1985, A&M)
**What Price Paradise* (1987, A&M)

Colourfield

**Virgins & Philistines* (1985, Chrysalis)
**Deception* (1987, Chrysalis)

Concrete Blond

**Concrete Blond* (1987, I.R.S.)

Anthologies

First Edition (Wavelength)
The Recorder (Bristol Recorder)
Recorder Three (Bristol Recorder)
New Musical Express Dancin' Master (New Musical Express, 1981)

New Wave, U.S.

*Cars

*Just What I Needed (1978, Elektra)
*My Best Friend's Girl (1978, Elektra)
*Let's Go (1979, Elektra)
*Shake It Up (1981, Elektra)
*Drive (1984, Elektra)

*The Cars (1978, Elektra)
Candy-O (1979, Elektra)
Panorama (1980, Elektra)
Shake It Up (1981, Elektra)
*Heartbeat City (1984, Elektra)

Rick Ocasek solo

Beatitude (1983, Geffen)
This Side of Paradise (1986, Geffen)

Ben Orr solo

The Lace (1986, Elektra)

*Talking Heads

Psycho Killer (1977, Sire)
*Take Me to the River (1978, Sire)
*Life during Wartime (1979, Sire)
*Burning Down the House (1983, Sire)

*77 (1977, Sire)
More Songs about Buildings and Food (1978, Sire)
Fear of Music (1979, Sire)
*Remain in Light (1980, Sire)
The Name of This Band Is Talking Heads (1982, Sire)
*Speaking in Tongues (1983, Sire)
Stop Making Sense (1984, Sire)
*True Stories (1986, Sire)
Naked (1987, Sire)

*Pere Ubu

*30 Seconds Over Tokyo/Heart of Darkness (1975, Hearthan)

*Final Solution/Cloud 149 (1976, Hearthan)

*Datapanik in the Year Zero (1978, Radar)
*The Modern Dance (1978, Blank)
*Dub Housing (1979, Chrysalis)
New Panic Time (1979, Chrysalis)
The Art of Walking (1980, Rough Trade)
*390 Degrees of Simulated Stereo Live (1981, Rough Trade)
The Song of the Bailing Man (1982, Rough Trade)

*Pretenders

*The Wait/Stop Your Sobbing (1978, Real)
*Brass in Pocket (1979, Sire)
*Kid/Tattoed Love Boys (1979, Real)
*Talk of the Town (1980, Real)
*Back on the Chain Gang (1983, Sire)
*Middle of the Road (1984, Sire)
*Show Me (1984, Sire)

*Pretenders (1979, Sire)
Extended Play (1981, Sire)
*Pretenders 2 (1981, Sire)
*Learning to Crawl (1984, Sire)
*Get Close (1986, Sire)

B-52's

*Rock Lobster (1979, Warner Bros.)

The B-52's (1979, Warner Bros.)
Wild Planet (1980, Warner Bros.)
Whammy! (1983, Warner Bros.)

Tubes

*White Punks on Dope (1977, A&M)
Don't Touch Me There (1978, A&M)
*Don't Want to Wait Anymore (1981, Capitol)
Talk to You Later (1981, Capitol)

She's a Beauty (1983, Capitol)

The Tubes (1975, A&M)
Young and Richy (1976, A&M)
Now (1977, A&M)
What Do You Want from Life?
(1978, A&M)
Remote Control (1979, A&M)
Completion Backward Principle
(1981, Capitol)
Outside Inside (1983, Capitol)
Love Bomb (1985, Capitol)

Grace Jones (1952-)

Portfolio (1977, Island)
Fame (1978, Island)
Muse (1979, Island)
Warm Leatherette (1980, Island)
Nightclubbing (1981, Island)
Living My Life (1982, Island)

Devo

Jocko Homo/Mongloid (1976,
Booji Boy Records)
Wip It (1980, Warner Bros.)

*Q: Are We Not Men? A: We Are
Devo* (1978, Warner Bros.)
Duty Now for the Future (1979,
Warner Bros.)
Freedom of Choice (1981, Warner
Bros.)
New Traditionalists (1981, Warner
Bros.)
Oh, No! It's Devo (1982, Warner
Bros.)
Shout (1984, Warner Bros.)

*Residents

Meet the Residents (1974, Ralph)
Third Reich'n'Roll (1975, Ralph)
Fingerprince (1976, Ralph)
Buster and Glen/Duck Stab! (1978,
Ralph)
**Not Available* (1978, Ralph)
**Eskimo* (1979, Ralph)

Residents Commercial Album (1980,
Ralph)
Mark of the Mole (1981, Ralph)
Intermission (1982, Ralph)
Tunes of Two Cities (1982, Ralph)

*Motels

*Only the Lonely (1982, Capitol)
*Suddenly Last Summer (1983,
Capitol)
Remember the Nights (1984,
Capitol)

Motels (1979, Capitol)
Careful (1980, Capitol)
**All Four One* (1982, Capitol)
**Little Robbers* (1983, Capitol)

Romantics

What I Like About You (1979,
Nemperor)
*Talking in Your Sleep (1983)
One in a Million (1984)

**The Romantics* (1979)
National Breakout (1980)
Strictly Personal (1981, Nemperor)
**In Heat* (1983)

Golden Palominos

The Golden Palominos (1981,
Celluloid)
Visions of Excess (1986, Celluloid)

Rainmakers

**The Rainmakers* (1986, Polygram)

Athens, Ga.

**Inside/Out--Various Artists* (1987,
I.R.S.)

Pearl Harbour

**Don't Follow Me, I'm Lost Too*
(1980, Warner Bros.)

Pearl Harbour and the Explosions
(1980, Warner Bros.)

Rachel Sweet (1962-)

Fool Around (1979, Stiff)
Protect the Innocent (1980, Stiff)
. . . And Then He Kissed Me (1981,
ABC)
Blame It On Love (1982, ABC)

*Blasters

*The Blasters (1981, Slash)

*Bus Boys

*Minimum Wage Rock & Roll (1980,
Arista)
*American Worker (1982, Arista)

*Go-Go's

*Our Lips Are Sealed (1981, I.R.S.)
*Vacation (1982, I.R.S.)
*We Got the Beat (1982, I.R.S.)
*Head over Heals (1984, I.R.S.)
*Turn to You (1984, I.R.S.)

*Beauty and the Beat (1981, I.R.S.)
*Vacation (1982, I.R.S.)
*Talk Show (1984, I.R.S.)

Belinda Carlisle (1958-) solo

Belinda (1986, I.R.S.)
Heaven on Earth (1987, MCA)

*Replacements

**Sorry Ma, Forgot to Take Out the
Trash* (1981, Twin Tone)
*Stink (1982, Sire)
*Let It Be (1985, Twin Tone)
*Tim (1985, Sire)
*Pleased to Meet Me (1987, Sire)

Lydia Lunch (1959-)

Queen of Siam (1980, ZE)
Eight-Eyed Spy (1981, Fetish)
Pre-Teenage Jesus (1981, ZE)

13.13 (1981, Ruby)

Romeo Void

A Girl in Trouble (Is a Temporary
Thing) (1984, Columbia)

It's a Condition (1981, 415)
Benefactor (1982, Columbia)
Never Say Never (1982, 415)
Instincts (1984, Columbia)

*Madonna

Holiday (1983, Sire)
*Borderline (1984, Sire)
*Like a Virgin (1984, Sire)
*Lucky Star (1984, Sire)
*Material Girl (1984, Sire)

*Madonna (1983, Sire)
*Like a Virgin (1984, Sire)

*Cindy Lauper

*All through the Night (1984,
Portrait)
*Girls Just Want to Have Fun (1984,
Portrait)
*She Bop (1984, Portrait)
*Time after Time (1984, Portrait)

*She's So Unusual (1983, Portrait)
*True Colors (1986, Portrait)

R.E.M.

Murmur (1983, IRS)
Reckoning (1984, IRS)
Fables of the Reconstruction (1985,
IRS)
*Dead Letter Office (1987, I.R.S.)

Bangles

All Over the Place (1984, Columbia)
Different Light (1986, Columbia)

Del-Fuegos

*The Longest Day (1985, Slash)

Jules Shear

*Demo--It Is (1987, Enigma)

The Eternal Return (1985, EMI
U.S.)

Beat Rodeo

Staying Out Late with Beat Rodeo
(1985, IRS)

Call

Reconciled (1986, Elektra)

Lone Justice

**Lone Justice* (1985, Geffen)
Shelter (1986, Geffen)

Hüsker Dü

Land Speed Record (1981, SST)
Flip Your Wig (1985, SST)
New Day Rising (1985, SST)
**Zen Arcade* (1985, SST)
Candy Apple Grey (1986, Warner
Bros.)
**Warehouse: Songs and Stories*
(1987, Warner Bros.)

Til' Tuesday

Voices Carry (1985, Epic)
**Welcome Home* (1986, Epic)

Cure

**Standing On the Beach--the Singles*
(1986, Elektra)

Hooters

And We Danced (1986, Columbia)
Day by Day (1986, Columbia)

Amore (1984, Columbia)
**Nervous Night* (1985, Columbia)

Tommy Keene

Strange Alliance (1982
Back Again, Try . . . (1983)
Places that Are Gone (1983)
Songs from the Film (1986, Geffen)

BoDeans

Fadeway (1986, Slash)
**Love & Hope & Sex & Dreams*
(1986, Slash)
She's a Runaway (1986, Slash)
Outside Looking In (1987, Slash)

Peter Case

Peter Case (1986, Geffen)

David & David

(David Ricketts; David Baerwald)

**Boomtown* (1986, A&M)

Smithereens

Beauty and Sadness (1983, Enigma)
**Especially for You* (1986, Enigma)

Rage to Live

**Rage to Live* (1986, Bar-None)

Meat Puppets

**Out My Way* (1986, SST)

Rainmakers

**The Rainmakers* (1986, Polygram)

Rock/Pop

*Hall & Oates

(Daryl Hall, 1949- ; John Oates, 1949-)

*Sara Smile (1976, RCA)
*She's Gone (1976, Atlantic)
*Rich Girl (1977, RCA)
*I Can't Go for That (No Can Do) (1981, RCA)
*Kiss on My List (1981, RCA)
*Private Eyes (1981, RCA)
*You Make My Dream (1981, RCA)
*Did It in a Minute (1982, RCA)
*Maneater (1982, RCA)
*Family Man (1983, RCA)
*One on One (1983, RCA)
*Say It Isn't So (1983, RCA)
*Adult Education (1984, RCA)
*Out of Touch (1984, RCA)
*Some Things Are Better Left Unsaid (1985, RCA)

Gulliver (1970, Elektra)
Past Times Behind (1971, Chelsea)
Whole Oates (1972, Atlantic)
Abandoned Luncheonette (1973, Atlantic)
Daryl Hall and John Oates (1975, Atlantic)
Bigger Than Both of Us (1976, RCA)
Beauty on a Back Street (1977, RCA)
Along the Red Ledge (1978, RCA)
Voices (1980, RCA)
Private Eyes (1981, RCA)
H2O (1982, RCA)
Big Bam Boom (1985, RCA)
Rock'n Soul, Part 1 (1986, RCA)

Daryl Hall solo

Three Hearts in the Happy Ending Machine (1986, RCA)

Huey Lewis and the News

*Do You Believe in Love? (1982, Chrysalis)
*Heart and Soul (1983, Chrysalis)
*The Heart of Rock & Roll (1984, Chrysalis)
*If This Is It (1984, Chrysalis)
*I Want a New Drug (1984, Chrysalis)
*Walking on a Thin Line (1984, Chrysalis)

Huey Lewis and the News (1980, Chrysalis)
Sports (1983, Chrysalis)
Fore! (1986, Chrysalis)

*Wham

*Wake Me Up before You Go-Go (1984, Columbia)
*Freedom (1985, Columbia)
*I'm Your Man (1986, Columbia)

Fantastic (1983, Columbia)
Make It Big (1985, Columbia)
Music from the Edge of Heaven (1986, Columbia)

Tears for Fears

*Head over Heels (1985, Mercury)
*Shout (1985, Mercury)

Songs from the Big Chair (1985, Mercury)
The Hurting (1986, Mercury)

*Sade

(Sade Adu)

*Smooth Operator (1985, CBS)
*The Sweetest Taboo (1986, Epic)

Diamond Life (1985, CBS)
Promise (1986, Epic)

*Paul Young (1956-)

Come Back and Stay (1984, Columbia)
No Parlez (1984, Columbia)
Everytime You Go Away (1985, Columbia)
Secret of Association (1985, Columbia)

*A-Ha

*Take On Me (1985, Warner Bros.)
*The Sun Always Shines on T.V. (1986, Warner Bros.)

Hunting High and Low (1985, Warner Bros.)
Scoundrel Days (1986, Warner Bros.)

*Power Station

*Communication (1985, Capitol)
*Some Like It Hot (1985, Capitol)

The Power Station (1985, Capitol)

Falco

Falco^3 (A&M)

Family

The Family (1986, A&M)

*Julian Lennon (1964-)

*Too Late for Goodbyes (1985, Atlantic)
*Valotte (1985, Atlantic)
*Well I Don't Know (1985, Atlantic)

Valotte (1985, Atlantic)
The Secret Value of Daydreaming (1986, Atlantic)

*Robert Palmer (1949-)

Pressure Drop (1975, Island)
Sneakin' Sally Through the Alley (1975, Island)

Some People Can Do What They Like (1976, Island)
Double Fun (1978, Island)
Secrets (1979, Island)
Clues (1980, Island)
Maybe It's Live (1982, Island)
Pride (1983, Island)
Riptide (1986, Island)

Teena Marie (1957-)

Wild and Peaceful (1979, Motown)
Irons in the Fire (1980, Motown)
Lady T (1980, Motown)
It Must Be Magic (1981, Motown)
Robbery (1983, Epic)
Starchild (1984, Epic)
Emerald City (1986, Epic)

Howard Jones

Human's Lib (1984, Eelktra)
Dream into Action (1985, Elektra)
One to One (1986, Elektra)

Bruce Hornsby

The Way It Is (1986, Capitol)

Crowded House

Crowded House (1986, Capitol)

Peter Cetera (1944-)

Solitude/Solitare (1986, Warner Bros.)

Eddy Money (1949-)

Can't Hold Back (1986, Columbia)

Timbuk 3

Greetings from . . . (1986, I.R.S.)

Mr. Mister

I Wear the Face (1984, RCA)
Welcome to the Real World (1986, RCA)

World Party

Private Revolution (1985, Chrysalis)

Robyn Hitchcock

Black Snake Diamond Role (1981)
City of Shame (1981)
Fegmania! (1985)
Gotta Let This Hen Out (1985)
Element Of Light (1987)

Billy Bragg

Lewis Stubbs Tears (Chrysalis)

Translator

Evening of the Harvest (1986,
     Columbia)

Bourgeois Tagg

Bourgeois Tagg (1986, Island)

Communards

Communards (1987)

Lou Ann Barton

Old Enough (1982, Spindeltop)
Forbidden Tones (1987, Spindletop)

Love and Rockets

Express (1987, Big Time)

Steve Tibbetts

Steve Tibbetts (1979, Frammis)
Yr (1981, Frammis)
Exploded View (1987, ECM)

System

Don't Disturb This Groove (1987,
     Atlantic)

Jason and the Scorchers

Still Standing (1987, Enigma)

Anthology

Woodstock (1970, Cotillion)

German Rock

Scorpions

*Rock You Like a Hurricane (1984, Mercury)

Fly to the Rainbow (1976, RCA)
In Trance (1976, RCA)
Taken by the Force (1978, RCA)
Love Drive (1979, Mercury)
Animal Magnetism (1980, Mercury)
Love at First Sting (1984, Mercury)
World Wide Live (1986, Mercury)

*Accept

Accept (1980, Passport)
Breaker (1981, Passport)

Breaker (1981, Brain)
Restless and Wild (1982, Heavy Metal Records)
Balls to the Wall (1984, Portrait)

*Can

*Spoon (1973, United Artists)

Monster Movie (1969, United Artists)
Tago Mago (1971, United Artists)
Ege Bamyasi (1973, United Artists)
Future Days (1974, United Artists)
Landed (1975, Virgin)
Soon over Babaluma (1975, United Artists)
Opener (1976, United Artists)
Unlimited Edition (1976, United Artists)
Flow Motion (1977, United Artists)
Saw Delight (1977, United Artists)
Cannibalism (1978, United Artists)
Out of Reach (1978, Peters)

Amon Dull 2

Yeti (1970, Liberty)
Dance of Lemmings (1971, United Artists)

Carnival in Babylon (1972, United Artists)
Phallus Dei (1972, Sonet)
Wolf City (1972, United Artists)
Viva La Trance (1974, United Artists)
Hijack (1975, IRL)

Kraftwerk

*Autobahn (1975, Vertigo)

Kraftwerk 1 (1971, Philips)
Kraftwerk 2 (1972, Philips)
Kraftwerk (1973, Vertigo)
Ralf and Florian (1973, Vertigo)
Autobahn (1974, Mercury)
Exceller 9 (1975, Vertigo)
Radio Activity (1975, Capitol)
Trans-Europe Express (1977, Capitol)
Man Machine (1978, Capitol)
Computer World (1981, Warner Bros.)

*Tangerine Dream

Alpha Centauri (1970, Ohr)
Electronic Meditation (1970, Ohr)
Atem (1972, Ohr)
Zeit (1972, Ohr)
Phaedra (1974, Virgin)
Live (1975, Virgin)
Rubycon (1975, Virgin)
Atem Alpha Centauri (1976, Virgin)
Richochet (1976, Virgin)
Stratosfear (1976, Virgin)
Sorcerer (1977, MCA)
Cyclone (1978, Virgin)
Force Majeure (1978, Virgin)
Tamgram (1980, Virgin)
Exit (1981, Virgin)
Thief (1981, Virgin)

*Soft Cell

Tainted Love (1982)

Faust

Faust (1972, Recommended)
So Far (1972, Recommended)

Canadian Hard Rock

Bryan Adams (1959-)

*Summer of '69 (1985, A&M)

Cuts Like a Knife (1983, A&M)
Reckless (1985, A&M)
Into the Fire (1987, A&M)

*Guess Who

*Shakin' All Over (1965, Scepter)
*Laughing/Undun (1969, RCA)
*These Eyes (1969, RCA)
*American Woman/No Sugar
    Tonight (1970, RCA)
*Hand Me Down World (1970, RCA)
*No Time (1970, RCA)
*Share the Land (1970, RCA)
*Albert Flasher (1971, RCA)
*Rain Dance (1971, RCA)
*Clap for the Wolfman (1974, RCA)
*Dancin' Fool (1974, RCA)
*Star Baby (1974, RCA)

Guess Who (1968, MGM)
Shakin' All Over (1968, Scepter)
Canned Heat (1969, RCA)
Wheatfield Soul (1969, RCA)
American Woman (1970, RCA)
Share the Land (1970, RCA)
Best of the Guess Who (1971, RCA)
So Long, Bannatyne (1971, RCA)
Live at the Paramount (1972, RCA)
Best of..., Vol. 2 (1973, RCA)
Artificial Paradise (1974, RCA)
Road Food (1974, RCA)
Born in Canada (1975, RCA)
Power in the Music (1975, RCA)
Greatest of... (1977, RCA)
All This for a Song (1979, HTK)

*Bachman-Turner Overdrive

*Let It Ride (1974, Mercury)

*Takin' Care of Business (1974,
  Mercury)
*You Ain't Seen Nothing Yet (1974,
  Mercury)
*Hey You (1975, Mercury)
*Roll On Down the Highway (1975,
  Mercury)
*Take It Like a Man (1976,
  Mercury)

Bachman-Turner Overdrive (1973,
  Mercury)
Bachman-Turner Overdrive 2 (1973,
  Mercury)
*Not Fragile (1974, Mercury)
Four Wheel Drive (1975, Mercury)
Head On (1975, Mercury)
**Best of . . .* (1976, Mercury)
Freeways (1977, Mercury)
Rock'n'Roll Nights (1978, Mercury)
Street Action (1978, Mercury)

*Hemispheres (1978, Mercury)
*Permanent Waves (1980, Mercury)
**Exit . . . Stage Left* (1981, Mercury)
*Moving Pictures (1981, Mercury)
*Signals (1982, Mercury)
**Grace under Pressure* (1984,
  Mercury)
*Power Windows (1986, Mercury)

*Pat Travers (1954-)

Pat Travers (1976, Poly.)
Makin' Magic (1977, Poly.)
Putting It Straight (1977, Poly.)
Heat in the Streets (1978, Poly.)
Go for What You Know (1979,
  Poly.)
Crash and Burn (1980, Poly.)
Radio Active (1981, Poly.)

*Rush

Rush (1974, Mercury)
Caress of Steel (1975, Mercury)
Fly by Night (1975, Mercury)
All the World's Stage (1976,
  Mercury)
*2112 (1976, Mercury)
*Jacob's Ladder (1980, Mercury)
*Spirit of the Radio (1980, Mercury)
*New World Man (1982, Mercury)
*The Big Money (1986, Mercury)

**2112* (1976, Mercury)
A Farewell to the Kings (1977,
  Mercury)
Archives (1978, Mercury)

Australian Rock

*Johnny O'Keefe

Wild One (1985, EMI)

*Easybeats

*Friday on My Mind (1966, EMI)
*Sorry (1966, EMI)
*Wedding Ring (1966, EMI)

*The Absolute Anthology, 1965-69 (1980, EMI)

*Daddy Cool

*Eagle Rock (1971, Warner Bros.)

*Daddy Who? Daddy Cool! (1971, Warner Bros.)
Teenage Heaven (1972, Warner Bros.)

Skyhooks

*Living in the Seventies (1975, Mushroom)
*Love on the Radio (1975, Mushroom)
*Love's Not Good Enough (1976, Mushroom)

*Living in the Seventies (1974, Mushroom)
*Ego Is Not a Dirty Word (1975, Mushroom)
Straight in a Gay Gay World (1976, Mushroom)
Guilty until Proven Insane (1977, Mushroom)
Live! Be in It (1978, Mushroom)
Best of ... (1979, Mushroom)
Hot for the Orient (1980, Mushroom)

*AC/DC

*You Shook Me All Night Long (1980, Atlantic)

*Back in Black (1981, Atlantic)

High Voltage (1976, Atco)
Let There Be Rock (1977, Atco)
*If You Want Blood You've Got It (1978, Atlantic)
Powerage (1978, Atlantic)
Highway to Hell (1979, Atlantic)
Back in Black (1980, Atlantic)
Dirty Deeds Done Dirt Cheap (1981, Atlantic)
*For Those About to Rock, We Salute You (1981, Atlantic)

*Little River Band

*It's a Long Way There (1976, Harvest)
*Help Is on the Way (1977, Harvest)
*Happy Anniversary (1978, Harvest)
*Reminiscing (1978, Harvest)
*Cool Change (1979, Capitol)
*Lady (1979, Harvest)
*Lonesome Loser (1979, Capitol)
*The Night Owls (1981, Capitol)
*Take It Easy on Me (1981, Capitol)
*Man on Your Mind (1982, Capitol)
*The Other Guy (1982, Capitol)
*We Two (1983, Capitol)
*You're Driving Me Out of My Mind (1983, Capitol)

*Little River Band (1975, Capitol)
After Hours (1976, Capitol)
Diamantina Cocktail (1977, Capitol)
Beginnings (1978, Capitol)
Sleeper Catcher (1978, Capitol)
First Under the Wire (1979, Capitol)
Backstage Pass (1980, Capitol)
Time Exposure (1981, Capitol)

*Split Enz

*I See Red (1979, Mushroom)
*I Got You (1980, Mushroom)

Mental Notes (1975, Mushroom)
Second Thoughts (1976, Mushroom)
Dizrhythmia (1977, Mushroom)

Frenzy (1979, Mushroom)
Beginning of the Enz (1980,
Mushroom)
True Colors (1980, A&M)
Waiata (1981, A&M)
Time and Tide (1982, A&M)

*Jo Jo Zep and the Falcons

*Hit and Run (1979, Mushroom)
*So Young (1979, Mushroom)
*Sweet Honey Sweet (1981,
Columbia)
*Tighten Up (1981, Columbia)

Don't Waste It (1976, Oz)
Whip It Out (1977, Oz)
So Young (1978, Oz)
Jo Jo Zep and the Falcons (1979,
Rockburg)
Screaming Targets (1979,
Mushroom)
Hats Off Step Lively (1980,
Mushroom)
Dexterity (1981, Mushroom)
Step Lively (1981, Columbia)

*Sports

*Mailed It to Your Sister (1978,
Mushroom)
*Reckless (1978, Mushroom)
*Who Listens to the Radio (1978,
Mushroom)
*Blue Hearts (1980, Mushroom)
*Strangers on a Train (1980,
Mushroom)
*Face the Tiger (1981, Mushroom)
*Softly Softly (1981, Mushroom)

Don't Throw Stones (1978,
Mushroom)
Reckless (1978, Mushroom)
Suddenly (1980, Mushroom)
Sondra (1981, Mushroom)

*Cold Chisel

*Choirgirl (1980, Elektra)
*My Baby (1980, Elektra)

*The Sanh (1980, Elektra)
*Star Hotel (1980, Elektra)

Cold Chisel (1978, WEA)
Breakfast at Sweethearts (1979,
WEA)
East (1980, Elektra)
Swingshift (1981, WEA)

*Midnight Oil

Midnight Oil (1978, Powderworks)
Head Injuries (1979, Powderworks)
Place without a Postcard (1981,
Powderworks)

*Mental as Anything

*Another Man's Sitting in My
Kitchen (Regular)
*The Nips Are Getting Bigger (1979,
Regular)
*If You Leave Me Can I Come Too
(1981, Regular)

Get Wet (1979, Regular)
Espresso Bongo (1980, Regular)
Cats and Dogs (1981, Regular)

*Rose Tattoo

Assault and Battery (1980, Mirage)
*Rock'n'Roll Outlaw (1980, Mirage)

*Men at Work

*Down Under (1982, Columbia)
*Who Can It Be Now (1982,
Columbia)
*Dr. Heckyll and Mr. Jive (1983,
Columbia)
*It's a Mistake (1983, Columbia)
*Overkill (1983, Columbia)

Business as Usual (1982, Columbia)
Cargo (1983, Columbia)
Two Hearts (1985, Columbia)

Celibate Rifles

Kiss, Kiss, Bang, Bang (1987, What
    Goes On)
Mina Mina Mina (1987, What Goes
    On)
The Turgid Miasma of Existence
    (1987, Rough Trade)

Saints

*I'm Stranded (1976, Sire)
*Everything's Fine (1978, Sire)
*Swing for the Crime (1978, Sire)

A Little Madness to Be Free (TVT)
Live in a Mud Hut (TVT)
 I'm Stranded (1977, Sire)
Eternally Yours (1978, Sire)
Prehistoric Sounds (1978, Harvest)
 Paralytic Tonight, Dublin Tomorrow
    (1980)
All Fools Day (1987, TVT)

Chris Bailey solo

What I Did On My Holidays (TVT)

*Divinyls

What a Life! (1986, Chrysalis)

*Inxs

Listen Like Thieves (1985, Atlantic)

*Hoodoo Gurus

Mars Needs Guitars! (1986, Big
    Time)

Angel City

Dark Room (1980, Epic)
Face To Face (1980, Epic)
Night Attack (1982, Epic)
Two-Minute Warning (1985, MCA)

Church

The Blurred Crusade (1982, Warner
    Bros.)
Heyday (1986, Warner Bros.)

Japanese Rock

*Yellow Magic Orchestra

Yellow Magic Orchestra (1979, A&M)
BGM (1981, A&M)

*Stomu Yamashita

Red Buddah (1974, Vanguard)
Go (1976, Island)
Go Too (1977, Arista)
Go--Live from Paris (1978, Island)

Heavy Metal

*Judas Priest

*Living after Midnight (1980, Columbia)

Rocka Rolla (1974, Gull)
Sad Wings of Destiny (1976, Gull)
Sin After Sin (1976, Columbia)
Hell Bent for Leather (1979, Columbia)
Unleashed in the East (1979, Columbia)
British Steel (1980, Columbia)
Point of Entry (1981, Columbia)
Creaming for Vengeance (1982, Columbia)
Defenders of the Faith (1984, Columbia)
Stained Glass (1987, Columbia)

Ratt

Out of the Cellar (1984, Atlantic)
Invasion of Your Privacy (1985, Atlantic)
Dancing under Cover (1986, Atlantic)

Quiet Riot

*Cum On Feel the Noize (1983, Pasha)

Condition Critical (1984, Pasha)
Mental Health (1984, Pasha)

*Mötley Crüe

*If Looks Could Kill (1983, Elektra)
*Smokin' in the Boys Room (1985, Elektra)

Shout at the Devil (1983, Elektra)
Too Fast for Love (1983, Elektra)
Theatre of Pain (1985, Elektra)

*Twisted Sister

Under the Blade (1982, Atlantic)
You Can't Stop Rock'n'Roll (1983, Atlantic)
Stay Hungry (1984, Atlantic)
Come Out and Play (1985, Atlantic)

*Fixx

Reach the Beach (1983, MCA)
Phantoms (1984, MCA)

*Iron Maiden

Iron Maiden (1980, EMI)
Killer (1981, EMI)
The Number of the Beast (1982, EMI)
Piece of Mind (1983, EMI)
Live after Death (1985, Capitol)
Somewhere in Time (1986, Capitol)

*Def Leppard

*Foolin' (1983, Mercury)
*Photograph (1983, Mercury)
*Rock of Ages (1983, Mercury)

Getcha Rocks Off (1978)
On Through the Night (1980, Mercury)
High'n'Dry (1981, Polydor)
Pyromania (1984, Mercury)
Hysteria (1987, Polydor)

*Firm

*Radioactive (1985, Atlantic)
*All the Kings Horses (1986, Atlantic)

The Firm (1985, Atlantic)
Mean Business (1986, Atlantic)

Alcatrazz

No Parole from Rock'n'Roll (1984, Rockshire)

Michael Schenker

Michael Schenker Group (1980, Chrysalis)
One Night at Budokan (1981, Chrysalis)
Assault Attack (1982, Chrysalis)
Built to Destroy (1983, Chrysalis)

Krokus

Krokus (1977, Mercury)
Painkiller (1978, Mercury)
Pay for It in Metal (1979, Mercury)
Metal Rendez-vous (1980, Ariola)
Hardware (1981, Ariola)
One Vice at a Time (1982, Ariola)
Headhunters (1983, Arista)

Ronnie James Dio

The Last in Time (1984, Warner Bros.)

Dio

Dio (1983, Phonogram)
Holy Diver (1983, Vertigo)

Rainbow

Ritchie Blackmore's Rainbow (1975, Polydor)
Rainbow Rising (1976, Polydor)
Long Live Rock'n'Roll (1978, Polydor)
Down to Earth (1979, Polydor)
Straight between the Eyes (1982, Polydor)

Dokken

Dokken (1982, Carrere)

Girlschool

Demolition (1980, Bronze)
Hit and Run (1981, Bronze)
Screaming Blue Murder (1982, Bronze)

Great White

Out of the Night (1982, Aegan)
Great White (1984, Eni)

Y & T

Yesterday and Today (1976, London)
Struck Down (1978, London)
Earthshaker (1981, A&M)
Black Tiger (1982, A&M)
Meanstreak (1983, A&M)
In Rock We Trust (1984, A&M)
Contagious (1987, Geffen)

Talas

Sink Your Teeth into That (1982, Relativity Records)
Live Speed On Ice (1984, Combat)

Rods

The Rods (1981, Arista)
Wild Dogs (1982, Arista)
In the Raw (1983, Shrapnel)

Helstar

Burning Star (1984, Combat)

Oz

The Oz (1982, Krak)

Tokyo Blade

Midnight Rendezvous (1984, Combat)

TNT

TNT (1984, Polygram)

Fastway

Fastway (1983, Columbia)

Helix

Breaking Loose (1979, Hands)

White Heather and Black Lace (1981, M&S)
No Rest for the Wicked (1983, Capitol)

Saxon

Saxon (1979, Saxon Carrere)
Strong Arms of the Law (1980, Carrere)
Wheels of Steel (1980, Saxon Carrere)
Denim and Leather (1981, Carrere)
The Eagle Has Landed (1982, Carrere)
Power and Glory (1983, Carrere)

Metallica

Kill 'em All (1984, Megaforce)
*Master of Puppets (1986, Elektra)

Manowar

Battle Hymn (1982, Liberty)
Into Glory Rides (1983, Music for Nations)

Mercyful Fate

Soul without Corpse (1982, Rave On)

Raven

Rock Until You Drop (1981, Neat)
Wiped Out (1982, Neat)
All For One (1983, Neat)
Athletic Rock (1983, Neat)

Exciter

Heavy Metal Maniac (1983, Shrapnell)

Vandenberg

Vandenberg (1982, Atco)

Kix

Atomic Bomb (1981, Atlantic)
Cool Kids (1983, Atlantic)

Bon Jovi

7800 Fahrenheit (1984, Mercury)
*Slippery When Wet (1986, Mercury)

W.A.S.P.

Winged Assassins (1984, Capitol)

Lita Ford

Dancin' on the Edge (1984, Mercury)

Billy Squire (1950-)

Stroke (1981, Capitol)
Everybody Wants You (1982, Capitol)

The Tale of the Tape (1980, Capitol)
Don't Say No (1981, Capitol)
*Emotions in Motion (1982, Capitol)
*Enough Is Enough (1986, Capitol)

Whitesnake

*Whitesnake (1987, Geffen)

Beastie Boys

Licensed to Ill (1987, Def Jam)

Cinderella

Night Songs (1986, Mercury)

Motorhead

Iron Fist (1982, Mercury)

Spinal Tap

Smell the Glove (1984, Polygram)

Queensryche

Operation Mindcrime (1987, EMI-Manhattan)

Zebra

Zebra (1983, Atlantic)
No Tellin' Lies (1984, Atlantic)

Later Soul

*Dramatics

*In the Rain (1971, Stax)
*Whatcha See Is Whatcha Get
  (1972, Stax)

*Whatcha See Is Whatcha Get (1972,
  Stax; 1978, Stax)
*Shake It Well (1977, ABC)

Ohio Players

*Funky Worm (1973, Westbound)
*Fire (1974, Mercury)
*Skin Tight (1974, Mercury)
*Love Rollercoaster (1975, Mercury)

First Impressions (1968, Trip)
Observations in Time (1969,
  Capitol)
*Pain (1972, Westbound)
Ecstasy (1973, Westbound)
*Pleasure (1973, Westbound)
*Fire (1974, Mercury)
*Ohio Players Gold (1976, Mercury)
Young and Ready (1981, Accord)

Shirley Brown

Woman to Woman (1974, Truth)

*Woman to Woman (1974, Stax)
Shirley Brown (1977, Arista)
For the Real Feeling (1979, Stax)

*Earth, Wind, and Fire

*Mighty Mighty (1974, Columbia)
*Shining Star (1975, Columbia)
*Sing a Song (1975, Columbia)
*Getaway (1976, Columbia)
*Got to Get You into My Life (1978,
  Columbia)
*September (1978, ARC)
*After the Love Has Gone (1979,
  ARC)
*Let's Groove (1981, ARC)

Earth, Wind, and Fire (1971,
  Warner Bros.)
*Last Days and Time (1972, Warner
  Bros.)
*The Need of Love (1972, Warner
  Bros.)
*Gratitude (1975, Columbia)
*Spirit (1976, Columbia)
*The Best of . . ., Vol. 1 (1978,
  Columbia)
*That's the Way of the World (1978,
  Columbia)
Powerlight (1983, Columbia)

*Commodores

*I Feel Sanctified (1974, Motown)
*Machine Gun (1974, Motown)
*Slippery When Wet (1975,
  Motown)
*Easy (1977, Motown)
*Fancy Dancer (1977, Motown)
*Just to Be Close to You (1977,
  Motown)
*Sweet Love (1977, Motown)
*Three Times a Lady (1978,
  Motown)
*Sail On (1979, Motown)
*Still (1979, Motown)

*Machine Gun (1974, Motown)
Greatest Hits (1978, Motown)

Lionel Richie (1950-) solo

*Lady (1980, Motown)
*Truly (1982, Motown)

Lionel Richie (1982, Motown)
Can't Slow Down (1983, Motown)
*Dancing on the Ceiling (1986,
  Motown)

*Bobby Womack (1944-)

*That's the Way I Feel About Cha
  (1972, United Artists)
*Woman's Gotta Have It (1972,
  United Artists)
*Harry Hippie (1973, United Artists)

*Lookin' for a Love (1974, United Artists)

Fly Me to the Moon (1968, Minit)
*Facts of Life (1973, United Artists)
*Greatest Hits (1974, United Artists)
*Safety Zone (1976, United Artists)
The Poet (1981, Beverly Glen)
Poet 2 (1984, Beverly Glen)

Bill Withers (1938-)

Ain't No Sunshine (1971, Sussex)
Lean on Me (1972, Sussex)
Use Me (1972, Sussex)

Just as I Am (1971, Sussex)
Still Bill (1972, Sussex)
*Best of . . . (1975, Sussex)

*Emotions

*So I Can Love You (1969, Volt)
Show Me How (1970, Volt)
*Best of My Love (1977, Columbia)

So I Can Love You (1970, Stax)
Untouched (1970, Stax)
*Flowers (1976, Stax)
*Best of . . . (1979, Stax)
New Affair (1981, ARC)

Pointer Sisters

Don't Try to Take the Fifth (1972, Atlantic)
*Yes We Can Can (1973, Blue Thumb)
*Fire (1978, Planet)
*He's So Shy (1980, Planet)
*Slow Hand (1981, Planet)
*I'm So Excited (1982, Planet; 1984, Planet)
*Automatic (1984, Planet)
*Jump (For My Love) (1984, Planet)

*The Pointer Sisters (1973, Blue Thumb)
Energy (1978, Planet)
Special Things (1980, Planet)
Black & White (1981, Planet)

Break Out (1983, Planet)

Raydio

*Jack and Jill (1978, Arista)
You Can't Change That (1979, Arista)

Ray Parker, Jr. (1954-)

*A Woman Needs Love (Just Like You Do) (1981, Arista)
*The Other Woman (1982, Arista)
*Ghostbusters (1984, Arista)

Raydio (1978, Arista)
Rock On (1979, Arista)
*Ray Parker, Jr.: Greatest Hits (1982, Arista)

Kool and the Gang

*Funky Man (1970, De-Lite)
*Funky Stuff (1973, De-Lite)
*Hollywood Swinging (1974, De-Lite)
*Jungle Boogie (1974, De-Lite)
Ladies Night (1979, De-Lite)
Celebration (1980, De-Lite)
Too Hot (1980, De-Lite)
Get Down on It (1982, De-Lite)
Joanna (1983, De-Lite)

*Live at the Sex Machine (1971, De-Lite)
*Good Times (1972, De-Lite)
*Wild and Peaceful (1973, De-Lite)
*Kool and the Gang Spin Their Top Hits (1978, De-Lite)
*Celebration (1980, De-Lite)
Emergency (1984, De-Lite)

*Whispers

Planets of Life (1969, Canyon)
Seems Like I Gotta Go Wrong (1970, Canyon)
Time Will Come (1970, Canyon)
Bingo (1974, Soul Train)
A Mother for My Child (1974, Soul Train)

*(Olivia) Lost and Turned Out
   (1978, Solar)
*And the Beat Goes On (1980,
   Solar)
*Lady (1980, Solar)
*It's a Love Thing (1981, Solar)

Greatest Hits (Janus)
One For the Money (1976, Solar)
The Whispers (1980, Solar)
Imagination (1981, Solar)
Best of . . . (1982, Solar)
So Good (1984, Solar)

*Shalamar

Uptown Festival (1977, Soul Train)
Take That to the Bank (1978, Solar)
Full of Fire (1980, Solar)
Right in the Socket (1980, Solar)
*The Second Time Around (1980,
   Solar)
*Make That Move (1981, Solar)
*Dead Giveaway (1983, Solar)

Uptown Festival (1977, Soul Train)
Big Fun (1979, Solar)
Three for Love (1981, Solar)
Friends (1982, Solar)
The Look (1983, Solar)
Heart Break (1984, Solar)

*Sly Johnson

*Back for a Taste (1973, Hi)
*Take to the River (1976, Hi)

Back for a Last of Your Love (1973,
   Hi)
Total Explosion (1976, Hi)

Odyssey

*Native New Yorker (1977, RCA)
*Weekend Lover (1978, RCA)

Odyssey (1977, RCA)

Rose Royce

*Car Wash (1976, MCA)
Do Your Dance (1977, Whitfield)

*I Wanna Get Next to You (1977,
   MCA)
Love Don't Live Here Anymore
   (1979, Whitfield)

Car Wash (1976, MCA)
Rose Royce 2/In Full Bloom (1977,
   Whitfield)
Rose Royce Strikes Again (1978,
   Whitfield)

*Rufus

Smoking Room (1974, ABC)
*Tell Me Something Good (1974,
   ABC)
*You Got the Love (1974, ABC)
Once You Get Started (1975, ABC)
*Sweet Thing (1976, ABC)
Ain't Nothing But Maybe (1977,
   ABC)
Better Days (1977, ABC)
Stop on By (1977, ABC)

Rufus (1973, ABC)
Rags to Rufus (1974, ABC)
Rufusized (1974, ABC)
Rufus . . . Featuring Chaka Khan
   (1975, ABC)
Ask Rufus (1977, ABC)
Street Player (1978, ABC)

*Chaka Khan (1953-) solo

*I'm Every Woman (1978, Warner
   Bros.)
*I Feel for You (1984, Warner Bros.)

Chaka (1978, Warner Bros.)
Naughty (1980, Warner Bros.)
What Cha Gonna Do for Me? (1981,
   Warner Bros.)
Echoes of an Era (1982, Elektra)
Chaka Khan (1982, Warner Bros.)
I Feel for You (1984, Warner Bros.)

King Sunny Ade

Aura (1984)

*Musical Youth

Youth of Today (1982)

*Luther Vandross (1951-)

*Never Too Much (1981, Epic)
*Bad Boy/Having a Party (1982,
  Epic)

*Never Too Much (1981, Epic)
*Forever, for Always, for Love (1982,
  Epic)
Busy Body (1983, Epic)
*Give Me the Reason (1987, Epic)

Freddie Jackson

*Just Like the First Time (1987,
  Capitol)

Gregory Abbott

*Shake You Down (1987, Columbia)

***Africa Bombattaa and Soul Sonic
  Force**

Planet Rock (1983)

Jeffrey Osborne (1948-)

Stay with Me Tonight (1984, A&M)

Anita Baker

The Songstress (1983, Beverly Glen)
*Rapture (1986, Elektra)

Cameo

She's Strange (Atlanta Artist)
Single Life (Atlanta Artist)
Cardiac Arrest (1977, Atlanta
  Artist)
Alligator Woman (1981, Atlanta
  Artist)
Style (1983, Atlanta Artist)
*Word Up (1987, Polygram)

Janet Jackson (1966-)

*Control (1986, A&M)

Fiona

Beyond the Pale (1986, Atlantic)

Jody Watley (1959-)

*Jody Watley (1987, MCA)

*Klymaxx

Meeting in the Ladies' Room (1985,
  Constellation)
*Never Underestimate the Power of a
  Woman* (1981, Solar)

*Whitney Houston (1963-)

Whitney
Whitney Houston (1985, Arista)

*Billy Ocean

Tear Down These Walls (1987, Jive)

Punk/Funk

*Rick James (1952-)

Mary Jane (1978, Gordy)
*You and I (1978, Gordy)
Bustin' Out (1979, Gordy)
High on Your Love Suite (1979, Gordy)
Love Gun (1979, Gordy)
Big Time (1980, Gordy)
*Give It to Me Baby (1981, Gordy)
*Super Freak, Part One (1981, Gordy)
*Cold Blooded (1983, Gordy)
*17 (1984, Gordy)

*Come Get It (1978, Gordy)
*Garden of Love (1980, Gordy)
*Street Songs (1981, Gordy)
*Throwin' Down (1982, Gordy)
*Cold Blooded (1983, Gordy)

*Prince (1960-)

*I Wanna Be Your Lover (1979, Warner Bros.)
Soft and Wet (1979, Warner Bros.)
Why You Wanna Treat Me So Bad? (1979, Warner Bros.)
*Uptown (1980, Warner Bros.)
When You Were Mine (1980, Warner Bros.)
*Controversy (1981, Warner Bros.)
*Let's Work (1981, Warner Bros.)
*Delirious (1983, Warner Bros.)
*Little Red Corvette (1983, Warner Bros.)
*1999 (1983, Warner Bros.)
*Let's Go Crazy (1984, Warner Bros.)
*Purple Rain (1984, Warner Bros.)
*When Doves Cry (1984, Warner Bros.)
*Raspberry Beret (1985, Warner Bros.)

For You (1978, Warner Bros.)
Prince (1979, Warner Bros.)

*Dirty Mind (1980, Warner Bros.)
*Controversy (1981, Warner Bros.)
*1999 (1982, Warner Bros.)
*Purple Rain (1984, Warner Bros.)
*Around the World In a Day (1985, Warner Bros.)
*Parade (1986, Paisley Park)
*Sign o' the Times (1987, Paisley Park)

Time

*The Stick (1981, Warner Bros.)

*The Time (1981, Warner Bros.)
*What Time Is It? (1982, Warner Bros.)
*Ice Cream Castle (1984, Warner Bros.)

Was (Not Was)

Was/Not Was (1981, Island)
Born to Laugh at Tornadoes (1983, Geffen)

Jesse Johnson

Shockadelica (1986, A&M)

Funk

*Sly and the Family Stone

(Sly Stone, 1944-)

I Ain't Got Nobody/I Can't Turn
You Loose (1967, Loadstone)
*Dance to the Music (1968, Epic)
*Life (1968, Epic)
*Everyday People/Sing a Simple
Song (1969, Epic)
*Hot Fun in the Summertime (1969,
Epic)
*I Want to Take You Higher (1969,
Epic)
*Stand (1969, Epic)
*Everybody Is a Star (1970, Epic)
*Thank You (Falettime Be Mice Elf
Agin) (1970, Epic)
*Family Affair (1971, Epic)
If You Want Me To Stay (1973,
Epic)

A Whole New Thing (1967, Epic)
Dance to the Music (1968, Epic;
1975, High Energy)
Life (1968, Epic; 1975, High
Energy)
Stand! (1969, Epic)
Greatest Hits (1970, Epic)
There's a Riot Goin' On (1971,
Epic)
Fresh (1973, Epic)
Anthology (1981, Epic)

*War

Spill the Wine (1970, United
Artists)
*All Day Music (1971, United
Artists)
*Slippin' into Darkness (1972,
United Artists)
*The World Is a Ghetto (1972,
United Artists)
*The Cisco Kid (1973, United
Artists)

*Gypsy Man (1973, United Artists)
*Low Rider (1975, United Artists)
*Why Can't We Be Friends? (1975,
United Artists)
*Summer (1976, United Artists)
Outlaw (1982, RCA)
You Got the Power (1982, RCA)

Eric Burdon Declares "War" (1970,
MGM)
All Day Music (1971, United
Artists)
The World Is a Ghetto (1972,
United Artists)
Deliver the Word (1973, United
Artists)
Why Can't We Be Friends? (1975,
United Artists)
Greatest Hits (1976, United Artists)
Outlaw (1982, RCA)

*Graham Central Station

Can You Handle It? (1974, Warner
Bros.)
Feel the Need (1974, Warner Bros.)
*Your Love (1975, Warner Bros.)

Graham Central Station (1974,
Warner Bros.)
Release Yourself (1974, Warner
Bros.)
Ain't No Bout-A-Doubt It (1975,
Warner Bros.)

Larry Graham (1944-) solo

One in a Million You (1980,
Warner Bros.)

One in a Million You (1980, Warner
Bros.)

*Parliament

*All Your Goodies Are Gone (1967,
Revilot)
*(I Just Wanna) Testify (1967,
Revilot)
*Up for the Down Stroke (1974,
Casablanca)

*Tear the Roof Off the Sucker (Give Up the Funk) (1976, Casablanca)
*Flash Light (1978, Casablanca)
Aqua Boogie (1979, Casablanca)

Osmium (1970, Invictus)
Up for the Down Stroke (1974, Casablanca)
Chocolate City (1975, Casablanca)
The Clones of Dr. Funkenstein (1976, Casablanca)
Funkentelechy vs. the Placebo Syndrome (1977, Casablanca)
Motor Booty Affair (1978, Casablanca)

*Funkadelic

*One Nation under a Groove (1978, Warner Bros.)
*(Not Just) Knee Deep, Part 1 (1979, Warner Bros.)

Free Your Mind . . . and Your Ass Will Follow (1970, Westbound)
Funkadelic (1970, Westbound)
Maggot Brain (1971, Westbound)
America Eats Its Young (1972, Westbound)
Cosmic Slop (1973, Westbound)
Standing on the Verge of Getting It On (1974, Westbound)
Let's Take It to the Stage (1975, Westbound)
Best of the Funkadelic Early Years (1977, Westbound)
One Nation under a Groove (1978, Warner Bros.)
Uncle Jam Wants You (1979, Warner Bros.)
Electric Spanking of War Babies (1981, Warner Bros.)

George Clinton (1940-) solo

Hydraulic Pump/One of Those Summers (1981, Hump)
Atomic Dog (1983, Capitol)

Computer Games (1983, Capitol)

R&B Skeletons in the Closet (1986, Capitol)

*Sweat Band

Sweat Band (1980, Uncle Jam)

*Bootsy's Rubber Band

*The Pinocchio Theory (1977, Warner Bros.)
*Rubber Duckie (1977, Warner Bros.)

Stretchin' Out in Bootsy's Rubber Band (1976, Warner Bros.)
Ahh . . . The Name Is Bootsy, Baby (1977, Warner Bros.)
Bootsy: Player of the Year (1978, Warner Bros.)
This Boot Is Made for Funk In (1979, Warner Bros.)
Ultra Wave (1980, Warner Bros.)

Brothers Johnson

(George Johnson, 1953- ; Lewis Johnson, 1955-)

*I'll Be Good to You (1976, A&M)
*Strawberry Letter 23 (1977, A&M)
*Stomp! (1980, A&M)

Look Out for #1 (1976, A&M)
Right On Time (1977, A&M)
Blam! (1978, A&M)
Light Up the Night (1980, A&M)

Rapping

*Millie Jackson (1943-)

Ask Me What You Want (1972, Spring)
A Child of God (1972, Spring)
My Man, a Sweet Man (1972, Spring)
It Hurts So Good (1973, Spring)
*If Loving You Is Wrong (I Don't Want to Be Right) (1974, Spring)

Millie Jackson (1972, Spring)
It Hurts So Good (1973, Spring)
Caught Up (1974, Spring)
Still Caught Up (1975, Spring)
Free and In Love (1976, Spring)
Feelin' Bitchy (1977, Spring)
Live and Outrageous (1982, Spring)

*Sugarhill Gang

*Rapper's Delight (1980, Sugarhill)
8th Wonder (1981, Sugarhill)
Lover in You (1981, Sugarhill)

Rapper's Delight (1979, Sugarhill)
8th Wonder (1982, Sugarhill)

Grandmaster Flash

(Joseph Saddler, 1957-)

Superrappin' (1979, Enjoy)
*Freedom (1980, Sugarhill)
*The Adventures of Grandmaster Flash on the Wheels of Steel (1981, Sugarhill)
*Birthday Party (1981, Sugarhill)
*The Message (1982, Sugarhill)

The Message (1982, Sugarhill)

*Kurtis Blow

Christmas Rappin' (1979, Sugarhill)
*The Breaks (1980, Mercury)
King Tim III (1980, Sugarhill)

Kurtis Blow (1980, Mercury)
Ego Trip (1984, Mercury)

*Run-D.M.C.

*Run-D.M.C. (1984, Profile)
King of Rock (1985, Profile)

Whodini

Back Is Black (1986, Jive)

Anthologies

The Great Rap Hits (1980, Sugarhill)

Reggae Music

REGGAE

Jimmy Cliff (1948-)

Daisy Got Me Crazy (1961, Trojan)
Wonderful World, Beautiful People (1970, Trojan)

Wonderful World, Beautiful People (1970, A&M)
The Harder They Come (1972, Mango)
Jimmy Cliff (1972, Trojan)

Desmond Dekker and the Aces

007 (Shanty Town) (1967, Pyramid)
The Israelites (1969, Pyramid)

Sweet Sixteen Hits (1978, Trojan)

Toots and the Maytalls

(Frederic "Toots" Hibbert, 1946-)

Do the Reggae (1968, Trojan)
Monkey Man (1970, Trojan)

Funky Kingston (1965, Island)
From the Roots (1973, Trojan)
Reggae Got Soul (1976, Island)
Best of the Toots and the Maytalls (1979, Trojan)

Pioneers

Long Shot Kick de Bucket (1969, Trojan)

Longshot Kick de Bucket (1970, Trojan)
Greatest Hits (1979, Trojan)

Bob Marley and the Wailers

(Bob Marley, 1945-81)

Judge Not (1961, Trojan)
Simmer Down (1964, Trojan)
Catch a Fire (1973, Island)
Get Up Stand Up (1973, Island)
I Shot the Sheriff (1973, Island)
Waiting in Vain (1977, Island)
Redemption Song (1980, Island)

Catch a Fire (1972, Island)
Burnin' (1973, Island)
African Herbsman (1974, Trojan)
Rasta Revolution (1974, Trojan)
Live (1975, Island)
Natty Dread (1975, Island)
Kaya (1978, Island)
Survival (1979, Island)
Uprising (1980, Island)

Peter Tosh (1944-88)

Legalize It (1975, Trojan)
Don't Look Back (1978, Rolling Stone)
Wanted (1981, EMI)

Legalize It (1976, Columbia)
Equal Rights (1977, Columbia)
Bush Doctor (1978, Rolling Stone)
Wanted Dread or Alive (1981, EMI)

Dennis Brown (1950-)

No Man Is an Island (1968, Golden Age)
Money in My Pocket (1972, Trojan)

Visions (1978, Gibbs)
Money in My Pocket (1981, Trojan)

Bunny Wailer

(Neville O'Reilly Livingston, 1947-)

Blackheart Man (1976, Island)
Bunny Wailer Sings the Wailers (1980, Mango)

Rock'n Groove (1981, King
  Solomonie)

Wailing Souls

Fire House Rock (1981,
  Greensleeves)
Wailing (1981, Jah Guidance)

Jacob Miller

Tenement Yard (1978, Top
  Ranking)
Dread, Dread (1979, United Artists)
Greatest Hits (1980, Top Ranking)

Gregory Isaacs

Meets Ronnie Davis (Joe Gibbs)
Mr. Isaacs (Shanty)
Cool Ruler (1978, Virgin Front
  Line)
Lonely Lover (1980, PRE)
Best of . . ., Vol. 2 (1981, Hit)
The Early Years (1981, Trojan)
More Gregory (1981, Mango)

I Roy

Presenting (1973, Trojan)
Crisus Time (1979, Caroline)
Whap'n Bap'n (1980, V.F.L.)

Joe Gibbs

African Dub Almighty (Joe Gibbs)
African Dub Chapter Two (Joe
  Gibbs)
African Dub Chapter Three (Joe
  Gibbs)
African Dub Chapter Four (Joe
  Gibbs)

U Roy

Version Galore (Treasure Isle)
U Roy (1974, Attack)
Dread in-a Babylon (1976, Virgin)
Jah Son of Africa (1979, State Line)

Gladiators

Trenchtown Mix-Up (1976, V.F.L.)
Proverbial Reggae (1977, V.F.L.)
Naturality (1978, V.F.L.)
Symbol of Reality (1982,
  Nighthawk)

Mighty Diamonds

Deeper Roots (1979, V.F.L.)
Reggae Street (1981, Shanty)
Vital Selection (1981, Virgin)

Ijahman

Haile I Hymn (1978, Mango)
Are We a Warrior? (1979, Mango)

Pablo Moses

A Song (1970, Mango)
I Man I Bring (1980, United Artists)
Pave the Way (1981, Mango)

Judy Mowatt

Black Woman (1979, Ashandan-
  Genesis)

Hugh Mundell

Africa Must Be Free, by 1983 (1979,
  Message)

Cedric Myton

Heart of the Congos (1980, Go Feet)
Face the Music (1981, Go Feet)

Culture

Two Sevens Clash (1977, Joe Gibbs)
Africa Stand Alone (1978, April)
Baldhead Bridge (1978, Joe Gibbs)
Cumbolo (1978, V.F.L.)
Harder Than the Best (1978, V.F.L.)
International Herb (1979, V.F.L.)
Vital Selection (1981, Virgin
  International)

Linval Thompson

Six Babyolon (1979, Clocktower)

Melodians

Sweet Sensation (1981, Mango)

Black Uhuru

Showcase Black Rose (1979, D Roy)
Red (1981, Mango)

Prince Far I

Message from the King (1979,
Virgin)

Anthologies

Creation Rockers, Vols. 1-6 (Trojan)
This is Reggae Music, Vols. 1-3
(Island)
The Harder They Come (1975,
Island)
Rockers (1979, Mango)
Monkey Business (1980, Trojan)
Rebel Music (1980, Trojan)
Taxi Presents Sounds of the Eighties
(1980, Taxi)
The Trojan Story (1980, Trojan)
The "King Kong" Compilation (1981,
Mango)
Sly and Robbie Present Taxi (1981,
Island)
Wiser Dread (1981, Nighthawk)
Calling Rastafari (1982, Nighthawk)

DUB

Augustus Pablo

Java (1972, Kaya)

King Tubby Meets Rockers Uptown
(1976, Clocktower)
Original Rockers (1979,
Greensleeves)
East of the River Nile (1981,
Message)

Burning Spear

(Winston Rodney, 1947)

Garvey's Ghost (1976, Island)

Marcus Garvey (1976, Island)
Harder Than the Rest (1979,
Mango)
Social Living (1980, Island)

Count Ossie and Mystic Revelation of Rastafari

Grounation (1974, Grounation)

Revolutionaries

Rockers Almighty Dub (Clocktower)

Anthology

Soul to Soul (1979, Tadd's)
21st-Century Dub (1987, Reachout
International)

SKA

Millie Small

My Boy Lollipop (1964, Smash)

Georgie Fame

(Clive Powell, 1943-)

Yeh, Yeh (1965, Imperial)
Get Away (1966, Imperial)
Bonnie and Clyde (1968, Epic)

Get Away (1966, Imperial)
Yeh, Yeh (1966, Imperial)
The Ballad of Bonnie and Clyde
(1968, Epic)

Prince Buster

Al Capone (1967, Blue Beat)

Fabulous Greatest Hits (1967,
Melodise)

Skatalites

Guns of Navarone (1967, Island)

Best of the Skatalites (Studio One)
Ska Authentic (Studio One)
African Roots (1978, United Artists)

Madness

One Step Beyond (1979, Stiff)
Baggy Trousers (1980, Stiff)
House of Fun (1981, Stiff)
Our House (1983, Geffen)

One Step Beyond (1979, Sire)
Absolutely (1980, Sire)

Selecter

Gangster/Selecter (1979, T-Tone)
Three Minute Hero (1980, Chrysalis)

Too Much Pressure (1980, Chrysalis)
Celebrate the Bullet (1981, Chrysalis)

English Beat

I Just Can't Stop It (1980, Sire)

Specials

Specials (1979, Two Tone)
More Specials (1980, Two Tone)

UB40

Red, Red Wine (1984, A&M)

Signing Off (1980, Gradmate)
Present Arms (1981, Deptford Fun City)
UB44 (1982, Deptford Fun City)
Labor of Love (1983, A&M)
The Singles Album (1983, Deptford Fun City)
Geffery Morgan (1984, A&M)

Anthologies

Club Ska '67 (1980, Mango)
Intensified! Originial Ska, 1962-66 (1979, Mango)
Intensified! Originial Ska, 1963-67 (1979, Mango)

ROCK STEADY

Alton Ellis

Rock Steady (1966, Treasure Isle)

Paragons

On the Beach (1967, Treasure Isle)
The Tide Is High (1967, Treasure Isle)
Wear You to the Ball (1967, Treasure Isle)

Return Of the Paragons (1981, Top Ranking)
Riding High (1981, Mango)

Heptones

Fatty Fatty (1966, Studio One)
Why Must I (1969, Studio One)
Hypocrities (1971, Studio One)
Freedom to the People (1972, Joe Gibbs)
Book of Rules (1976, Island)
Mama Say (1976, Island)

Heptones on Top (1970, Studio One)
Freedom Line (1971, Studio One)
Night Food (1976, Island)
Party Time (1977, Mango)
On the Run (1982, Shanty)

English Beat

Best Friend (1980, Go Feet)
Hands Off . . . She's Mine (1980, Go Feet)
Mirror in the Bathroom (1980, Go Feet)

Doors to Your Heart (1981, Sire)
Too Nice to Talk To (1981, Sire)

Specials

A Message to You Rudy (1980,
  Chrysalis)
Ghost Town (1981, Chrysalis)

Anthology

Catch This Beat (1980, Island)

New Age Music

Tony Scott

Music for Zen Meditation (1964,
  Vanguard)

Sandy Bull

E. Pluribus Unum (1969, Vanguard)

Will Ackerman

In Search of the Turtle's Navel
  (1975, Windham Hill)

George Winston

December (1982, Windham Hill)

Andreas Vollenweider

*Behind the Gardens--Behind the
  Wall--Under the Tree* (FM/CBS)
Cavern Magica (FM/CBS)
White Winds (FM/CBS)
Down to the Moon (1986 ,
  Windham Hill)

Kitaro

(Masanori Takahashi)

My Best (1986, Gramavision
Tenku (1986, Windham Hill)

David Sylvian

*Brilliant Trees (1984)
*Gone to Earth (1986)

David Hykes

Harmonic Meetings (1985, Celestial
  Harmonies)

Black Notes

Flux (1985)

Patrick O'Hearn

Ancient Dreams (1986, Private
Music)

Jerry Goodman

On the Future of Aviation (1986,
Private Music)

Terry Riley

The Harp of New Albion (1986,
Celestial Harmonies)

Index

The Author

Mirek Kocandrle is an assistant professor at the Berklee College of Music in Boston, Massachusetts, where he created and teaches courses on the history of rock'n'roll and on rock arranging.

An active performing musician on trumpet and electric bass, he has performed with Roy Orbison, the Bee Gees, the Platters, the Coasters, the Drifters, and others. He has been active on the local music scene since 1978 as leader of his own big band and jazz-rock group, and as sideman. He has also served in the Australian Army Band in Canberra, Australia, his home town; he now resides with his wife, Nancy, and his son, Rudy, in Harrisville, Rhode Island.